MW01527716

Getting Started

With

Microsoft Access 7.0

For Windows 95

Getting Started With Microsoft Access 7.0 For Windows 95

Henry Gaylord

Pace Computer Learning Center
School of Computer Science and Information Systems
Pace University

Babette Kronstadt
David Sachs

Series Editors
Pace Computer Learning Center
School of Computer Science and Information Systems
Pace University

JOHN WILEY & SONS, INC.

New York / Chichester / Brisbane / Toronto / Singapore

Trademark Acknowledgments:

Microsoft is a registered trademark of Microsoft Corporation
Excel for Windows is a trademark of Microsoft Corporation
Word for Windows is a trademark of Microsoft Corporation
PowerPoint for Windows is a trademark of Microsoft Corporation
Microsoft Office is a trademark of Microsoft Corporation
Windows is a trademark of Microsoft Corporation
Microsoft Access is a registered trademark of Microsoft Corporation
1-2-3 is a registered trademark of Lotus Development Corporation
WordPerfect is a registered trademark of WordPerfect Corporation
IBM is a registered trademark of International Business Machines Corporation
Paradox is a registered trademark of Borland International, Inc.
Microsoft Encarta is a registered trademark of Microsoft Corporation

Portions of this text were adapted from other texts in this series and from Pace University Computer Learning Center manuals.

Copyright © 1997 by John Wiley & Sons, Inc.

All rights reserved.

Reproduction or translation of any part of this work beyond that permitted by Sections 107 and 108 of the 1976 United States Copyright Act without the permission of the copyright owner is unlawful. Requests for permission or further information should be addressed to the Permissions Department, John Wiley & Sons, Inc.

ISBN 0-471-15869-0

Printed in the United States of America

10 9 8 7 6 5 4 3 2 1

Printed and bound by Banta Company

Preface

Getting Started with Microsoft Access 7.0 for Windows 95 provides a step-by-step, hands-on introduction to *Microsoft Access*. It is designed for students with basic PC and Windows skills who have little or no experience with *Microsoft Access*. Basic skills are taught in short, focused activities which build to create actual applications.

Key Elements

Each lesson in *Getting Started with Microsoft Access 7.0 for Windows 95* uses eight key elements to help students master specific database concepts and skills and develop the ability to apply them in the future.

- **Learning objectives**, located at the beginning of each lesson, focus students on the skills to be learned.

- **Project orientation** allows the students to meet the objectives while creating a real-world application. Skills are developed as they are needed to complete projects, not to follow menus or other artificial organization.

- **Motivation** for each activity is supplied so that students learn *why* and *when* to perform an activity, rather than how to follow a series of instructions by rote.

- **Bulleted lists of step-by-step general procedures** introduce the tasks and provide a handy, quick reference.

- **Activities with step-by-step instructions** guide students as they apply the general procedures to solve the problems presented by the projects.

- **Screen displays** provide visual aids for learning and illustrate major steps.

- **Independent projects** provide opportunities to practice newly acquired skills with decreasing level of support.

- **Feature reference** at the end of the book allows students to have a single place to look for commands to carry out the activities learned in the book.

Stop and Go

The steps for completing each *Microsoft Access* feature introduced in this book are covered in two ways. First they are described clearly in a bulleted list, which can also be used for reference. Then the steps are used in a hands-on Activity. Be sure to wait until the Activity to practice each feature on the computer.

Taking Advantage of Windows

Getting Started with Microsoft Access 7.0 for Windows 95 provides a balanced approach to using a Windows application. The use of the mouse and buttons for carrying out commands is emphasized. However, familiarity with the menus is developed so that students can take advantage of the wider range of options available in menu commands. Shortcut keys are introduced when appropriate. The convenient **Feature Reference** at the end of the book summarizes menu commands and mouse and keyboard shortcuts for each of the features covered in the lessons. Students can use this both to review procedures or learn alternate ways of carrying out commands.

Flexible Use

Getting Started with Microsoft Access 7.0 for Windows 95 is designed for use in an introductory computer course. As a "getting started" book, it does not attempt to cover all of the features of the software. However, the topics included in later lessons allow instructors to provide opportunities for individualized or extra credit assignments or use the book in short courses focused specifically on *Microsoft Access*. While designed to be used in conjunction with lectures or other instructor supervision, basic concepts are explained so that students can use the book in independent learning settings. Students should be able to follow specific instructions with minimal instructor assistance.

Data Disk

Data disks are provided for distribution to the students. The projects use files from the data disk so that the focus of the lesson is on the new skills being learned in each project. Initial projects require that students develop applications from the beginning, and later projects build on those applications. Enough explanation is always included so that students understand the full application that they are building.

Acknowledgments

While the author has written the words, this book represents the work and effort of many individuals and organizations. Babette Kronstadt provided energetic leadership and orchestrated the production of not only this book but all of Pace's books in the *Getting Started* series. Joe Knowlton worked miracles with the layout and text formatting. Sylvia Russakoff patiently and exhaustingly examined the text and activities, locating many of my errors and offering innumerable suggestions.

I received enormous institutional support from Pace University and the School of Computer Science and Information Systems (CSIS). In particular, much personal support and personal leadership for the work has come from the Dean, Dr. Susan Merritt.

From another perspective, this book is also a product of the Pace Computer Learning Center which is a loose affiliation of approximately 15 faculty and staff who have provided more than 7,000 days of instruction to over 60,000 individuals in corporate settings throughout the United States and around the world during the past nine years. My shared experiences in the development and teaching of these non-credit workshops was an ideal preparation for writing this book. In addition, none of the books for Wiley would have been possible without the continuing support of Dr. David Sachs, the director of the Computer Learning Center.

My thanks also go to the many people at Wiley who provided needed support and assistance. The editor, Beth Lang Golub, assistant editor David Kear, and production editor Lenore Belton have all been very responsive to our concerns and helpful in all of the Pace Computer Learning Center's writing projects.

Henry Gaylord

May, 1996
White Plains, New York

vi

Contents

2 WORKING WITH A TABLE'S DATA

3 MULTIPLE TABLES

4 QUERIES

5 MULTIPLE CRITERIA AND MULTI-TABLE QUERIES   137

6 REPORTS   165

7 CALCULATIONS AND ACTION QUERIES   199

Windows 95 Basics

Objectives

In this lesson you will learn to:

- Understand what *Windows 95* is
- Run *Windows 95*
- Identify the Desktop icons
- Use the mouse
- Open and close windows

- Identify the parts of a window
- Move and resize windows
- Maximize, Minimize, and Restore Windows
- Use menus and dialog boxes
- Shut down *Windows 95*

WHAT IS WINDOWS 95?

Windows 95 is the newest version of *Windows*, the program from Microsoft Corporation that lets you organize, run, and manage your programs and documents at the computer. Over the last few years, *Windows* has grown tremendously in importance and is now the standard operating system for IBM and other compatible brands of personal computers.

This lesson will introduce the basics of *Windows 95,* covering material that will prepare you for *Windows 95* application programs. If you are already familiar with *Windows 95* you may skip this lesson. For a complete introduction to *Windows 95*, refer to *Getting Started with Windows 95,* John Wiley & Sons, 1996.

BEGINNING WINDOWS VOCABULARY

Window	A four-sided frame within which a program, document, or message to the user is enclosed. Almost everything you do in the *Windows* environment will take place inside a window.
Icon	A small picture used to represent a program or document.
Desktop	The background screen of *Windows 95,* which holds all icons and windows.
Mouse	A small hand-held device used for giving commands to the computer.
Operating system	A type of software program that every computer must have. It works behind the scenes to direct the flow of data in the computer and makes it possible for you to organize and manage your documents.

Table Basics - 1

Windows 95 features will be covered in two ways—in **bulleted lists** and in **numbered activities**. **Read** the bulleted instructions carefully. Then, **carry out** the **numbered** instructions in the Activity. Remember **not** to carry out the bulleted items on your computer. The icon in the margin will remind you to wait for the Activities before carrying out instructions.

1

RUNNING WINDOWS 95

Every computer must have an operating system, and *Windows 95* is now the operating system for your computer. To run *Windows 95*, all you need to do is turn on your computer!

Instructions for all Activities:

- Read and follow each numbered instruction.
- Read italicized text. It provides additional information you will need to know.
- Read **PROBLEM SOLVERS** only if you cannot proceed.

Activity Basics.1: Running Windows 95

1. Turn on your personal computer.

   The boot-up procedure may take longer than you expect. Make sure there is no disk in the floppy drive. Some systems display a Welcome screen before the Desktop appears.

   If you are using Windows 95 on a network, you may be asked to sign on. You must type your User ID and password. If you need help, ask your instructor or lab assistant.

2. You will see the Desktop, the opening screen of *Windows 95*. Your monitor screen should look similar to Figure BAS - 1.

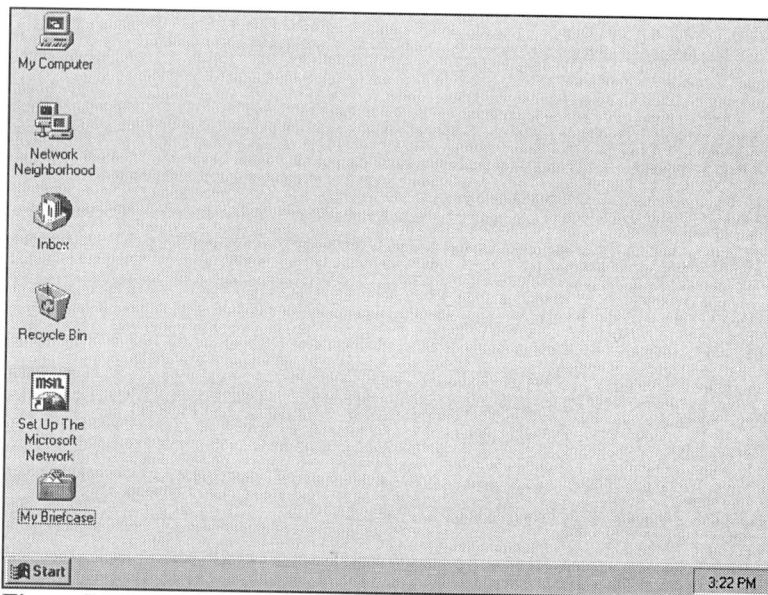

Figure BAS - 1

✓ **PROBLEM SOLVER:** *If the Windows 95 Desktop does not appear, your computer may have been set to run a different program or a different operating system when you boot up. Ask you instructor or lab assistant for help.*

3. Leave the computer on for the next activity.

WHAT IS ON THE DESKTOP?

The Desktop (Figure BAS - 1) is displayed when you run *Windows 95*. The icons on the Desktop may vary slightly, depending on how your computer was set up (see Table BAS - 2).

	My Computer	My Computer contains the contents of the drives on your computer.
	Inbox	The Inbox holds the electronic mail messages you have sent and received using Microsoft Exchange.
	Network Neighborhood	This icon appears if your computer is connected to a network. It contains all the computers and shared resources, such as printers, that are part of the network.
	Recycle Bin	The Recycle Bin is used to hold files you are planning to delete. The files are held in the Recycle Bin until you delete them or restore them.
	Microsoft Network	Microsoft Network is a new online service offered to all *Windows 95* users. It provides connectivity to the Internet and many other features.
	My Briefcase	My Briefcase helps you keep important files up-to-date when you work on them on the road and at your home or office. It is installed if you choose the Portable option or the Custom option during the *Windows 95* setup.
	Start Button	The **Start** button is your gateway to the programs, documents, settings, and all other features on your computer. It is located on the Taskbar.
	Taskbar	The Taskbar extends from the **Start** button across the bottom of the screen to the clock. It displays the name of all open windows in *Windows 95*.

Table BAS - 2

USING THE MOUSE

You need to learn to use the mouse before you begin to explore *Windows 95*. If you already use the mouse comfortably, you may skip to the next section, *Parts of a Window*.

To Use the Mouse:

Point	Touch the point of the arrow to a spot on the screen.
	Pointing highlights menu choices and positions your mouse pointer for the next action. It is important to touch the object you are pointing to. It is best to get near the center of the object rather than the edge.
Click	Lightly press and immediately release the *left* mouse button. Occasionally, the right mouse button will be specified.
	Clicking is used to highlight or select an object so that the next action taken will affect it. Clicking also opens and closes menus, chooses menu items, and closes or resizse windows.
Drag	Point to an object on-screen, press the left mouse button and hold it down while sliding the mouse. The object you are pointing to will move on-screen along with the mouse arrow.
	Dragging performs different tasks such as moving objects or text, resizing windows, and highlighting text in documents.
Double-click	Click and release the mouse button twice in rapid succession. Click quickly and lightly. Do not move the mouse as you click.
	Double-clicking is used to open windows and run programs.

Table BAS - 3

To Hold and Move the Mouse:

- Put the palm of your hand on the mouse. Your fingers should rest lightly on the mouse buttons.

- Slide the mouse around the mouse pad or flat surface next to your computer. The mouse must be guided by the palm of your hand, *not* by your fingers.

Activity Basics.2: Using the Mouse

In this activity you will practice using the mouse.

1. Turn on your computer, if it is not already on.

2. At the Desktop, place the palm of your right hand on the mouse and move it slowly on the mouse pad or flat surface. Watch the movement of the mouse pointer onscreen.

    The index finger of your right hand should rest easily on the left mouse button.

    If you are left-handed, move the mouse to the left side of the computer and hold it with your left hand.

3. Point to the icon labeled **My Computer**. Do not click the mouse button.

    Remember to touch the arrow point to the icon (see Figure BAS - 2).

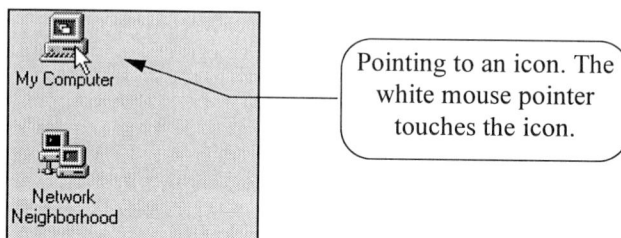

Pointing to an icon. The white mouse pointer touches the icon.

Figure BAS - 2

4. Point to the **Start** button in the lower left corner of your screen.

    ✓ **PROBLEM SOLVER:** *If the Start button is not visible, point to the bottom of the screen, and the button will appear.*

5. Point to the **Recycle Bin** icon.

6. Keeping your mouse pointer on the **Recycle Bin**, click the left mouse button. Keep your hand steady as you click.

    Both the icon and its label will change color. The icon is now selected. You will learn more about selected objects later.

    ✓ **PROBLEM SOLVER:** *If the mouse does not work, or works incorrectly, its settings may have been changed. Ask your instructor for assistance.*

7. Click on a blank part of the Desktop to unselect the **Recycle Bin** icon.

8. Click on the **My Computer** icon to select it.

9. Click on a blank part of the Desktop to unselect the icon.

10. Point to the **Start** button again.

11. When you see the mouse pointer on the **Start** button, click.

    *The **Start** menu will open (see FigureBAS - 3).*

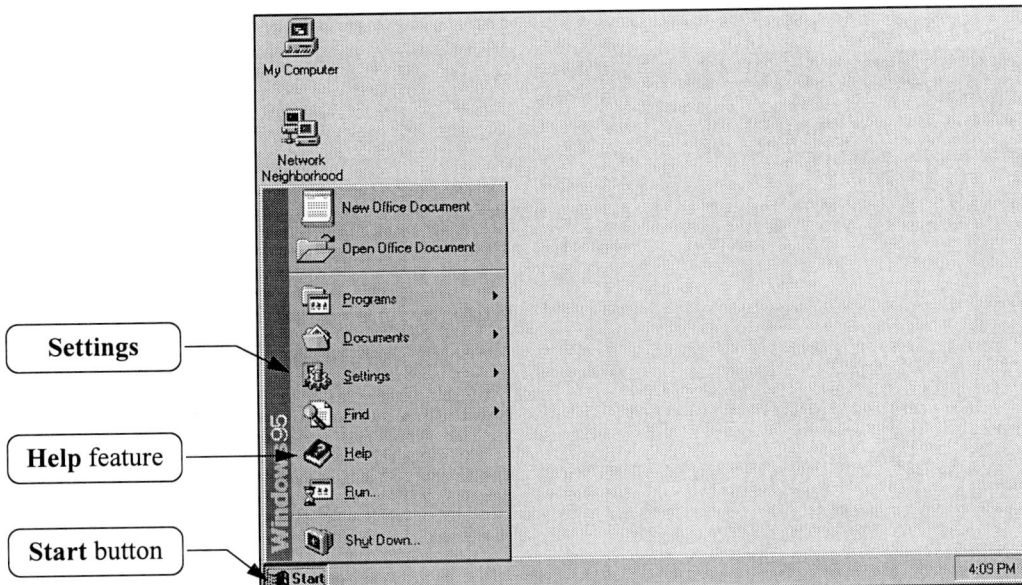

Figure BAS - 3   **The Start Menu**

12. Now point to **Settings** (Figure BAS - 3). Notice the triangle pointing to the right.

    The triangle indicates that Settings contains another group of choices. As you point to Settings, a smaller list containing three items opens (Figure BAS - 4).

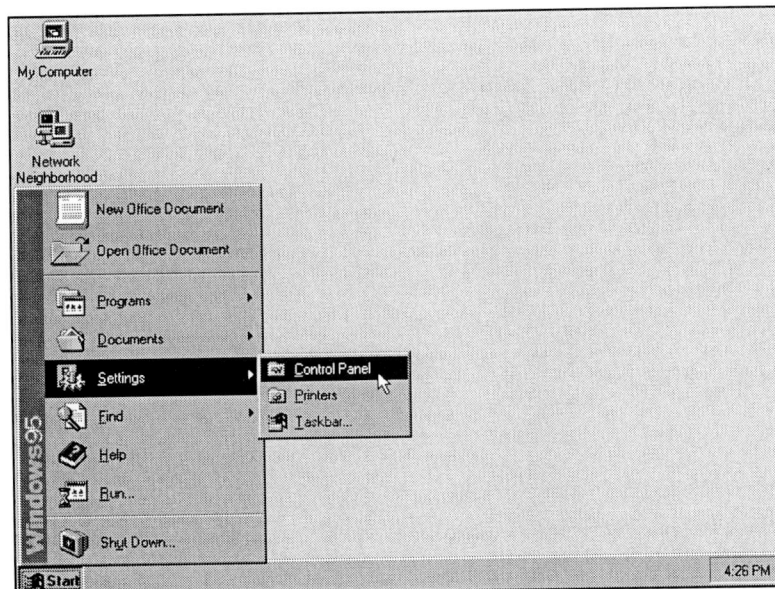

Figure BAS - 4

13. Point to the **Start** button and click again to close the **Start** menu.

14. Leave your computer on for the next activity.

PARTS OF A WINDOW

Figure BAS - 5 shows the elements of a typical *Windows 95* window.

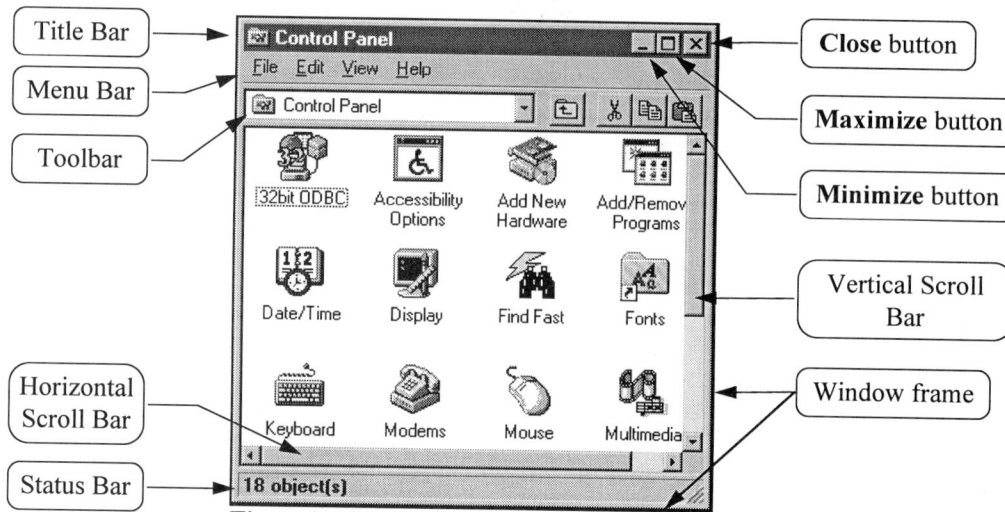

Title Bar
Menu Bar
Toolbar

Close button
Maximize button
Minimize button

Vertical Scroll Bar

Horizontal Scroll Bar
Status Bar

Window frame

Figure BAS - 5

OPENING, CLOSING, MOVING, AND SIZING WINDOWS

To work easily in *Windows 95*, you will need to be able to be able to open and close windows, as well as move them around the Desktop and change their size.

To open a window:

- Point to an icon on the Desktop or in a window.
- Double-click.

To close a window:

- Point to the **Close** button [X] in the upper right corner of the window.
- Click.

To move a window:

- Drag the **Title Bar** (see Figure BAS - 5) of the window to the new location.

  The TitleBar is the colored band at the top of a window that contains its name.

To size a window:

- Point to a side or corner of the window frame.

  When the mouse pointer touches the window frame, it is displayed as a double-headed arrow. Do not proceed until you see the double-headed arrow.

- Drag the window frame to resize the window.

  Dragging one of the four sides will move only that side, while dragging one of the corners will change two sides of the window at once.

MAXIMIZING, MINIMIZING, AND RESTORING WINDOWS

There are two preset sizes for windows— **Maximized** and **Minimized**— that can be chosen by clicking buttons that appear on every window. Another button, **Restore**, will return a window to its previous size.

A *maximized* window fills the entire screen. This setting gives you the best view of a window's contents, but blocks all other windows.

When a window is *minimized*, its name appears on the Taskbar but its contents cannot be seen. When a window is *restored*, it returns from maximized or minimized to its previous size.

To maximize a window:

- Click on the **Maximize** button ☐ , which is the middle button at the right end of the Title Bar.

To restore a window:

- If a window has been maximized, it will not contain a **Maximize** button, but will contain a **Restore** button 🗗 instead. Clicking **Restore** will return a window to its previous size.

To minimize a window:

- Click on the **Minimize** button ▬ to the left of the **Maximize/Restore** button.

Activity Basics.3: Working with Windows on the Desktop

In the next two activities, you will open, close, resize, move, maximize, minimize and restore windows.

1. Turn on your computer, if it is not already on.

2. At the Desktop, double-click on the icon called **My Computer**.

    *The **My Computer** window will open. Figure BAS - 6 shows the **My Computer** window with large icons displayed. If your screen does not match the figure, at the Menu Bar click on the word **View** and then, on the drop-down menu, click on **Large Icons**.*

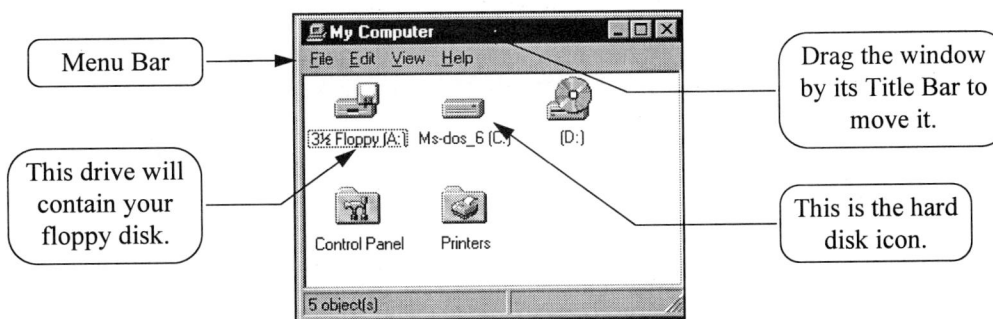

Figure BAS - 6

*If the **My Computer** window fills the entire screen, click the **Restore** button near the upper right corner of the window to make it smaller.*

3. Click and drag the window by its Title Bar (Figure BAS - 6) to a different place onscreen.

As you start to drag, the outline of the window will appear. Position the outline where you want the window moved and release the mouse button.

4. Touch any one of the four sides of the window with the mouse pointer.

   The mouse pointer will appear as a double-headed arrow.

5. Change the size of the window by dragging the frame.

6. Touch one of the four *corners* of the window with the mouse pointer and drag to change the window's size.

   When the double-headed arrow is positioned diagonally, you will move two sides of the window simultaneously.

7. In the **My Computer** window, double-click on the icon for the hard disk (**C**).

   *A second window will open that lists the contents of the hard drive. This window may be bigger or smaller than the **My Computer** window.*

   PROBLEM SOLVER: *If this new window covers the entire screen, follow the instructions in italics at the end of Step 2 to Restore the window.*

   PROBLEM SOLVER: *If there is no icon for the hard drive, it may have been deliberately hidden when Windows 95 was set up in your lab. Double-click on another icon instead and continue with Step 8.*

8. Move the two windows next to each other so that they do not overlap (see Figure BAS - 7). You may need to make one smaller.

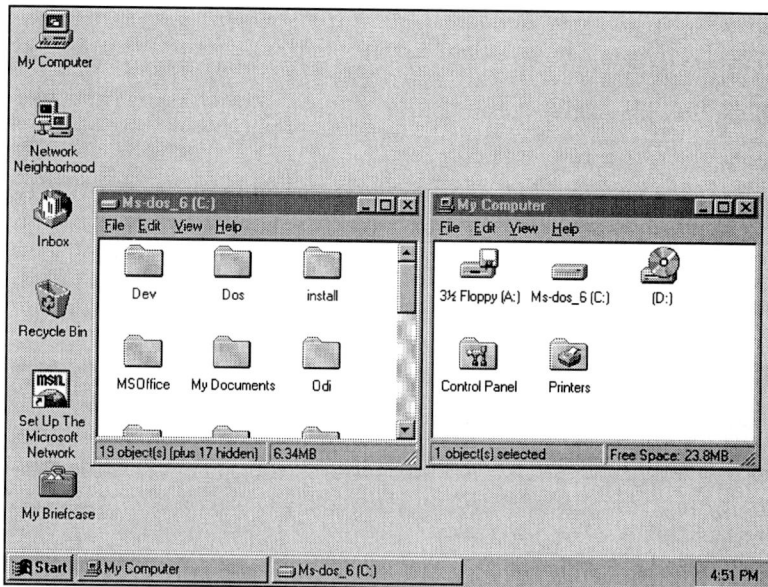

Figure BAS - 7

It will take at least several maneuvers to accomplish this. Take your time.

PROBLEM SOLVER: *If one window covers the other, move the one in front aside by dragging its Title Bar.*

9. Click the **Close** button (the **X** in the upper right corner) of the **My Computer** window.

10. Close the hard drive window.

    The Desktop should have no windows open at this point.

11. Leave the computer running for the next activity.

Activity Basics.4: Using Maximize, Minimize, and Restore

1. Turn on your computer, if it is not already on.

2. At the Desktop, double-click on the **Recycle Bin** icon (see Figure BAS - 8). Be careful not to move the mouse while you are double-clicking.

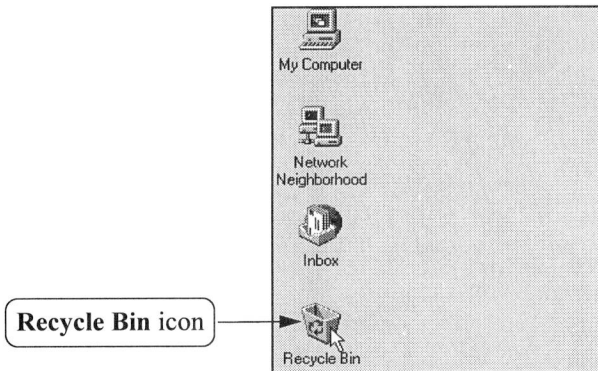

Figure BAS - 8

The Recycle Bin window opens.

3. Click the **Maximize** button on the Recycle Bin window, if it is showing. If not, continue with Step 4.

4. Click the **Restore** button. Remember that the **Maximize** and **Restore** buttons occupy the same location.

   Now the Recycle Bin window returns to its previous size.

5. Click the **Minimize** button.

   *The **Recycle Bin** window is minimized. All that is visible is its name on the Taskbar at the bottom of the screen. This lets you know that the Recycle Bin has not been closed.*

6. On the Taskbar, click on **Recycle Bin** to restore the window.

7. **Close** the Recycle Bin.

8. Double-click on the **My Computer** icon to open it.

9. In the **My Computer** window, double-click on the icon for the **Control Panel**.

   PROBLEM SOLVER: *If the **Control Panel** icon is not visible, increase the size of the **My Computer** window.*

10. **Maximize** the **Control Panel** window if it is not already maximized.

    Notice that both open windows are listed on the Taskbar.

11. Close the **Control Panel** window.

12. Close the **My Computer** window.

13. Close any other windows that are open.

    PROBLEM SOLVER: *If the **Close** button is not visible on any of these windows, drag the Title Bar to the left until you can see the **X**.*

14. Leave the computer running for the next activity.

RUNNING A PROGRAM FROM THE START MENU

The *Windows 95* Start Menu holds listings for all the programs you can run. You reach the Start Menu by clicking the **Start** button at the left edge of the Taskbar. The Start Menu displays both programs and program groups. Program groups may be identified by a triangle pointing to the right next to its name. Pointing to a program group name opens a list of all programs in that group. If you point to the wrong program group, slide your mouse pointer back to the left and the group will close. Do not click until you are pointing to the name of the program you want to run. Then, click to run the program.

To run a program:

- Click on the **Start** button;

- Point to **Programs**;

- Point to the program you want to run, or to a program group;

- When you are pointing to the name of the program you want to run, click the left mouse button.

Activity Basics.5: Running a Program

1. Point to the **Start** button and click to open the **Start** menu.

2. Point to **Programs**. Do not click.

3. Examine the list which opens. Notice that program groups are listed at the top.

4. Point to the **Accessories** program group. Examine the list of Accessory programs.

5. Slide the mouse pointer back to **Programs**. Notice how the Accessory list closes.

6. On the second panel, point to the listing for Microsoft Word. If this program is not listed, choose another program.

7. Click to run the program.

8. When the program has opened, click its **Close** button to close the program.

MENUS AND DIALOG BOXES

In addition to working with icons, buttons, and windows, you will be using menus and dialog boxes to give commands to your computer.

A *menu* is a list of commands. When you click on a menu name on a Menu Bar (pictured in Figure BAS - 6), a list of related commands drops down onto your screen (hence the term *drop-down menu*). You then click on the command of your choice. When a window contains a Menu Bar, you will find it directly below the Title Bar. Some menu commands have keyboard shortcuts associated with them, and these shortcuts are noted on the menus.

When you examine menu commands you will notice three possibilities. First, the menu command may appear in a light gray color. This means the command is not currently available.

Second, the command may be followed by three dots (an ellipsis). This means the computer needs more data before it can execute the command. A *dialog box,* a small window containing areas where you can provide information, will open automatically. The dialog box may contain areas in which to type, lists to select from, boxes to check, and buttons to click.

Third, if the command is neither gray nor followed by an ellipsis, it will be carried out as soon as you choose it.

To use a menu:

- Point to the menu name (e.g., **File**) on the Menu Bar and click to open (see Figure BAS - 9).

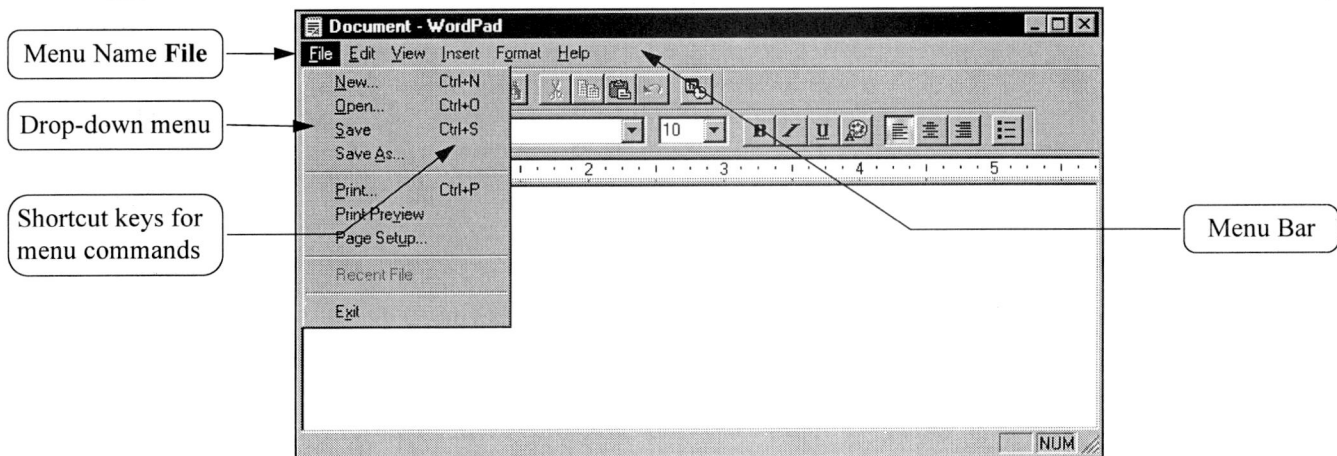

Menu Name **File**

Drop-down menu

Shortcut keys for menu commands

Menu Bar

Figure BAS - 9

- To choose a command from the menu, point to the word on the menu and click.

  ALTERNATE MOUSE METHOD: *Keep the mouse button down when you click on the menu name and drag down the menu, releasing the button at the command you want.*

- To close a menu without choosing a command, click again on the menu name on the Menu Bar.

Using Menus with the Keyboard

Although you may be comfortable with the mouse by now, you should also learn the keystrokes for using menus. In situations where both hands are on the keyboard, you may prefer to open a menu without having to reach for the mouse.

To use a menu with the keyboard:

- To activate the Menu Bar, press the **ALT** key (found on either side of the **SPACEBAR**).
- Tap the underlined letter of the menu name of your choice (e.g., the **F** on the **File** menu).

  The menu will open, meaning that a list of commands will drop down onto your screen.

- To choose a command, tap the underlined letter of the command.
- To close a menu, press the **ESC** key (in the upper left corner of the keyboard). This closes the menu that is open, but keeps the Menu Bar activated in case you want to use a different menu.
- To deactivate the Menu Bar, press the **ALT** key.

To use a dialog box:

- When a dialog box opens, use the following procedures to change the settings to meet your needs (see Figure BAS - 10).

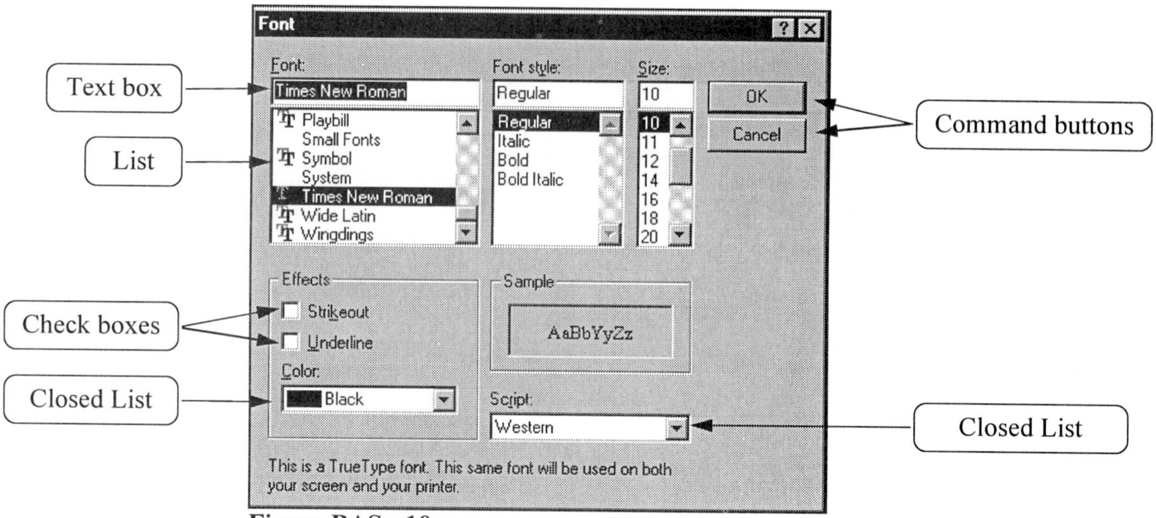

Figure BAS - 10

- ○ Type in the **text boxes**.
- ○ Select items from **open lists** by clicking on the item of your choice.
- ○ If a list is **closed**, click on the ↓ to open the list. If less than the entire list is visible, you may click the down and up arrows next to the list to see more choices. This is called *scrolling* the list.
- ○ If there is a set of **check boxes** (square), click on the appropriate one(s). You may select as many as you wish, or none at all. If a box is checked, click on it again to uncheck it.
- ○ If there is a set of **buttons** (round), click on the appropriate one. Because only one may be selected at a time, clicking on one removes the previous selection (not displayed).
- ○ Some dialog boxes have more than one panel. Click on the appropriate **index tab** to reach the screen of your choice (not displayed).

- You may use the mouse or the **TAB** key to move from one section of the box to another.
- When the dialog box has been filled as desired, click **OK** to carry out the instructions or **Cancel** to remove the dialog box. The **OK** and **Cancel** buttons are called *command buttons*.

KEYBOARD ALTERNATIVE: *Instead of clicking on* ***OK****, press the* ***ENTER*** *key. Instead of clicking on* ***Cancel****, press the* ***ESC*** *key, in the upper left corner of your keyboard.*

- Some dialog boxes contain a **Help** icon, located to the left of the **Close** button. Clicking on the **Help** icon and then on the element of the dialog box you are interested in displays a description of the element and how to use it.

Activity Basics.6: Using Menus and Dialog Boxes

In this activity you will work with menus and dialog boxes.

1. Turn on your computer, if it is not already on.
2. At the Desktop, double-click on the **My Computer** icon. Is the Toolbar showing?

   The Toolbar, a row of buttons positioned below the Menu Bar may or may not appear.

3. **Maximize** the window, if necessary, by clicking on its **Maximize** button.
4. At the Menu Bar, click on the word **View**. Is there a check next to **Toolbar**?

If so, the Toolbar is displayed. If not, the Toolbar is not displayed. The display of the Toolbar is turned on and off by clicking on the Toolbar command on the View menu.

5. If there is no check, click on **Toolbar**. If there is a check, click on **View** to close the menu.

   The Toolbar will be displayed (see Figure BAS - 5). A Toolbar is a row of buttons that appears directly below the Menu Bar. Each button is associated with a command.

6. Click on the **View** menu again and see if there is a check in front of the **Status Bar** command.

7. If there is no check, click on **Status Bar**. If there is a check, click on **View** to close the menu.

   The Status Bar will be displayed at the bottom of the window, directly above the Taskbar. It displays additional information about the contents of the window.

8. Click on **View** again and examine the next four menu items: **Large Icons**, **Small Icons**, **List**, and **Details**.

   These choices refer to how the contents of the window are displayed.

9. Click on **Large Icons**.

   Notice the appearance of the window with large icons displayed.

10. Click on **View** and click on **Small Icons**.

    Notice the difference between large and small icons.

11. Click on **View** and click on **List**.

    List arranges the icons in a vertical list.

12. Click on **View** and click on **Details**.

    The Details command adds information about the icons.

13. Now that you have examined all the choices, return to **Large Icons**.

14. At the Menu Bar, click on **HELP**.

15. Click on **About Windows 95**.

16. Read the screen and click on **OK**.

17. Click on **View** again and click on **Options**.

18. Click on the **File Types** index tab.

19. To scroll the list, click on the down triangle to the right of the list of file types. Examine the list as you scroll.

20. Click on the **View** index tab and notice the two check boxes. Do they contain checks?

21. Click on each box at least twice and watch the checks appear and disappear. Leave the boxes the way you found them.

22. Click on **Cancel** to close the **Options** dialog box without carrying out any changes you made.

23. Close the **My Computer** window.

24. Click on the **Start** button. Click on the **Shut Down...** command.

    The ellipsis tells you that a dialog box will open.

25. Do **not** click on **Yes** or you will shut down your computer. Instead, click on the **Help** command button.

26. Follow the directions in the **Help** box to learn about the **Shut Down Windows** box.

27. Close the **Windows Help** box when you are finished.

28. Leave your computer running for the final activity.

CLOSING WINDOWS 95

Don't shut your computer down merely by turning it off! When you exit improperly from *Windows 95*, files that should be deleted when you exit the program are not, and, instead, stay permanently on your system. Sooner or later this will cause a problem.

To exit from Windows 95:

- Click on the **Start** button [Start].
- Click on the **Shut Down** command.
- When the **Shut Down Windows** dialog box appears, click on the **Yes** button.
- Turn off your computer when you see the message that says you may do so.

Activity Basics.7: Closing Windows 95

1. Close any windows that are open on the Desktop.
2. Click on the **Start** button.
3. Click on **Shut Down** and **Yes** in the **Shut Down Windows** dialog box (see Figure BAS - 11).

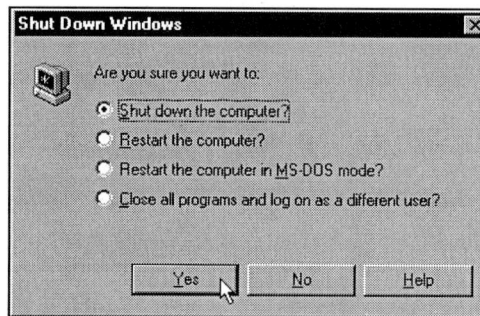

Figure BAS - 11

The fourth option will not be present unless you are working on a network.

4. Turn off your computer when you are permitted to do so.

SUMMARY

This introduction has covered the essential terms and procedures needed to open programs and perform basic tasks in *Windows 95*.

KEY TERMS

Cancel button	Icon	Operating System
Check boxes	Inbox	Point
Click	List	Program Group
Closed List	Maximize	Recycle Bin
Command buttons	Menu	Restore
Control Panel	Microsoft Network	Start button
Desktop	Minimize	Start menu
Dialog box	Mouse	Taskbar
Double-click	My Briefcase	Text box
Drag	My Computer	Toolbar
Drop-down list	Network Neighborhood	Window
Hard drive	Open list	

Introduction to Access

Objectives

In this lesson you will learn:

- What a database is
- How to start Microsoft *Access*
- The parts of the screen
- How to use the toolbar in *Access*
- Database terminology

- How to use the Help System
- How to exit from *Access*
- The typographical conventions used in this book

PURPOSE OF THE INTRODUCTION

Unlike the other lessons in this book, which contain specific steps to complete database projects, this introduction will discuss databases and Microsoft *Access* in general. It will start with how to get *Access* running, review the Windows 95 aspects of *Access*, point out the features that are different from other Windows 95 programs you may have used, and examine the Help system. It will also explain several terms that are used in database work. The final section describes the typographical conventions used by this book.

WHAT IS MICROSOFT *ACCESS*?

Every business and institution needs to keep lists of facts. A customer list, an inventory list, a sales invoice list, and a list of course enrollments would be but four examples. Such lists are called *database tables*, and the facts and figures they contain are called *data*. To work with these database tables on the computer, businesses and institutions, as well as individuals, use database programs. One such program is Microsoft *Access*.

Access is a powerful, yet remarkably straightforward, database tool. It is a *RDBMS*, or Relational Database Management System, which means it handles multiple lists of data simultaneously. It allows you to organize, edit, search for, report on, and perform calculations on your data. Since most people dislike keeping and working on long lists of data on paper, using *Access* on a computer makes an otherwise tedious job quick and painless; many would say fun.

One goal of a database program is the simple creation, maintenance, and organization of data. *Access* will streamline such routine tasks. The ultimate goal of databases is deriving summary information. Examples would include the total of all invoices, a list of customers by state, or the average price for each category of products. *Access* is equally adept at these tasks. This book will explore the necessary rudimentary jobs, as well as many of the summary tasks.

GETTING STARTED

Access is a Windows program. That is good news, because if you know how to start and work with any other Windows 95 program, you already know a portion of how to work with *Access*. This book assumes you have previously used a mouse, and that you know how to run Windows 95 on the computer you are using, as well as the fundamentals of operating Windows 95. Any basic procedures that are unique to *Access* will be discussed in this introduction.

Because *Access* is a Windows 95 program, and both *Access* and Windows 95 can be customized in various ways, there might be small differences between the appearance of your screen and the illustrations in this book. For example, the thickness of the Active Window Border can be changed in Windows 95 from the normal value of 1 to any number desired. If someone set the border to a width of 20, every window would look peculiar in every Windows 95 program, including *Access*. They would still work the same way, however. By simply setting the border value back to 1, all would appear normal again.

Like any Windows program, there are ways to perform operations with the mouse and with the keyboard. While *Access* was designed for a mouse, occasionally a key combination is easier. This book will favor whichever method is easier, although both ways will be described.

> The steps for completing each *Access* feature introduced in this book are covered in two ways. First, they are described in a **bulleted** list, that can also be used for reference. The steps are used in a hands-on *Activity*. Be sure to wait until the numbered instructions in the *Activity* to practice each feature on the computer.

To start *Access*:

- Turn on the computer so that Windows 95 is running.

- Click on the Start button on the Taskbar.

- Click on Programs in the menu that opens.

- Find *Microsoft Access* in the list of programs and click on it.

Activity I.1: Starting Access

1. Turn on the computer and start Windows 95.

2. Click on the **Start** button on the Taskbar.

3. Click on **Programs** in the menu that opens.

4. Click on *Microsoft Access*.

THE *ACCESS* INTRODUCTORY DIALOG BOX

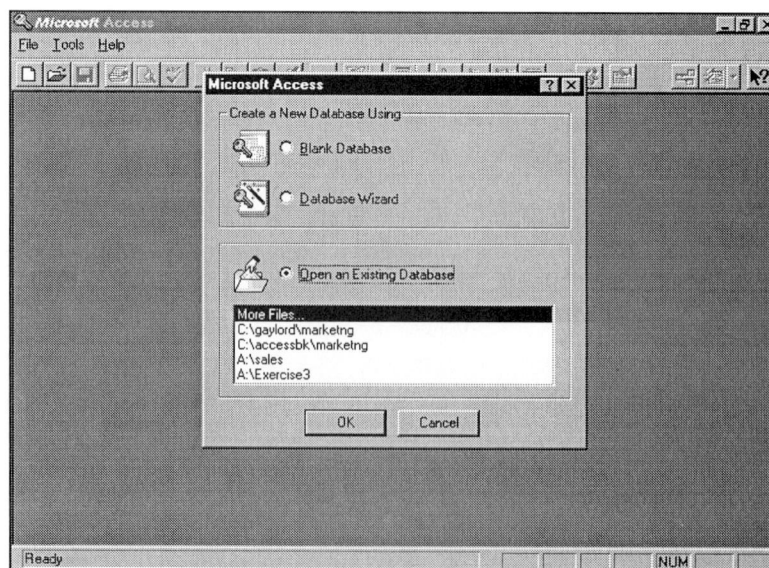

Figure I - 1

When *Access* first begins, you may see a dialog box that says *Microsoft Access* on the top line like Figure I - 1. Since you cannot do anything in *Access* without a database being open, *Access* asks which existing database you want opened, or whether you would like to create a new database. If this dialog box does not open automatically, someone who previously used the same computer turned this option off. We will see how to correct this option shortly.

The bottom panel of the dialog box lists the four most recently used databases. If one of those is the one you need opened, merely click on the name and click the **OK** button. If you need an unlisted database opened, click on **More Files** and click the **OK** button. If you have not yet created the database, pick one of the two options in the top panel. Blank Database will create a new database with whatever name you choose in any folder you want. The choice Database Wizard opens a dialog box with choices for a blank database or one of the 22 built-in designs for the most common business and home uses. While the built-in designs can often save you a great deal of design time and are a terrific source of ideas, we will not use them in this book since none of them match the designs we will produce. In personal or business projects, however, the built-in designs may be just what you need.

Making a choice in the introductory dialog box:

- If the name of the desired database is showing, click on that name and click the **OK** button.

- If the name of the desired database is not showing, click on **More Files** and click the **OK** button.

- To begin a new blank database, choose **Blank Database** in the upper panel and click **OK**.

- To begin a new database using one of the Wizard's 22 built-in designs, pick **Database Wizard** in the upper panel and click **OK**.

Activity I.2: Using the Introductory Dialog Box to Open a Database

Since you have just run *Access*, the introductory dialog box should be on the desktop. (If it is not open, begin with Step 3.)

1. In the introductory dialog box, click on the **Open an Existing Database** option (see Figure I - 1). If the **marketng** database is listed in the lower list, click on it, click the **OK** button, and skip Steps 2-5.

2. If **marketng** is not showing in the introductory dialog box, click on **More Files** and continue with Step 4.

3. If *Access* was already open from a previous activity, if the introductory dialog box did not open automatically, or if you clicked the **Cancel** button in the introductory dialog box so that it closed, click on the **FILE** menu and pick **Open Database**.

4. Make certain the correct drive and folder are chosen in the **Look in:** list. Your instructor or lab assistant can tell you what the correct folder and drive are for the "Data Disk" for this book.

   Your choice for Look in: will almost certainly be different from the folder in the illustration.

5. Click on **marketng** and click **Open**.

THE *ACCESS* SCREEN

The **marketng** database will open onto the *Access desktop* (see Figure I - 2). The desktop should resemble a typical Windows screen with a Title Bar at the top, the Menu Bar on the second line, the *toolbar* (probably) on the third line, and the *Status Bar* (probably) at the bottom. If your screen resembles, but doesn't look exactly like Figure I - 2, we will adjust it in this section so it matches.

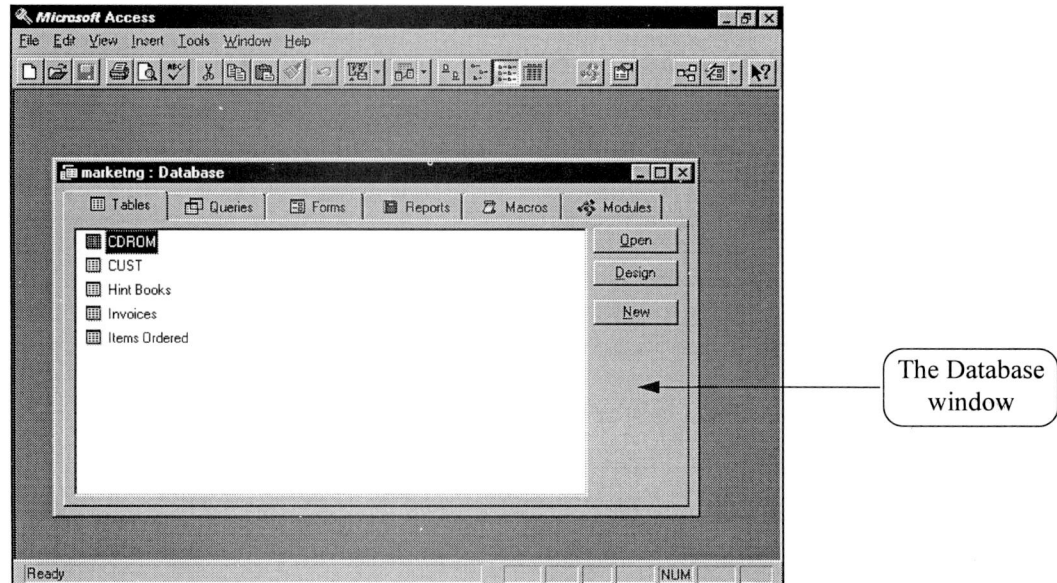

The Database window

Figure I - 2

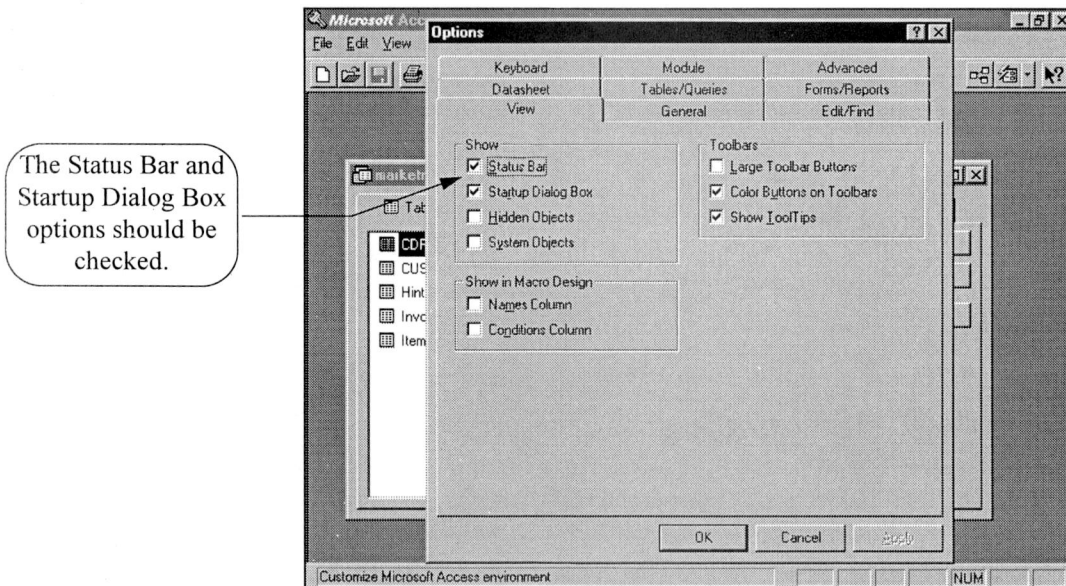

The Status Bar and Startup Dialog Box options should be checked.

Figure I - 3

The Status Bar

The bottom line of the window is the *Status Bar* (see Figure I - 2). Its left section displays various messages about the current operation. Some of the more useful messages describe the currently highlighted menu selection or the toolbar button that the mouse pointer is on top of. In the indented boxes on its right end, *Access* names the toggle keys like Caps Lock and Num Lock, which are currently turned on. It is important to read the Status Bar during operations in *Access* to obtain its information.

Displaying the Status Bar if it was hidden:

- Click on the **TOOLS** menu.

- Pick **Options**.

- In the **Options** dialog box on the **View** tab, check **Status Bar** in the **Show** section so that a check mark shows (see Figure I - 3).

- Click the **OK** button.

Displaying the introductory dialog box if it did not automatically appear:

- Click on the **TOOLS** menu.

- Pick **Options**.

- In the **Options** dialog box on the **View** tab, check **Startup Dialog Box** in the **Show** section so that a check mark shows (see Figure I - 3).

- Click the **OK** button.

The Toolbar

The third line at the top of the window is the *toolbar* (see Figure I - 2). It contains buttons that provide shortcuts to the most frequently used activities in *Access*. The toolbar will automatically switch among the 19 built-in toolbars to supply the appropriate tools for the item you are currently working on.

The last person to use this copy of *Access* might have turned off the option to see the toolbar. If so, you will see in the next activity how to make it reappear. Similarly, the last user may have displayed additional toolbars. Normally, only one toolbar should be showing at a time and *Access* automatically selects the appropriate one. Thus, we will remove any extra toolbars in the next activity, as well.

The toolbar is normally displayed on the third line at the top of the window. However, some *Access* users prefer other locations on the desktop. It can be moved to any position within the program window by moving the mouse pointer on top of a gap between two buttons or onto the border area next to a button, holding down the left mouse button, and dragging the toolbar someplace else. A toolbar in the middle of the screen is called a "floating" toolbar. If the toolbar is floating, its proportions can be customized by dragging the side frames.

To display the default toolbar on the third line of the window:

- With no database on the workspace, open the **FILE** menu and pick **Toolbars**. (Were there a database on the workspace, then **Toolbars** would be in the **VIEW** menu.)

- In the list of toolbars that is displayed (see Figure I - 4), click the check box in front of the name **Database** so that a check mark shows.

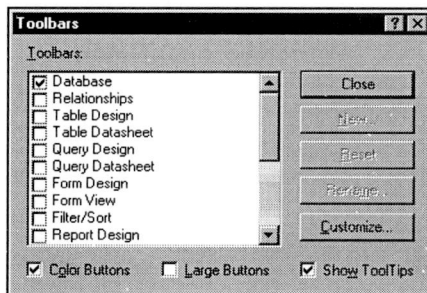

Figure I - 4

- If any other toolbar names have check marks in front of them, click on their check boxes one at a time to remove the checks. There are more names than can show at one time in the list, so you may need to use the scroll bar to scroll down to look for additional checks.

- Close the list of toolbars by clicking the **Close** button.

- If the toolbar is not on the third line of the window, move the mouse pointer onto an unoccupied area beside any button, hold down the left mouse button, and drag the toolbar toward the top of the window. When the mouse pointer is just below the menu bar and about 1/3 of the way across the screen, the dotted–line frame that represents the shape the toolbar will take will become a wide rectangle just one button tall. Release the mouse button and the toolbar should be positioned on the third line of the window (see Figure I - 2).

Activity I.3: Adjusting the Screen Display

We will verify that the Status Bar is displayed, the introductory dialog box will appear the next time *Access* is started, and that only the appropriate toolbar is displayed on the third line at the top of the desktop.

1. If no database is currently open, follow the steps in Activity I.2 to open marketng.

2. Click on **Options** in the **TOOLS** menu.

3. Click on the **View** tab at the top of the dialog box to select that page of options.

4. If **Status Bar** does not have a check mark in front of it in the **Show** section of the **Options** dialog box, click on its check box so a check mark appears (see Figure I - 3).

5. If **Startup Dialog Box** does not have a check mark in front of it in the **Show** section of the **Options** dialog box, click on its check box so a check mark appears.

   The introductory dialog box will appear the next time you begin Access.

6. Click the **OK** button.

7. Pick **Toolbars** in the **VIEW** menu.

8. If the top name, **Database**, does not have a check mark to the left of its name, click the mouse on the check box so it is checked (see Figure I - 4).

   A check mark will appear next to the name in the list and the toolbar will appear on the screen, probably on the third line.

9. If any other name besides **Database** has a check mark, click on that name's check box to remove the check and hide its toolbar. Repeat this step until only **Database** is checked.

   You may need to use the scroll bar to scroll down to look for additional checks

10. Close the list by clicking on the **Close** button.

    Only the toolbar shown in Figure I - 2 should be showing.

11. If the toolbar is not on the third line of the window, move the mouse pointer onto a blank area beside any button and hold down the left mouse button. Don't release the mouse button until the end of Step 12.

12. Drag the toolbar toward the top of the window by moving the mouse with the button still held down. When the mouse pointer is just below the menu bar and about 1/3 of the way across the screen, the dotted–line frame that represents the shape the toolbar will take will become a wide rectangle just one button tall. Release the mouse button.

    Your screen should now match Figure I - 2. This is the normal starting configuration for Access.

THE MOUSE POINTER

There are several different shapes for the mouse pointer, depending on what tool or item the mouse pointer is on top of. First, you must not confuse the mouse pointer with the text cursor. The text cursor is a blinking vertical bar that will only be seen within text while you are typing or ready to type. Clicking the mouse button while the mouse pointer is on top of some text will cause the text cursor to move to that spot. Otherwise, there is no relationship between the two.

The various mouse pointer shapes include the regular diagonal arrow (⟍) for choosing items on the screen like a menu, various double-headed arrows (for example ↔) for sizing items, a solid black arrow (↓) for picking an entire column or row, a solid black double-headed arrow with a bar between the arrows (↔) for sizing columns, various hands (for example ✋) for moving items on designs like a report design, a diagonal arrow with a question mark (⟍?) for clicking on an item about which you need to see help, and the hourglass (⧗) for those occurrences when an operation will take a little time. These mouse pointers will be described at each place in the book when they are encountered. For the moment, simply be ready to see many different shapes.

USING THE TOOLBAR BUTTONS

As mentioned previously, the *toolbar buttons*, which are sometimes called tools, are shortcuts to the most common operations in *Access*. There is nothing the toolbar buttons can do that cannot be accomplished through the menus or with a key combination; it's just much quicker with the toolbar buttons. For example, the second button on the toolbar is the **Open Database** tool. Therefore, to initiate opening a database, you could either click on the **FILE** menu and then click on **Open Database** in that menu, or you could make a single click on the toolbar button. Clearly, one click is quicker than two. Often the difference is even greater. For example, making text bold requires four clicks with the menu, but only one with the toolbar.

While the picture on each button is usually easy to associate with the button's purpose, to see a description of any tool on the toolbar, move the mouse pointer on top of the tool without pressing any mouse buttons, and read the Status Bar message. Additionally, the name of the tool will appear in a colored box immediately below the button when the mouse pointer pauses on top of a tool for a second or two. Those names are called "Tool Tips."

To use a toolbar tool:

- Click the left mouse button once while the mouse pointer is on top of the tool.
- If a dialog box opens, fill out the dialog box.

Activity I.4: Using the Toolbar Tools

To practice with the toolbar tools, we will open the **marketng.mdb** database again, and make some changes to the appearance of its table listings.

1. If any database is currently open, pick **Close** in the **FILE** menu to close it.

2. Move the mouse pointer on top of the first button on the toolbar. Do **not** press the mouse button.

   What is the name of this first tool and what does it do? Read the Tool Tips name and the Status Bar description to find out.

3. Move the mouse pointer on top of the second button on the toolbar. Note its name, **Open Database**, and its description, then press the left mouse button once on top of it to activate it.

   *The **Open** dialog box appears, just as it would if we were to choose **FILE/Open Database** in the menu.*

4. Set the drive and folder and click the mouse button on top of the name **marketng** in the list of database names (see Figure I - 5).

   Review Activity I.2 if you are not certain where to set the drive and folder.

5. Click the **Open** button.

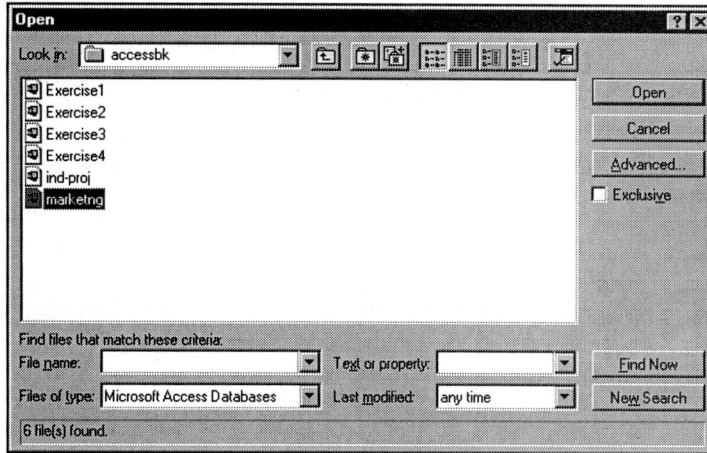

Figure I - 5

6. Click once on the tab at the top of the database window that says **Tables** to make certain you are looking at the list of table names (see Figure I - 2).

7. Click the **Large Icons** button on the toolbar and examine the icons and table names in the **Database** window (see Figure I - 6).

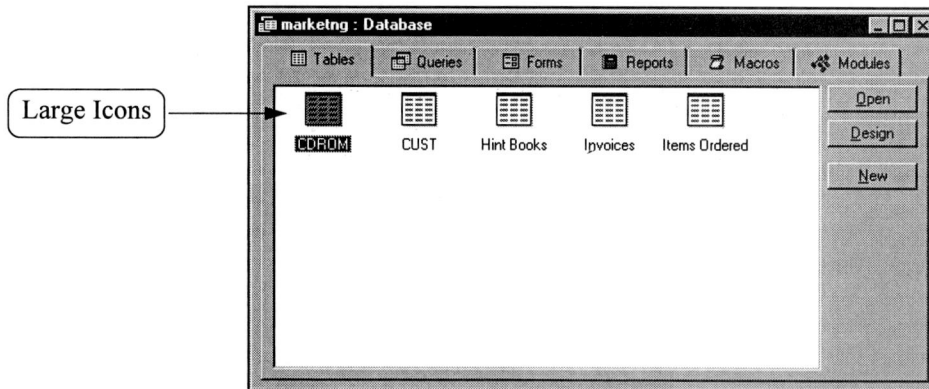

Figure I - 6

The equivalent menu command is VIEW/Large Icons.

8. Click the **Small Icons** button on the toolbar (see Figure I - 7).

9. Click the **Details** button on the toolbar (see Figure I - 8).

   What are the equivalent menu commands for these two buttons?

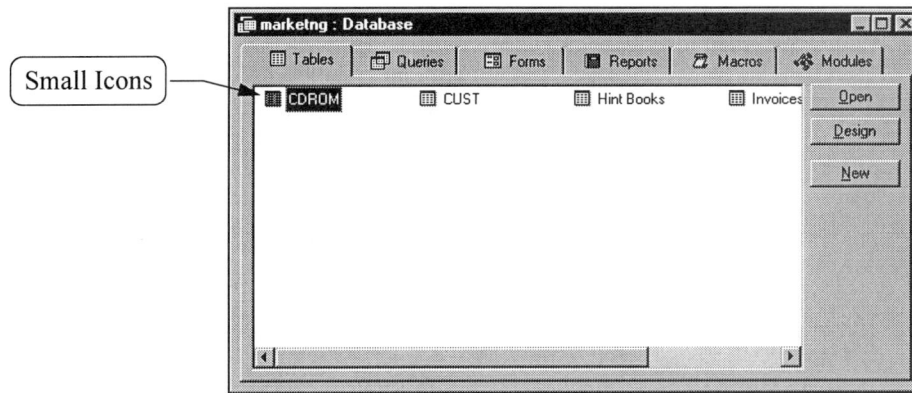

Figure I - 7

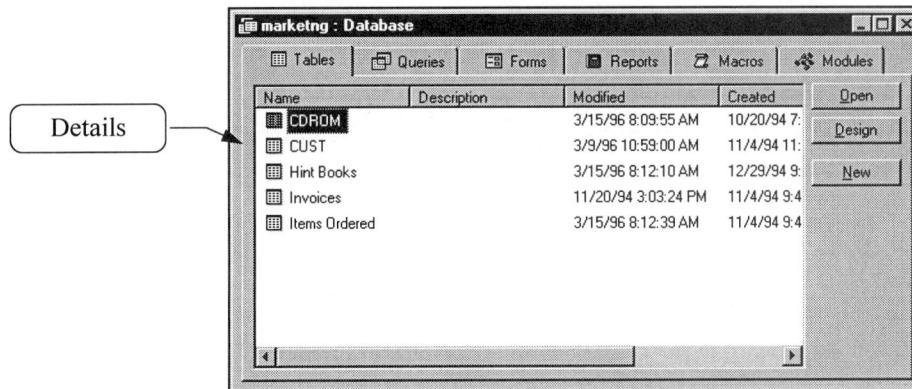

Figure I - 8

10. Click the **List** button on the toolbar (see Figure I - 9).

*List is the default view for the names listed in the **Database** window.*

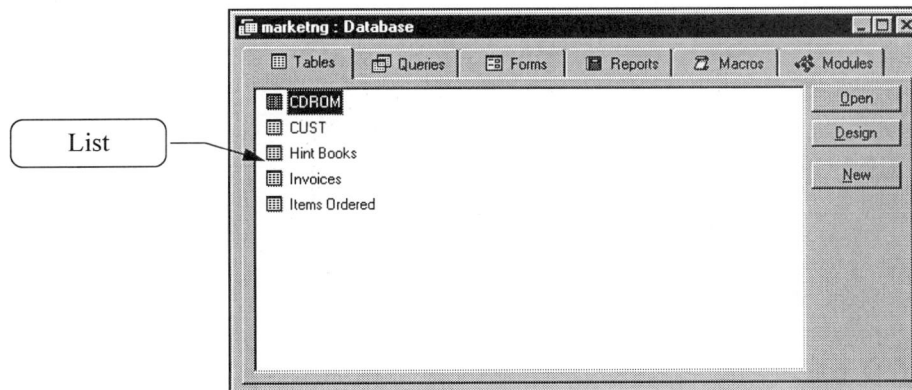

Figure I - 9

11. Click once on the name **Hint Books** in the list of Tables.

12. Click the **Open** button at the right edge of the **Database** window to open the table.

13. Press the **TAB** key four times to move the highlight from the **CD ID** column to the **Price** column.

14. On the toolbar, move the mouse pointer on top of the 12th button, the **Sort Descending** button, and click the mouse button once to activate it.

    *The listings should be reordered so that they go from highest price to lowest (see Figure I - 10). To accomplish this sorting through the menu would have required clicking on the **RECORDS** menu, then **Sort** within that menu, and finally on **Descending** in the submenu.*

Hint Books : Table

CD ID	CDROM Name	Book Title	Cost	Price	Quantity in Stock
V01	Vortar the Barbarian	Vortar - Tricks and Tips	$8.00	$15.95	8
S03	Scourge - The Game	Scourge - Hints & Tips	$7.50	$13.95	43
Z02	Zulu Encounter	The Unauthorized Zulu Encounter Boc	$6.95	$12.98	11
T01	Tuffy Goes to the Moon	Tuffy Goes to the Moon	$4.25	$6.95	18
*			$0.00	$0.00	0

Record: 1 of 4

Figure I - 10

15. Move the mouse pointer on top of the remaining toolbar buttons to see what their names and descriptions are. Do **not** press the mouse button.

16. Click on **Close** in the **FILE** menu to close the data table.

17. Click the **No** button when *Access* asks "Do you want to save changes to the design of the table 'Hint Books'?" so the sorted order will not become permanent (see Figure I - 11).

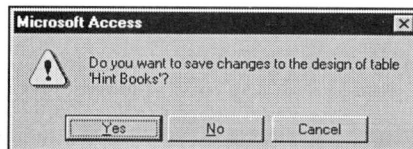

Microsoft Access

Do you want to save changes to the design of table 'Hint Books'?

Yes No Cancel

Figure I - 11

Microsoft Access

File Tools Help

The Access Desktop

Ready NUM

Figure I - 12

The database window disappears and the database is closed. The menu bar reverts to its minimal form. Most of the toolbar buttons become pale, indicating they are inactive. The desktop should resemble Figure I - 12. When no database is open there is no data to work on, so Access removes most of the data tools, namely the menus and toolbar buttons.

18. Pick **Close** in the **FILE** menu to close the database.

TERMS

There is a set of terms that you will encounter again and again within this or any book that discusses databases. Since it is important to understand what those terms mean, we will describe them here.

- *Data* are the facts and figures that are stored by *Access*. Names, addresses, telephone numbers, and prices are typical data elements.

- A *table* is a single set of data. It might be a list of customers, a list of sales, or an inventory list.

- A *database* in *Access* is a grouping of one or more tables of data, report designs, forms, queries, macros, and modules, comprising an entire accumulation of data and the tools to work with those data.

- A *record* is a single listing within the table of data. Thus, a table with 25 listings has 25 records.

- A *field* is a column of similar data. For example, in Figure I - 10 the Hint Books table has six fields: CD ID, CDROM Name, Book Title, Cost, Price, and Quantity in Stock.

- The *field name* is the title or heading given to a field.

THE HELP SYSTEM

As with all major Windows 95 programs, there is an extensive help system available any time you get stuck or need more information about any *Access* topic. Either the Help menu or the **F1** key will open the Microsoft *Access for Windows 95* **Help Topics** window. If you have used Help in any other Windows 95 program, you already know most of how the Help system works.

The Help window contains four tabs for different ways of locating information in the Help system. Table I - 1 outlines each different method.

Help Window Tab	**How the Window Works**
Contents	A list of topics about which you might want additional information. Double-click a topic and a list of sub-topics opens beneath it. Double-click a sub-topic and a window opens addressing that subject.
Index	A lengthy list of terms. Scroll down the list and double-click the term about which you need more information. Either a sub-list will open or information about the requested term will appear. To find a topic, you may also type the first few letters to cause the list to scroll automatically.
Find	Find creates a list of each word or phrase in the help topics, then allows you to search that list.
Answer Wizard	Attempts to search the help topics based on English language sentences that you type.

Table I - 1

Once on a specific screen of information within the Help system, that screen can contain three types of items. The information to be read will be displayed as text. A word or phrase that is underlined with a solid line (and will be green on a color screen) is a *jump term*. A *jump term* is the name of another topic that you might want to jump to in order to see the information on its screen. A dotted–underlined phrase (which will also be green on a color screen) will pop open a box of information without changing topics. To activate either kind of underlined item, move the mouse pointer on top of the phrase and click the left mouse button once. When you move the mouse on top of an underlined term, the mouse pointer will change to a hand with a pointing index finger (🖑).

In *Access,* the pop-up box from a dotted–underlined phrase could contain two different types of information. If the dotted–underlined item is part of a sentence, you will get a definition of the word or phrase in a pop-up box. Those terms are called *glossary terms*. When you are finished reading the definition, click again anywhere on the screen to close the definition box. If the item stands alone on its line, it represents a list of additional topics that are related to the current screen. Since all of the related topics in the pop-up box will be jump terms (underlined with a solid line), you may click on one to jump to that new topic.

The three buttons at the top of the window *(see Figure I - 13)* will return to the **Help Topics** window, move **Back** to any previous topic one screen at a time, and open a sub-menu of **Options** that include printing the current screen's information and copying the information.

To use the Help system:

- Click on **HELP** in the menu bar.

- Click on **Microsoft Access Help Topics** or **Answer Wizard** to open the Help system.

- Click on the tab for the method you wish to use to locate the specific information you desire.

- Choose any jump terms or dotted–underlined terms to display associated topics.

Activity I.5: Using the Help System

To experience the Help system, we will look for information about the toolbar.

1. Click the mouse on the **HELP** menu to open that menu.

2. In the **HELP** menu, click on **Microsoft Access Help Topics**.

    The tab last selected in the Help system is the tab that displays.

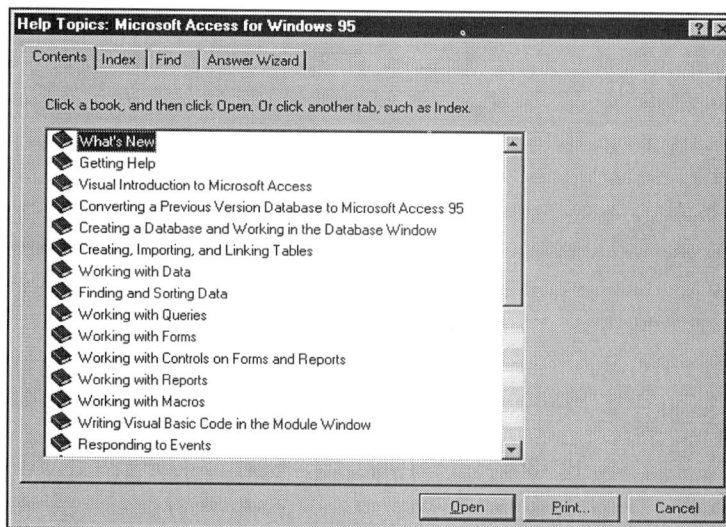

Help Topics: Microsoft Access for Windows 95

Contents | Index | Find | Answer Wizard

Click a book, and then click Open. Or click another tab, such as Index.

- What's New
- Getting Help
- Visual Introduction to Microsoft Access
- Converting a Previous Version Database to Microsoft Access 95
- Creating a Database and Working in the Database Window
- Creating, Importing, and Linking Tables
- Working with Data
- Finding and Sorting Data
- Working with Queries
- Working with Forms
- Working with Controls on Forms and Reports
- Working with Reports
- Working with Macros
- Writing Visual Basic Code in the Module Window
- Responding to Events

Open | Print... | Cancel

Figure I - 13

3. Click on the **Contents** tab.

    *The **Contents** list appears (see Figure I - 13).*

4. Scroll down in the list of topics to **Reference Information** and either double-click that topic or click on it once to highlight it and click the **Open** button.

5. Click on **Glossary** in the list of sub-topics that appears under **Reference Information** (see Figure I - 14) and click the **Display** button.

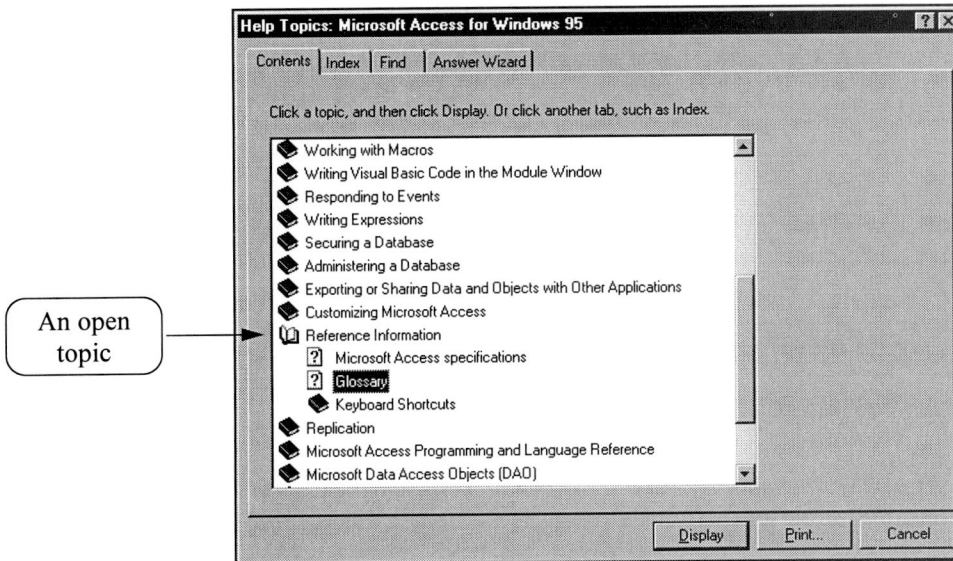

Figure I - 14

6. As we are looking for information about the toolbars, click the **T** button near the top of the window to jump to the Ts in the **Glossary** list.

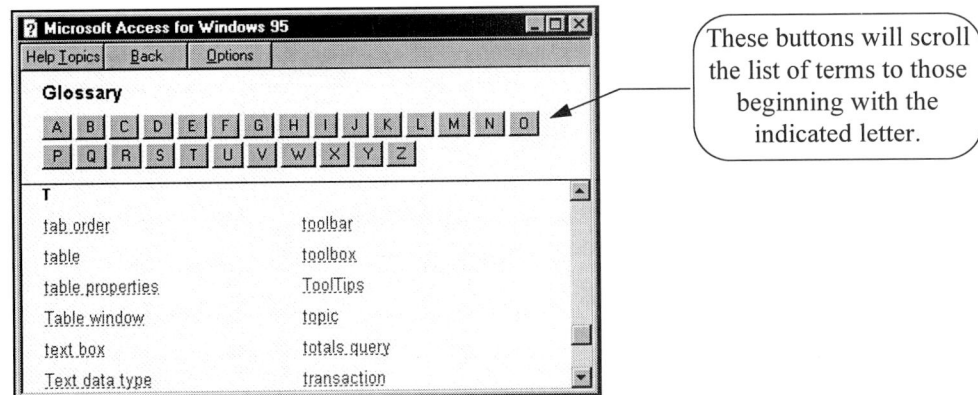

Figure I - 15

7. The dotted–underlined term **toolbar** should be showing at the top of the right column (see Figure I - 15). Click on **toolbar** to see a glossary definition of that term (see Figure I - 16).

    *The mouse pointer becomes a hand with a pointing index finger when on top of the term. If you cannot see the term **toolbar**, you will need to scroll down until it appears.*

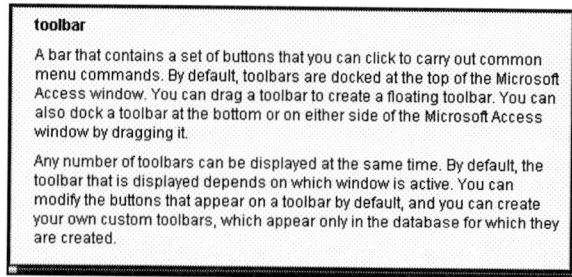

toolbar

A bar that contains a set of buttons that you can click to carry out common menu commands. By default, toolbars are docked at the top of the Microsoft Access window. You can drag a toolbar to create a floating toolbar. You can also dock a toolbar at the bottom or on either side of the Microsoft Access window by dragging it.

Any number of toolbars can be displayed at the same time. By default, the toolbar that is displayed depends on which window is active. You can modify the buttons that appear on a toolbar by default, and you can create your own custom toolbars, which appear only in the database for which they are created.

Figure I - 16

8. Click the mouse button again (anywhere on the screen) when you are finished examining the definition. The **glossary definition** box disappears.

9. Click the **Help Topics** button to return to the **Help Topics** window.

10. Click on the **Index** tab at the top of the window (see Figure I - 17).

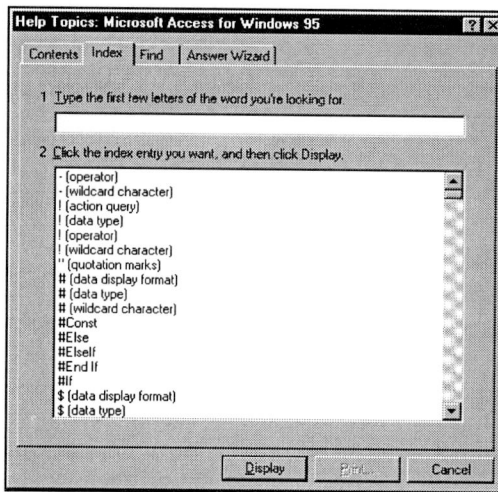

Figure I - 17

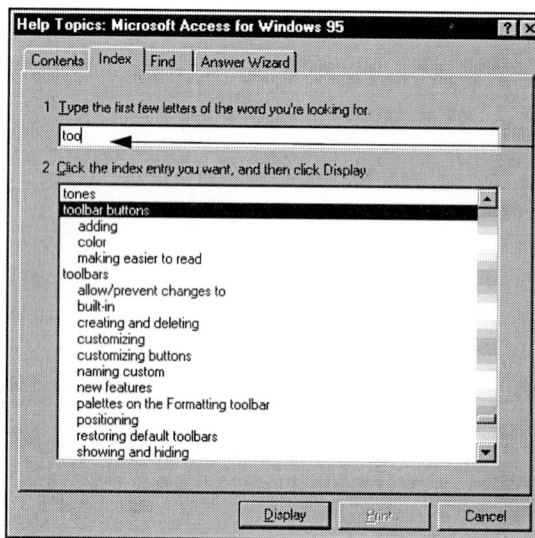

Type the starting letters of the desired topic.

Figure I - 18

11. Begin typing the first three letters of **toolbars** one letter at a time.

    *When you type the **t**, the list of topics scrolls to the ts. When you type the second letter, **o**, it scrolls to topics beginning with to. The third letter brings the list to the desired topic, **toolbars** (see Figure I - 18).*

12. Scroll down in the list under **toolbars** and click on **ToolTips**. Click the **Display** button.

13. A sub-list of **Topics Found** opens (see Figure I - 19).

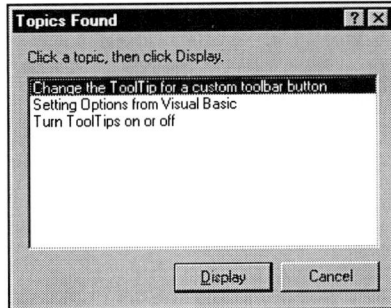

Figure I - 19

14. Click on **Turn ToolTips on or off** and click the **Display** button.

    The directions for accomplishing that task appear in a window (see Figure I - 20). We will not carry out those directions, but the method is outlined.

15. Click on the **Help Topics** button to return to the **Help Topics** window.

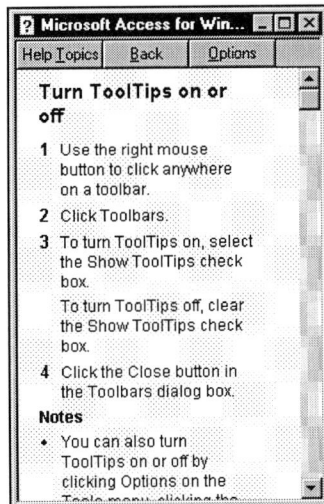

Figure I - 20

16. Click on the **Answer Wizard** tab (see Figure I - 21).

    *The question that is showing in the text box in Step 1 of the **Answer Wizard** screen will be the last question asked of the Wizard.*

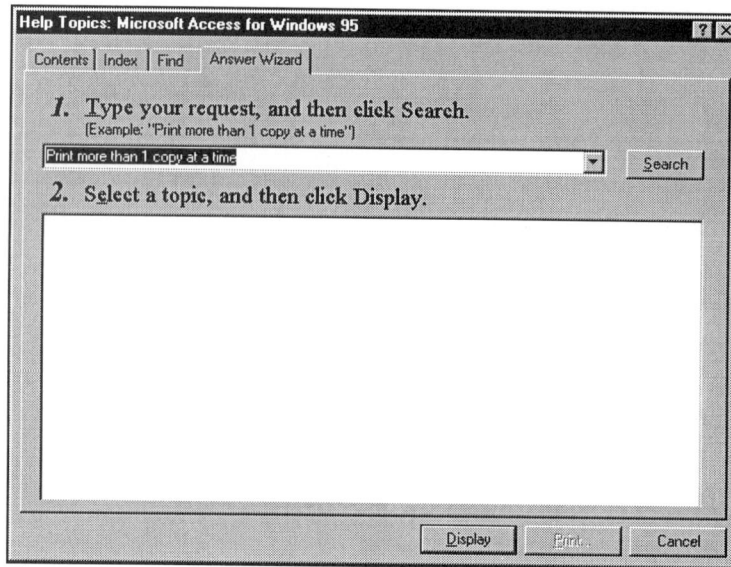

Figure I - 21

17. Type: **how do I move a toolbar** and click the **Search** button (see Figure I - 22).

18. In the list of topics under **How Do I**, click on **Move toolbars to another screen location** and click the **Display** button.

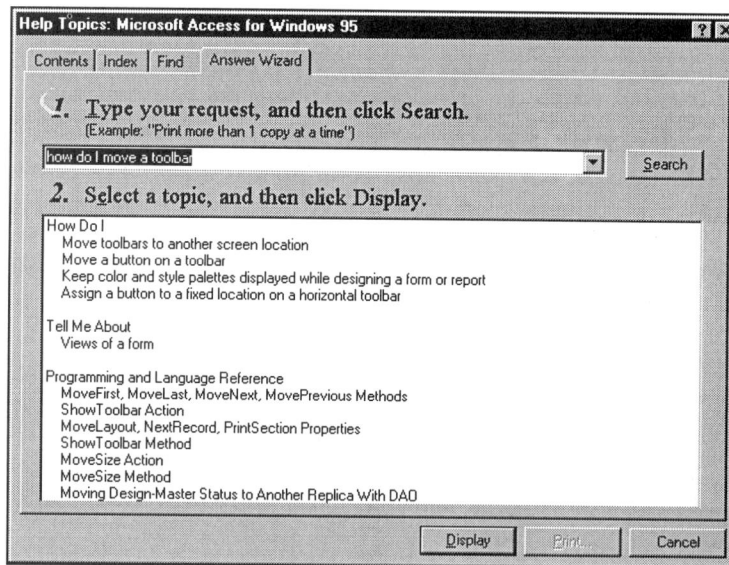

Figure I - 22

The steps are listed in a window (see Figure I - 23). You do not need to carry out these steps now.

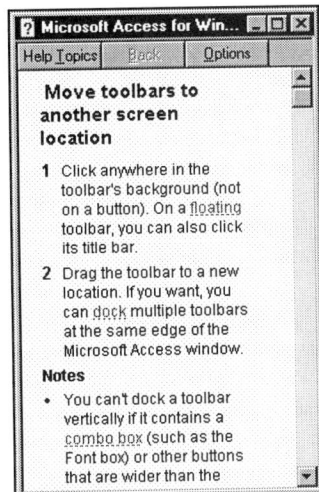

Figure I - 23

19. Click the mouse on the **Help Topics** button to return to the **Help Topics** window.

20. Click the **Cancel** button to close the Help system and return to *Access*.

EXITING FROM ACCESS

Although *Access* automatically saves the data you type, there is no guarantee it has saved yet. Thus, you must **never** turn the computer off without properly exiting from *Access*. There is nothing you can do to prevent the electricity from going off occasionally, and that may cause some problems and force you to have to repair a database once in a while (Repair Database is in the **TOOLS** menu when no database is open on the desktop), but do not do it to yourself by turning the computer off prematurely.

Also, if you are using a floppy diskette for your data, **never** switch floppy diskettes while a database is open in *Access*, even if you switch programs first. *Access* is expecting that same diskette to be there at all times, and will complain if it cannot locate it, and may even overwrite the second diskette.

It is also important to properly exit from Windows as problems can occur otherwise.

To exit from *Access*:

- Click on **Exit** in the **FILE** menu.

- If there are design changes that have not been saved yet, *Access* will ask in an alert box (see Figure I - 24 for a typical example) whether to save them or not before exiting.

- If you get an alert box, click **Yes** to save and exit, **No** to exit without saving, and **Cancel** to cancel the request to exit and return to where you were in *Access*.

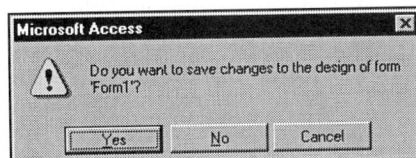

Figure I - 24

Activity I.6: Exiting from Access

If you will be stopping rather than moving on to Lesson 1, you should exit from *Access*.

1. Click on the **FILE** menu.
2. Click on **Exit**.

CONVENTIONS FOLLOWED IN THIS BOOK

Table I - 2 explains the conventions used in this book when giving instructions.

Task	Notation in the Book	What To Do
Highlighting a choice or activating a button with the mouse	click on, click the mouse button	Move the mouse pointer on top of the menu name, button, or choice in a list and press the left mouse button once.
Selecting from a list with the mouse	double-click on	Move the mouse pointer on top of the choice in a list and click the left mouse button two times rapidly without moving the mouse.
Moving or sizing an object with the mouse	drag the mouse	Move the mouse on top of the item to be moved or sized, hold down the left mouse button, move the mouse with the button still held down until the position or size of the object is as desired, and release the mouse button.
Choosing a menu command	Pick **MENU/Command** Choose **MENU/Command**, then **Submenu Command**	(1) Move the mouse pointer on top of the **MENU** name and click the left mouse button once. (2) Within the menu that opens, move the mouse pointer on top of the desired **Command** name and click the left mouse button once. (3) If a submenu appears, move the mouse pointer on top of the desired **Submenu Command** name in the submenu and click the left mouse button once.
Pressing a key	Press **ENTER**	Press the **ENTER** key on the keyboard.
Using a key combination	Press **SHIFT+TAB**	Hold down the first key (**SHIFT**) and, while it is down, tap the second key (**TAB**).

Table I - 2

SUMMARY

In this introduction you have run *Access*, explored its screen components, used its basic tools (the menu and the toolbar, among others), and run the Help system. The major terms were also defined. You opened a supplied database and opened a table within that database. You closed the table, closed the database, and exited from *Access*. As these are the fundamentals that you will use throughout the lessons in this book, feel free to come back to review some procedures or terms. Keep in mind that the Help system is an enormous source of information about *Access* and should be used.

KEY TERMS

Data
Database
Field
Field Name
Glossary Term

Jump Term
RDBMS
Record
Status Bar
Table

Tool
Tool Tips
Toolbar
Toolbar Button

1 Creating Databases and Tables

Objectives

In this lesson you will learn how to:

- Create a new database
- Design and create a data table
- Distinguish between the data types in *Access*

- Enter data into a table
- Modify the structure of a table
- Create a primary key

PROJECT DESCRIPTION

The project that we will pursue through these lessons is that of a small retailer of CDROMs for computers. This lesson will begin by creating the employee file, which will contain the employees' names, identification numbers, date of hire, salary, phone extension, and any important notes. Subsequent lessons will build other components using tables of invoices, products, and customers. All of these tables of data will fit together by the final lesson into a system of related tables, in what is called a Relational Database Management System or RDBMS.

At the end of this first lesson you will have created the table of data shown in **Figure 1 - 1**.

	Employee ID	First Name	Last Name	Date Hired	Salary	Commissioned	Extension	Notes
▶	8	Ruth	Koslow	7/5/90	$39,000.00	☐	7903	Moved from Hawaii.
	5	Gina	Brown	1/20/92	$32,000.00	☐	7901	Previous job with MTV.
	8	Herman	Nutley	10/4/93	$36,000.00	☐	7910	
	9	Sarah	Smith	2/5/94	$29,000.00	☐	7905	
	10	Daphne	Green	3/1/94	$26,000.00	☐	7911	Hired on a trial basis.
	11	George	Jeffers	5/27/94	$29,000.00	☐	7904	Experience in electroni
✳	0				$0.00	☐		

Figure 1 - 1

THE DATABASE

A database in *Access* is a container that can hold tables of data, report and label designs, screen designs called forms, queries for selecting subsets of listings, and programming. Since the tables, reports, forms, queries, macros, and modules that you create to put together a system for obtaining information are called *objects*, the database contains all of the objects for one system of data.

The employee table that we will create in this lesson must be contained within such a database, so we must create the database first.

> **REMEMBER:** Read the bulleted list that follows, but do not actually perform the steps until you reach Activity 1.1.

To create a database:

- If you have just started *Access*, click the **Blank Database** option in the introductory dialog box and click the **OK** button.

- If *Access* is already running with some other database open or an empty desktop, choose **FILE/New Database** in the menu, or click the **New Database** button ▯ on the toolbar. In the **New** dialog box on the **General** tab, click on **Blank Database** and click the **OK** button.

- In the **File New Database** dialog box, pick the desired location for Save in. The Save as type selection should be **Microsoft Access Databases.**

- In the **File Name** text box, replace **db1** with the name by which the database will be recorded, and click the **Create** command button.

Activity 1.1: Creating the Database

1. Run *Access*.

2. In the Introductory dialog box (see Figure 1 - 2), click on **Blank Database** in the **Create a New Database Using** section.

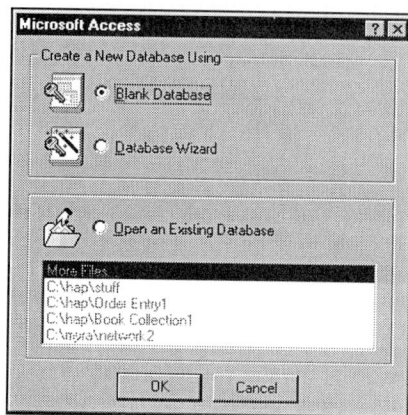

Figure 1 - 2

*If Access was already running with a database open on the desktop or an empty desktop, pick **FILE/New Database** and click on **Blank Database** on the **General** tab instead (see Figure 1 - 3).*

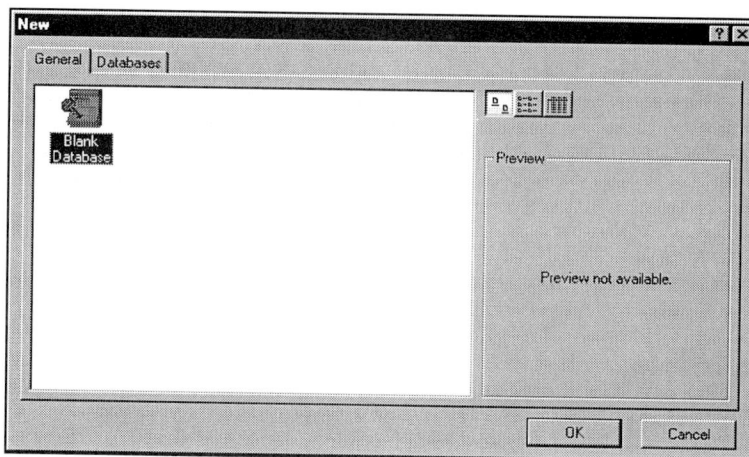

Figure 1 - 3

3. In the **File Name** text box of the **File New Database** dialog box, type: **SALES** as in Figure 1 - 4.

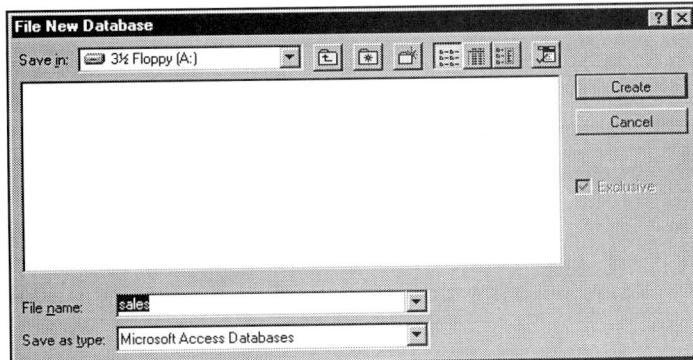

Figure 1 - 4

Even though you do not normally see any extension on the filename, .mdb which stands for Microsoft database, is added automatically by Access.

4. Check to make certain that the currently selected **Save in:** location is correct, and that **Save as type** says **Microsoft Access Databases**.

5. Click the **Create** button and the database will be created and opened on the workspace (see Figure 1 - 5).

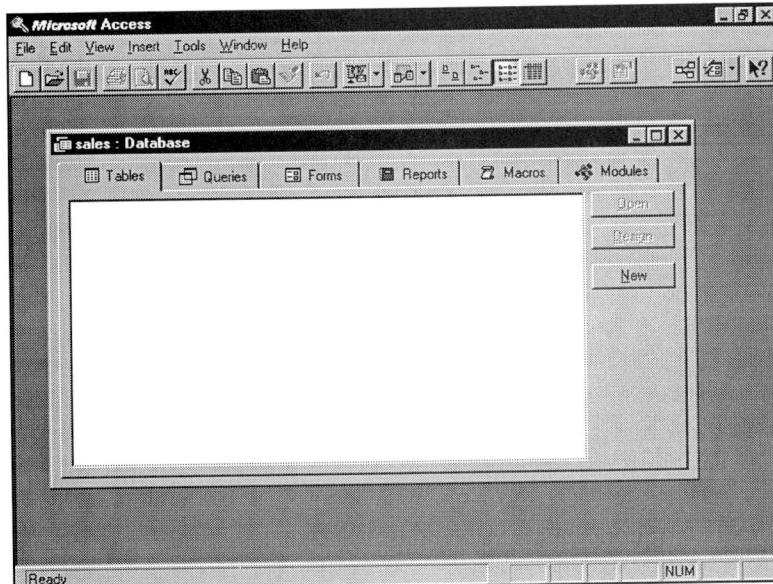

Figure 1 - 5

Creating Objects

Now that the database exists, we are ready to create the table to hold the employee data. The most direct way to create an object like a table is to click on the tab for the design category at the top edge of the **Database** window (Tables, Reports, etc.), and click the **New** button at the right side of the window.

There are five ways to proceed with the creation of a new table (see Figure 1 - 6):

- **Datasheet View** lets you type sample data into a grid and *Access* will guess what type of data each column contains. For really simple tables this method might be satisfactory, but the burden is on the user to make certain that all of *Access'* guesses were correct. Checking and correcting the guesses can often take as long as creating the table directly, and in practice this method is not normally a good choice.

- **Design View** is usually the best choice for creating a new table. A grid is filled in with the actual design rather than sample data and the user has complete control over the details of the table design. We will use Design View in the following activity.

- The **Table Wizard** contains 25 business designs and 20 personal table designs ready to be used by merely selecting the needed type. With some minor modifications these designs can often suit a user's needs. The difficulty is that the designers of *Access* could not guess all of an individual's or corporation's needs. Thus, these ready-to-run table designs often are close, but not quite perfect. As with Datasheet View, you could spend as long fine tuning the built-in design as you would if you created it yourself.

- **Import Table** lets you create in *Access* a copy of a table recorded by some other program. We will explore importing data in Lesson 3.

- **Link Table** enables you to use within the current database data that is recorded somewhere else, like in another database. We will examine linking in Lesson 3, as well.

When you create something within *Access*, the name you give it may be up to 64 characters long. Any characters except the exclamation point, period, accent mark, or square brackets are legal; thus, spaces are allowed.

The names of tables and other objects should fully describe their function. As there are hardly any restrictions, you should not name a table **EMPL** when it could be **Employees**. Similarly, **Equipment In Use** is better than **EQPINUSE**, and **Accounts Receivable** fully describes a table whereas **AR** or **ACCTRECV** is potentially confusing.

To create a table:

- Click the **Table** tab at the top of the **Database** window.

- Click the **New** button on the right side of the **Database** window.

- Select **Design View** to design a data table from scratch, or pick one of the other methods.

- Assuming you selected **Design View**, fill in the grid with the names for the columns, data types, and descriptions.

- Save the design.

Filling in the Table Grid

The window for designing tables has three columns in the top section and a group of *Field Properties* in two groups in the lower section. To fill in the three columns, type the desired *Field Name* for a field in your table following the same rules as for the names of objects (see Creating Objects above), select a *Data Type* (see the next section), and optionally enter a description of the field. The description will not only remind you or another person of the purpose for the field, but also will be displayed on the Status Bar during data entry. Thus, the description is an excellent place to include instructions that will be automatically displayed during data entry.

The *Field Properties* in the lower section of the window control the details and options for each field. Only one field's properties show at a time, and, as you move from field to field in the upper portion of the window, the Field Properties for that current field are shown. Such options as the length of a text field and the specific variety of a numeric field are set with Field Properties.

Data Types

There are nine types of data that can be stored in an *Access* table. Additionally, the numeric type has six varieties. When designing a table, you must plan carefully and select the proper type for each column of data. The details of each type and variety are listed in Table 1 - 1 below. Pay particular attention to the limitations, as that often dictates what type cannot be used for a specific purpose.

Data Type	Subtype	Size Limitation	Special Characteristics
Text		1-255 characters	Most common field type
Memo		0-64,000 characters	May have not only text, but tabs, carriage returns, font changes, etc.
Number			
	Byte	An integer from 0 to 255	Requires 1 character of storage
	Integer	An integer from -32,768 to 32,767	Requires 2 characters of storage
	Long Integer	An integer from -2,147,483,648 to 2,147,483,647	Requires 4 characters of storage
	Single	A decimal with up to 7 decimal places from $-3.4*10^{38}$ to $3.4*10^{38}$	Requires 4 characters of storage
	Double	A decimal with up to 15 decimal places from $-1.797*10^{308}$ to $1.797*10^{308}$	Requires 8 characters of storage
	Replication ID		Deals with replication of databases which is beyond the scope of this book
Date/Time		A date or a time or both	From the year 100 to 9999
Currency		Up to $999 trillion with 4 decimal places	2 decimal places is the default
Counter			Automatically numbers each record when the record is entered; the number assigned cannot be changed
Yes/No		Only Yes or No	
OLE Object		Up to 1 gigabyte	A picture or other binary file
Lookup Wizard		Looks up a value from another table	Like choosing from a drop-down list

Table 1 - 1

Activity 1.2: Creating a Table

In this activity you will create the fields that are needed in the **Employees** table. The business will need the name, an identification number, the hired date, the salary, the phone extension, and a place for important notes.

1. Click the **Table** tab at the top edge of the **Database** window.
2. Click the **New** button at the right side of the **Database** window.

3.   Select **Design View** in the **New Table** dialog box (see Figure 1 - 6) and click **OK**.

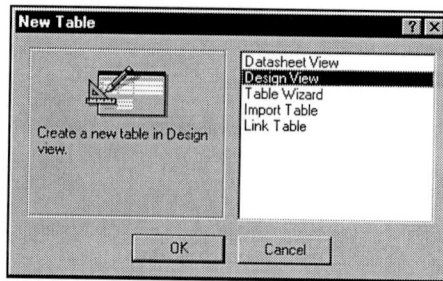

Figure 1 - 6

*The **Table** window that opens is where you define the fields for the new table (Figure 1 - 7).*

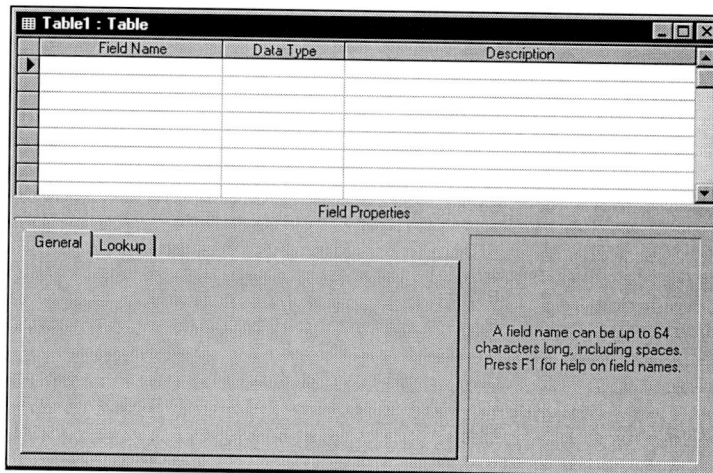

Figure 1 - 7

4.   On the first row in the **Field Name** column, type the name of the first field: **Employee ID**

5.   Press the **TAB** key to move to the **Data Type** column.

6.   **Text** is the default data type, but we want the Employee IDs to be numbers. Therefore, we must change the **Data Type**. Click the drop-down list arrow to open the list of data types and select **Number** (see Figure 1 - 8).

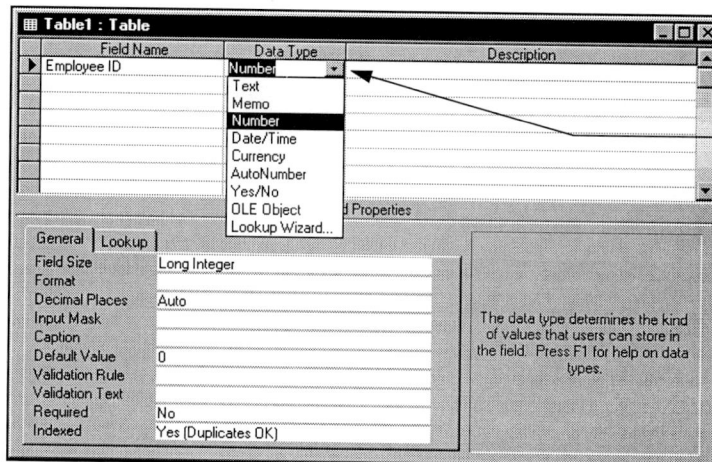

Figure 1 - 8

*The **Field Properties** list in the lower section of the **Table** window contains the options for the current field. Notice that the **Field Size** of the **Employee ID** field is set to Long Integer (see Figure 1 - 8). That would allow much larger numbers than are needed. Since the company is small, we will need only two or three digits. Also, the Employee ID numbers will not need decimal places, so we can use **Integer** as the **Field Size**.*

*The Status Bar mentions that the **F6** key will switch panes from the upper section to the lower and vice versa. Alternatively, clicking the mouse within the lower section or the upper section will move to that pane.*

7. Press the **F6** key to switch to the lower pane.

8. Click on the arrow to open the drop-down list and select **Integer** (see Figure 1 - 9).

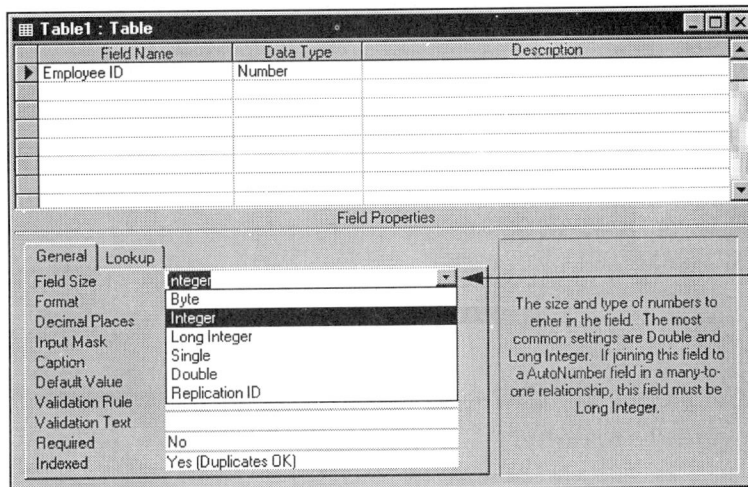

After pressing **F6** to switch to the lower section, make certain the **General** tab is selected and click here to open the list of number sizes.

Figure 1 - 9

9. Press **F6** to return to the upper pane.

10. Press **TAB** to move to the **Description** column.

11. Enter the description: **Consecutive numbers assigned upon hiring**

12. Press **TAB** to move to the second line.

13. On the second row in the **Field Name** column, type the field name: **First Name**

14. Press the **TAB** key to move to the **Data Type** column.

15. Since **Text**, the default data type, is correct, merely press **TAB** to move to the **Description** column.

    It is possible that someone changed the default data type to another type. If Text is not the default, merely open the drop-down list and click on Text.

    *The **Field Properties** list in the lower section of the **Table** dialog box shows the size of the First Name field as 50 characters wide. That is wider than needed.*

16. Press the **F6** key to switch to the lower pane.

17. Replace the 50 on the **Field Size** line with **15** as shown in Figure 1 - 10.

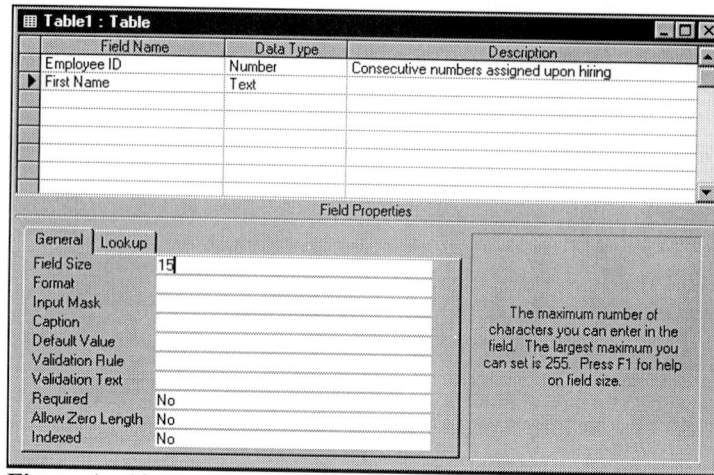

Figure 1 - 10

18. Press **F6** to return to the upper pane.

19. As it is obvious what a first name is, we do not need a description, so press **TAB** to move to the third line.

20. Enter the remaining five fields as displayed in the last five lines of Table 1 - 2. When finished, the grid should look like Figure 1 - 11.

Field Name	Data Type	Size (in lower pane)	Description
Employee ID	Number	Integer	Consecutive numbers...
First Name	Text	15	
Last Name	Text	20	
Date Hired	Date/Time	(size is automatic)	
Salary	Currency	(size is automatic)	
Extension	Text	4	
Notes	Memo	(size is automatic)	

Table 1 - 2

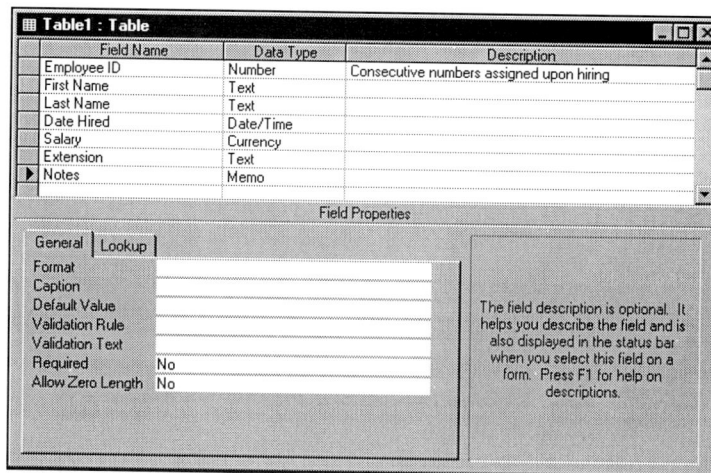

Figure 1 - 11

*Notice that the **Extension** was created as a Text field even though a phone extension contains only digits and looks like a number. When a field will contain only digits, but they are never involved in calculations, it is usually more efficient to make them text fields. Zip codes and area codes are two more examples.*

SAVING THE DESIGN

With the design completed, you need to save the table structure into the database. Here you decide on a descriptive name. Since this table contains data on the employees, you will name it **Employees**.

Should you try to close the table without saving, *Access* will ask whether you want to save the design. You may save it by choosing **Yes** and entering a name for the table, or discard the design with **No** if you really do not want it.

To save a table design:

- Choose **FILE/Save** in the menus.

- Type the desired name for the table.

- Click on the **OK** button.

Activity 1.3: Saving the Table Design

We will save the table with the name **Employees**.

1. Select **FILE/Save**.

2. In the **Save As** dialog box, type the name for this table: **Employees** and click the **OK** button (see Figure 1 - 12).

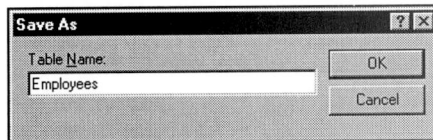

Figure 1 - 12

3. When *Access* says **There is no primary key defined...Do you want to create a primary key now?** click the **No** button (see Figure 1 - 13).

   We will discuss primary keys in a few pages and assign one at that time.

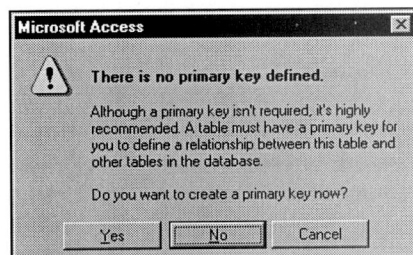

Figure 1 - 13

Access will record the table design in the Sales database.

4. Since we are finished with the design, close the **Employees: Table** window with **FILE/Close**.

*The new table **Employees** will be listed in the **Table** section of the **Sales** database (*Figure 1 - 14*).*

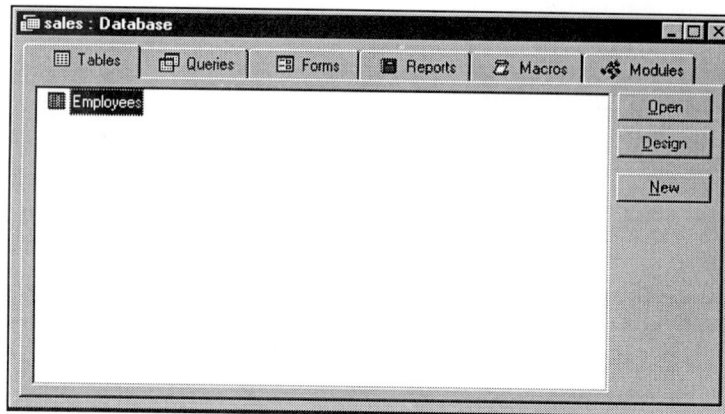

Figure 1 - 14

ENTERING DATA IN A TABLE

The next step is to enter the data into the new Employees table. To type new data into a table, open the table, move to the desired place in the table, and type each item of data.

When you first move onto a line, a rightward pointing triangle at the left edge of the table indicates the current record. As soon as you begin typing, that triangle changes to a pencil. The pencil means data have been typed on that line, but not yet saved. Saving data is automatic; you do not need to make any menu choices or click any buttons to tell *Access* to save the data you have typed. The moment you move to a different record, the previous line of typing is saved. Thus, there is never more than a single line of unsaved data. Even if you close the table without telling *Access* to save the active record, *Access* saves the line automatically. When saved, the pencil icon disappears and the triangle marks the new line.

To move to the proper field while entering data into an *Access* table:

- The **TAB** key, the **ENTER** key, or the **RIGHT ARROW** key will move to the next field.

- Should you need to back up to a previous field, press either the **SHIFT+TAB** key combination or the **LEFT ARROW**.

- You may click the mouse in any field to move the cursor there.

- If you are in the last field, the **TAB, ENTER,** or **RIGHT ARROW** keys wrap around to the first field on the next line so that you are ready to type another record.

Keep the following points in mind while entering data in an *Access* table:

- If you move back to a field that already contains data, the entire set of characters in that field will be selected. Should you begin typing when the whole field is highlighted, the first character you type will replace the entire previous set of characters! While this is handy when replacing outdated data, it might happen accidentally. Either the **Undo** button on the toolbar, or the **EDIT/Undo Typing** command in the menu will restore the field contents.

- To substitute a cursor for the highlighting, press the **F2** key to switch out of Replace mode and into Character Edit mode. Alternatively, click the mouse in the field. When you click the mouse on a field, it places the cursor within that field in Character Edit mode rather than Replace mode.

To fix typing errors while entering data:

- If you notice a typing error before moving to a new field, press the **BACKSPACE** key to remove the error, and then retype.

- Should you notice an error in a previous field, either move to the field and retype the entire entry, or click the mouse cursor next to the mistaken character(s), press the **BACKSPACE** key to remove characters to the left of the cursor or press the **DELETE** key to erase characters to the right of the cursor, and retype the required characters.

Activity 1.4: Entering Data into the Table

In this activity you will enter the data for the six employees of the company.

1. Click on the **Table** tab at the top of the **Database** window if it is not already selected.

2. Select the table name **Employees** by clicking on it.

3. Click the **Open** button at the right side of the **Database** window. Alternatively, you may double-click the table name to automatically open it.

   *The triangle at the left edge of the table (see Figure 1 - 15) should mark the current line and the cursor should be blinking in the **Employee ID** field. Notice the description for the **Employee ID** field on the left end of the Status Bar.*

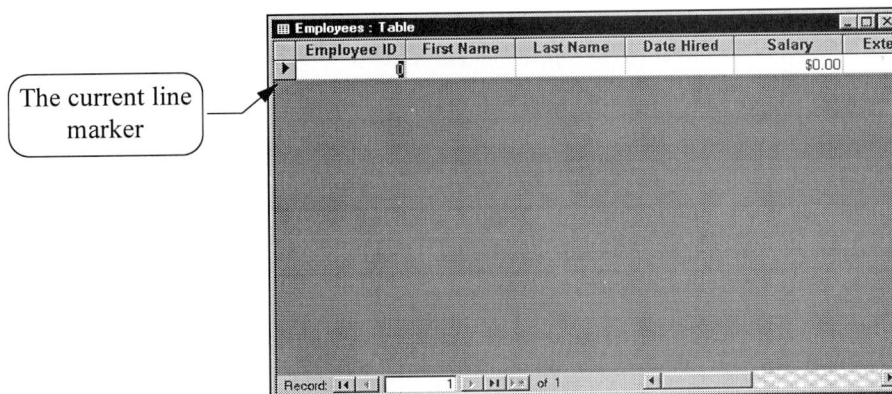

The current line marker

Figure 1 - 15

4. Type **3** for the first employee's ID number and press the **TAB** key to move to the next field.

   The pencil icon should show at the left edge of the table indicating that this record is now being typed (see Figure 1 - 16).

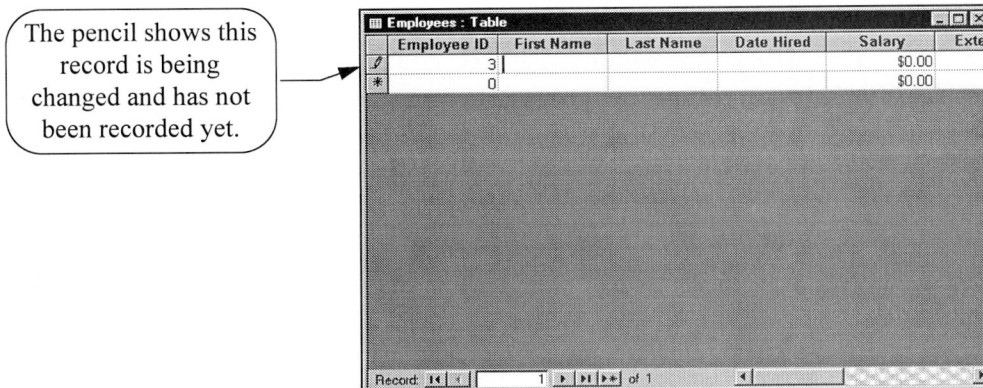

The pencil shows this record is being changed and has not been recorded yet.

Figure 1 - 16

5. In the **First Name** field, type: **Ruth** and press **TAB**.

6. For **Last Name** enter: **Koslow** and move to the next field.

7. In **Date Hired** type: **7/5/90** and move to the next field.

8. Enter: **39,000** for **Salary**.

    Although you may type them, you do not need to type a dollar sign or comma. Nor is it necessary to enter the decimal point and two zeros any time the decimal places are .00. Those will be added automatically when you leave the field.

9. Move to **Extension** and type: **7903**.

    If the table scrolls within the window, that is normal when the fields cannot all fit within the width of the current window frame. As you move within the table, Access will automatically scroll the table so that you can see the field on which you are working. To scroll the table yourself, use the scroll bars.

10. Press **TAB** to move to the **Notes** field and type: **Moved from Hawaii.**

    If the contents of a field are too long for the displayed width of the field, the characters will scroll. We will see later how to adjust the width of a column.

11. Press **TAB** to finish this record and move to the next line.

    The pencil icon disappears, the previous record is saved to disk, and the triangle marks the next line.

12. Type the five additional records as shown in **Table 1 - 3**.

13. As we are finished with data entry, close the table with **FILE/Close**.

    The current record is automatically saved and the table window is closed.

Employee ID	First Name	Last Name	Date Hired	Salary	Extension	Notes
5	Gina	Brown	1/20/92	32,000	7901	Previous job with MTV.
8	Herman	Nutley	10/4/93	36,000	7910	
9	Sarah	Smith	2/5/94	29,000	7905	
10	Daphne	Green	3/1/94	26,000	7911	Hired on a trial basis.
11	George	Jeffers	5/27/94	29,000	7904	Experience in electronics.

Table 1 - 3

MODIFYING A TABLE

After working with a table of data for a while, it usually becomes evident that some alterations need to be made. Perhaps new requirements demand changes, or you might see a better way of accomplishing your objectives.

The company decides that placing the sales staff on a base salary plus commissions will spur sales. Non-sales staff will continue with a full salary. Thus, the employee table needs to record who is on commission by adding a new field.

To modify a table's structure:

*   While the table name is highlighted in the **Database** window, click the **Design** button.

- Move to any field that needs to be altered and type any changes or select any different options.

- To insert a new field, move to the field that currently occupies the position where you want the new field to be and choose **INSERT/Field**. On the new blank line, type the new name, data type, and description.

- To add a new field at the end of the current group of fields, click on the blank line just below the last field and type the new name, data type, and description.

- To remove a field, click on the gray block just to the left of the field name. The entire line will be highlighted. Press the **DELETE** key or pick **EDIT/Delete Row** and confirm the deletion.

Activity 1.5: Modifying the Table Structure

You decide to insert the new Commissioned field between Salary and Extension.

1. With the highlight on the table **Employees**, click the **Design** button at the right side of the Database window.

2. Click the mouse pointer on the field name **Extension** to move onto that line.

3. Choose **INSERT/Field** to insert a new line, which will push Extension and Notes down a row (see Figure 1 - 17).

4. Type the new field name: **Commissioned** and press **TAB**.

5. Select a **Yes/No** field type by typing the letter **Y** and pressing **TAB**.

    Each data type except Counter begins with a unique letter; thus, to select the type, merely type the first letter and press TAB. To select Counter, type the first two letters.

6. For the **Description** type: **Checked means base salary plus commissions; Unchecked means full salary.**

    The size of a Yes/No field is automatic, so you do not need to change the Field Properties.

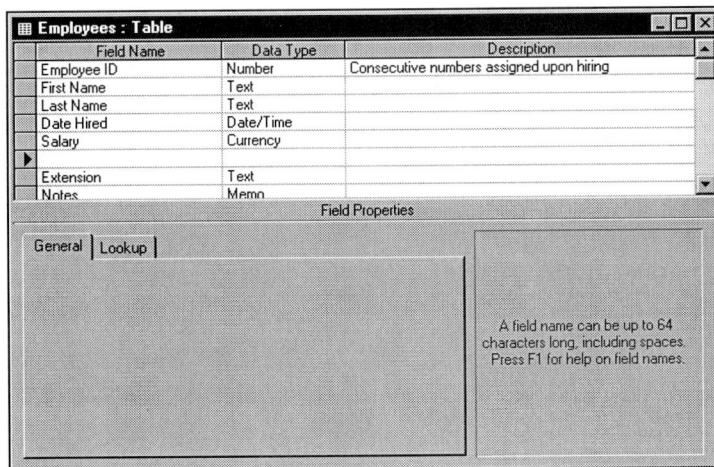

Figure 1 - 17

7. Save this alteration with **FILE/Save**.

    If you are continuing on to the next section now, do not close the table design.

    We will update the data by filling in whether the employees are on commission or not in the next lesson.

PRIMARY KEY FIELDS

If the data in a table is kept in order, finding a particular listing is much quicker. For example, since the telephone book is in alphabetical name order, to locate the name Quinn, one could open the book in the exact middle and look at the first name on the page to see whether Quinn was further along in the book or in the first half of the book. Supposing Quinn is further along than the middle, you can ignore the first half of the book, for you know Quinn cannot be there. If you then divided the second half in half again and looked to see which of those quarters Quinn was in, you would have narrowed the search down to only one fourth of all listings in just two tries. Continuing in a similar fashion, you could search thousands of listings in about a dozen tries.

If, however, the names in the telephone book were not in order, you would need to read every name to locate a particular listing, a process that could take thousands of tries to search thousands of records. *Access* reaps the same benefit from having the records in order, and, thus, has what is called a *primary key* to keep the records in order.

A *primary key* can consist of one or more fields in the table design. Normally you designate which field or fields will make up the primary key, although *Access* will ask whether it should establish the primary key the first time you save a table design that does not have one. If allowed, *Access* will select a counter type of field; if there is no counter field, *Access* will insert one and designate it the primary key.

You should select as a primary key a single field that will have unique values in it, like an ID field, or a combination of fields that taken together will be unique. Uniqueness is a requirement of a primary key. Once established, *Access* will not accept either duplicate entries in a primary key field (or the combination of fields), or an empty primary key field.

Primary key fields are often a requirement for multiple table operations. For example, when a relational system uses several tables simultaneously, editing across multiple tables is not allowed without primary keys. Thus, you often must designate primary keys.

To designate a primary key field:

- Select the field in the table design window.
- Either choose **EDIT/Primary Key** or click the **Primary Key** button on the toolbar.
- A key symbol will appear on the gray block at the left edge of the line for that field.

Activity 1.6: Assigning a Primary Key

We will select the **Employee ID** field as the primary key since it contains a unique value for each employee.

1. If you are not still in the **Employees: Table** design window (see Figure 1 - 18), select the table name **Employees** and click the **Design** button.

2. Click anywhere on the line for the **Employee ID** field.

   The triangle icon will appear on the left end of the Employee ID line.

3. Click the **Primary Key** button on the toolbar or choose **EDIT/Primary Key**.

   A key icon will appear to the left of the field name (see Figure 1 - 18).

4. Select **FILE/Save** to save the design.

   This altered design is saved over the previous version of Employees, so the table design has been updated.

5.   Select **FILE/Close**.

The key icon denotes a primary key.

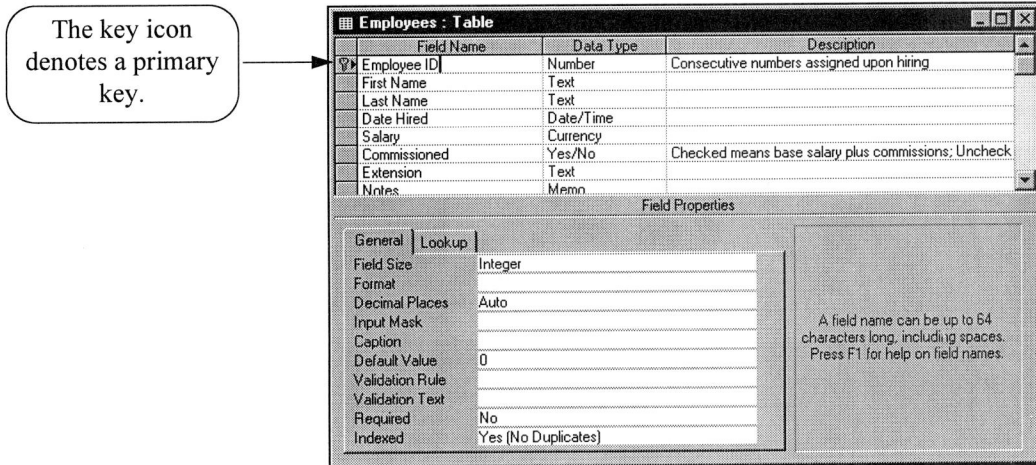

Figure 1 - 18

PRINTING A TABLE

When you need a paper copy of the data in a table, the table can be printed. This is a quick printout, not a designed report. On a table printout all fields are included. Also, no calculations, font changes, titles, or other frills are included. It is a dump of the data onto paper. In a later lesson we will explore designed reports.

To print a table:

- Either open the table or move the highlight onto the table name in the database window.

- Choose **FILE/Print** in the menu.

- In the **Print** dialog box, set any options.

- Click the **OK** command button.

- Alternatively, you may click the **Print** button on the toolbar. The **Print** button prints immediately without allowing for any options to be changed.

Activity 1.7: Printing a Table

1.   The highlight should still be on **Employees**.

2.   Click the mouse on the **FILE** menu to open it, then pick **Print** within that menu by clicking on that choice.

   Alternatively, you could press Ctrl+P.

3.   In the **Print** dialog box (see Figure 1 - 19), **All** should be the option for Print Range and Copies should have a 1 in the text box.

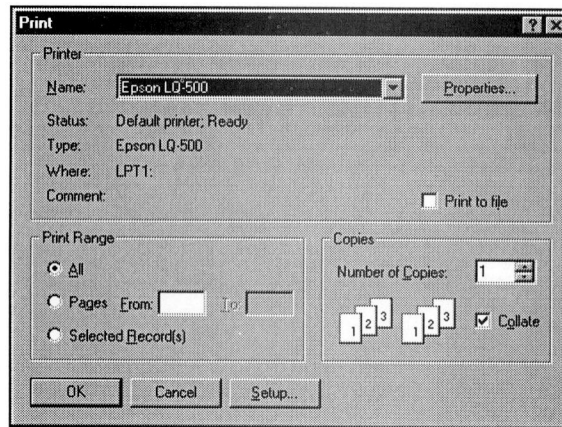

Figure 1 - 19

Your computer will probably have a different printer listed at the top of the dialog box.

4. Click the **OK** button.

5. Select **FILE/Close** to close the **SALES** database.

SUMMARY

In this project you created a database to hold the various designed objects that we will need and built the first table for that database. You entered records into the table, modified the structure of the table, and established a primary key. In Lesson 2 you will further develop your editing and searching capabilities. Lesson 3 will then add more tables to Sales by importing the data from other sources.

KEY TERMS

Data Type	Field Properties	Table
Database	Object	
Field Name	Primary key	

INDEPENDENT PROJECTS

The following four independent projects give you a chance to work with *Access* in creating databases and tables. The first two projects give explicit directions to complete the steps. The third leaves more of the decisions and details to you. The fourth project merely outlines the project and leaves most of the planning to you. The projects continue in each lesson, building on the previous lesson's project.

Independent Project 1.1: The School Newspaper

The school newspaper needs your help. They are currently recording the advertisements they solicit in composition books. However, they are going to need summary statistics and the thought of performing them by hand is not appealing.

They ask you to design a table for recording the ads. The paper records they show you have six columns of data: Ad Number, Purchased By, Size, Price, Date Paid, and Salesperson ID. Ad Number is a unique number that is preprinted on each sheet the sales force uses to write up a sale.

Since it is unique, Ad Number will be the primary key. Size is a two–letter code representing the size of the ad. (See the **Description** column for the meanings of the four possible codes.) Salesperson ID is the letter plus two–digit code for the salesperson. The structure of the table is outlined in Table 1 - 4.

Field Name	Data Type	Size (in lower pane)	Description
Ad Number	Number	Integer	Number on Solicitation sheet
Purchased By	Text	30	
Size	Text	2	FP=Full page, HP=Half page, QP =Quarter page, EP=Eighth page
Price	Currency	(Size is automatic)	
Date Paid	Date/Time	(Size is automatic)	
Salesperson ID	Text	3	Letter plus 2 digits for salesperson.

Table 1 - 4

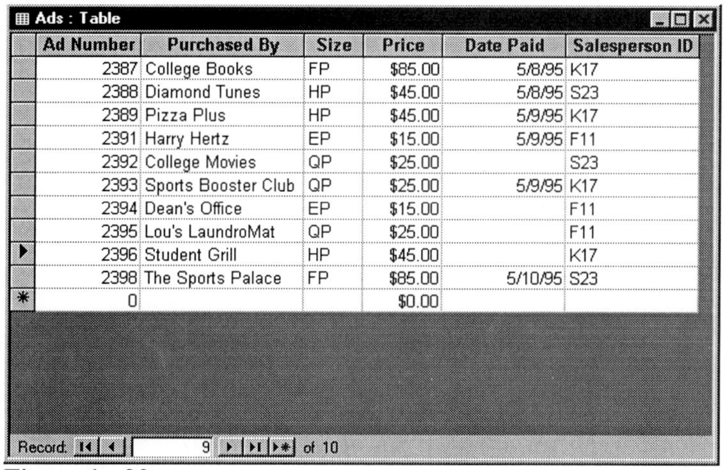

Figure 1 - 20

Figure 1 - 20 shows the data you will need to get started.

1. Run *Access*.

2. Begin creating a new database to hold the newspaper ads (and any other data they may eventually need to record) by clicking the **Blank Database** option in the introductory dialog box. Click **OK**. (Use **FILE/New Database** or click the **New Database** button on the toolbar if *Access* was already running with a different database or no database open on the desktop. Then, pick **Blank Database** on the **General** tab and click **OK**.)

3. Make certain **Save in** is correct. For example, if you will be using the A: drive and that is not currently selected, click on the drop-down arrow for the **Save in:** list and click on **A:**.

4. Type the name for the new database, **Exercise1**, in the **File name:** box of the **File New Database** dialog box and click on the **Create** button.

5. **Maximize** the *Access* window if it does not already cover the entire screen.

6. Make sure the **Table** tab is selected and click on the **New** button to begin a new table.

7. Choose **Design View** in the **New Table** dialog box and click **OK**.

8. Fill in the six fields as shown in Table 1 - 4. Remember to set the **Size** for each field (except the automatic ones) in the lower section of the window.

9. Make **Ad Number** the primary key by clicking anywhere on the line for **Ad Number** and clicking the **Primary Key** button on the toolbar. The key icon will appear on the record selector.

10. Save the table by picking **FILE/Save**, entering the name: **Ads** and clicking the **OK** button.

11. Close the Table window with **FILE/Close**.

12. With the highlight on **Ads**, click on the **Open** button to open the table for data entry.

13. Enter the 10 records shown in Figure 1 - 20. Be careful to match the upper– or lower–case characters for each entry. Some of the entries will scroll and be partially hidden since they are longer than the width that is currently showing for the column. That is perfectly all right. You will correct the situation in the next lesson.

14. When finished, close the table with **FILE/Close**.

    The newspaper had previously kept the ads for different issues of the paper on separate sheets in the ad book. That will not work in a database table, so you realize after working with the data a while that the table will need an additional column to record the issue of the newspaper. Rather than the issue number, which would not mean much by itself, you decide to add the date of issue to the table structure.

15. With the highlight on **Ads**, click the **Design** button to open the design of the table.

16. Click on the next available line, line 7.

17. Type the field name: **Issue Date** and press **TAB** to move to the **Data Type** column.

18. It will be a **Date/Time** field, so type a **D** and press **TAB**. The size will be automatic. No description is necessary.

19. Save the altered design with **FILE/Save**.

20. Close the table with **FILE/Close**.

21. Click on the **Open** button to open **Ads**.

22. Move to the **Issue Date** column and enter: **5/20/95** for all 10 records. (As a shortcut, type **5/20/95** in the first record, move down with the **DOWN ARROW**, and press the Ditto key for each of the remaining records. The Ditto key is **CTRL+'** , that is hold down **CTRL** and tap the apostrophe. Continue until all 10 are done. The **Ditto** key copies into the current field whatever is in the field immediately above.)

23. Print the table with **FILE/Print** or the **Print** button on the toolbar. Click the **OK** button in the Print dialog box if you used **FILE/Print**.

24. Close the table with **FILE/Close**.

25. Close the database with **FILE/Close**.

26. If you are finished with *Access*, exit from *Access* with **FILE/Exit**.

Independent Project 1.2: The Bookstore

The local bookstore has asked you to create a database to keep track of the books that it stocks and their publishers. The owner has written out the items that need to be recorded. That list names Title, Author, Year of Publication, Publisher Code, Price, and Quantity in Stock.

After reviewing the owner's plans, you spot one problem with the list. You want to include a primary key, but nothing in the list is sure to be unique. Therefore, you decide to add to the six suggested fields a Book Code as the first field in the design. The resulting table structure is displayed in Table 1 - 5. The data you are given to get started and test the table is shown in Figure 1 - 21.

Field Name	Data Type	Size (in lower pane)	Description
Book Code	Text	6	Unique code of 3 letters and 2 digits
Title	Text	40	
Author	Text	40	
Year of Publication	Text	4	4–digit year
Publisher Code	Text	4	2 letters plus 2 digits
Price	Currency	(Size is automatic)	
Quantity in Stock	Number	Integer	

Table 1 - 5

Book Code	Title	Author	Year of Publication	Publisher Code	Price	Quantity in Stock
ATL11	Art Through Life	Jane Rick	1994	AW30	$22.95	86
CAL28	Calculus	Henry Slate	1977	TT12	$42.95	152
ECC22	Economically Correct	Lester Dane	1974	CE03	$32.95	81
EMP19	Even More Poems	Sina Grant	1976	BP07	$21.00	47
LOP18	Lots of Poems	Sina Grant	1973	BP07	$18.00	7
LUI81	Look Up In The Sky	Bruce Tipple	1989	TT12	$28.95	63
MOR47	Modern Russian	Igora Bylov	1990	CE03	$28.50	59
MUC17	Music Composition	Eliza Smith	1985	AW30	$32.95	127
MUH16	Music Harmony	Eliza Smith	1986	AW30	$32.95	86
POG17	The Physics of Glass	Kate Rice	1993	BP07	$7.95	80
PWM51	Philosophize With Me	Whyle Jones	1975	TT12	$30.95	115
WOH23	World of History	James Dyce	1988	CE03	$34.95	39
*					$0.00	0

Figure 1 - 21

1. Run *Access*.

2. Begin creating a new database to hold the book list (and later the publishers) by clicking the **Blank Database** option in the introductory dialog box. Click **OK**. (Use **FILE/New Database** or click the **New Database** button on the toolbar if *Access* was already running with a different database or no database open on the desktop. Then, pick **Blank Database** on the **General** tab and click on **OK**.)

3. Make certain **Save in:** is correct. For example, if you will be using the A: drive and that is not currently selected, click on the drop-down arrow for the **Save in:** list and click on **A:**.

4. Type the name for the new database, **Exercise2**, in the **File name:** box of the **File New Database** dialog box and click on the **Create** button.

5. **Maximize** the *Access* window if it does not already cover the entire screen.

6. Make sure the **Table** tab is selected and click the **New** button to begin a new table.

7. Click **Design View** in the **New Table** dialog box and click **OK**.

8. Fill in the seven fields as shown in Table 1 - 5. Remember to set the Size for each field (except the automatic one) in the lower section of the window.

9. Make **Book Code** the primary key by clicking anywhere on its line and clicking the **Primary Key** button on the toolbar. The key icon will appear to the left of the field name.

10. Save the table by picking **FILE/Save**, entering the name: **Books** and clicking on the **OK** button.

11. Close the Table window with **FILE/Close**.

12. With the highlight on **Books**, click on the **Open** button to open the table for data entry.

13. Enter the 12 records shown in Figure 1 - 21. Be careful to match the upper– or lower–case characters for each entry. Some of the entries will scroll and be partially hidden since they are longer than the width that is currently showing for the column. That is perfectly all right. You will correct the situation in the next lesson.

14. When finished, close the table with **FILE/Close**.

    The bookstore owner comes to you with the realization that she forgot to include the Cost of a book, which is an important piece of data. You need to modify the table structure to add the Cost.

15. With the highlight on **Books**, click the **Design** button to open the design of the table.

16. Since **Cost** should be placed before **Price**, press the **DOWN ARROW** five times to move onto the line that currently contains the **Price** field.

17. When on the line with **Price**, press the **INSERT** key (or pick **INSERT/Field**) to open a new line, which will push **Price** down to line 7.

18. Type the field name: **Cost** and press **TAB** to move to the **Data Type** column.

19. Cost will be a **Currency** field, so type a **C** and press **TAB**. The size will be automatic. No description is necessary.

20. Save the altered design with **FILE/Save**.

21. Close the table with **FILE/Close**.

22. Click on the **Open** button to open **Books**.

23. Move to the **Cost** column and enter the values shown in the **Cost** column in Figure 1 - 22.

Book Code	Title	Author	Year of Pub	Publisher Code	Cost	Price	Quantity in Stock
ATL11	Art Through Life	Jane Rick	1994	AW30	$13.50	$22.95	86
CAL28	Calculus	Henry Slate	1977	TT12	$25.40	$42.95	152
ECC22	Economically Correct	Lester Dane	1974	CE03	$19.95	$32.95	81
EMP19	Even More Poems	Sina Grant	1976	BP07	$12.60	$21.00	47
LOP18	Lots of Poems	Sina Grant	1973	BP07	$10.80	$18.00	7
LUI81	Look Up In The Sky	Bruce Tipple	1989	TT12	$17.00	$28.95	63
MOR47	Modern Russian	Igora Bylov	1990	CE03	$17.00	$28.50	59
MUC17	Music Composition	Eliza Smith	1985	AW30	$19.50	$32.95	127
MUH16	Music Harmony	Eliza Smith	1986	AW30	$19.50	$32.95	86
POG17	The Physics of Glass	Kate Rice	1993	BP07	$4.75	$7.95	80
PWM51	Philosophize With Me	Whyle Jones	1975	TT12	$18.50	$30.95	115
WOH23	World of History	James Dyce	1988	CE03	$20.95	$34.95	39
					$0.00	$0.00	0

Figure 1 - 22

24. Print the table with **FILE/Print** or the **Print** button on the toolbar. Click on the **OK** button if you used the menu.

25. Close the table with **FILE/Close**.

26. Close the database with **FILE/Close**.

27. If you are finished with *Access*, exit from *Access* with **FILE/Exit**.

Independent Project 1.3: The Real Estate Office

During a summer job in a real estate office the manager learns of your work with databases, and asks you to create a database for the listings of commercial properties. He shows you a sample sheet that contains commercial offers, which lists 10 items of data: street address of the building, city, state, zip code, size in square feet, floor of the building, whether it is to purchase or rent, price, date it becomes available, and the code for the agency that holds the listing.

In order to include a primary key, a unique code number has been created for each listing. Thus, the 11 fields should be given the names in Table 1 - 6. The data you are given to get started and test the table is shown in Figure 1 - 23

Field Name	Description
Code	2 letters plus 2 digits (Primary Key)
Address	
City	
State	
Zip	
Size	Number of square feet
Floor	Number of the floor in the building
Purchase or Rent	The letter P or R
Price	
Available	Date available for occupancy
Agency Code	2 letters plus 2 digits

Table 1 - 6

Code	Address	City	State	Zip	Size	Floor	Purchase or Rent	Price	Available	Agency
ES52	5 Elm St.	Greenwich	CT	06830	4800	1	R	$72,000.00	6/1/95	SC18
FA28	18 Frost Ave.	Greenwich	CT	06830	3700	2	R	$52,000.00	8/1/95	RR11
GP25	12 Gedney Place	Danbury	CT	06810	8900	3	R	$105,000.00	7/15/95	SC18
LW17	1 Lewis Way	Danbury	CT	06810	12000	2	R	$140,000.00	7/1/95	PP24
MC29	Maple Court	New Canaan	CT	06840	450	1	P	$125,000.00	4/1/95	PP15
MS11	22 Main St.	Stamford	CT	06901	5500	10	R	$75,000.00	5/20/95	RR11
RP12	2 Research Park	Stamford	CT	06902	18000	1	P	$3,400,000.00	6/1/95	PP15
RP13	3 Research Park	Stamford	CT	06902	18000	1	P	$3,400,000.00	6/1/95	GW14
RP15	5 Research Park	Stamford	CT	06902	21000	1	P	$4,100,000.00	8/1/95	RP12
RR19	952 River Rd.	Stamford	CT	06901	3750	6	R	$49,000.00	9/1/95	PP24
*					0	0		$0.00		

Figure 1 - 23

1. Create a new database named **Exercise3** to hold the commercial real estate listings with **FILE/New Database** or by clicking the **New Database** button on the toolbar or the choice in the introductory dialog box.

2. In **Exercise3**, create a table. Fill in the **Primary Key** field together with the remaining 10 fields named in Table 1 - 6. Carefully choose a data type for each, and remember to set the size for each text and number field in the lower section of the table design window. Examine the data in Figure 1 - 23 to help decide the sizes. Make certain that the field named **Size** (in square feet) is a number field of type **Long Integer**.

3. Save the table with the name: **Commercial Listings** and close the design window.

4. Open **Commercial Listings** for data entry.

5. Enter the 10 records shown in Figure 1 - 23.

6. When finished, close the table.

*The manager notices that the agent's name is not included and requests an addition to the table design. A field named **Agent** should be added to the structure. It will contain the data shown in Figure 1 - 24.*

7. Open the design of **Commercial Listings**.

8. Put the new field **Agent** at the end of the table. Examine the names in Figure 1 - 24 to see what size to make the field.

9. **Save** and close the design.

10. Open the table and enter the values shown in the **Agent** column in Figure 1 - 24.

Code	Address	City	State	Zip	Size	Floor	Purc	Price	Available	Agency	Agent
ES52	5 Elm St.	Greenwich	CT	06830	4800	1	R	$72,000.00	6/1/95	SC18	Brown
FA28	18 Frost Ave.	Greenwich	CT	06830	3700	2	R	$52,000.00	8/1/95	RR11	Funchall
GP25	12 Gedney Place	Danbury	CT	06810	8900	3	R	$105,000.00	7/15/95	SC18	Equat
LW17	1 Lewis Way	Danbury	CT	06810	12000	2	R	$140,000.00	7/1/95	PP24	Smith
MC29	Maple Court	New Canaan	CT	06840	450	1	P	$125,000.00	4/1/95	PP15	Green
MS11	22 Main St.	Stamford	CT	06901	5500	10	R	$75,000.00	5/20/95	RR11	Wuthen
RP12	2 Research Park	Stamford	CT	06902	18000	1	P	$3,400,000.00	6/1/95	PP15	Ruth
RP13	3 Research Park	Stamford	CT	06902	18000	1	P	$3,400,000.00	6/1/95	GW14	Purcell
RP15	5 Research Park	Stamford	CT	06902	21000	1	P	$4,100,000.00	8/1/95	RP12	Williams
RR19	952 River Rd.	Stamford	CT	06901	3750	6	R	$49,000.00	9/1/95	PP24	Smith
					0	0		$0.00			

Figure 1 - 24

11. **Print** the table.

12. **Close** the table.

13. **Close** the database.

14. If you are finished with *Access*, exit from *Access*.

Independent Project 1.4: The Veterinarian

The local veterinarian needs you to help with a database of the pets she tends. Since she likes to keep up on the names and ages of each pet she sees, the database will need to include the pet's name, date of birth (as closely as it is known), weight, color, and type of animal, as well as the owner's name, address, and phone number. She gives you the list shown in Table 1 - 7 to get started.

In this project you are to do most of the planning as well as the creating of the database and table. While the data are listed in Table 1 - 7, you must determine the table name, field names, and data types. In this project you will build the table for the pets; in Lesson 3 you will include a table for the owners' data.

To include a primary key, you must create a unique code number for each pet. Whatever you call that field, you will probably want it to be the first field in the table.

Carry out the following steps using *Access*.

1. Study Table 1 - 7 to plan the structure of the data table.

2. Create a new database to hold the veterinarian's data.

3. In that new database, create the pet table. Be sure to include a Primary Key. IMPORTANT: You must name the field with the codes for the owners **Owner Code** in order to work with the table containing the owners' data that will be added in Lesson 3.

NAME	DATE OF BIRTH	WEIGHT			OWNER CODE
Homer	2/15/94	35	dark brown	dog	AS19
Fifi	9/1/89	14	yellow	cat	AS19
Wild Thing	3/5/94	22	gray	dog	AS19
Runner	10/1/91	840	brown	horse	AS19
Spot	1/1/92	49	brown	dog	DW11
Fluffy	4/1/94	15	white	cat	MU25
George	8/15/91	67	brown	dog	MU25
Kuddles	7/1/92	12	orange	cat	MU25
Sir Strut	5/1/90	915	gray	horse	TR12
Yoshi	6/1/95	0.25	brown	hamster	TR12
Clank	7/1/94	13	gray	armadillo	WE31
Lilly	2/1/93	13	black	cat	PS14
Homer	1/1/92	75	white	dog	PS14
Sneaker	5/15/90	12	orange	cat	PS14

Table 1 - 7

4. Enter the data shown in Table 1 - 7.

   After examining your design, the veterinarian notices that Date of Last Visit needs to be added to the table.

5. Add a field for **Date of Last Visit** and enter a different date for each pet, but each date must be within the last 12 months.

6. **Print** the table.

7. **Close** the database.

8. If you are finished with *Access*, exit from *Access*.

2 Working with a Table's Data

Objectives

In this lesson you will learn how to:

- Open an existing database
- Move about within an *Access* table
- Size the fields in a table
- Move the fields within a table

- Edit a table's data
- Search for matching listings
- Delete records

PROJECT DESCRIPTION

In this lesson we will change the data within a table and the appearance of the table. Changing the data means editing the table. Since the data are recorded magnetically, editing it is a simple matter of typing the new values over the old data. Usually the appearance of a table will need adjusting by changing the display widths of fields, and sometimes the positions of fields.

While the editing is a straightforward task, locating the record that needs editing is often a bigger challenge. With thousands of listings in a table, you would not want to read every entry searching for the desired record. The computer program must perform that task for you since it can search many times faster than a human. Thus, we will also see how to search for matching records in this lesson.

After sizing the columns, editing some of the data, and deleting one record, the **Employee** table will look like Figure 2 - 1.

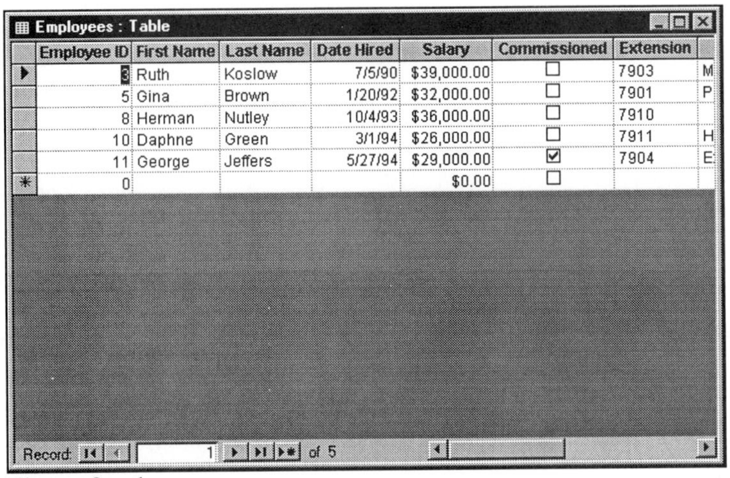

Employee ID	First Name	Last Name	Date Hired	Salary	Commissioned	Extension	
3	Ruth	Koslow	7/5/90	$39,000.00	☐	7903	M
5	Gina	Brown	1/20/92	$32,000.00	☐	7901	P
8	Herman	Nutley	10/4/93	$36,000.00	☐	7910	
10	Daphne	Green	3/1/94	$26,000.00	☐	7911	H
11	George	Jeffers	5/27/94	$29,000.00	☑	7904	E
0				$0.00	☐		

Record: 1 of 5

Figure 2 - 1

OPENING A DATABASE

To work with the objects in a database you must open that database.

To open an existing database:

- If you have just run *Access* and the introductory dialog box is open, click on the **Open an Existing Database** option, click on the name of the database if it is showing or click on **More Files**, and click the **OK** button.

- If Access is already running with another database or with no database open, choose **FILE/Open Database** or click the **Open Database** button ⌷ on the toolbar.

- Pick the correct drive and directory for **Look in** if they are not already the right choices.

- Click on the desired database name and click **Open**.

Activity 2.1: Opening the SALES Database

1. If you have just run *Access*, the Introductory dialog box will be on the desktop, so click on the **Open an Existing Database** option. If the **Sales** database is listed in the lower list, click on it, click the **OK** button, and skip Steps 2-5.

2. If Sales is not showing in the introductory dialog box, click on **More Files** and continue with Step 4.

3. If *Access* was already open, pick **FILE/Open Database**.

4. Make certain the correct drive and folder are chosen in the **Look in** list.

5. Click on **Sales** and click **Open**.

MOVING ABOUT WITHIN A TABLE

Before you can change any data in a table you must move to the position of that data. There are ways to move about within a table using the mouse or the keyboard. While the arrow keys may be best for navigating short distances, data tables often consist of thousands of records. Moving from the first to the thousandth listing with only the arrow keys would be impractical. Thus, the following methods are important for faster and more efficient navigation.

To move about a table with the mouse:

- Click the mouse on any field that is visible to position the cursor within that field.

- The *Navigation Buttons* are the five buttons with triangles on their faces on the left half of the bottom line of the window frame (see Figure 2 - 2). The first button jumps to record 1 and the fourth button jumps to the last record. The second and third Navigation buttons jump to the preceding and next records, respectively. The cursor remains in the same field during these moves. The fifth button jumps to a new record, which would be the next row below the last record.

- Between the Navigation buttons is the current **Record** number indicator (see Figure 2 - 2). Clicking the mouse on that number places the cursor next to its digits, so that you can delete the current value and type the number of the record to which you want to jump. After pressing **ENTER**, you will be placed on the desired record.

- The *scroll bars* at the right edge of the table window and in the right half of the bottom line of the window frame will scroll to a section of the table not currently showing in the window (see Figure 2 - 2). The scroll bars do not actually move the cursor, and, thus, it is possible to scroll the table so that the cursor cannot be seen. Once you have scrolled far enough to see the desired data, click the mouse on that field to position the cursor there. Each scroll bar only appears when actually needed, that is, when the table actually extends beyond the window boundary.

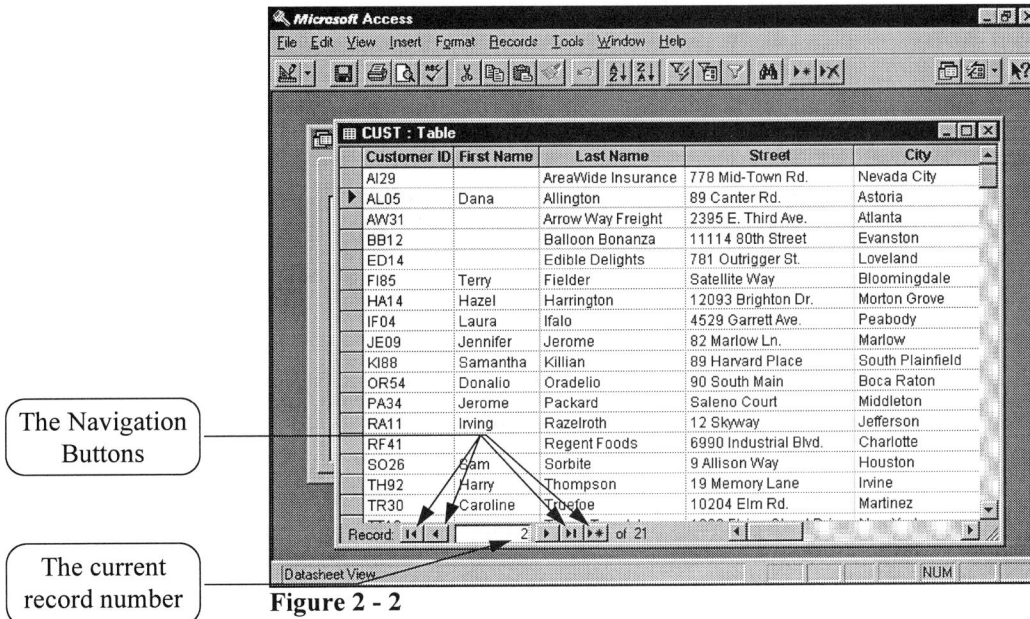

The Navigation Buttons

The current record number

Figure 2 - 2

Activity 2.2: Navigating Within a Table with the Mouse

1. The **Sales** database should be open.

2. Make certain the **Table** tab is selected.

3. Select the **Employees** table and click the **Open** button at the right edge of the Database window to open that table into a window.

4. Notice between the Navigation buttons that the current record number is **1**.

5. Click the **Last Record** button (fourth Navigation button) to jump to the last record.

The Navigation line should now say **Record: 6 of 6** *as in Figure 2 - 3*.

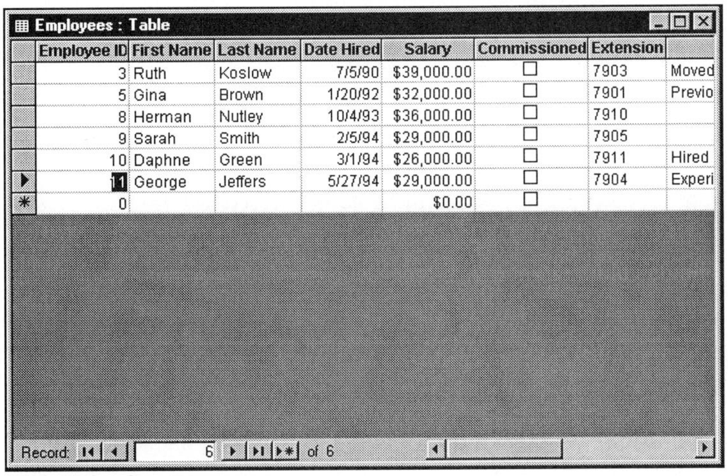

Figure 2 - 3

6. Click on the **Previous Record** button (second Navigation button) to jump to the preceding record.

7. Click on the **First Record** button to jump to record 1.

8. Click the mouse on the number **1** of **Record: 1 of 6** between the Navigation buttons and remove the 1 with either the **BACKSPACE** or the **DELETE** key. Type **4** and press the **ENTER** key to jump to record 4.

9. Click three times the rightward pointing arrowhead at the right end of the scroll bar on the bottom edge of the table's window to scroll to the right so that you can see the last field in the table. Notice that you can no longer see the selection highlight on the **Employee ID** field (see Figure 2 - 4).

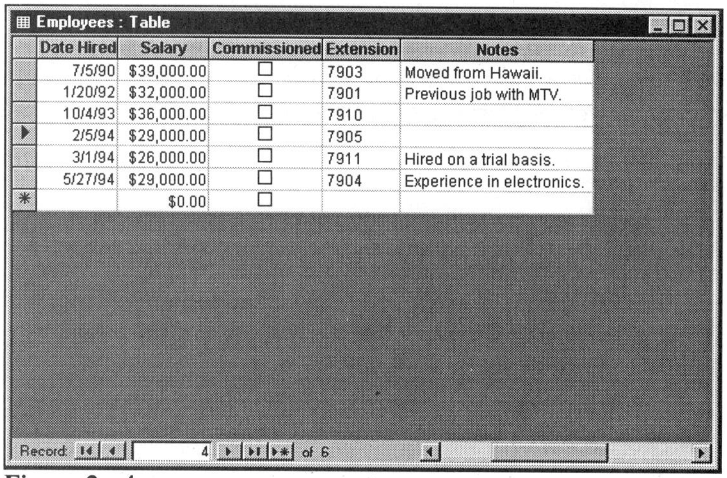

Date Hired	Salary	Commissioned	Extension	Notes
7/5/90	$39,000.00	☐	7903	Moved from Hawaii.
1/20/92	$32,000.00	☐	7901	Previous job with MTV.
10/4/93	$36,000.00	☐	7910	
2/5/94	$29,000.00	☐	7905	
3/1/94	$26,000.00	☐	7911	Hired on a trial basis.
5/27/94	$29,000.00	☐	7904	Experience in electronics.
	$0.00	☐		

Record: |◄| ◄ | 4 | ► |►|| |►* | of 6

Figure 2 - 4

10. Scroll back to the first field so you can see the cursor and selection highlight in the **Employee ID** field.

To move about a table with keys:

- The **arrow keys** move one line up or down or one field to the left or right in the direction of the arrow. (If the vertical cursor is blinking in the field rather than the entire field being highlighted, then the **LEFT ARROW** moves one character to the left and the **RIGHT ARROW** moves one character to the right.)

- The **TAB** key moves to the next field and **SHIFT+TAB** moves to the previous field. (The **ENTER** key will usually move to the next column, but not in every situation. Thus, **TAB** is preferred.)

- **PGUP** (or **PAGE UP**) and **PGDN** (or **PAGE DOWN**) move up or down the number of records showing in the window; that is, they jump to the next screenful of records.

- **HOME** jumps to the first field and **END** jumps to the last field. (If the vertical cursor is blinking in the field rather than the entire field being highlighted, then **HOME** jumps to the beginning of the field and **END** jumps to the end of the field.)

- **CTRL+HOME** jumps to the first field in the first record when the field is highlighted.

- **CTRL+END** jumps to the last field on the last record when the field is highlighted.

Activity 2.3: Navigating Within a Table with Keys

1.   Press the **UP ARROW** key to move to record **3**.

2.   Press **CTRL+END** to jump to the last field of the last record.

3.   Press **CTRL+HOME** to jump to the first field of record 1.

4.   Press the **DOWN ARROW** to move to record **2**.

5.   Press **END** to jump to the last field within record 2.

6.   Press **HOME** to jump to the first field of the current record.

7.   Press **TAB** four times to move to the **Salary** field.

8.   Click the mouse pointer in the middle of the name **Koslow** in record 1. Press the **LEFT ARROW** and **RIGHT ARROW** keys a few times each to move from character to character within the field.

9.   With the vertical cursor still blinking within the name Koslow, press the **HOME** key to jump to the beginning of the characters and press the **END** key to jump to the end of the entry.

10. Close the table with **FILE/Close**.

SIZING FIELDS

When a table is created, all fields, no matter what data type or designed size, are displayed at the default of 1 inch wide. Thus, you usually need to change the display width of the majority of columns. The gray rectangle that contains the field name at the top of each column of data is called the *field selector*. You can use the mouse to either drag the line at the right edge of the field selector until the width looks right, or double click the same line to have *Access* perform a "best fit." *Best fit* means that *Access* will check all entries showing in the field to determine which is the longest. It will then adjust the field width to either the longest entry showing in the column or the field name, whichever is longer.

When you change the widths of the columns in a table, you may save the new column widths immediately with **FILE/Save Layout**. Alternatively, when you close the table *Access* will ask whether to save the changes. By not saving the changes, the new column widths were temporary. Should you save them, they will be permanent.

Changing the field widths in this manner does not restructure the table; it only displays the fields in a different width for viewing purposes.

To change the display width of a column:

•   Move the mouse pointer on top of the line at the right edge of the desired field selector (see Figure 2 - 5). The mouse pointer will become a double-headed left-and-right pointing arrow. Hold down the mouse button and drag the mouse to the left to narrow the column or to the right to widen it.

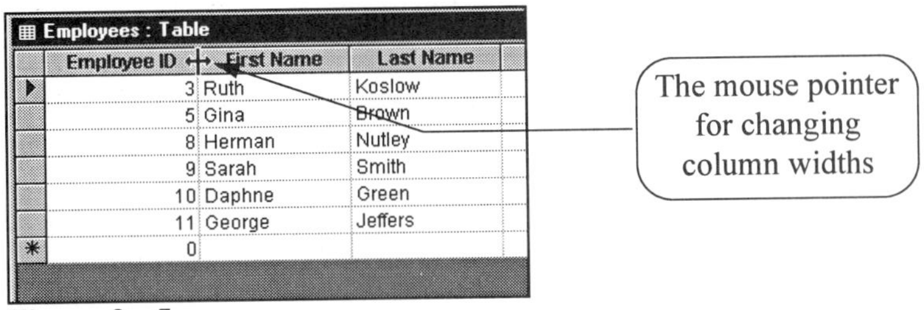

Figure 2 - 5

- To achieve a best fit for the whole column, double-click the line on the right edge of the field selector.

Activity 2.4: Sizing a Table's Fields

1. The **Sales** database should be open.
2. Make certain the **Table** tab is selected.
3. Click on the **Employees** table and click the **Open** button at the right side of the **Database** window to open that table into a window.

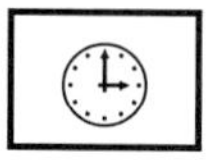

SHORTCUT: *To open a table, double-click on the table name.*

4. Move the mouse pointer on top of the right edge of the field selector for the **Employee ID** field. When the mouse cursor shape is a double-headed left-and-right arrow, hold down the mouse button and drag the line to the left until it is between the two letters **pl** of Employee. Release the mouse button.

Four or five letters will probably now show in the title (see Figure 2 - 6) since the name had been centered so that there was extra space ahead of the field name. Notice that you may hide part of the field name.

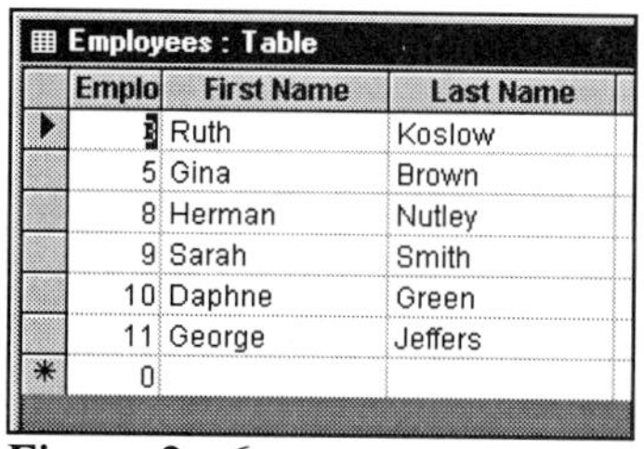

Employees : Table

Emplo	First Name	Last Name
3	Ruth	Koslow
5	Gina	Brown
8	Herman	Nutley
9	Sarah	Smith
10	Daphne	Green
11	George	Jeffers
0		

Figure 2 - 6

5. Increase the width of the same field so that the entire field name, **Employee ID**, shows.
6. Narrow the width of the **First Name** field so that the field name just fits (see Figure 2 - 7).

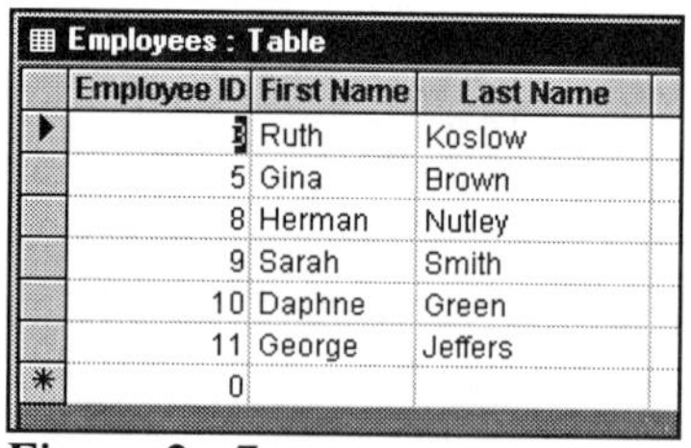

Employees : Table

Employee ID	First Name	Last Name
3	Ruth	Koslow
5	Gina	Brown
8	Herman	Nutley
9	Sarah	Smith
10	Daphne	Green
11	George	Jeffers
0		

Figure 2 - 7

7. Move the mouse on top of the line at the right edge of the field selector for the **Last Name** column and double-click the mouse button to do a best fit.

The field width should adjust to the size of the field name since that name is longer than any data item in the column.

8. Perform a best fit on the **Date Hired, Salary, Commissioned,** and **Extension** columns.

*You may need to scroll with the scroll bar to get to the right edge of the **Extension** field's selector box.*

9. Widen the **Notes** field so that it reveals the entire length of every note.

10. Choose **FILE/Save Layout** to record the new widths.

MOVING FIELDS

On occasion you may need one or more fields in a different position while viewing the table. Perhaps you need to see the first and last columns simultaneously. You may move fields to new positions either temporarily or permanently. Moving fields does not restructure the table; it only repositions the fields for viewing purposes. To move them, merely select the field and drag the field selector to a new position. When you close the table you will be asked whether or not to save the layout changes and make them permanent.

To move a field:

- Click the mouse on the field selector at the top of the desired column. The entire column will be highlighted.

- Move the mouse cursor back on top of the field selector, hold down the mouse button, and drag the field to a new position. As you drag the field, you will see a thick highlight on top of the line that separates one column from another. When the highlight is in the position that you want the field to occupy, release the mouse button.

Activity 2.5: Moving Fields

You will move the **Notes** field in-between **Last Name** and **Date Hired** so that you can see the names and notes simultaneously.

1. The **Employees** table should still be open. If not, open it.

2. Press the **END** key to jump to the **Notes** field.

3. Move the mouse on top of the field selector and click the mouse button to select the entire **Notes** column (see Figure 2 - 8).

Last Name	Date Hired	Salary	Commissioned	Extension	Notes
▶ Koslow	7/5/90	$39,000.00	☐	7903	Moved from Hawaii.
Brown	1/20/92	$32,000.00	☐	7901	Previous job with MTV.
Nutley	10/4/93	$36,000.00	☐	7910	
Smith	2/5/94	$29,000.00	☐	7905	
Green	3/1/94	$26,000.00	☐	7911	Hired on a trial basis.
Jeffers	5/27/94	$29,000.00	☐	7904	Experience in electronics.
＊		$0.00	☐		

Figure 2 - 8

4. Move the mouse back on top of the field selector and hold down the mouse button. Drag the mouse to the left until the highlight that jumps from separator line to separator between the fields is between **Last Name** and **Date Hired** (see Figure 2 - 9). Release the mouse button.

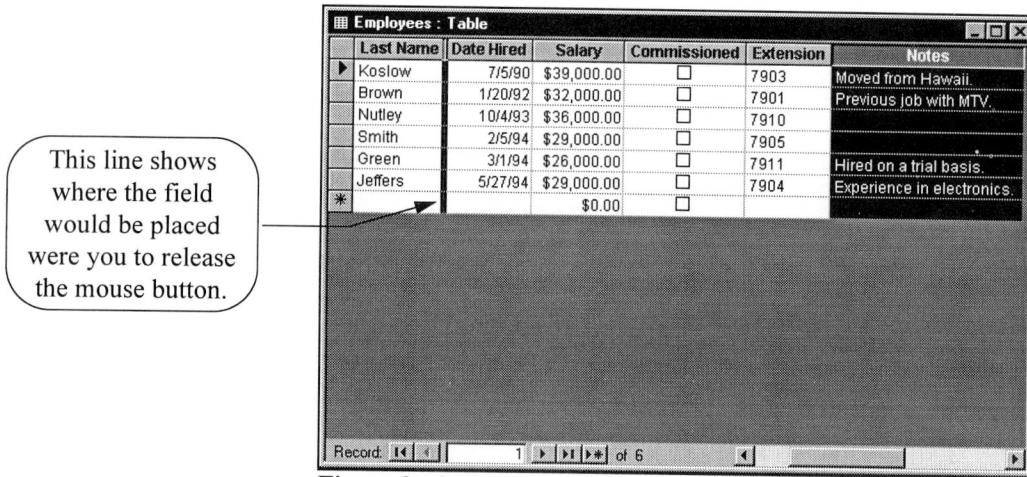

This line shows where the field would be placed were you to release the mouse button.

Figure 2 - 9

5. Press the **HOME** key to jump to the first field.

   Notice that you can now see the ID, names, and notes simultaneously.

6. Choose **FILE/Close** to close the table.

7. As the change of position of the **Notes** field was only intended to be temporary, answer **Save changes to the layout of table 'Employees'?** by clicking the **No** button (see Figure 2 - 10).

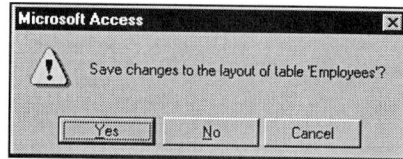

Figure 2 - 10

EDITING A TABLE'S DATA

To edit the data in an *Access* table, move to the data that needs to be changed and type over the old entry with a new entry. The table is always in edit mode.

To replace an entire field's entry:

• If you use the keys or Navigation buttons to move to a field, the entire entry in the field will be highlighted (see Figure 2 - 11). While the entry is highlighted, the next character you type would replace the entire entry.

When highlighted any typed character would replace the entire entry.

Figure 2 - 11

- Should you accidentally erase an entire entry while it is highlighted, choose **EDIT/Undo Typing** immediately. If you only notice the accident after you have moved to another record, you can still choose **EDIT/Undo Saved Record**, but only if you have not edited any other record yet.

To edit a few characters within a field:

- To switch to a moveable cursor within the field, either press the **F2** Edit Mode key, or click the mouse within the field. Once the cursor is blinking within the field (see Figure 2 - 12), you may use the **LEFT** and **RIGHT ARROW** keys to move from character to character, press **BACKSPACE** or **DELETE** to remove characters, and insert new characters.

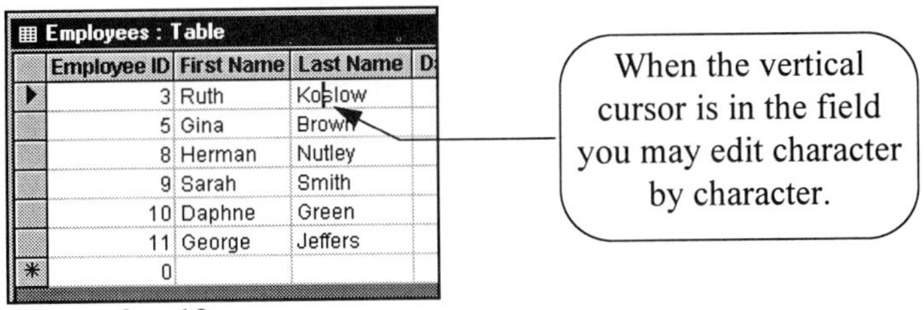

When the vertical cursor is in the field you may edit character by character.

Figure 2 - 12

- To overstrike existing characters and replace them, press the **INSERT** key. **OVR** will appear on the Status Bar. Since you usually need to insert characters, be sure to press **INSERT** again to return to insert mode when you are finished overstriking.

- To return to Navigation mode so that the entire entry is highlighted and the movement keys function normally, press **F2** again, or move to another field with **TAB**, or the **UP** or **DOWN ARROW** keys.

While editing (or entering) data, you do not need to do anything to save the changes. The moment you move to a different record, any data changes are registered. Thus, at no time is more than one record unsaved.

Activity 2.6: Editing Data

Sarah Smith has received a raise; she now makes $31,000. We need to correct her record. Also, Sarah and George Jeffers are on commission, so we need to update that field. Finally, we will add the note **Looking for a new job** to Sarah's **Notes** field.

1. Select the **Employees** table and click on the **Open** button at the right side of the **Database** window to open that table into a window.

2. If the Status Bar shows an **OVR** at the right end, press the **INSERT** key to return to insert mode. The **OVR** should not show.

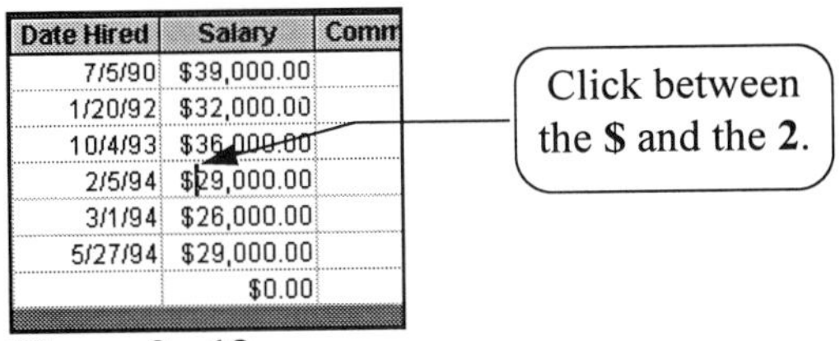

Click between the $ and the 2.

Figure 2 - 13

3. Click the mouse between the **$** and the **2** of Sarah Smith's **Salary** to move to that field and position the cursor (see Figure 2 - 13). If the vertical insertion bar is not blinking between the **$** and **2**, press the **LEFT ARROW** or **RIGHT ARROW** keys until it is.

4. Press the **DELETE** key twice to remove the **29**.

5. Type **31** to insert the new value.

6. Press the **TAB** key to move to the **Commissioned** field.

   *A small dotted box will appear within the check box in the **Commissioned** field.*

7. Click the mouse on the box to check the box (see Figure 2 - 14).

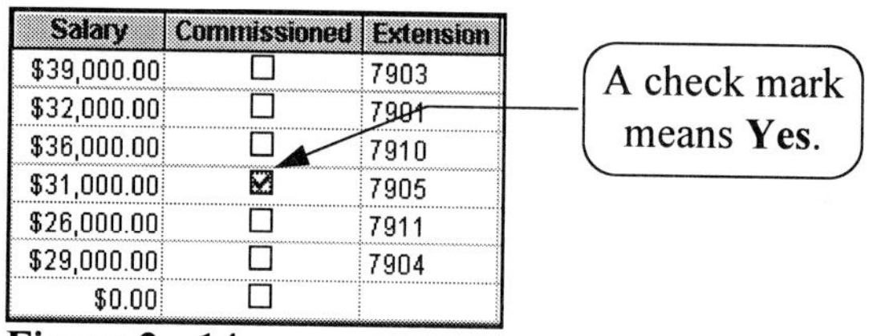

Figure 2 - 14

8. Press the **TAB** key twice to move to the **Notes** field.

9. Enter: **Looking for a new job.** in the **Notes** field.

10. Click the mouse on the **Commissioned** field of **George Jeffers'** record.

    *If you cannot see the last name Jeffers, press **HOME** to jump to the first field, move onto the record for George Jeffers, and press **TAB** several times to move to the **Commissioned** field.*

11. Check the box by clicking the mouse on the box.

12. Press **TAB** to move to the next field.

13. Choose **FILE/Close** to close the table.

    The changes are automatically saved. We will print the new data.

14. With the highlight on the table name, **Employees**, click on the **Print** button on the toolbar.

SEARCHING FOR RECORDS

While the typing of changes to the data in a table is relatively straightforward, finding the record, especially as the table gets large, can be more difficult. With hundreds or thousands of records you cannot take the time (nor would you want to) to read every name or code number looking for a matching value. The program can search much faster and does not tire of reading data.

To search for a value in a table:

- Choose **EDIT/Find** or click the **Find** button on the toolbar.

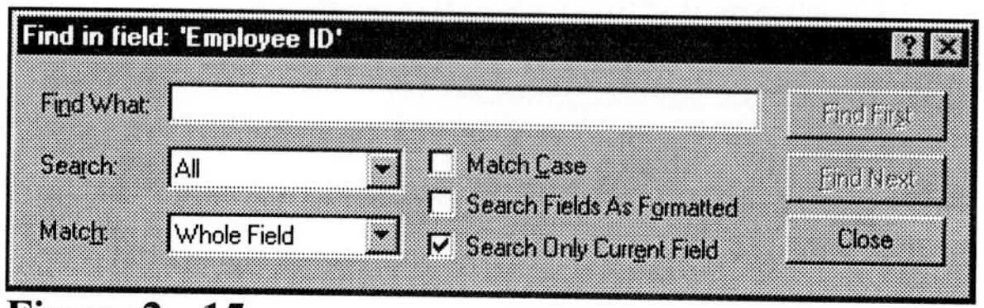

Figure 2 - 15

- In the **Find** dialog box (see Figure 2 - 15), type the value to be located in the **Find What** text box.

- The choice for **Search** should be **All** unless you are certain you wish to search only toward the top (**Up**) or bottom (**Down**) of the table.

- In the **Match:** list, pick either **Any Part of Field** to look for the desired characters embedded anywhere within a field's entry, **Whole Field** to require an exact match of all characters, or **Start of Field** to match only the starting characters for as many characters as you enter.

- Check the **Search Only Current Field** option if you positioned the cursor in the appropriate field and want to limit the search to only that field. The name of the current field is displayed in the title bar of the dialog box. Uncheck this option to search every column in the table.

- Check **Match Case** only if you have typed correctly capitalized characters and want to restrict matches to that capitalization.

- **Search Fields as Formatted** allows for dollar signs, commas, and other characters that show in the table even though they may not have been typed. If those special characters must be matched, check this option.

- The three command buttons will locate the first match in the table (**Find First**), the next match (**Find Next**), or **Close** the dialog box. Since you might need to continue the search several times to locate a record, the dialog box remains open until you close it.

- Should the dialog box obscure the data that you need to see, drag it higher or lower on the screen by dragging its Title Bar, as you would with any window.

Activity 2.7: Searching for Matching Records

Because of an approaching project, we need to find the two employees with experience in television (with MTV) and electronics.

1. Select the **Employees** table and click the **Open** button at the right side of the **Database** window to open that table.

2. Click on the **Find** button on the toolbar.

3. In the **Find** dialog box, type: **mtv** in the **Find What** text box (see Figure 2 - 16).

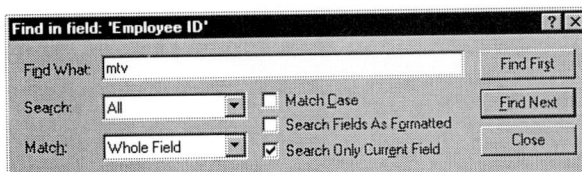

Figure 2 - 16

4. For **Match:**, open the drop-down list and choose **Any Part of Field**.

5. Uncheck **Search Only Current Field**.

6. Leave **Match Case** unchecked. **All** is the best choice for **Search**. Click the **Find First** button.

   The triangle on the record selectors at the left end of each row will jump to Brown and the record number between the Navigation buttons will show record 2 (see Figure 2 - 17). MTV should be highlighted.

The triangle marks the matching record. Close the dialog box to work with the record.

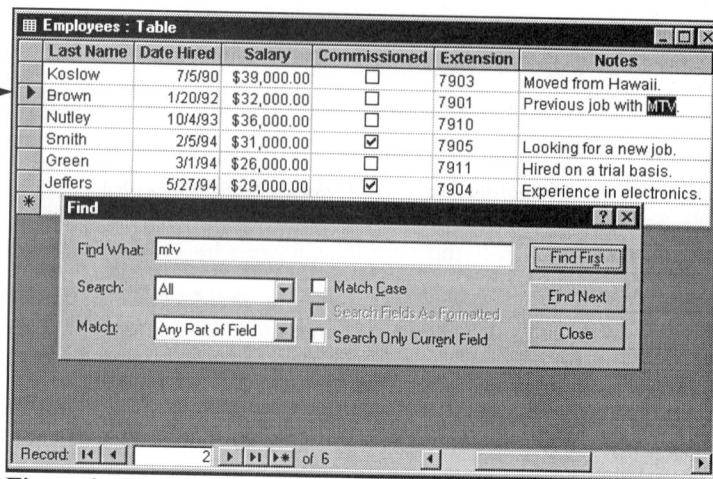

Figure 2 - 17

7. In the **Find** dialog box, type: **electronics** on top of **mtv** in the **Find What:** text box to replace the earlier characters.

8. **Match** should remain as **Any Part of Field**.

9. **Search Only Current Field** should not be checked.

10. Leave **Match Case** unchecked, and **All** is again the best choice for **Search**. Click the **Find First** button.

    The triangle on the record selectors at the left end of each listing will jump to Jeffers and the record number between the Navigation buttons will show 6 (see Figure 2 - 18). **Electronics** *will be highlighted.*

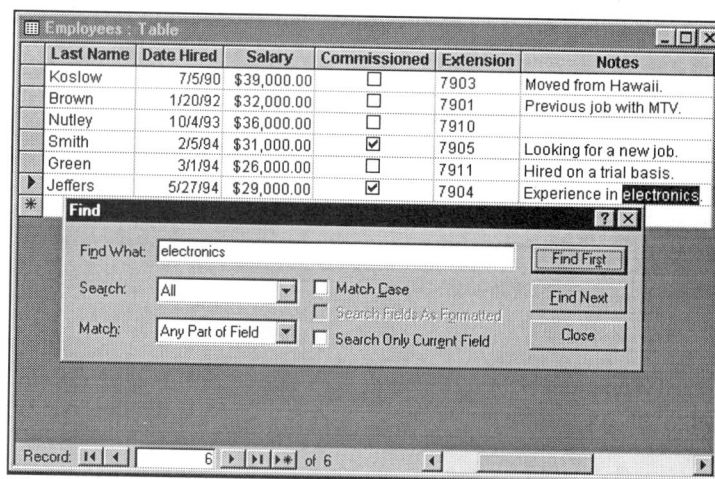

Figure 2 - 18

11. Perhaps there is someone else with electronics experience, so click on the **Find Next** button.

    The message **Microsoft Access finished searching the records. The search item was not found.** *appears (see Figure 2 - 19). Since you previously found the first match, and there are no additional matches toward the end of the table, there can be no other matches.*

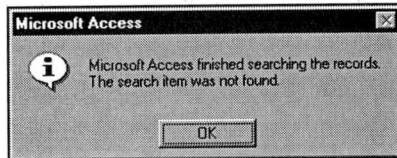

Figure 2 - 19

12. Click on **OK**.

13. Click on the **Close** button to close the **Find** dialog box.

14. Press the **HOME** key to see the full name and Employee ID of the person with electronics experience.

Activity 2.8: Editing a Matching Record

After asking Gina Brown about her MTV experience, it turns out she actually worked for CTW, Children's Television Workshop, not MTV. You need to correct the inaccurate data.

1. If the **Employees** table is not already open, click on the **Open** button.

2. Click on the **Find** button on the toolbar.

3. In the **Find** dialog box, replace electronics with: **mtv** in the **Find What:** text box.

   Access remembers what you searched for the last time in case you need to repeat that search.

4. All other choices are still correct, so click on the **Find First** button.

   Brown will again become the selected record and MTV will be highlighted.

5. Click on the **Close** button to close the dialog box.

   You must close the Find dialog box to work with the data.

6. Since **MTV** is highlighted, merely type: **Children's Television Workshop**, and the new name will replace the old (see Figure 2 - 20).

Figure 2 - 20

7. To adjust the column width for this longer note, double-click the line at the right edge of the field selector.

Activity 2.9: Searching for an Exact Match

We need to locate the employee whose ID number is 9. Were we to leave **Any Part of Field** as the choice for **Match:**, *Access* would stop at every field that contains a 9. The extensions, salaries, and hired dates have many 9s in them. It would take a while to work through the unwanted 9s before arriving at Employee ID number 9. Therefore, we need to change the choice for **Match:** to **Whole Field**.

1. If the **Employees** table is not already open, click on the **Open** button.

2. Click on the **Find** button on the toolbar.

3. In the **Find** dialog box, replace **mtv** with: **9** in the **Find What** text box.

4. Click on the drop-down arrow for the **Match** list and pick **Whole Field** (see Figure 2 - 21).

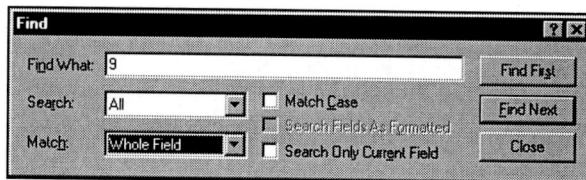

Figure 2 - 21

5. Click on **Find First**.

    The Employee ID for Sarah Smith should be highlighted on record 4.

6. Close the **Find** dialog box by clicking on the **Close** button.

7. Close the table with **FILE/Close**.

    Because you have made changes to the column width of the Notes field, the message for saving the layout changes appears.

8. Click **Yes** to save the layout changes.

DELETING RECORDS

Records can be deleted by merely selecting the record or records, and either pressing the **DELETE** key or choosing **EDIT/Delete Record** in the menu. When you delete, *Access* will ask you to confirm or cancel the deletion. If you confirm the deletion with the **Yes** button, the record(s) are permanently erased, and the operation cannot be undone. If you select the **Cancel** button, the records are restored and no deletion takes place.

Selecting one or more records is accomplished by moving the mouse on top of the *record selector* (the gray block at the left edge of each record) and clicking the mouse button for a single record, or dragging the mouse across several rows' selectors to select a group of neighboring records. The **EDIT** menu also has two selection choices. **Select Record** will select the current record and **Select All Records** will select every record.

To delete a record:

*   Select the record or records to be deleted.

*   Press the **DELETE** key or choose **EDIT/Delete Record** in the menu.

*   Confirm the deletion by clicking the **Yes** button.

Activity 2.10: Deleting a Record

Sarah Smith has left the company. We need to delete her record.

1. Select the **Employees** table and click on the **Open** button.

2. Click the mouse on the record selector at the left edge of the line for Sarah Smith (see Figure 2 - 22).

Figure 2 - 22

The mouse pointer will become a rightward pointing arrow on top of the record selector. The entire row will be highlighted when you click the mouse button.

3. Press the **DELETE** key.

4. Confirm the deletion by clicking the **Yes** button in the **You are about to delete 1 record(s)...** alert box (see Figure 2 - 23).

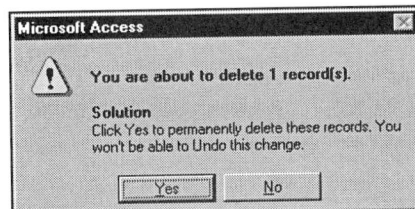

Figure 2 - 23

5. Print the table by clicking the **Print** button on the toolbar.

6. Close the table with **FILE/Close**.

7. Close the database with **FILE/Close**.

SUMMARY

In this project you have made several different types of changes to a table. You have sized the fields and moved them into different positions. You have edited the data and searched for the listings that needed editing. You have deleted a record. In Lesson 3 you will add additional tables to the database, and in Lesson 4 you will find complete sets of matching records and work with multiple tables at one time.

KEY TERMS

Best Fit
Field Selector

Navigation Buttons
Record Selector

Undo

INDEPENDENT PROJECTS

Independent Project 2.1: The School Newspaper

This Independent Project continues the Newspaper Ad database you began in Independent Project 1.1. In this project you will edit the table to make some changes to the data, size the fields, move a field, delete a record, and search for listings.

The following changes need to be made. When finished, the table should look like Figure 2 - 24.

- Pizza Plus has changed their ad number 2389 to a Full Page. They paid the larger fee on 5/11/95.

- The Student Grill paid for ad number 2396 on 5/12/95.

- College Movies has canceled its ad number 2392.

Ad Number	Purchased By	Issue Date	Size	Price	Date Paid	Salesperson
2387	College Books	5/20/95	FP	$85.00	5/8/95	K17
2388	Diamond Tunes	5/20/95	HP	$45.00	5/8/95	S23
2389	Pizza Plus	5/20/95	FP	$85.00	5/11/95	K17
2391	Harry Hertz	5/20/95	EP	$15.00	5/9/95	F11
2393	Sports Booster Club	5/20/95	QP	$25.00	5/9/95	K17
2394	Dean's Office	5/20/95	EP	$15.00		F11
2395	Lou's LaundroMat	5/20/95	QP	$25.00		F11
2396	Student Grill	5/20/95	HP	$45.00	5/12/95	K17
2398	The Sports Palace	5/20/95	FP	$85.00	5/10/95	S23
0				$0.00		

Figure 2 - 24

1. Run *Access*.

2. In the introductory dialog box, click on the **Open an Existing Database** option and click on **Exercise1** if it is showing in the list of files. If it is not showing, click on **More Files**. Click **OK**.

3. If *Access* was already running, open the **Exercise1** database with **FILE/Open Database** or by clicking the **Open Database** tool on the toolbar. Make certain you have the correct drive location in **Look in** and click on the name **Exercise1**. Click on the **Open** button.

4. Maximize the *Access* window if it does not already cover the entire screen.

5. Open the **Ads** table by clicking on the name in the list of tables and clicking the **Open** button.

6. To change Pizza Plus's ad number 2389 to a Full Page, begin by searching for that ad number. Click on the **Find** button on the toolbar, type **2389** into the **Find What** text box, and click the **Find First** button.

7. The triangle record marker should move to record 3. Click on the **Close** button.

8. Press **TAB** twice to move to the **Size** field.

9. The **HP** should be highlighted, so merely type: **FP** to replace the old value.

10. Press **TAB** again to jump to the **Price** column and enter: **85**

11. Press **TAB** once more and change the Date Paid to **5/11/95**. You can either retype the entire date, or press **F2** to switch into edit mode and change the 9 to an 11.

12. To fill in the Date Paid for the Student Grill ad number 2396, begin by searching for that ad number. Click on the **Find** button on the toolbar, type **2396** into the **Find What** text box, uncheck the **Search Only Current Field** option, and click on the **Find First** button.

13. The triangle record marker should already have moved to record 9, but to see the record click on the **Close** button.

14. Press **TAB** four times to move to the **Date Paid** field.

15. Enter: **5/12/95**

16. To remove the College Movies ad number 2392, begin by searching for that ad number. Click on the **Find** button on the toolbar, type **2392** into the **Find What** text box, check that the **Search Only Current Field** option is not checked, and click on the **Find First** button.

17. The triangle record marker should move to record 5. Click on the **Close** button.

18. Click the mouse on the gray **selector box** at the left end of that record to select the entire listing for College Movies.

19. Press the **DELETE** key and click the **Yes** button in the alert box that appears.

20. Press the **END** key to jump to the **Issue Date** field.

21. Click the mouse on the gray **selector** at the top of the column (where the field name is) to select the entire **Issue Date** column.

22. Move the mouse back on top of the selector, hold down the left mouse button and drag that field to the left until the dark highlight is between **Purchased By** and **Size**. Release the mouse button to drop the field and reposition it there.

23. Press the **HOME** key to jump to the first field.

24. Resize the **Ad Number** field by moving the mouse on top of the right edge of its selector (at the top of that column) and either dragging the line until it is the proper size or double-clicking to do a best fit.

25. Similarly, resize the remaining fields (see Figure 2 - 24).

26. Print the table by clicking on the **Print** button on the toolbar.

27. Close the table with **FILE/Close**. Answer **Save changes to the layout of table 'Ads'?** by clicking **Yes**.

28. Close the database with **FILE/Close**.

29. If you need to exit from *Access*, do so properly.

Independent Project 2.2: The Bookstore

This Independent Project continues the Bookstore database you began in Independent Project 1.2. In this project you will edit the table to make some changes to the data, size the fields, delete a record, and search for listings.

The following changes need to be made:

- The book with code ALT11 ("Art Through Life") has the wrong publisher code. Instead of AW30, it should be TT12.

- The music students have purchased their texts so that the Quantity in Stock of MUC17 ("Music Composition") has dropped from 127 to 85, and the Quantity in Stock of MUH16 ("Music Harmony") has dropped from 86 to 48.

- The Author of LUI81 ("Look Up In The Sky") is incorrect. Instead of Bruce Tipple, it should be Bruce Tiggle.

- LOP18 ("Lots of Poems") is being discontinued, so it should be deleted.

  When finished, the table should look like Figure 2 - 25.

Book Code	Title	Author	Year of Pub	Publisher Code	Cost	Price	Quantity in Stock
ATL11	Art Through Life	Jane Rick	1994	TT12	$13.50	$22.95	86
CAL28	Calculus	Henry Slate	1977	TT12	$25.40	$42.95	152
ECC22	Economically Correct	Lester Dane	1974	CE03	$19.95	$32.95	81
EMP19	Even More Poems	Sina Grant	1976	BP07	$12.60	$21.00	47
LUI81	Look Up In The Sky	Bruce Tiggle	1989	TT12	$17.00	$28.95	63
MOR47	Modern Russian	Igora Bylov	1990	CE03	$17.00	$28.50	59
MUC17	Music Composition	Eliza Smith	1985	AW30	$19.50	$32.95	85
MUH16	Music Harmony	Eliza Smith	1986	AW30	$19.50	$32.95	48
POG17	The Physics of Glass	Kate Rice	1993	BP07	$4.75	$7.95	80
PWM51	Philosophize With Me	Whyle Jones	1975	TT12	$18.50	$30.95	115
WOH23	World of History	James Dyce	1988	CE03	$20.95	$34.95	39
					$0.00	$0.00	0

Figure 2 - 25

1. Run *Access*.

2. In the introductory dialog box, click on the **Open an Existing Database** option and click on **Exercise2** if it is showing in the list of files. If it is not showing, click on **More Files**. Click on **OK**.

3. If *Access* was already running, open the **Exercise2** database with **FILE/Open Database** or by clicking the **Open Database** tool on the toolbar. Make certain you have the correct drive location in **Look in:** and click on the name **Exercise2**. Click on the **Open** button.

4. Maximize the *Access* window if it does not already cover the entire screen.

5. Open the **Books** table by clicking on the name in the list of tables and clicking on the **Open** button.

6. Maximize the table window by clicking its **Maximize** button.

7. To change the publisher code for ALT11 ("Art Through Life") from AW30 to TT12, you need to locate the record. It is the first record, so you don't need to search.

8. Press **TAB** four times to move to the **Publisher Code** field.

9. The **AW30** should be highlighted, so merely type: **TT12** to replace the old value.

10. To update the Quantity in Stock for the two music texts, begin by searching for the first book's code number. Click on the **Find** button on the toolbar, type **MUC17** into the **Find What** text box, and make certain the **Search Only Current Fields** option is not checked. Match: should say **Whole Field**, **Match Case** should not be checked, and **Search:** can be **All**. Click the **Find First** button.

11. The triangle record marker should move to record 8. Click on the **Close** button.

12. Press the **END** key to jump to the **Quantity in Stock** field.

13. The **127** should be highlighted, so merely type: **85** to replace the old value.

14. To update the Quantity in Stock for the second music text, search for the Book Code by clicking on the **Find** button on the toolbar, typing **MUH16** into the **Find What** text box, and clicking the **Find First** button. All the other options remain the same as in the first search.

15. The triangle record marker should move to record 9. Click on the **Close** button.

16. Press the **END** key to jump to the **Quantity in Stock** field.

17. The **86** should be highlighted, so merely type: **48** to replace the old value.

18. To correct the Author's name for **LUI81** ("Look Up In The Sky"), click the **Find** button on the toolbar, type **LUI81** into the **Find What** text box, and click the **Find First** button.

19. The triangle record marker will jump to record 6. Click on the **Close** button.

20. Press **TAB** twice to move to the **Author** field.

21. You need to correct only two letters, so press the **F2** key to get an insertion bar rather than the full field highlight.

22. Move over to the **pp** and delete those two characters. Then type: **gg** in their place so the name becomes Bruce Tiggle.

23. LOP18 ("Lots of Poems") is being discontinued and should be deleted. Since it is the preceding record (record 5), merely click the mouse on the gray **selector box** at the left end of LOP18 (record 5) to select the entire listing.

24. Press the **DELETE** key and click the **Yes** button in the alert box that appears.

25. Resize the **Year of Publication** field so that only **Year of Pub** shows. To do this, move the mouse on top of the right edge of its selector (at the top of the **Year of Publication** column) and drag that line to the left until it is between the **b** and **l** of the word Publication (see Figure 2 - 25).

26. Resize the remaining fields to a Best Fit by double-clicking on the right edge of the field selector box of each field (see Figure 2 - 25).

27. Print the table by clicking the **Print** button on the toolbar.

28. Close the table with **FILE/Close**. Answer **Save changes to the layout of table 'Books'?** by clicking **Yes**.

29. Close the database with **FILE/Close**.

30. If you need to exit from *Access*, do so properly.

Independent Project 2.3: The Real Estate Office

This Independent Project continues the Real Estate Office database you began in Independent Project 1.3. In this project you will edit the table to make some changes to the data, size the fields, move a field, delete a record, and search for listings.

The following changes need to be made.

- Property MC29 will take longer to prepare than was originally estimated, so the date when it will be available should be 5/15/95 instead of 4/1/95.

- The rental price on 1 Lewis Way, Danbury has been lowered to $125,000.

- MS11 has been leased and should be deleted.

When finished, the table should look like Figure 2 - 26.

	Code	Address	City	State	Zip	Available	Size	Floor	Purc	Price	Agency	Agent
▶	ES52	5 Elm St.	Greenwich	CT	06830	6/1/95	4800	1	R	$72,000.00	SC18	Brown
	FA28	18 Frost Ave.	Greenwich	CT	06830	8/1/95	3700	2	R	$52,000.00	RR11	Funchall
	GP25	12 Gedney Place	Danbury	CT	06810	7/15/95	8900	3	R	$105,000.00	SC18	Equat
	LW17	1 Lewis Way	Danbury	CT	06810	7/1/95	12000	2	R	$125,000.00	PP24	Smith
	MC29	Maple Court	New Canaan	CT	06840	5/15/95	450	1	P	$125,000.00	PP15	Green
	RP12	2 Research Park	Stamford	CT	06902	6/1/95	18000	1	P	$3,400,000.00	PP15	Ruth
	RP13	3 Research Park	Stamford	CT	06902	6/1/95	18000	1	P	$3,400,000.00	GW14	Purcell
	RP15	5 Research Park	Stamford	CT	06902	8/1/95	21000	1	P	$4,100,000.00	RP12	Williams
	RR19	952 River Rd.	Stamford	CT	06901	9/1/95	3750	6	R	$49,000.00	PP24	Smith
*							0	0		$0.00		

Figure 2 - 26

1. Run *Access* and maximize the window.

2. Open **Exercise3**.

3. Open the **Commercial Listings** table.

4. Change the **Available** date for MC29 (Maple Court, New Canaan) from 4/1/95 to **5/15/95**.

5. Locate **1 Lewis Way** in Danbury and change its **Price to $125,000**.

6. To remove the listing for **MS11** (22 Main St., Stamford), click on its **selector**, then press the **DELETE** key and click the **Yes** button in the alert box that appears.

7. Resize all fields to a Best Fit by double-clicking on the right edge of the field selector box of each field (see Figure 2 - 26).

8. Resize **Purchase or Rent** so that only **Purc** shows in the title (see Figure 2 - 26).

9. Move the **Available** field between **Zip** and **Size**.

10. **Print** the table.

11. **Close** the table. **Save** layout changes.

12. **Close** the database.

13. If you need to exit from *Access*, do so properly.

Independent Project 2.4: The Veterinarian

This Independent Project continues the Veterinarian database you began in Independent Project 1.4. In this project you will edit the table to make some changes to the data, size the fields, move a field, delete a record, and search for listings.

Make the following changes.

- Wild Thing's weight has increased to 30 pounds.

- Spot is much older than his family thought; change his date of birth to 1/1/88.

- The owner of Sir Strut has sold the horse to a breeder several hundred miles away. Delete that record from the table.

- Set the width of each field in the table to fit the data as closely as possible.

- Move the field that contains the type of animal (dog, cat, etc.) immediately to the right of the name field.

Lesson

3 Multiple Tables

Objectives

In this lesson you will learn how to:

- Import tables from other *Access* databases
- Link to tables in other *Access* databases
- Rename a table

- Design a multiple table system
- Create a form
- Use a form

PROJECT DESCRIPTION

In this lesson we will begin to explore the need for multiple tables to hold the data that a typical business generates. Usually it is neither efficient nor desirable to combine all of the data into a single table. To obtain the extra data needed to work with multiple tables, we will build upon the **Sales** database by *importing* and *linking* to existing tables of data from other *Access* databases that are supplied on the student diskette. Once we have several tables of data, we will see how the tables fit together in a system of tables, a Relational Database System. We will also create and use forms, an alternative way to view and work with the data in a single table or a pair of related tables.

When this lesson concludes, the **Sales** database will contain five tables, as shown in Figure 3 - 1.

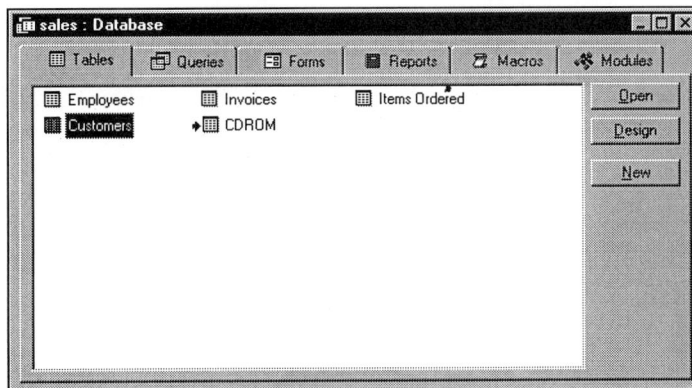

Figure 3 - 1

IMPORTING A TABLE FROM ANOTHER *ACCESS* DATABASE

Our need to acquire additional tables is not the only reason to copy a table from one database to another. In *Access* only one database may be open at a time. Because of this, if there is a table of data that will be needed in two different databases, you must either make a second copy of the table by importing the table into the second database, or link from the second database to the original copy of the table in the first database.

Importing a table will make a new copy of the table. Of course, if you create a second copy of a table, you must keep both copies up to date by editing them. Since that is usually an undesirable task, linking is commonly employed. We will discuss linking in the next section of this lesson.

Sometimes you need a second copy of a table of data, either to work with separately, or as a model from which to continue. Importing the table structure or the structure together with the data will produce that second copy of a table. Possibly someone else in the office has created the very table you need, but it resides in another *Access* database. Whatever the reason, you may often need to import a copy of a table from a different *Access* database.

To import a table from another *Access* database:

- With the database open, select **FILE/Get External Data/Import** in the menu.

- In the **Import** dialog box, pick **Microsoft Access** in the **Files of type** drop-down list.

- Choose the appropriate file location in the **Look in** drop-down list and the folder in the large central panel.

- Click on the name of the database that contains the desired table and click the **Import** button.

- In the **Import Objects** dialog box, select the tab for the desired type of object, click on the name of the object itself, and click the **OK** button.

Activity 3.1: Importing a Table

1. Open the **Sales** database by repeating the steps in Activity 2.1.

2. Choose **FILE/Get External Data/Import**.

3. In the **Import** dialog box, pick **Microsoft Access** as the desired source of the data in the **Files of type** drop-down list (see Figure 3 - 2).

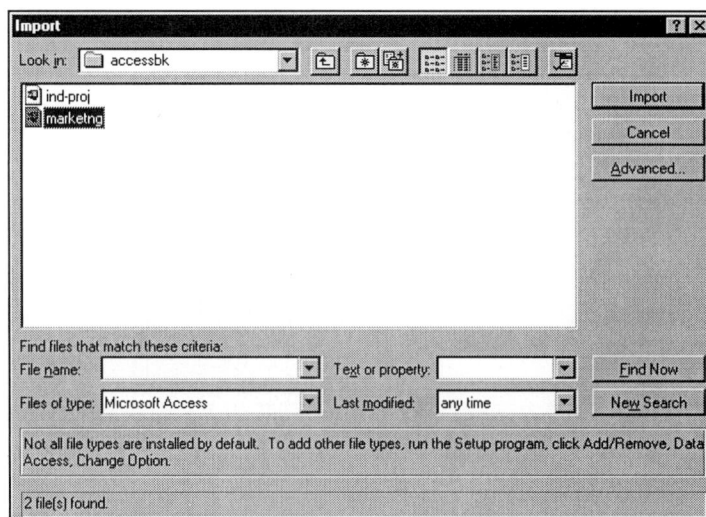

Figure 3 - 2

4. Open the **Look in** drop down list and pick the appropriate drive if it is not already correct. Then, if the correct folder is not selected, double-click on the needed folder name.

5. Click on **marketng** and click the **Import** button.

6. The **Tables** tab should be selected. Click on **Invoices** in the list of tables and click on the **OK** button (see Figure 3 - 3).

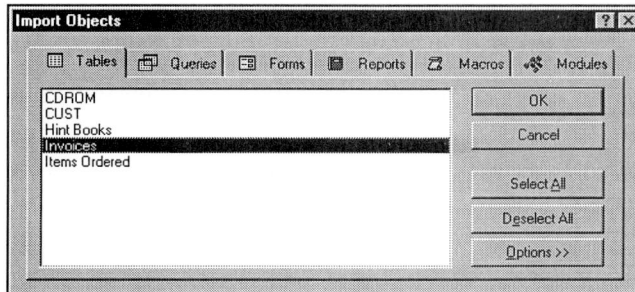

Figure 3 - 3

When the import is finished, Invoices will be listed as a table (see Figure 3 - 4).

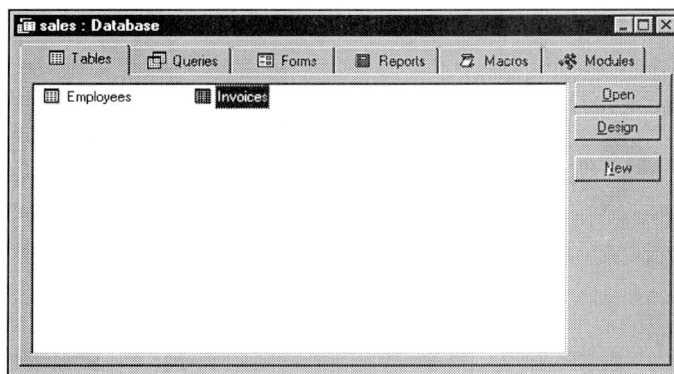

Figure 3 - 4

7. Click on the new name **Invoices** to select it, and click the **Open** button to examine the imported data.

The new data table should look like Figure 3 - 5.

Figure 3 - 5

8. After looking at the new table, close it with **FILE/Close**.

Importing Additional Tables

We will import two more tables from the **marketng** database.

Activity 3.2: Importing Additional Tables

1. Select **FILE/Get External Data/Import**.

2. In the **Import** dialog box, make sure **Microsoft Access** is the desired source of the data in the **Files of type:** list.

3. Click on **marketng** and click **Import**.

   *Access remembers the previous drive and folder so they are probably already correct. If not, you will need to choose the drive in the **Look in** list and the folder in the central panel.*

4. Make sure the **Tables** tab is selected and pick **Items Ordered** in the list of table names. Click the **OK** button.

5. Repeat Steps 1-3 to begin importing an additional table from **marketng**.

6. Pick **CUST** and click on the **OK** button.

7. Click on the new name **Items Ordered** to select it, and click the **Open** button to examine the imported data (see Figure 3 - 6).

Invoice #	Line #	Quantity Sold	CD ID	Back Ordered	Expected Delivery
14902	1	20	F01	N	
14902	2	100	E04	N	
14902	3	25	C01	N	
14903	1	20	C01	N	
14903	2	5	F01	N	
14903	3	10	E04	N	
14903	4	5	P02	N	
14904	1	55	E04	N	
14904	2	3	P02	N	
14904	3	100	C01	N	
14905	1	10	C02	N	
14905	2	5	C01	N	
14906	1	2	E04	N	
14907	1	1	T02	Y	6/11/95
14907	2	1	E06	N	
14908	1	125	E04	N	

Record: 1 of 45

Figure 3 - 6

Customer ID	First Name	Last Name	Street	City
AI29		AreaWide Insurance	778 Mid-Town Rd.	Nevada City
AL05	Dana	Allington	89 Canter Rd.	Astoria
AW31		Arrow Way Freight	2395 E. Third Ave.	Atlanta
BB12		Balloon Bonanza	11114 80th Street	Evanston
ED14		Edible Delights	781 Outrigger St.	Loveland
FI85	Terry	Fielder	Satellite Way	Bloomingdale
HA14	Hazel	Harrington	12093 Brighton Dr.	Morton Grove
IF04	Laura	Ifalo	4529 Garrett Ave.	Peabody
JE09	Jennifer	Jerome	82 Marlow Ln.	Marlow
KI88	Samantha	Killian	89 Harvard Place	South Plainfield
OR54	Donalio	Oradelio	90 South Main	Boca Raton
PA34	Jerome	Packard	Saleno Court	Middleton
RA11	Irving	Razelroth	12 Skyway	Jefferson
RF41		Regent Foods	6990 Industrial Blvd.	Charlotte
SO26	Sam	Sorbite	9 Allison Way	Houston
TH92	Harry	Thompson	19 Memory Lane	Irvine
TR30	Caroline	Truefoe	10204 Elm Rd.	Martinez

Record: 1 of 21

Figure 3 - 7

8. After looking at the new data, close the table with **FILE/Close**.

9. Click on the new name **CUST** to select it, and click the **Open** button to examine its data (see Figure 3 - 7).

10. Close the table with **FILE/Close**.

LINKING TO A TABLE IN ANOTHER *ACCESS* DATABASE

To avoid having to keep both an imported copy of a table and the original table up-to-date, linking can be used. Linking a table establishes a link to the original table without producing another copy of it. Once linked, you can use the data in all the normal ways like editing, printing reports, and adding new listings from either database.

The only restriction on a linked table is that you may not restructure the table within the database in which it is linked; you would need to open the database that actually contains the table to change the table's design.

To link to a table in another *Access* database:

- Select **FILE/Get External Data/Link Tables** in the menu.

- In the **Link** dialog box, pick **Microsoft Access** as the desired **Files of type:**.

- In the **Look in** drop-down list pick the desired drive. From the directory folders, pick the desired folder.

- Click on the database name and click the **Link** button.

- In the **Link Tables** dialog box, select the table from the **Tables** list.

- Click the **OK** button.

The table should be included in the list of tables in the **Database** window. It will show an arrow at the left of the name and icon indicating that this is only a link to the table.

Activity 3.3: Linking a Table

1. Select **FILE/Get External Data/Link Tables**.

2. In the **Link** dialog box, pick **Microsoft Access** in the **Files of type** list.

3. Make certain the drive/folder are correct in **Look in**.

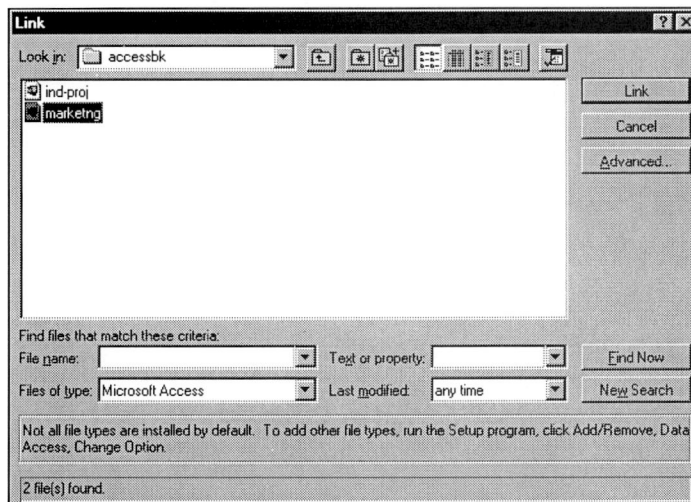

Figure 3 - 8

4.   Click on **marketng** and click the **Link** button (see Figure 3 - 8).

5.   Pick **CDROM** in the **Tables** list and click the **OK** button (see Figure 3 - 9).

Figure 3 - 9

6.   When the linking is finished, **CDROM** will appear in the table list with an arrow in front of the icon (see Figure 3 - 10).

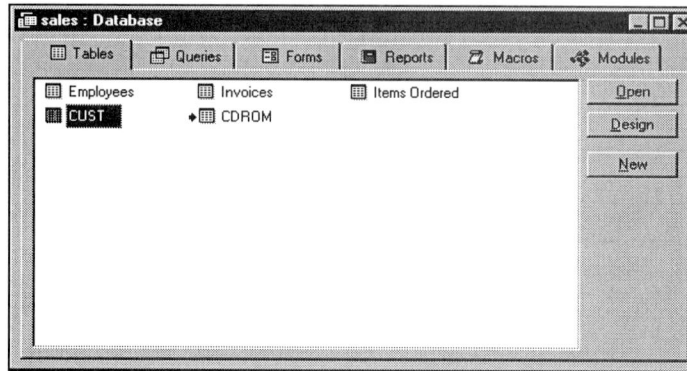

Figure 3 - 10

7.   Click on the name **CDROM** to select the table.

8.   Choose **Open** to view the table (see Figure 3 - 11).

CD ID	Title	Cost	Price	Quantity in Stock	Release Date	Notes
C01	Comsumers, Consumers	$179.00	$299.00	17	4/1/95	DOS
C02	Clip Art 200,000	$65.00	$109.00	290	5/2/95	Windows
E04	Every Household Listed	$179.00	$299.00	58	1/5/95	DOS
E05	Encyclopedia Galactica	$299.00	$499.00	12	1/18/95	MPC
E06	Every Poem Printed	$89.00	$149.00	40	4/2/95	DOS
E07	Everything There Is to Know	$77.00	$129.00	60		Windows
F01	99,000 Fonts	$59.00	$99.00	34	1/15/95	Windows
F02	Fog Scenes	$5.99	$9.99	130	2/12/95	Windows - B&W
L01	Legal Assistant to the Rescue	$417.00	$695.00	17		DOS
P01	Programming in Every Language	$599.00	$999.00	17	3/10/95	Windows
P02	Perfect Paragraph 8.0	$477.00	$795.00	72	5/1/95	Windows
S03	Scourge - The Game	$41.00	$69.00	89	2/15/95	MPC
T02	Too Small to See	$29.00	$49.00	2	2/16/95	Windows
T03	Telephone Poles of the World	$29.00	$49.00	15	5/14/95	MPC
U02	Universal Language Translator	$47.99	$79.95	4	5/2/95	Windows
*		$0.00	$0.00	0		

Figure 3 - 11

The table appears normal in every way, and is, except that you cannot restructure it. You may, of course, add new data, edit the existing records, print reports, and query its data in the regular ways.

9.   Click the **Print** button on the toolbar to print the table.

10. Close the table with **FILE/Close**.

Notice that the icon in front of the table name has an arrow, signifying that a link points to the original table.

RENAMING A TABLE

An imported copy of a table may have a different purpose from the original and, thus, need a new name. Or the original name may have been created by someone else who was not descriptive enough. Perhaps the table you need to import has the same name as one of your existing tables. Whatever the reason, you may need to rename a table.

As a quick reminder, *Access*' rules allow up to 64 characters in a name, with any characters except the five between the parentheses (` . [ ] !) being legal.

To rename a table:

*   Make certain the table is not open. A table cannot be renamed while it is open.

*   The highlight must be on top of the name of the table in the **Database** window.

*   Select **EDIT/Rename**.

*   In the box that appears around the existing table name, type the new name and press **ENTER**.

Activity 3.4: Renaming a Table

Whoever created the **CUST** table did not name it very well. CUST could be an abbreviation for several things. A fully spelled out name would be much more descriptive and useful.

1.   If the **CUST** table is open on the workspace, close it with **FILE/Close**.

2.   Click once on the name **CUST** so that it is highlighted in the table list of the **sales** database.

3.   Select **EDIT/Rename**.

4.   In the box, type the new name **Customers** (see Figure 3 - 12) and press **ENTER**.

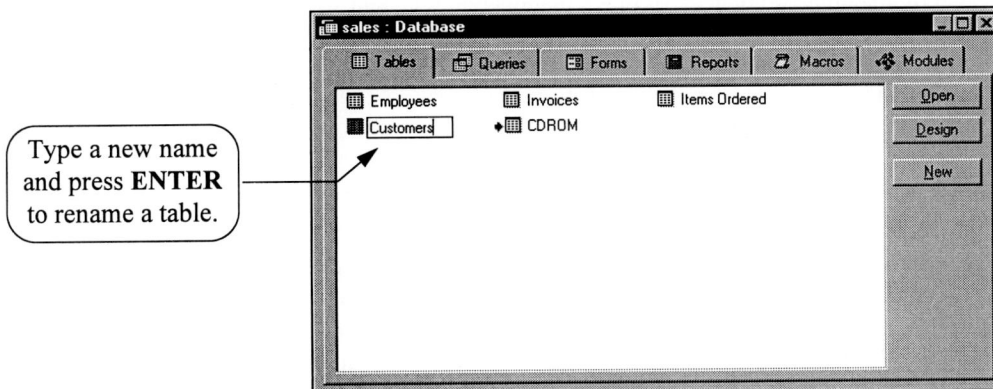

Type a new name and press **ENTER** to rename a table.

Figure 3 - 12

If you type a long name, some of it may disappear behind the next icon.

A RELATIONAL SYSTEM OF TABLES

As you gain experience developing tables of data, you will encounter situations that cause various design problems. For example, suppose the CDROM company asks you to design a table to record customer purchases. You might try a single table like Figure 3 - 13, but when you begin filling in the data an immediate problem occurs. Data begin to get duplicated. Redundant data usually signals a poor design and taxes the system in the following five ways.

Customer	Employee	Last Name	Invoice #	Quantity Sold	Title	Price
Arrow Way Freight	Daphne	Green	14902	20	99,000 Fonts	$99.00
Arrow Way Freight	Daphne	Green	14902	100	Every Household Listed	$299.00
Arrow Way Freight	Daphne	Green	14902	25	Comsumers, Consumers	$299.00
Edible Delights	Daphne	Green	14903	20	Comsumers, Consumers	$299.00
Edible Delights	Daphne	Green	14903	5	99,000 Fonts	$99.00
Edible Delights	Daphne	Green	14903	10	Every Household Listed	$299.00
Edible Delights	Daphne	Green	14903	5	Perfect Paragraph 8.0	$795.00
AreaWide Insurance	George	Jeffers	14904	55	Every Household Listed	$299.00
AreaWide Insurance	George	Jeffers	14904	3	Perfect Paragraph 8.0	$795.00
AreaWide Insurance	George	Jeffers	14904	100	Comsumers, Consumers	$299.00
Your Trip Travel	George	Jeffers	14905	10	Clip Art 200,000	$109.00
Your Trip Travel	George	Jeffers	14905	5	Comsumers, Consumers	$299.00
Timed Travel, Inc	George	Jeffers	14906	2	Every Household Listed	$299.00
Jerome	George	Jeffers	14907	1	Too Small to See	$49.00
Jerome	George	Jeffers	14907	1	Every Poem Printed	$149.00
Arrow Way Freight	Daphne	Green	14908	125	Every Household Listed	$299.00
Yorko	George	Jeffers	14909	1	Everything There Is to Know	$129.00
Yorko	George	Jeffers	14909	1	Every Poem Printed	$149.00
Yorko	George	Jeffers	14909	1	Fog Scenes	$9.99
Yorko	George	Jeffers	14909	1	Encyclopedia Galactica	$499.00
Regent Foods	Daphne	Green	14910	30	Perfect Paragraph 8.0	$795.00
Balloon Bonanza	Daphne	Green	14911	5	Every Household Listed	$299.00
Balloon Bonanza	Daphne	Green	14911	2	Perfect Paragraph 8.0	$795.00
Harrington	George	Jeffers	14912	1	Every Poem Printed	$149.00
Oradelio	Daphne	Green	14913	1	Too Small to See	$49.00
Arrow Way Freight	Daphne	Green	14915	50	Comsumers, Consumers	$299.00

A poor table design because of massive duplication

Figure 3 - 13

- A data entry person is wasting time and effort retyping every character that is duplicate data.

- Disk space is wasted recording the redundant data.

- Inconsistencies will occur among the duplicated data when changes are made, as some of it will get updated and some may not.

- *Access* will slow down as it works its way through more data than is necessary.

- Typing errors will proliferate since more data entry is being done than is required.

To eliminate data duplication, divide some of the data into separate tables. While entire books are devoted to this topic, there are two fundamental situations that with experience you can begin to recognize.

- When an indeterminate number of fields needs to be included.

- When data items will occur over and over again.

As an example of the first situation, suppose you need to record customer purchases of CDROMs. You will need to record the customer's name and address, of course, but how many CDROMs will the customer purchase at a time? There is no way of telling. Therefore, you cannot design a table based on the customer, with a separate column for each CDROM ordered (see Figure 3 - 14). You don't know how many columns to create. If you create too few columns, the remainder of the order will not fit, and if you create too many fields, every order for a single CDROM will waste the space reserved in each additional column. Such a design fails either way.

Customer	Street	State	Title1	Qty1	Title2	Qty2	Title3	Qty3
Arrow Way Freight	2395 E. Third Ave.	GA	Comsumers, Consu	25	Every Household L	100	99,000 Fonts	20
Edible Delights	781 Outrigger St.	CO	Perfect Paragraph	5	Every Household L	10	99,000 Fonts	5
AreaWide Insuranc	778 Mid-Town Rd.	CA	Comsumers, Consu	100	Perfect Paragraph	3	Every Household L	55
Your Trip Travel	1290 Joshua Dr.	CO	Comsumers, Consu	5	Clip Art 200,000	10		
Timed Travel, Inc	1000 Flying Cloud D	NY	Every Household L	2	Every Poem Printed	1		
Jerome	82 Marlow Ln.	NH	Too Small to See	125				
Arrow Way Freight	2395 E. Third Ave.	GA	Every Household L	125				
Yorko	546 Troddle St.	IL	Encyclopedia Gala	1	Everything There Is	1	Every Poem Printed	1
Regent Foods	6990 Industrial Blvd.	NC	Perfect Paragraph	30				
Balloon Bonanza	11114 80th Street	IL	Every Household L	5	Perfect Paragraph	2		
Harrington	12093 Brighton Dr.	IL	Every Poem Printed	1				
Oradelio	90 South Main	FL	Too Small to See	1				
Edible Delights	781 Outrigger St.	CO	Clip Art 200,000	25				
AreaWide Insuranc	778 Mid-Town Rd.	CA	Clip Art 200,000	50				
Fielder	Satellite Way	IL	Programming in Any	1				
Truefoe	10204 Elm Rd.	GA	Everything There Is	1	Encyclopedia Gala	1		
Ifalo	4529 Garrett Ave.	MA	Fog Scenes	1				
Thompson	19 Memory Lane	CA	Too Small to See	1	Encyclopedia Gala	1	Scourge - The Gam	1
Packard	Saleno Court	WI	Every Household L	110				
Udarell	Heather Lane	CA	Fog Scenes	1				
Killian	89 Harvard Place	NJ	Encyclopedia Gala	1				
Allington	89 Canter Rd.	NY	Legal Assistant to th	1				
Sorbite	9 Allison Way	TX	Programming in Any	1				
						0		0

> A poor table design because there is no way to anticipate how many titles a customer will order

Figure 3 - 14

On the other hand, and as an example of the second situation where data will repeat over and over, you might try to record each CDROM ordered in a separate record (see Figure 3 - 13). But then, if you keep track of the customer's name and address, a customer who orders 10 CDROMs will have 10 records with his or her name and address repeated on every line! That design fails because of redundancy.

Customer ID	First Name	Last Name	Street	State		Invoice #	Date of Sale	Customer ID
AI29		AreaWide Insurance	778 Mid-Town Rd.	CA		14902	6/2/95	AW31
AL05	Dana	Allington	89 Canter Rd.	NY		14903	6/2/95	ED14
AW31		Arrow Way Freight	2395 E. Third Ave.	GA		14904	6/2/95	AI29
BB12		Balloon Bonanza	11114 80th Street	IL		14905	6/2/95	YT01
ED14		Edible Delights	781 Outrigger St.	CO		14906	6/2/95	TT10
FI85	Terry	Fielder	Satellite Way	IL		14907	6/2/95	JE09
HA14	Hazel	Harrington	12093 Brighton Dr.	IL		14908	5/19/95	AW31
IF04	Laura	Ifalo	4529 Garrett Ave.	MA		14909	6/3/95	YO19
JE09	Jennifer	Jerome	82 Marlow Ln.	NH		14910	6/3/95	RF41
KI88	Samantha	Killian	89 Harvard Place	NJ		14911	6/4/95	BB12
OR54	Donalio	Oradelio	90 South Main	FL		14912	6/1/95	HA14
PA34	Jerome	Packard	Saleno Court	WI		14913	5/20/95	OR54
RF41		Regent Foods	6990 Industrial Blvd.	NC		14915	6/2/95	AW31
SO26	Sam	Sorbite	9 Allison Way	TX		14916	6/7/95	ED14
TH92	Harry	Thompson	19 Memory Lane	CA		14917	6/7/95	AI29
TR30	Caroline	Truefoe	10204 Elm Rd.	GA		14919	6/8/95	FI85
TT10		Timed Travel, Inc	1000 Flying Cloud Drive	NY		14920	6/8/95	TR30
UD20	Susan	Udarell	Heather Lane	CA		14921	6/9/95	IF04
YO19	Larry	Yorko	546 Troddle St.	IL		14922	6/10/95	TH92
YT01		Your Trip Travel	1290 Joshua Dr.	CO		14924	6/10/95	PA34
						14925	6/11/95	UD20
						14926	6/11/95	KI88
						14927	6/12/95	AL05
						14928	6/12/95	SO26

> Enter each customer once in a separate customer table.

> Repeat only the Customer ID in a separate orders table, not the entire customer name, address, and phone number.

Figure 3 - 15

The solution to both design problems is to split the data into separate tables (see Figure 3 - 15). Record each customer only once in a separate customer table. Do not enter the CDROM order there, but give each customer a code number and enter that code on each order. Since the code number will be very short, we will not mind typing it on each order, even if the same customer orders over and over so that his or her code is repeated many times.

Since we cannot anticipate how many items will be on an order, make one table for the customer's order as a whole (an invoice with order number, date, sales person, etc.—each item that has a predetermined number of entries), and a separate table that lists the items on the order with one item in each record (see Figure 3 - 16). To know which order an item belongs to, record the order number along with each item. Since the order number will be short, we won't mind if it is repeated on each of the 10 lines of an order for 10 items.

Invoice #	Employee ID	Date of Sale	Customer ID
14902	10	6/2/95	AW31
14903	10	6/2/95	ED14
14904	11	6/2/95	AI29
14905	11	6/2/95	YT01
14906	11	6/2/95	TT10
14907	11	6/2/95	JE09
14908	10	5/19/95	AW31
14909	11	6/3/95	YO19
14910	10	6/3/95	RF41
14911	10	6/4/95	BB12
14912	11	6/1/95	HA14
14913	10	5/20/95	OR54
14915	10	6/2/95	AW31
14916	10	6/7/95	ED14
14917	11	6/7/95	AI29
14919	10	6/8/95	FI85
14920	11	6/8/95	TR30
14921	11	6/9/95	IF04
14922	11	6/10/95	TH92
14924	10	6/10/95	PA34
14925	11	6/11/95	UD20
14926	11	6/11/95	KI88
14927	10	6/12/95	AL05
14928	11	6/12/95	SO26
	0		

Invoice #	Line #	Quantity	CD ID	Back Ordered
14902	1	20	F01	N
14902	2	100	E04	N
14902	3	25	C01	N
14903	1	20	C01	N
14903	2	5	F01	N
14903	3	10	E04	N
14903	4	5	P02	N
14904	1	55	E04	N
14904	2	3	P02	N
14904	3	100	C01	N
14905	1	10	C02	N
14905	2	5	C01	N
14906	1	2	E04	N
14907	1	1	T02	Y
14907	2	1	E06	N
14908	1	125	E04	N
14909	1	1	E07	N
14909	2	1	E06	N
14909	3	1	F02	N
14909	4	1	E05	N
14910	1	30	P02	N
14911	1	5	E04	N
14911	2	2	P02	N
14912	1	1	E06	N
14913	1	1	T02	Y
14915	1	50	C01	N

Enter each invoice once in a separate table.

Because there could be any number of items ordered on an invoice, enter the items in a separate table.

Figure 3 - 16

To test your understanding of these two database design problems, try determining which of the two problems each of the following examples resembles.

- A design to keep track of the computer equipment each employee is using. How many pieces of equipment (computer, printer, screen, mouse, etc.) would each employee have?

- One or more tables to keep track of the publisher's name and address for each CDROM title, where many CDROMs may come from the same publisher.

- A list of the people who are contacts at each publisher. Could there be more than one contact?

- A design for the family members (dependents) of each employee. Could a family have 10 members? 12? 14?

Now that you understand the necessity for multiple tables, we will actually use multiple tables in the next sections with forms, as well as in most of the remaining lessons.

CREATING A FORM

A form is an alternative arrangement of the fields in a table (see Figure 3 - 17). Rather than the straight columns and rows of a table, a form may have any field placed anywhere you please. Normally a form displays only one record at a time so the user can focus on a single listing. Because a form allows great freedom in design, you may not only arrange some or all of the fields in any order on the screen, but you may add titles, instructions, boxes and lines, colors, calculations, and graphics to enhance the design. Forms can also display two or more related tables at a time.

Designing a form from scratch would be a lengthy and tedious process as you would need to place every field and every label individually, adjust the appearance and alignment of those items, and add any other details you wanted. Fortunately there is a *Wizard* that can perform all of the tedious work for you. The *Form Wizard* is a built-in set of instructions that is programmed to help you design a form. The *Wizard* offers a number of options, and then creates the form for you based on your choices. We will make use of the *Form Wizard* and save a great deal of time and effort.

Figure 3 - 17

To create a form:

- Click on the **Forms** tab at the top of the **Database** window.

- Click on the **New** button at the right edge of the **Database** window.

- Click in the top part of the **New Form** dialog box the listing for the particular Wizard you want to use.

- Select a table from the **Choose the table or query...** drop-down list in the lower part of the **New Form** dialog box.

- Click on the **OK** button.

- Select the desired options in each step of the **Form Wizard**.

- Click on the **Finish** button.

- Save the form.

Activity 3.5: Creating a Form

We will create a standard form (see Figure 3 - 17) for the **Employees** table that includes all eight fields. The choice **AutoForm: Columnar** uses all fields in the most common design, thus creating the form without asking for any selection of options.

1. Click on the **Forms** tab at the top of the **Database** window (see Figure 3 - 18).

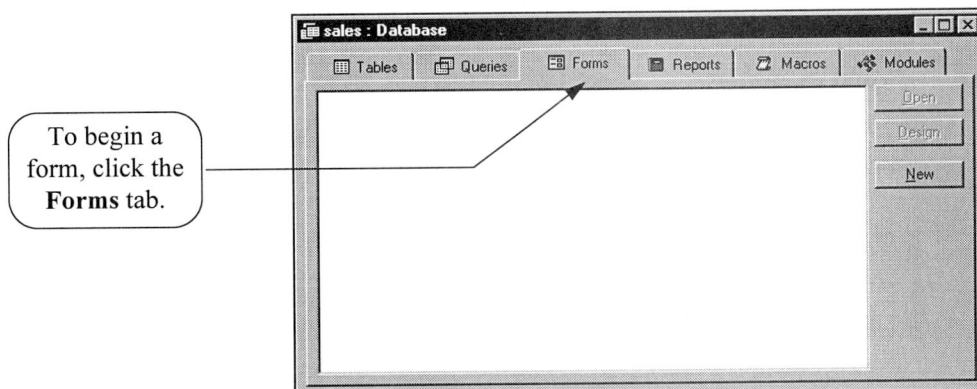

To begin a form, click the **Forms** tab.

Figure 3 - 18

2. Click the **New** button at the right edge of the **Database** window.

3. Select **Employees** from the **Choose the table or query where the object's data comes from** drop-down list (see Figure 3 - 19).

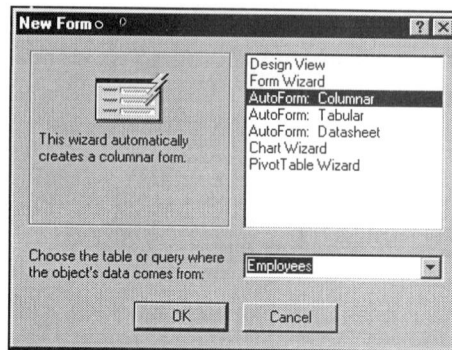

Figure 3 - 19

4. Click the **AutoForm: Columnar** Wizard (see Figure 3 - 19).

5. Click on **OK**.

   After a brief delay while the Form Wizard does all of the design work, the form will appear on the workspace ready to use (see Figure 3 - 17).

6. To save the design choose **FILE/Save**, make certain the name **Employees** is entered, and click **OK** (see Figure 3 - 20).

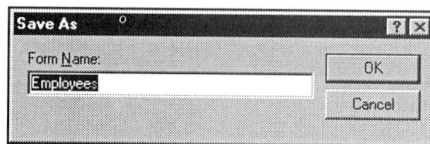

Figure 3 - 20

7. Do not close the form.

USING A FORM

You work with this form the same way as in a table, except that the movement is mostly vertical instead of horizontal. The data are the same; editing is the same; searching is the same. It is the same table of data, just reorganized visually.

To use a form:

- Open the form.

- View the data, edit the existing data, or type new data.

- Print the form, if you wish.

- Close the form.

Activity 3.6: Using a Form

A form is used to view or edit the data, or to enter new data. A form may also be printed. We will view the existing listings in **Employees**, and then enter a new record on the form.

1. If the **Employees** form is not already open on the screen, click on the **Forms** tab at the top of the **Database** window, click on the name **Employees** to highlight it, and click the **Open** button at the right edge of the **Database** window.

   *The current record number between the Navigation buttons should say **Record: 1 of 5** (see Figure 3 - 21).*

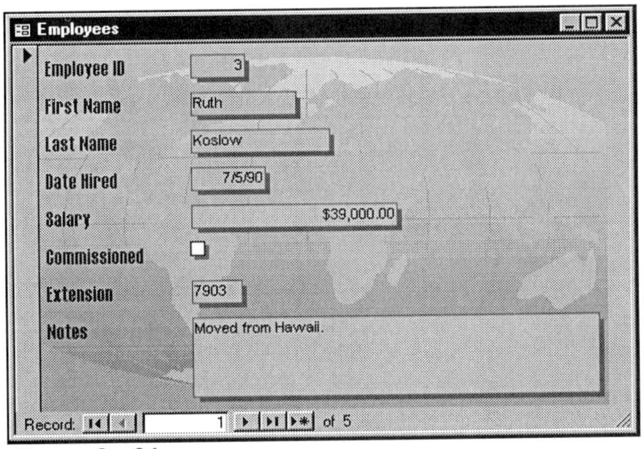

Figure 3 - 21

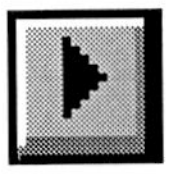

2. View record 2 by pressing the **PGDN** (or **PAGE DOWN**) key.
3. View record 3 by clicking the **Next Record** Navigation button.
4. Jump to the last record by clicking the **Last Record** Navigation button.
5. To begin a new record, press the **PGDN** key or click the **Next Record** button.

   *The record number should be **Record: 6 of 6** (see Figure 3 - 22).*

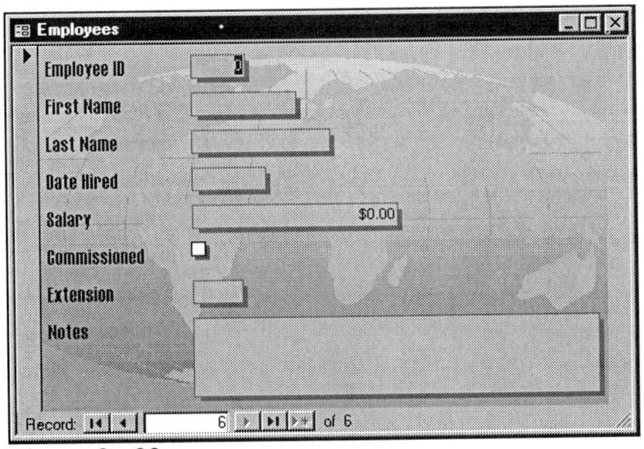

Figure 3 - 22

6. For the **Employee ID**, enter: **12** and press **TAB** to move to the next field.

7. Fill in the **First Name** by typing: **Gary** and press **TAB**.

8. For **Last Name** type: **Lamp** and press **TAB**.

9. His **Date Hired** is: **2/1/95**.

10. Enter: **28,000** for **Salary**.

11. The **Commissioned** field is a check box just like those in a dialog box. Check the box for this new employee since he is on commission. Press **TAB** to continue.

12. The **Extension** is: **7905**

13. Press the **TAB** key to move into the **Notes** field. There are no Notes for this employee yet, so we are finished with this first additional record (see Figure 3 - 23).

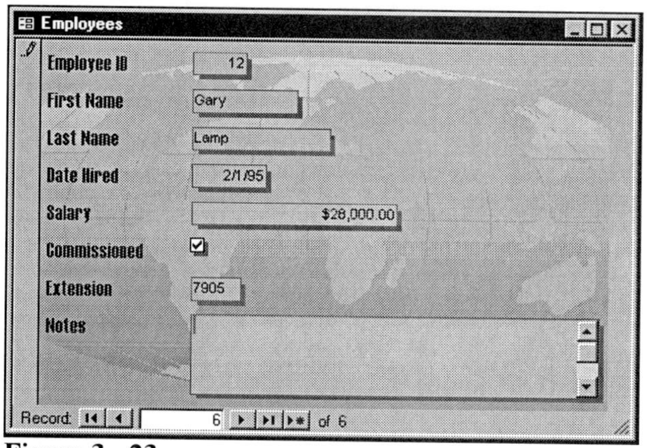

Figure 3 - 23

14. Add a record for yourself by pressing the **TAB** key to move to the next record, record 7.

15. For your **Employee ID**, enter: **1** and press **TAB** to move to the next field.

16. Fill in your first name in the **First Name** field and press **TAB**.

17. Type your last name in the **Last Name** field and press **TAB**.

18. For **Date Hired** enter the current date and move to the next field.

19. Enter: **32,000** for your **Salary**.

20. You are not on commission, so leave the box for the **Commissioned** field unchecked. Press **TAB** to continue.

21. Your **Extension** is: **7900**

22. In your **Notes** field enter: **Experience with the Access database program.**

23. Close the form with **FILE/Close**.

*The new form **Employees** will be listed in the Forms section of the **Database** window. If you were to view the **Employees** table, you would, of course, see the new records there, too.*

PRINTING A FORM

Although a form is primarily intended to be used on the computer screen, it can be printed. Printing a form is not an efficient way to print the data in a table, but the method is straight-forward.

To print a form:

- Click on the **Forms** tab at the top of the **Database** window.
- Click on the name of the form.
- Click the **Print** button on the toolbar.

Activity 3.7: Printing a Form

We will print the form we just created (see Figure 3-24).

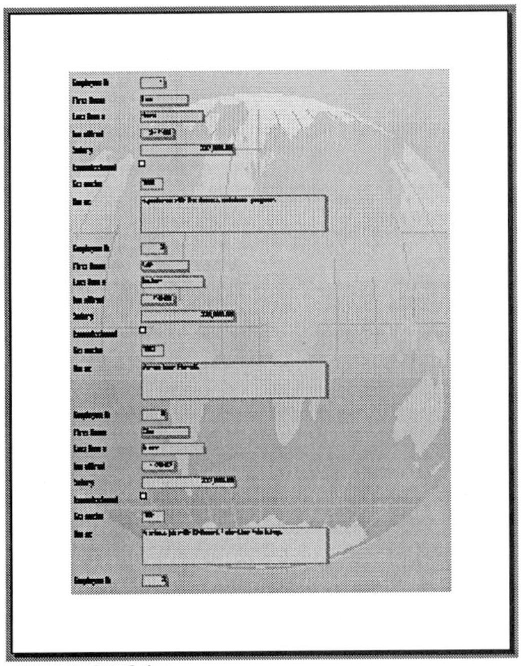

Figure 3 - 24

1. Click on the **Forms** tab at the top of the **Database** window.
2. Click on **Employees**.
3. Click on the **Print** button on the toolbar.

A MULTI-TABLE FORM

Two or more tables can be displayed on the same form. One of the tables would be the main table and would occupy the main part of the form; the other table would be the secondary table and would be embedded on the main table's form (see Figure 3 - 25). The two tables would be related by a field that is common to both tables. That common field is the basis of the link or relationship between the pair of tables. Once there is such a link, *Access* will display only the records from the secondary table that go with the current record in the main table. *Access* figures out which records go together (are related) and displays them on the form simultaneously.

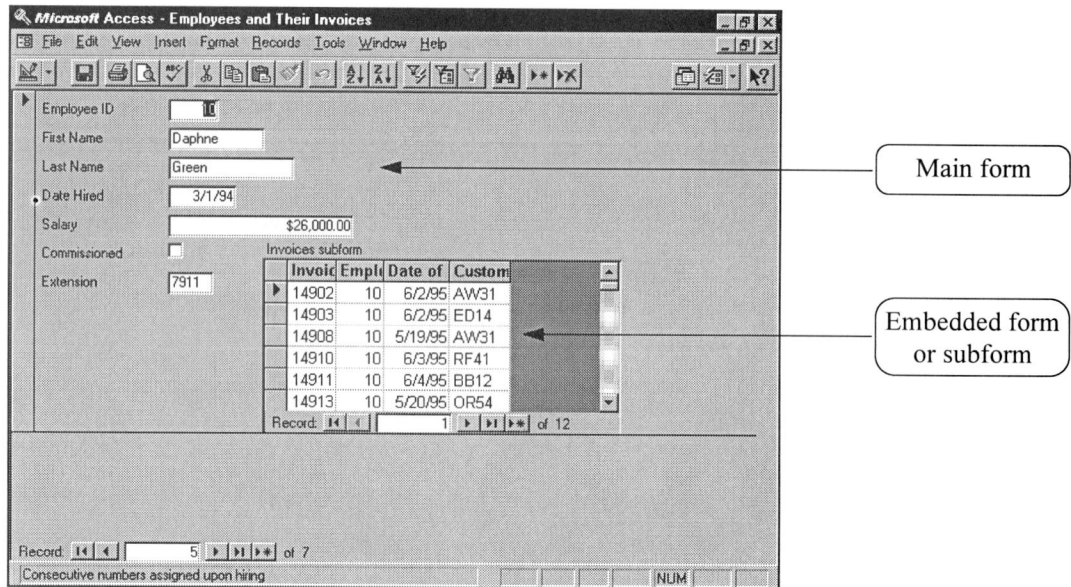

Figure 3 - 25

Remembering the discussion of relational tables two sections ago, we will create a form with data from both the **Employees** and the **Invoices** tables. Both tables contain the linking field **Employee ID**. **Employees** will be the main table, and a subform listing **Invoices** will be embedded on it (see Figure 3 - 25).

To create a main form with an embedded subform:

- Create the main form with either an AutoForm choice or with the Form Wizard.
- Switch to the design screen for the form.
- Add a Subform using the **Subform Wizard**.
- Size and place the subform.
- Save the combined form.

Activity 3.8: Creating a Main Form with a Subform

We need to work with the employees and the invoices they have sold, so we will create a main form for the employees and embed on it a subform for the invoices. This form will display the employees one at a time, with all the invoices they have sold in the subform embedded on the main form. The common field is **Employee ID**.

1. Click on the **Forms** tab at the top of the **Database** window followed by the **New** button at the right edge of the **Database** window.

2. Click on **FormWizard** in the list of choices at the top of the **New Form** dialog box.

3. Open the drop-down list in the bottom part of the **New Form** dialog box and pick **Employees** (see Figure 3 - 26).

4. Click the **OK** button.

5. Click the >> button to transfer all fields into the **Selected Fields** list.

   *The **Tables/Queries** list should say **Table: Employees** since we selected the **Employees** table as the basis of this design.*

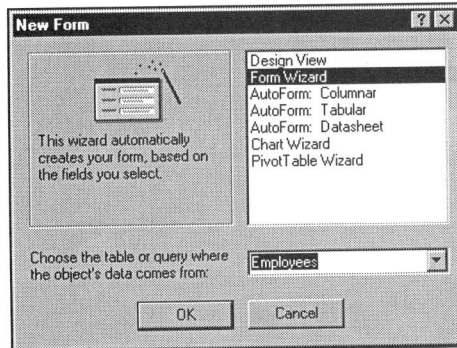

Figure 3 - 26

6. Since we do not want the **Notes** field on the form, click on that field name at the bottom of the list of fields (if it is not already highlighted) and click the < button to send that one field back to the **Available Fields:** list (see Figure 3 - 27).

7. Click the **Next** button.

Click the double arrow button to include all fields.

Then click on the **Notes** field name and click on the back arrow to exclude Notes.

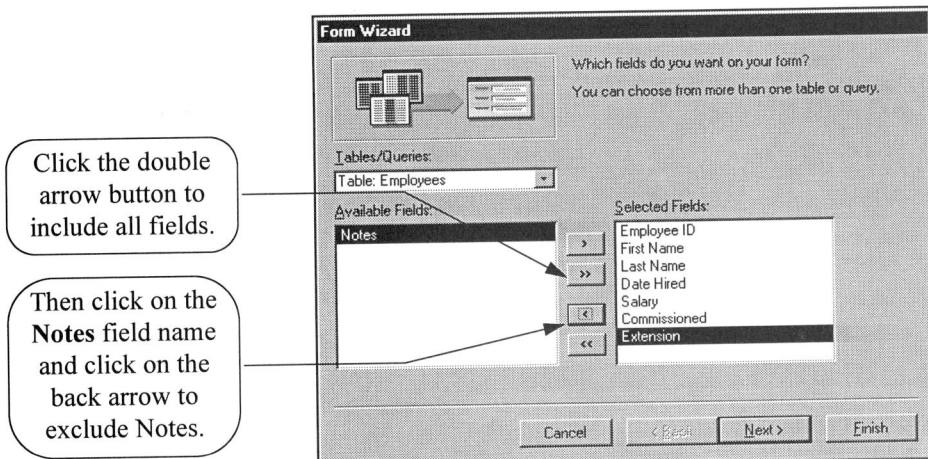

Figure 3 - 27

8. In the next **Form Wizard** dialog box, **Columnar** is the correct choice for the form layout, so just click the **Next>** button (see Figure 3-28).

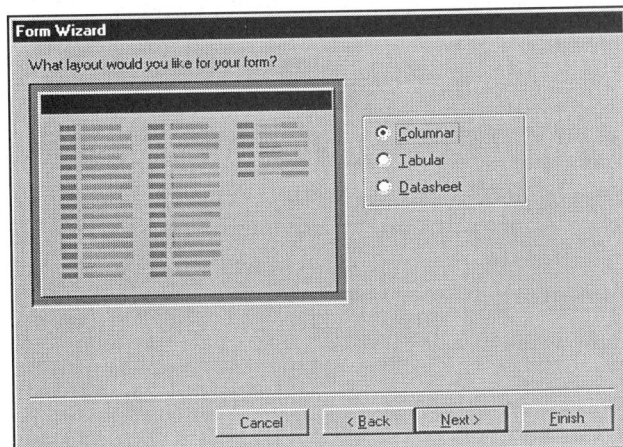

Figure 3 - 28

9. We will use **Standard** style, so click on **Standard** in the **What style would you like?** dialog box and click **Next>** (see Figure 3 - 29).

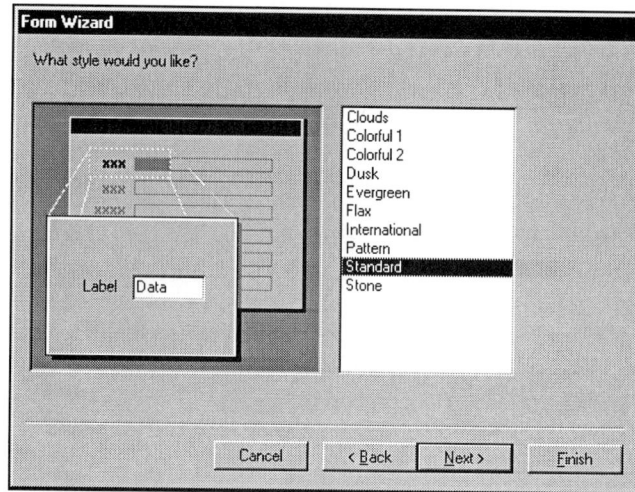

Figure 3 - 29

10. For **What title do you want for your form?** type **Employees and Their Invoices**

The title is the name by which the form will be recorded in the database. Therefore, you cannot use a title that is already the name of another form.

11. Click on the choice **Open the form to view or enter information.**, do not choose to Display Help..., and click the **Finish** button (see Figure 3 - 30).

The Wizard goes to work designing the main form and it opens onto the desktop.

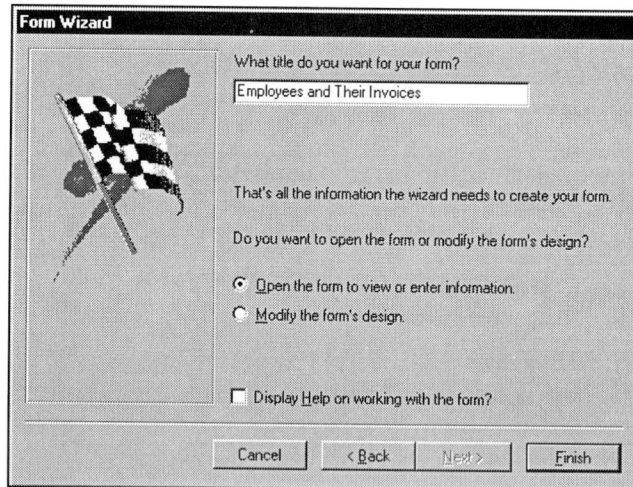

Figure 3 - 30

12. **Maximize** the form window (see Figure 3 - 31).

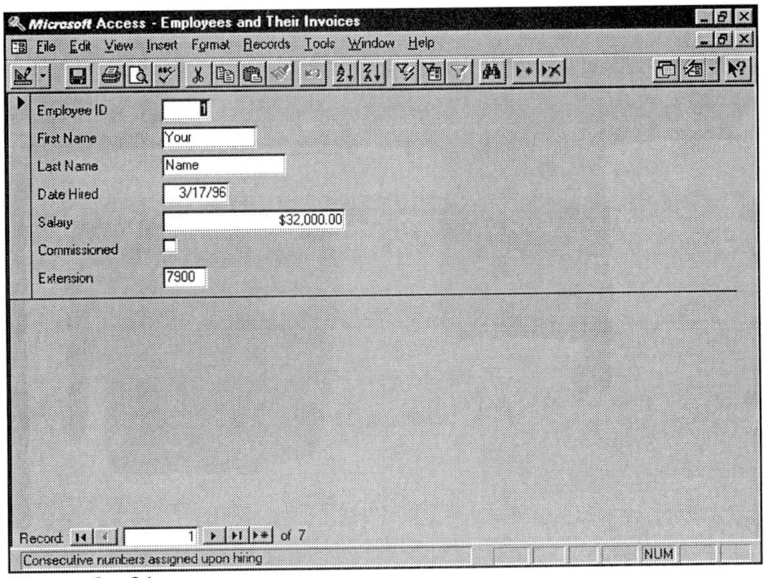

Figure 3 - 31

13. Click the **Form View** button to switch to the design of the form (see Figure 3 - 32).

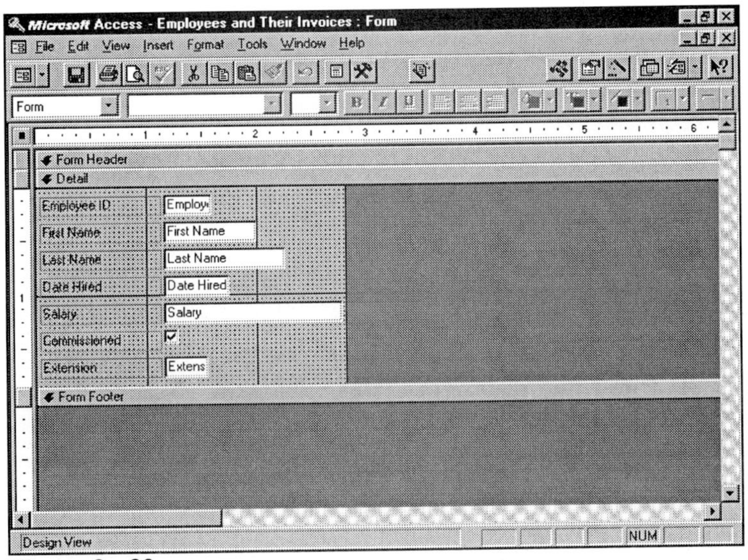

Figure 3 - 32

14. To add some room on this main form for the Invoices subform, pick **EDIT/Select Form** in the menus.

15. Choose **VIEW/Properties**.

   The Properties List for the Form will open. The Properties List contains every detail of how the form will look and operate.

16. Click on the **Format** tab at the top of the dialog box and scroll down the list until you see the line labeled **Width** (see Figure 3 - 33).

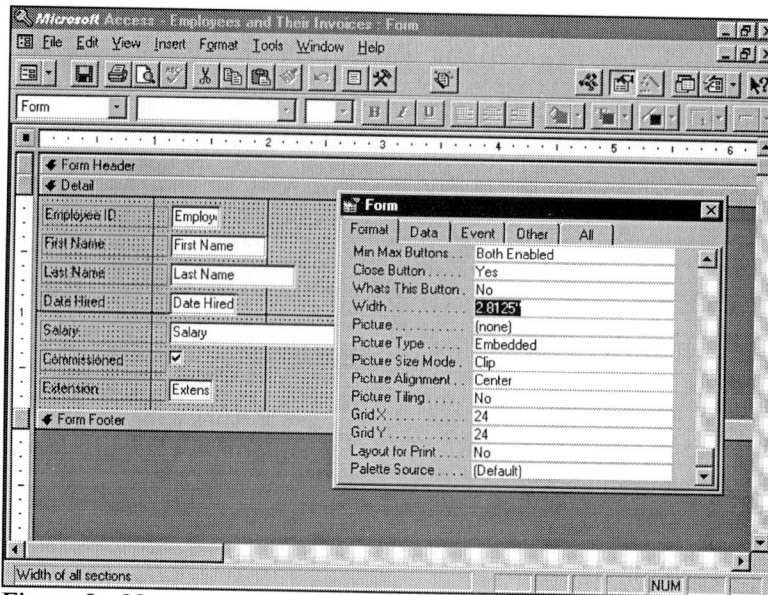

Figure 3 - 33

17. Click on the line for the **Width** and replace the current measurement with **6** to widen the form design to 6 inches.

    You do not need to type the inch marker (").

18. Close the Properties List with **VIEW/Properties**.

    *The form design background should now extend to the 6 inch mark on the top ruler as shown in Figure 3 - 34. If the ruler is not showing, pick **VIEW/Ruler** in the menus. Also, these illustrations show the grid dots. If they are not showing, you may pick **VIEW/Grid**, although there is no need to have the grid showing.*

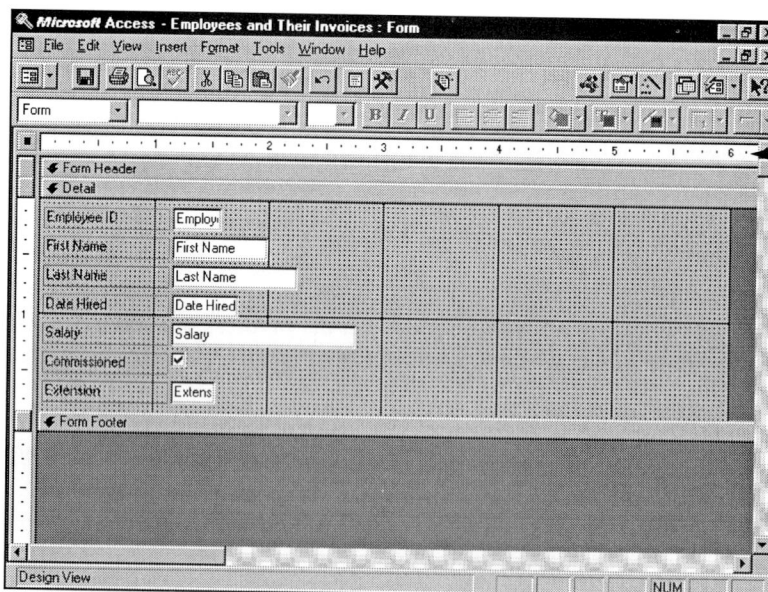

The top ruler

Figure 3 - 34

19. Pick **VIEW/Toolbox**.

The toolbox will appear wherever the last person who used Access left it; thus, it could be anywhere on the screen and in almost any rectangular proportion. As it is the buttons that we need, the position and shape are only a matter of convenience. Since the toolbox is a toolbar, you may drag it to a better position, if you choose.

20. Make certain the **Control Wizards** button in the toolbox is activated (pressed in). If it is not pressed in, click on it to turn on the Control Wizards (see Figure 3-35).

21. Click the **Subform/Subreport** button in the toolbox and move onto the design screen.

The mouse cursor should be a small cross together with a tiny shape that matches the shape on the Subform/Subreport button.

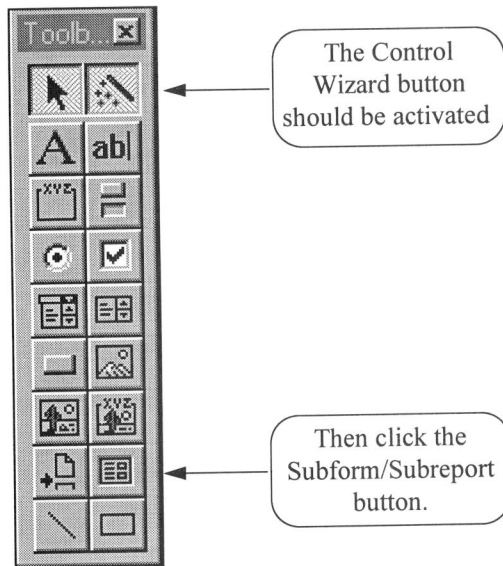

The Control Wizard button should be activated

Then click the Subform/Subreport button.

Figure 3 - 35

22. Move the mouse pointer cross to a position of approximately 2 inches on the top ruler and 1.5 inches on the left–hand ruler and click the mouse button once. You may need to move the toolbox first if it is in the way.

*The **Subform/Subreport Wizard** dialog box will appear on the screen (see Figure 3-36).*

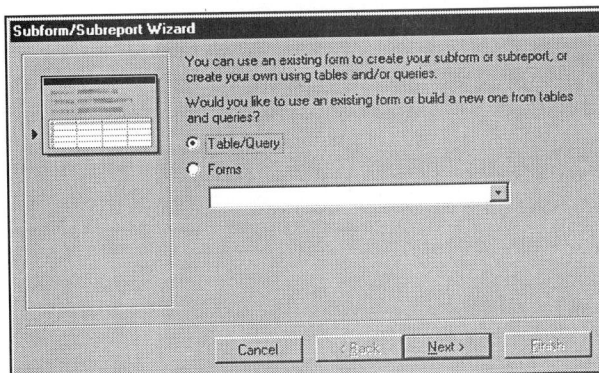

Figure 3 - 36

23. Click on the choice **Table/Query** and click the button that says **Next**.

24. Open the drop-down list of **Tables and Queries** and choose **Table: Invoices**.

25. Click the **>>** button to send all four fields from the **Available Fields** list to the **Selected Fields** list (see Figure 3-37).

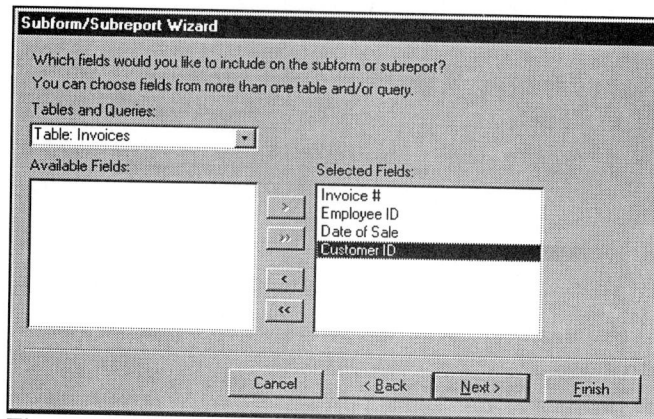

Figure 3 - 37

26. Click the **Next** button.

27. Pick **Choose from a list** if it is not already selected and click on **Show Invoices for each record in Employees using Employee ID** (see Figure 3-38). Click the **Next** button.

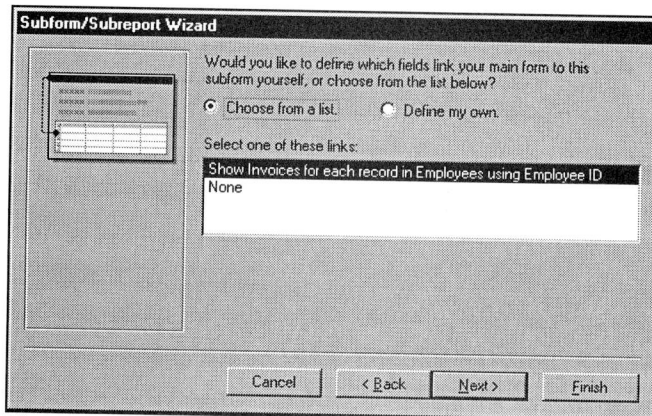

Figure 3 - 38

28. The suggested name **Invoices subform** is fine so click the **Finish** button. Do not check **Display Help**....

    The Wizard creates the subform for you and displays it on the form design (see Figure 3-39).

29. **Maximize** the window.

    As there may be many lines of invoices, we want to increase the height of the subform. To change the Invoices Subform, it must be the selected object on the form design because the Properties List applies to whatever the active object is.

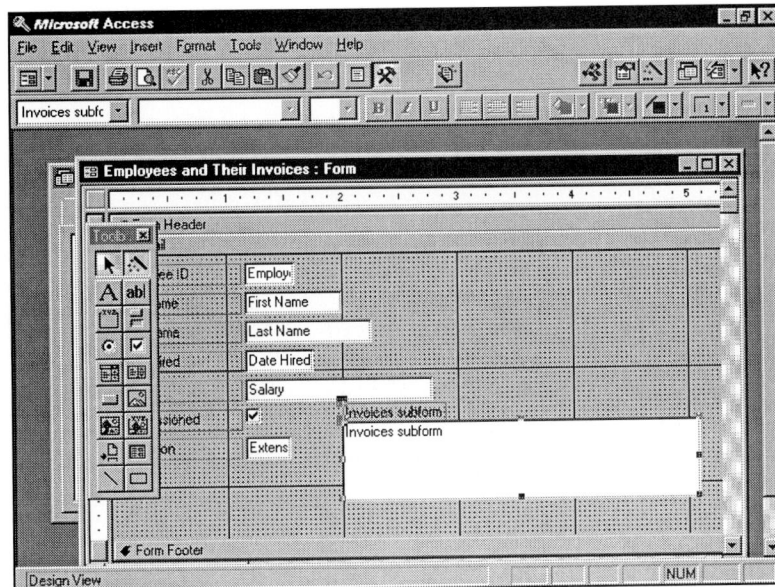

Figure 3 - 39

30. Only if the Invoices Subform does not already have tiny blocks on all of its sides as in Figure 3 - 39, click once on the Invoices Subform to select it.

31. Pick **VIEW/Properties**.

32. In the Properties List, click the **Format** tab if it is not already selected.

33. Move to the line for the **Height** and replace the current value with **1.5** (see Figure 3-40).

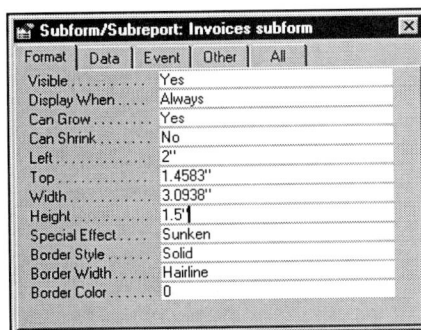

Figure 3 - 40

34. Close the Properties List with **VIEW/Properties**.

35. Click the **Form View** button to view the form.

36. Press **PGDN** (or **PAGE DOWN**) four times to get to **Daphne Green** (see Figure 3 - 25).

As Daphne is a salesperson, she has invoices associated with her Employee ID number. Notice that her number, 10, is listed on every one of the invoices that shows in the embedded subform.

37. Press **PGDN** (or **PAGE DOWN**) once to get to **George Jeffers**. He is in sales and has many invoices listed.

38. Press **PGDN** (or **PAGE DOWN**) once more to get to **Gary Lamp**. He is in sales, but is so new he does not have any sales yet (see Figure 3 - 41).

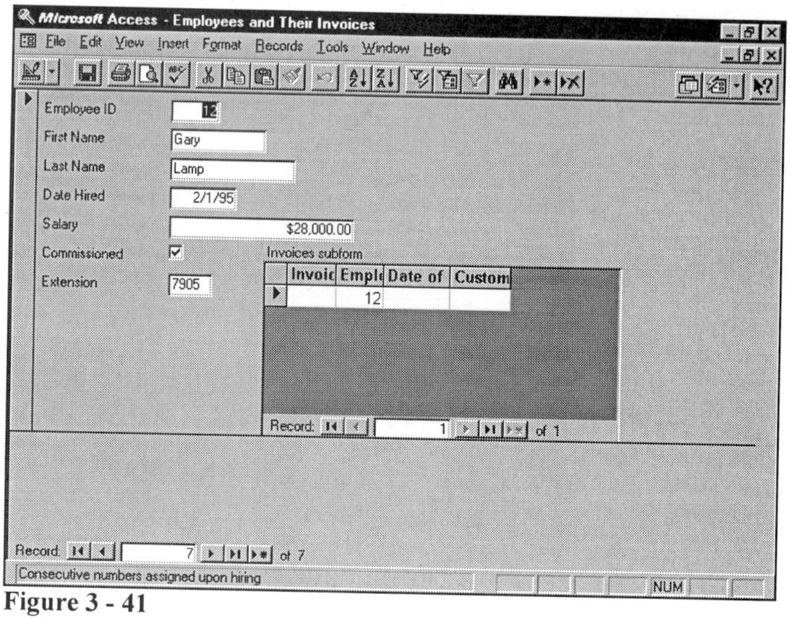

Figure 3 - 41

39. Save the design with **FILE/Save**.

40. Close the form with **FILE/Close**.

*Both new forms plus the Invoices Subform will be listed in the **Database** window.*

41. Restore the size of the **Database** window.

Operations with multiple tables like this multi-table form are much simpler if you name the matching fields in each table the exact same thing. In this past example, the *Access* Subform/Subreport Wizard figured out that **Employee ID** was the common field because the field name was the same in both tables. You are not required to make the names identical, but it makes many operations with multiple tables much simpler.

SUMMARY

In this lesson we have assembled a group of tables to compliment the **Employees** table that we created in Lesson 1, by importing from and linking to other *Access* databases. Once we had the tables, we began to work with multiple tables, examining the need for common fields between pairs of tables and creating a form that displayed data from two tables simultaneously.

In the next two lessons we will carry the multiple table idea one step further by seeing how to join separate but related tables. We will also learn how to select subsets of the data in a table based on matching specified values.

KEY TERMS

Link
Form
Form Wizard

Import
Relational Database System
Subform Wizard

INDEPENDENT PROJECTS

Independent Project 3.1: The School Newspaper

This Independent Project continues the Newspaper Ad database from Independent Project 2.1. In this project you will import the table containing the salespersons' names, rename the table, and create a form for entering ads. Finally, you will use that form to type in a new ad.

The table of names was typed by someone else who works for the newspaper and saved as **SF** (short for Sales Force) in the **IND-PROJ** database that is on the Student Data Diskette. You might ask why are the salespersons' names in a separate table? Why not include them right in the **Ads** table? Because the same sales people sell many ads, and their names would be repeated over and over in **Ads**. In **SF**, each salesperson is entered just once and given a code number. Only the short code number is included in each record.

The table of names looks like Figure 3-42.

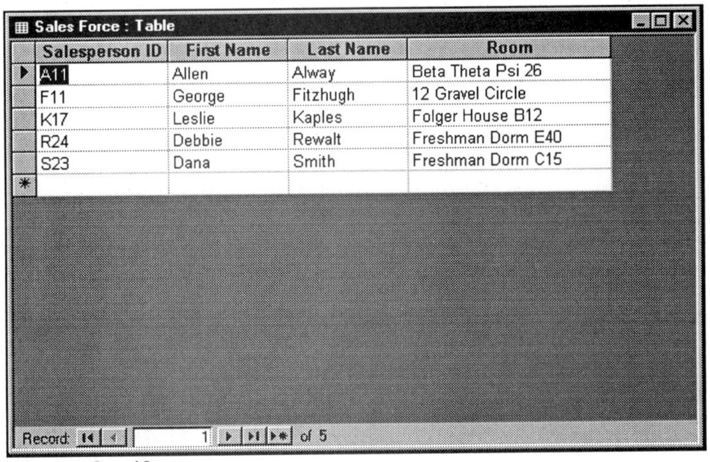

Salesperson ID	First Name	Last Name	Room
A11	Allen	Alway	Beta Theta Psi 26
F11	George	Fitzhugh	12 Gravel Circle
K17	Leslie	Kaples	Folger House B12
R24	Debbie	Rewalt	Freshman Dorm E40
S23	Dana	Smith	Freshman Dorm C15

Record: 1 of 5

Figure 3 - 42

When finished with the form, it should resemble Figure 3 - 43.

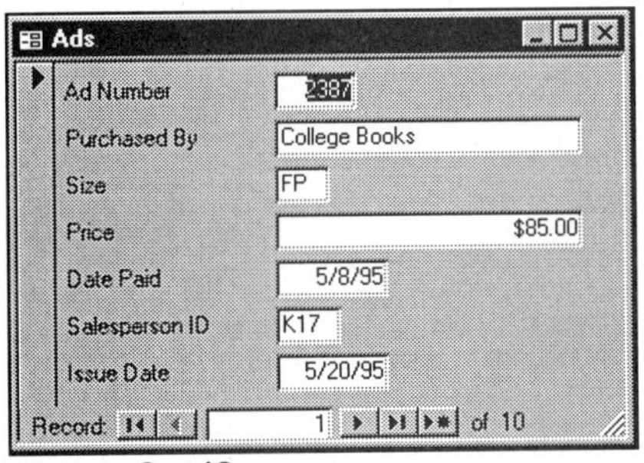

Ads	
Ad Number	2387
Purchased By	College Books
Size	FP
Price	$85.00
Date Paid	5/8/95
Salesperson ID	K17
Issue Date	5/20/95

Record: 1 of 10

Figure 3 - 43

1. Run *Access*.

2. Open the **Exercise1** database in the Introductory dialog box. Alternatively, pick **FILE/Open Database** or click the **Open Database** tool on the toolbar, and then click on the name **Exercise1** and click the **Open** button.

3. **Maximize** the *Access* window if it does not already cover the entire screen.

4. Begin importing the **SF** (Sales Force) table from the **Ind-Proj** database on the Student Data Diskette by picking **FILE/Get External Data/Import**.

5. In the **Import** dialog box, make certain the **Files of type:** list has **Microsoft Access** showing. Make any adjustments to the drive or folder in the **Look in:** list.

6. From the list of available databases, click on **ind-proj** and click the **Import** button.

7. On the **Tables** tab, click on **SF** and click the **OK** button.

8. If it is not already highlighted, click once on the name **SF** to select it in the Database window.

9. To rename the table pick **EDIT/Rename** and enter the new name **Sales Force** in the text box. Press the **ENTER** key to conclude the typing.

10. Open **Sales Force** by clicking the **Open** button. It should look like Figure 3-42.

11. Close **Sales Force** by picking **FILE/Close**.

12. Begin creating the form by clicking on the **Forms** tab at the top of the Database window.

13. Click the **New** button.

14. Pick **AutoForm: Columnar** in the list at the top of the **New Form** dialog box.

15. Open the drop-down list to **Choose the table or query where the object's data comes from:** and click on **Ads**.

16. Click the **OK** button.

17. When the form appears on the desktop, it is designed, but has not been saved yet. Save the design with **FILE/Save**, and enter the name **Ad Sales**. Click on **OK**.

18. Press the **PGDN** key several times to examine the data.

19. Click the **New Record** button to jump to a new blank record at the end of the table.

20. Enter ad number **2399**. It was purchased by **College Movies** as a **QP** (Quarter Page Size) at **$25** and was paid on **5/12/95**. Enter these first five data items in the appropriate fields.

21. This sale was made by Debbie Rewalt, her first sale! Her ID number is R24, so type that value into the **Salesperson ID** field. Press **TAB** to jump to **Issue Date** and enter **5/20/95**.

22. Print the form by clicking the **Print** button on the toolbar.

23. Close the form with **FILE/Close**.

24. Close the database with **FILE/Close**.

25. If you need to exit from *Access*, do so properly.

Independent Project 3.2: The Bookstore

This Independent Project continues the Bookstore database from Independent Project 2.2. In this project you will import the table containing the publishers' names, rename the table, and create a form that includes both the book data and the publishers' names on one screen. Finally you will use that form to enter a new book and a new publisher.

The table of publishers was typed by a clerk at the bookstore and saved as **PUB** (short for Publishers) in the **IND-PROJ** database that is on the Student Data Diskette. You might ask why are the publishers' names in a separate table? Why not include them right in the **Books** table? Because the same publishers supply many books, and their names would be repeated over and over in the **Books** table. In **PUB**, each publisher is entered just once and given a code number. Only the short code number is included on each book listing. Of course, to combine both **PUB** and **Books** on the same form, the matching code numbers must be in the **Books** table, too. You can check **Books** to make certain they are.

The table of publishers' names looks like Figure 3 - 44. When finished with the form, it should resemble Figure 3 - 45.

1. Run *Access*.

2. Open the **Exercise2** database in the Introductory dialog box. Alternatively, pick **FILE/Open Database** or click the **Open Database** tool on the toolbar, and then click on the name **Exercise2** and click the **Open** button.

3. **Maximize** the *Access* window if it does not already cover the entire screen.

4. Begin importing the **PUB** (Publishers) table from the **Ind-Proj** database on the Student Data Diskette by picking **FILE/Get External Data/Import**.

5. In the **Import** dialog box, make certain the **Files of type** list has **Microsoft Access** showing. Make any adjustments to the drive or folder in the **Look in:** list.

6. From the list of available databases, click on **ind-proj** and click the **Import** button.

7. On the **Tables** tab, click on **PUB** and click the **OK** button.

8. If it is not already highlighted, click once on the name **PUB** to select it in the **Database** window.

9. To rename the table to something better, pick **EDIT/Rename** and enter the new name **Publishers** in the text box. Press the **ENTER** key to conclude the typing.

10. Open **Publishers** by clicking the **Open** button. It should look like Figure 3 - 44. Press the **END** key to jump to the last field.

Publisher Code	Name	Address	City	State	Zip	Area Code	Phone	Fax
AW30	Atlantic Works	5856 Mane St.	New Market	NH	03857	403	436-7442	436-7440
BB29	Bulky Books	1285 N. Rasty St.	San Jose	CA	95124	408	559-9317	559-0018
BP07	Books Plus	Midway Court	Huntsville	AL	35805	205	430-7192	430-7190
CE03	College Editions	871 Cotina Ave.	Colorado Springs	CO	80949	719	260-4545	260-4546
PP01	Prime Publications	18 Riverside Rd.	Astoria	NY	11103	718	545-6018	545-9996
TM02	Treatise Marketplace	132 Sawmill Rd.	Wheaton	IL	60187	708	665-1412	665-1512
TT12	Texts and Tomes	15 Tyler Way	Sandy	UT	84093	801	772-4591	772-8002
VO11	Volumes	2 West Way	Ashville	NC	28806	704	665-0891	665-1170

Figure 3 - 44

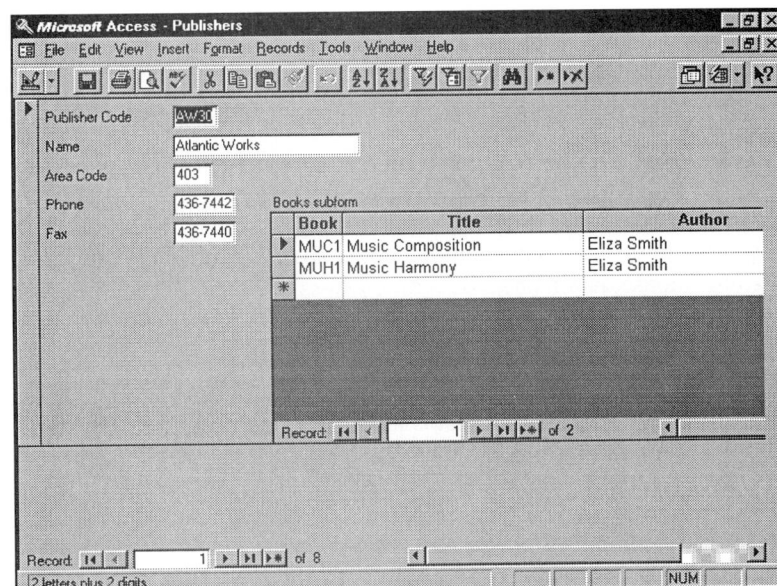

Figure 3 - 45

11. Close **Publishers** by picking **FILE/Close**.

12. Begin creating the form by clicking on the **Forms** tab at the top of the **Database** window.

13. Click the **New** button.

14. Click on **Form Wizard** in the list of methods at the top of the **New Form** dialog box. Open the list of tables by clicking the drop-down arrow and choose **Publishers**. Then, click the **OK** button.

15. Since we will include only the **Publisher Code, Name, Area Code, Phone,** and **Fax** fields on this form, make certain the highlight is on **Publisher Code** in the **Available Fields** list and click on the single arrow head button pointing to the right to start with that one field.

16. Click on the single arrow head once more to send the **Name** field to the **Selected Fields** list.

17. Click on the field name **Area Code** and click on the single arrow head to include it.

18. Similarly, click the single arrow head two more times to send the next two fields, **Phone** and **Fax** over to the **Selected Fields** list.

19. Click **Next**.

20. Click on **Columnar** for the layout and click **Next**.

21. In the third dialog box you pick the style for the form. **Standard** is recommended as the simplest to work with, but any style will do. Pick a style and click **Next**.

22. Enter the title (the name by which this form will be recorded in the database) and choose whether to go to the form to view information or to the design. The title **Publishers** is already in the text box so leave it alone. Make certain **Open the form to view or enter information** is the selected option, and click the **Finish** button.

23. **Maximize** the form window.

24. Click the **Form View** button to switch to the design.

25. Choose **EDIT/Select Form**.

26. Pick **VIEW/Properties**.

27. On the **Format** tab of the Properties List, scroll down to **Width** and type **6** over the current value.

28. Close the Properties List with **VIEW/Properties**.

29. If the Toolbox is not already showing on the screen, pick **VIEW/Toolbox**.

30. Make certain the **Control Wizards** button is pressed in.

31. Click on the **Subform/Subreport** button and move the mouse pointer onto the design.

32. Position the small cross at about 2 inches on the top ruler and 1 inch on the left–side ruler and click the mouse button once.

33. Choose **Table/Query** as the source and click the **Next** button.

34. Click the >> button to include all fields in the **Selected Fields** list and click the **Next** button.

35. Make certain **Choose from a list** is the selected option and that **Show Books for each record in Publisher using Publisher Code** is highlighted. Click **Next**.

36. Keep the suggested name **Books subform** and click the **Finish** button.

37. **Maximize** the form window.

38. With the **Books subform** still selected (there will be little handles on each side and corner), pick **VIEW/Properties**.

39. On the **Height** line in the Properties List, type **2**, to replace the original value.

40. Pick **VIEW/Properties** to close the Properties List.

41. Save the modifications to the form design with **FILE/Save**.

42. Click the **Form View** button to run the form.

43. Press the **PGDN** key seven times, pausing between each press to examine the data. Notice that four publishers have no books in the **Books** table yet. The other four have from two to four each.

44. To make sure the form works, you will enter one new book and one new publisher. To start the new book, you must search for the correct publisher. Click the **Find** button on the toolbar, enter: **BB29** (the code for Bulky Books) in the **Find What** text box, make certain **Search** says **All** and that **Search Only Current Field** is checked, and click the **Find First** button.

45. **Close** the **Find** dialog box.

46. Click the mouse in the typing box in the **Book Code** column (the first column) in the subform.

47. Enter book code **CHC18**. The title is **Chemical Compendium**. There is no Author so press the **TAB** key to skip to the **Year of Publication** field. The fields in the subform may not scroll, so you may need to click the lower scroll bar to scroll to the right.

48. Type in the Year of Publication as **1995** and skip over the Publisher Code as that is already filled in correctly and must not be changed. The Cost is **34.50** and the Price is **49.95**. Leave the Quantity in Stock as **0**.

49. To enter the new publisher, click the mouse on the current **Publisher Code** field on the main form. You will probably need to scroll back to the left to see the **Publisher Code** field at the top of the form.

50. Click the **New Record** Navigation button at the very bottom of the screen (not in the subform) to jump to a new record.

51. Type: **AA15** for the Publisher Code, **Authors Away** as the Name, **415** for the Area Code, **326-8899** in the **Phone** field, and **326-9988** for the Fax number.

52. Close the form with **FILE/Close**.

53. Print the form by clicking the **Print** button on the toolbar.

54. Close the database with **FILE/Close**.

55. If you need to exit from *Access*, do so properly.

Independent Project 3.3: The Real Estate Office

This Independent Project continues the Real Estate Office database from Independent Project 2.3. In this project you will import the table containing the agencies' names and create a form that includes both the properties and the agencies' names on one screen. Finally you will use that form to enter a new commercial real estate listing and a new agency.

The table of agencies was typed by a colleague at the real estate office and saved as Agencies in the **IND-PROJ** database that is on the Student Data Diskette. You might ask why are the agencies' names in a separate table? Why not include them right in the **Commercial Listings** table? Because the same agency supplies many commercial listings, and their names would be repeated over and over in the **Commercial Listings** table. In **Agencies**, each office and its associated data are entered just once and given a code number. Only the short code number is included on each commercial property listing. Of course, to combine both **Agencies** and **Commercial Listings** on the same form, the matching code numbers must be in the **Commercial Listings** table, too. You can check **Commercial Listings** to make certain they are.

The table of agencies' names looks like Figure 3 - 46. When finished with the form, it should resemble Figure 3 - 47.

Agency Code	Agency Name	Address	City	State	Zip	Area Code	Phone 1	Phone 2	Fax
GW14	George Winkle	80 N. Main St.	New Canaan	CT	06840	203	972-9538		972-9625
PP15	Priceless Properties	817 Glable Lane	Stamford	CT	06903	203	359-1111		359-1212
PP24	Profitable Properties	452 Elm Ave.	Danbury	CT	06810	203	748-3471	748-3472	748-0102
RP12	Right Properties	125 Ridgeway	Danbury	CT	06810	203	748-9410	748-9010	748-9411
RR11	Regal Real Estate	17 North Way W.	Stamford	CT	06905	203	359-0050	359-0060	359-0055
SC18	Smith and Cross	7612 Main St.	Greenwich	CT	06830	203	661-2831		661-2001

Figure 3 - 46

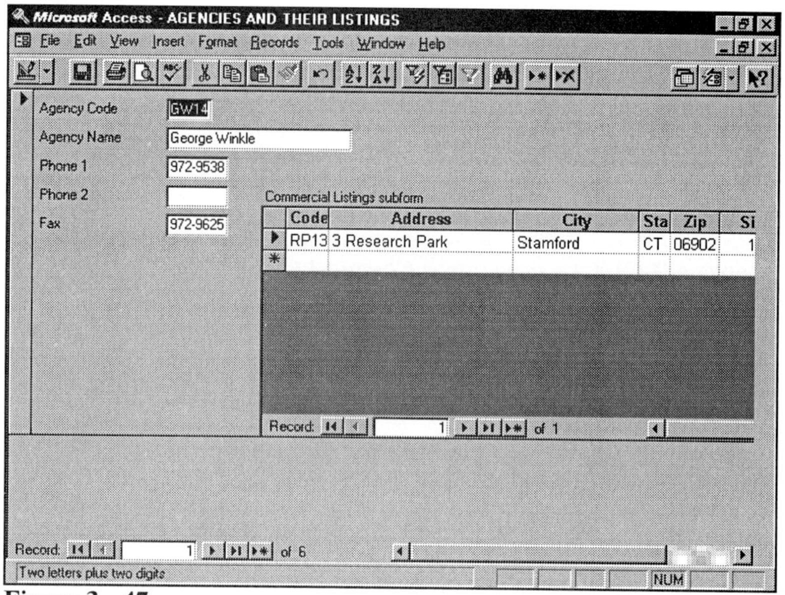

Figure 3 - 47

1. Run *Access* and maximize the window.

2. Open the **Exercise3** database.

3. Import the **Agencies** table from the **Microsoft Access** database named **Ind-Proj** on the Student Data Diskette.

4. Open **Agencies**. It should look like Figure 3 - 46.

5. Close **Agencies**.

6. Begin creating the form by clicking on the **Forms** tab at the top of the database window.

7. Use the **Form Wizard** to create a form for the **Agencies** table.

8. From **Agencies** include the **Agency Code, Agency Name, Phone 1, Phone 2**, and **Fax** fields.

9. The layout should be **Columnar**.

10. Pick **Standard** as the style.

11. Make the title **AGENCIES AND THEIR LISTINGS** and open the form to view or enter information.

12. **Maximize** the form window.

13. Switch to the design screen and select the entire form with **EDIT/Select Form**.

14. View the properties list and set the form's width to 6 inches.

15. Make certain the Control Wizard is activated and use the toolbox to add a subform at about 2 inches on the top ruler and about 1 inch on the left ruler.

16. Choose **Table/Query** as the data source in the Subform/Subreport Wizard dialog box.

17. Choose **Commercial Listings** as the table for the subform and include all fields.

18. Pick **Choose from a list** and then **Show Commercial Listings for each record in Agencies using Agency Code.**

19. Accept the name **Commercial Listings subform.**

20. **Maximize** the form design window.

21. With the **Commercial Listings subform** selected, open the Properties List and change the **Height** to **2** inches.

22. Save the modified design.

23. Run the form (see Figure 3 - 47).

24. Press the **PGDN** key five times, pausing between each press to examine the data.

25. A new listing at 6 Research Park, Stamford, has been announced. The listing agent will be RP12, Right Properties. Locate that real estate agency in the top portion of the form, and then enter the new listing from the data shown in Table 3 - 1 into the embedded portion of the form. You may need to scroll across the embedded form to see all the fields.

Field Name	Data
Code	RP16
Address	6 Research Park
City	Stamford
State	CT
Zip	06902
Size	19,000
Floor	1
Purchase or Rent	P
Price	$3,900,000
Available	10/1/95
Agency Code	RP12
Agent	Williams

Table 3 - 1

26. To enter the new real estate agency and click in the **Agency Code** field in the main part of the form and click the **New Record** button

27. Type **CP19** for the Agency Code, **Colonial Properties** as the Agency Name, **359-8372** for Phone 1, and **359-0573** in the **Fax** field.

28. Print the form by clicking the **Print** button on the toolbar.

29. Close the form with **FILE/Close.**

30. Close the database with **FILE/Close.**

31. If you need to exit from *Access*, do so properly.

Independent Project 3.4: The Veterinarian

This Independent Project continues the Veterinarian database from Independent Project 2.4. In this project you will import the table containing the owners' names and create a form that includes both the pets and the owners' names on one screen. Finally, you will use that form to enter a new owner and her pet.

The table of owners is already typed and has been saved as **Pet Owners** in the **IND-PROJ** database that is on the Student Data Diskette. Be sure you can answer the question of why the owners' names and addresses are in a separate table rather than included right in the pets table.

Complete the following tasks:

1. Import the **Pet Owners** table from the Student Data Diskette.

2. Open **Pet Owners** and examine the data in it.

3. Use the **Form Wizard** to create a form for the **Pet Owners** table and embed on it a subform for **Pets**. The link should be **Show Pets for each record in Pet Owner using Owner Code**. It should match the form illustrated in Figure 3 - 48, except that the embedded subform will have the field names you made up and the **Code** and **Date of Last Visit** fields will have the dates you entered.

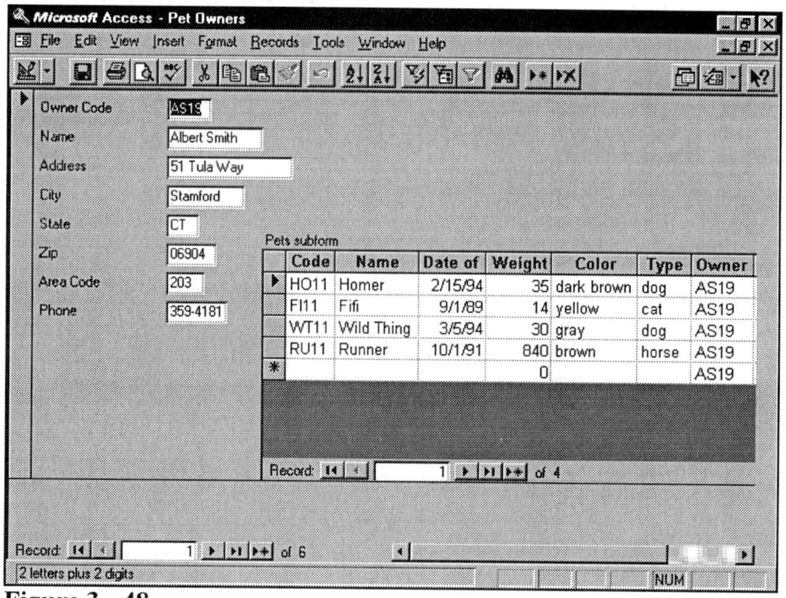

Figure 3 - 48

4. Use the form to enter a new pet for Dan Wilson. The pet is a black horse named Wilhelm that weighs 940 pounds. It was born about 6/15/90.

5. Use the form to enter a new owner. He is Monty Wright and lives at 56 Wildwood Terrace, Stamford, CT, 06905. His phone number is (203) 359-4415.

6. **Print** the form.

Queries

Objectives

In this lesson you will learn how to:

- Set up a select query
- Select the fields to be included

- Sort the query result
- Specify single criteria for selecting records

PROJECT DESCRIPTION

A *query* is a search for all the records within a table that contain a specific value. For example, you might need a list of all of your customers who ordered a particular CDROM title.

In this lesson, we will run several queries based on the CDROM table in order to extract various groups of listings, check inventory levels, and gather other pertinent information. We will match a single value at a time in this lesson. In the next lesson, we will use queries with multiple matching values, as well as multiple tables to access data from more than one source.

When you complete this lesson, you will have two queries listed in the database window (see Figure 4 - 1).

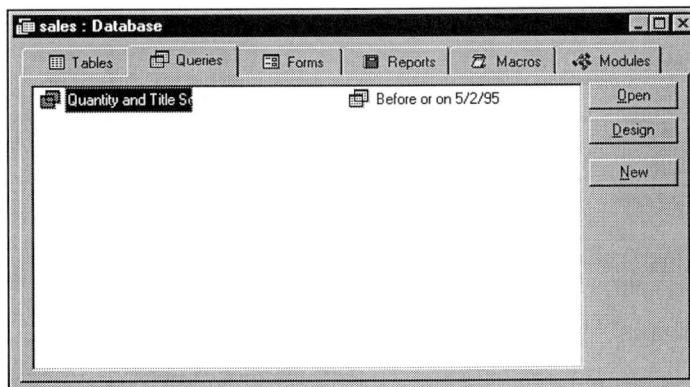

Figure 4 - 1

QUERYING A TABLE

During editing we searched for matching listings one at a time; with queries you get the complete set of matches all at once. A query also allows sorting the resulting listings, as well as selecting which fields will be included and in what order. Once designed, a query may be saved, or merely used temporarily and discarded. If saved, reports and forms can be designed for queries, the same as for tables. Since we are selecting the fields and records, this type of query is called a *Select Query*.

Access uses what is called *Query by Example*. This means that, rather than type out a lengthy instruction in words, in *Access* you merely fill in a diagram by giving an example of the value you want matched. For example, to work with only records of customers who live in New York, you would type the example "NY" in the **State** field. The example of what you want matched is also called the *criterion*. Query by Example is abbreviated QBE, and, thus, the grid in the bottom half of the Select Query window is called the *QBE grid* (see Figure 4 - 2).

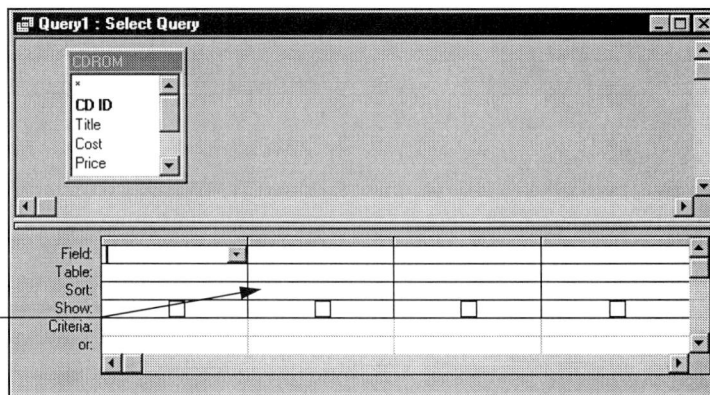

The QBE grid

Figure 4 - 2

The resulting answer from a select query is called a *dynaset*. Dynaset stands for "dynamically linked datasheet," which is a fancy way of saying that the listings resulting from a query can be directly edited and any changes to the data will automatically be made in the original table as well.

When you begin a new query, there are five choices in the initial dialog box. Design View is the most flexible way to design a query and the one this book will employ. The **Simple Query Wizard** will ask a few simple questions and then handle the remainder of the design for you. While the **Simple Query Wizard** sounds inviting, the amount of design work it actually accomplishes for you is minimal and can actually slow you down. Additionally, you almost always need to add details to what little that Wizard can accomplish. Therefore, this book will use Design View to set up queries. The reader should feel free to experiment with the **Simple Query Wizard**. The **Crosstab Query** Wizard, **Find Duplicates Query Wizard**, and **Find Unmatched Query Wizard** are very handy for the advanced user, but beyond the level of this book.

A SINGLE TABLE QUERY

For our first query we will produce a list of each CDROM Title and its Quantity in Stock. We begin by opening the Select Query window.

To set up a Select Query:

- Click the **Queries** tab at the top of the **Database** window.

- Click the **New** button at the right edge of the **Database** window.

- In the list in the **New Query** dialog box, choose **Design View**.

- Add the desired table or tables from the **Show Table** dialog box.

Activity 4.1: Setting up a Select Query

The first step is to initiate the query and choose the table whose data will be the basis of the search.

1. Open the **Sales** database by picking it in the Introductory dialog box and clicking **OK** or with **FILE/Open Database**, clicking on **SALES**, and clicking on **Open**.

   *Before clicking on **Sales** you may need to pick the correct drive and folder.*

2. Click on the **Queries** tab (see Figure 4 - 3).

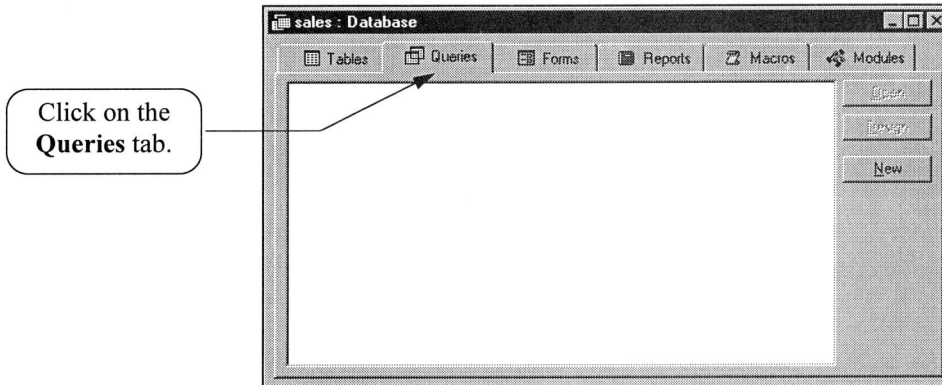

Figure 4 - 3

3. Click the **New** button at the right edge of the database window.

4. In the **New Query** dialog box, click on **Design View** (see Figure 4 - 4) and click the **OK** button.

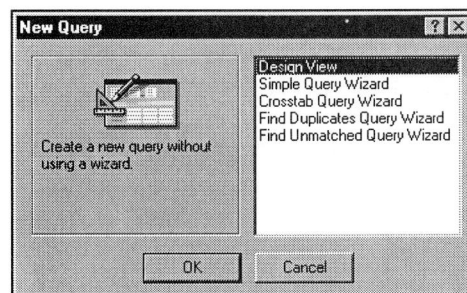

Figure 4 - 4

*The **Query1: Select Query** window opens with the **Add Table** dialog box on top of it (see Figure 4 - 5).*

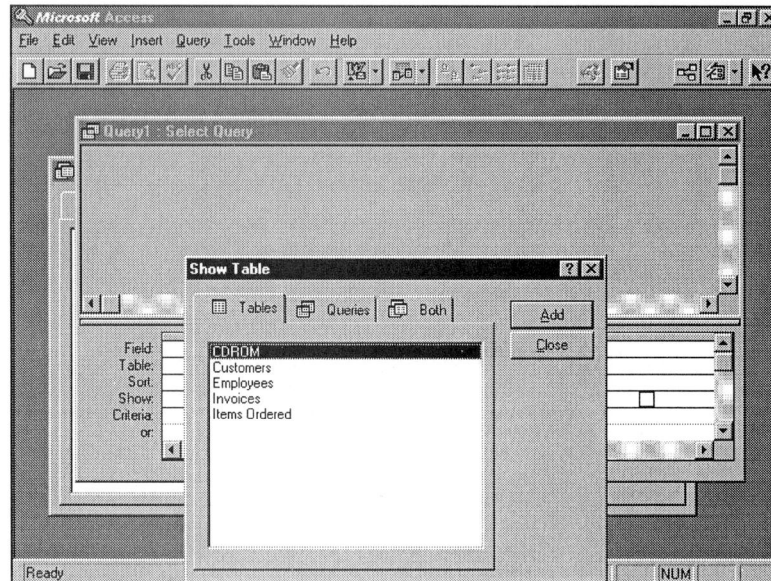

Figure 4 - 5

5. Since we are interested in selected data from the **CDROM** table, make certain the **Tables** tab is selected, pick **CDROM** from the list of tables, and click the **Add** button to place a list of its fields in the top half of the **Select Query** window (see Figure 4 - 6).

6. Since **CDROM** is the only table in which we are interested, click the **Close** button to close the **Show Table** dialog box.

The list of CDROM fields is shown in the upper section of the Query window.

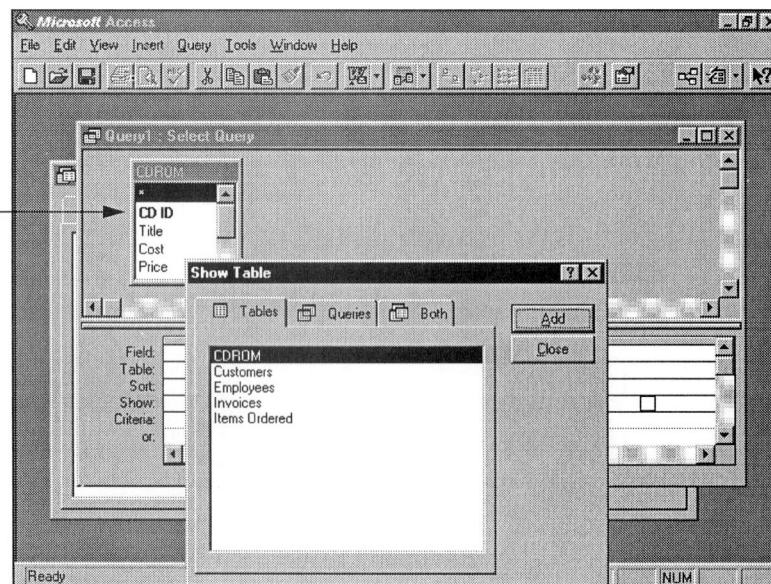

Figure 4 - 6

SELECTING THE FIELDS

There are four methods for choosing the fields that you want to see in the result.

To select the fields to be included in the result:

- Double– click the name in the field list in the top half of the query window. That field name will occupy the next available column in the QBE grid. This is probably quickest.

- Click on and drag the name from the field list down to the QBE grid. Either drag the name to an empty column, or, if the column is already occupied, the new name will be inserted and the existing name will be pushed to the right. This method is best for controlling the placement of a field.

- In the desired column in the QBE grid, click on the **Field** line. Then, click the drop-down arrow to open the list of available fields and select the field name from the list. This is a good method for changing a field selection.

- Type the desired field name directly on the **Field** line in the desired column. This is the slowest method, but does not require the mouse.

The **Query View** button is a drop–down list button. That means that it has a drop-down arrow associated with it and, if you click the arrow, a list of related choices will open below the toolbar. Usually you will not need to open the drop-down list as the most common choice is usually showing on the button itself and will change as you switch in and out of the design or the dynaset.

To view the resulting dynaset:

- Click the **Query View** button ▦▾ on the toolbar or pick **VIEW/Datasheet** in the menus.

To return to the query design:

- Click the **Query View** button ▨▾ on the toolbar or pick **VIEW/Query Design** in the menus. The button will have changed to the **Design View** button.

Activity 4.2: Selecting the Desired Fields and Viewing the Result

Since we need only the Title and Quantity in Stock, we will select only those two fields to be included in the field list. For the first field we will drag the field name down into the QBE grid. For the second field we will speed things up by double-clicking to include the field name.

1. In the list of fields in the top half of the **Query1: Select Query** window, click on the name **Title** to highlight it.

2. Move the mouse cursor back on top of the highlighted name, hold down the mouse button, and drag its icon (it will become a small rectangle) down onto the **Field** line in the first column of the QBE grid. Release the mouse button.

   While dragging the mouse, wherever a circle with a slash appears, that is an inappropriate area for the field name. Do not release the mouse button in such an area.

*The name **Title** will appear on the **Field** line in the first column, the table name will be shown on the **Table** line, and a check mark will check the box on the Show: line indicating that the field will be shown in the resulting dynaset (see Figure 4 - 7).*

The **Title** field has been installed in the first column of the QBE grid.

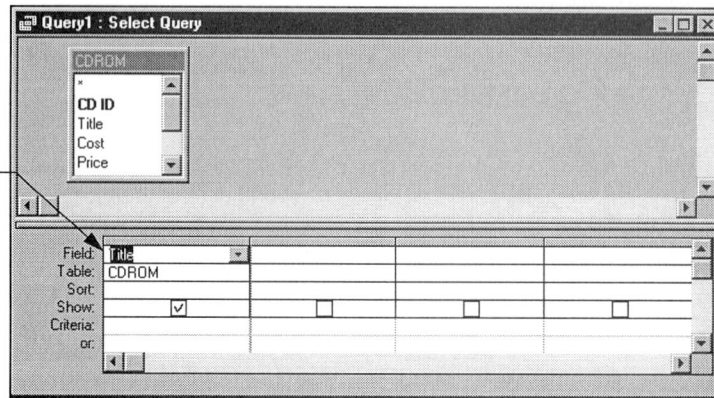

Figure 4 - 7

3. In the list of fields in the top half of the **Query1: Select Query** window, scroll down until you can see Quantity in Stock and double-click on the name **Quantity in Stock** to include it in the second column of the QBE grid (see Figure 4 - 8).

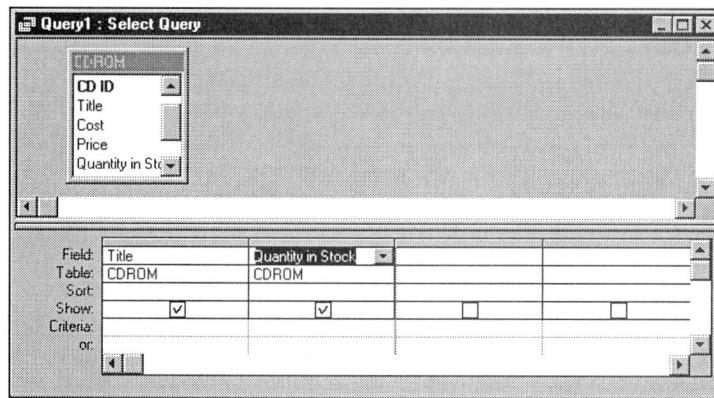

Figure 4 - 8

4. Click the **Query View** button on the toolbar to view the result.

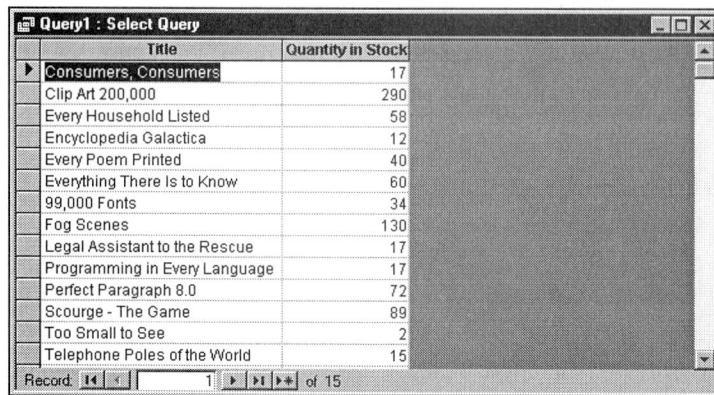

Title	Quantity in Stock
Consumers, Consumers	17
Clip Art 200,000	290
Every Household Listed	58
Encyclopedia Galactica	12
Every Poem Printed	40
Everything There Is to Know	60
99,000 Fonts	34
Fog Scenes	130
Legal Assistant to the Rescue	17
Programming in Every Language	17
Perfect Paragraph 8.0	72
Scourge - The Game	89
Too Small to See	2
Telephone Poles of the World	15

Record: 1 of 15

Figure 4 - 9

All 15 records are listed, but only the two selected fields are included (Figure 4 - 9). This result is a dynaset.

5. Click the **Query View** button on the toolbar to return to the query design.

SORTING THE DYNASET

A query can sort the resulting dynaset based on any field or combination of fields in the table. You fill in the **Sort** line in the QBE grid in one or more columns. With a multiple field sort, the column furthest on the left will be sorted first, followed by each additional column that contains a sort specification from left to right. The column(s) used to sort may be shown in the dynaset by leaving the **Show** box checked, or hidden by unchecking the **Show** box.

To sort a dynaset:

• Include the field you wish to sort by in the QBE grid.

• Move onto the **Sort** line of the column you wish to sort by. A drop-down list arrow will appear.

• Open the drop-down list by clicking its arrow and choose either **Ascending** or **Descending**.

Activity 4.3: Sorting by Quantity In Stock

We want to sort the dynaset by the **Quantity in Stock** field.

1. Since the **Quantity In Stock** field is already in the QBE Grid, click the mouse on the **Sort** line in that column.

2. Click on the drop-down arrow to open the list of sort options (see Figure 4 - 10).

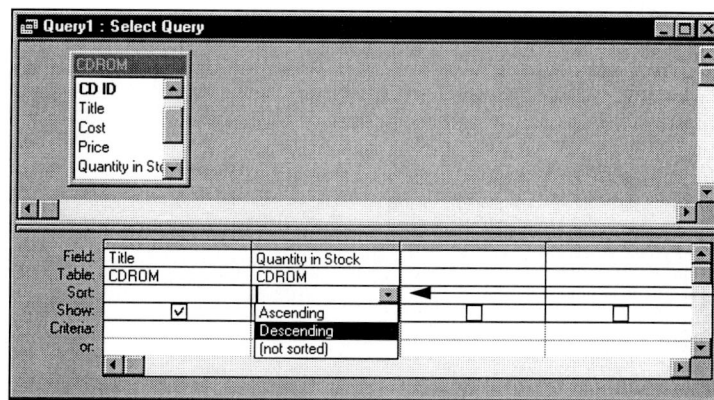

Figure 4 - 10

3. Choose **Descending** to sort the quantities from largest to smallest.

4. Click the **Query View** button on the toolbar to view the result (see Figure 4 - 11).

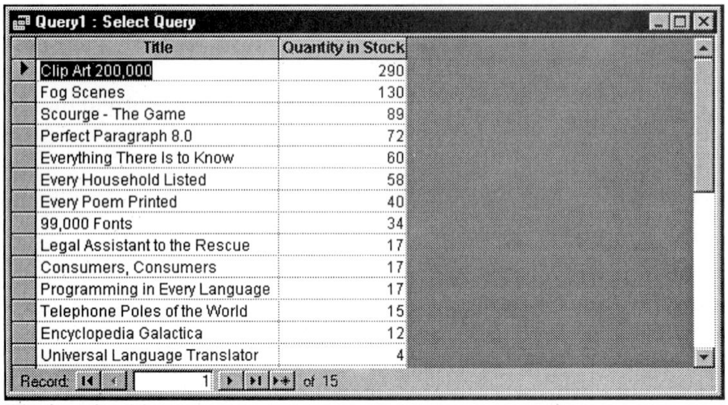

Figure 4 - 11

All 15 records are still listed, but they are now sorted into order by descending quantity.

5.   Print this result by clicking the **Print** button.

6.   Click the **Query View** button on the toolbar to return to the query design.

Activity 4.4: Inserting a Field and Sorting by Two Fields

The **Price** field is not in the QBE grid yet, so we must add it. We could easily put it in the third column, but we want it in the second column. To insert a field, drag its name down to the QBE grid on top of an existing name on the **Field** line and release the mouse button. The field that was in that column will move to the right to make room for the new field.

1.   Click the mouse once on the field name **Price** in the list in the top section of the window to highlight that name.

2.   Drag **Price** down to the QBE grid and drop it on top of **Quantity in Stock**.

     Quantity in Stock *will move over to the third column (see* Figure 4 - 12*).*

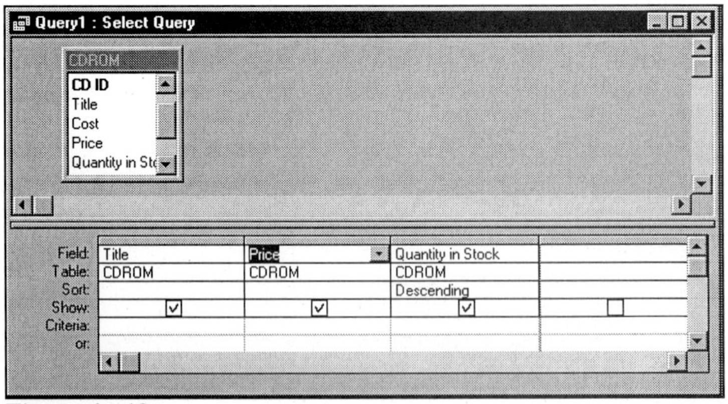

Figure 4 - 12

3.   Click the mouse on the **Sort** line in the **Price** column.

4. Open the list of sort options by clicking the drop-down list arrow and choose **Ascending**.

   Because we have two columns being sorted, Access will sort first by the column on the left. Thus, the prices will be in ascending order. Then, whenever two products have the same price, those two will be in descending quantity order.

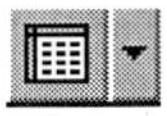

5. Click the **Query View** button on the toolbar to view the result (Figure 4 - 13).

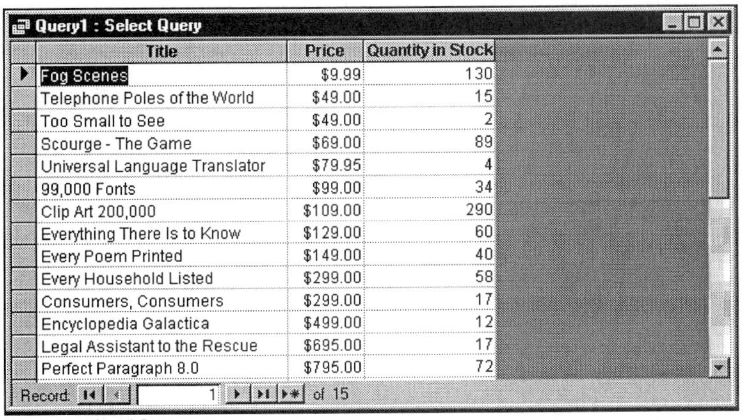

Title	Price	Quantity in Stock
Fog Scenes	$9.99	130
Telephone Poles of the World	$49.00	15
Too Small to See	$49.00	2
Scourge - The Game	$69.00	89
Universal Language Translator	$79.95	4
99,000 Fonts	$99.00	34
Clip Art 200,000	$109.00	290
Everything There Is to Know	$129.00	60
Every Poem Printed	$149.00	40
Every Household Listed	$299.00	58
Consumers, Consumers	$299.00	17
Encyclopedia Galactica	$499.00	12
Legal Assistant to the Rescue	$695.00	17
Perfect Paragraph 8.0	$795.00	72

Record: 1 of 15

Figure 4 - 13

Note the pair of products with a price of $49.00 and check that their two quantities are in descending order. Also examine the pair priced at $299.00.

6. Print this result by clicking the **Print** button.

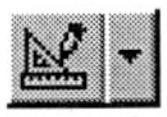

7. Click the **Query View** button on the toolbar to return to the query design.

REMOVING A FIELD FROM THE QBE GRID

Either a single field can be removed from the query design, or all fields can be deleted.

To delete a single field from the QBE grid:

- Move to the field in the QBE grid.

- Choose **EDIT/Delete Column** in the menu.

To delete all fields from the QBE grid:

- Pick **EDIT/Clear Grid**.

Activity 4.5: Deleting the Price Field

1. Click the mouse on any line of the **Price** column in the QBE grid.

2. Pick **EDIT/Delete Column** in the menu to remove the **Price** field.

   *The **Quantity in Stock** field slides back over to the second column.*

SORTING BY TWO FIELDS THAT ARE NOT IN LEFT TO RIGHT ORDER

Since *Access* sorts the fields that have sort specifications in the QBE grid from left to right, what if that is not the desired order? To see how to accomplish an out-of-order sort we will sort by **Quantity in Stock** in descending order and **Title** in ascending order even though **Title** will be the first field displayed in the dynaset.

To sort by fields that are not in left-to-right order:

- Place the fields you want to see in the dynaset in the desired order.

- Insert a second copy of the field that is the most important field for sorting, placing it to the left of the second most important field for sorting.

- Set the sort order specification (ascending or descending) in this new copy of the most important field, but uncheck the **Show** box so that the field will not show in the result. Thus it will sort, but not show.

- In the original copy of the most important field for sorting, leave the **Show** box checked so it will display, but do not set a sort option.

Activity 4.6: Sorting by Quantity, then Title

1. The query design with **Title** in the first column and **Quantity in Stock** in the second column should still be open.

2. Click on the **Quantity in Stock** field name in the list in the upper section of the window.

3. Drag that field name down into the QBE grid and drop it on top of **Title** in the first column.

   Title will move over to the second column (see Figure 4 - 14).

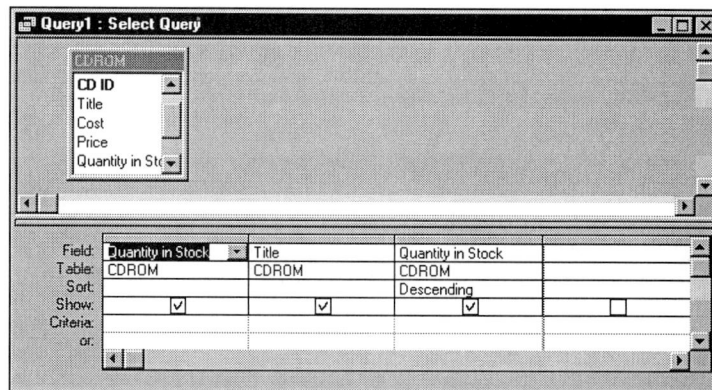

Figure 4 - 14

4. Click on the **Sort** line in the first column (the first Quantity in Stock), open the drop-down list, and choose **Descending**.

5. Remove the check on the **Show** line for this first column (the first Quantity in Stock) so it will sort but not display.

6. Click on the **Sort** line under the third column (the second Quantity in Stock) and delete the word **Descending** or pick **(Not Sorted)** from the drop-down list on the **Sort** line (see Figure 4 - 15).

Leave the check in the Show box of this second Quantity in Stock field as this one, which is to the right of Title, should display.

Uncheck the **Show** box when the column should not be displayed.

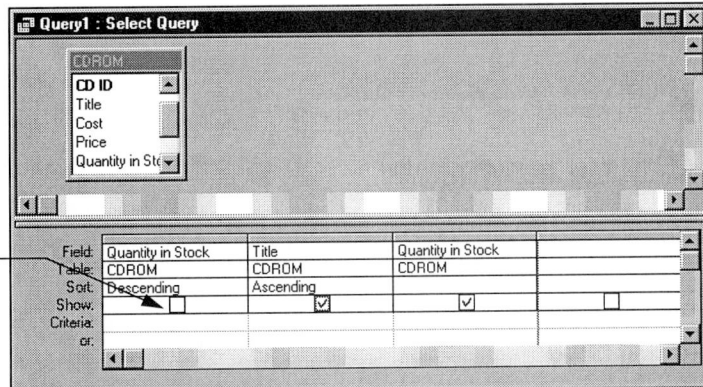

Figure 4 - 15

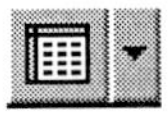

7. Click on the **Sort** line under **Title** and pick **Ascending** (see Figure 4 - 15).

8. Click the **Query View** button on the toolbar to view the result (Figure 4 - 16).

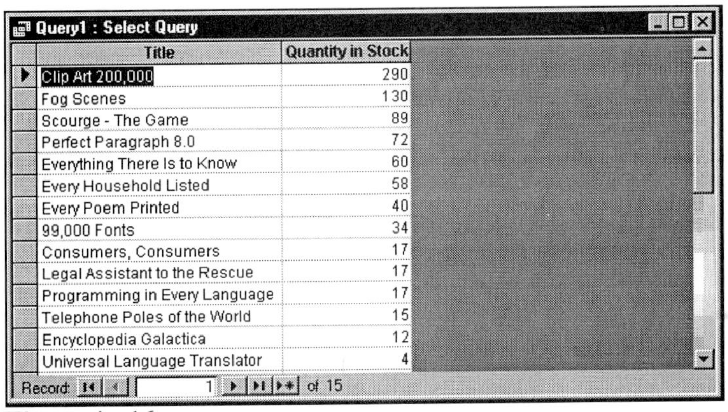

Figure 4 - 16

Examine the three listings with a quantity of 17. They should be in alphabetical order by Title.

9. Print this result by clicking the **Print** button.

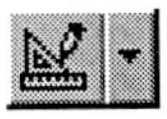

10. Click the **Query View** button on the toolbar to return to the query design.

SAVING A QUERY DESIGN

While a query is often used to temporarily view a result, sometimes the answer is important or useful enough to save the query so it can be rerun whenever needed.

To save a query:

• Choose **FILE/Save**.

• Type the desired name (up to 64 characters) in the **Query Name** text box of the **Save As** dialog box.

• Click **OK**.

Activity 4.7: Saving the Query

1. Choose **FILE/Save**.

2. Type the name: **Quantity and Title Sort** and click **OK** (see Figure 4 - 17).

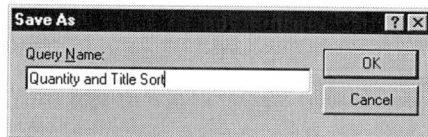

Figure 4 - 17

3. Choose **FILE/Close**.

   The name will appear in the Queries list of the Database window, and could be reopened any time that query was needed again.

SELECTING MATCHING RECORDS WITH A QUERY

Perhaps the most valuable ability of a query is to select only those records that match some criterion that you specify. You specify the value to be matched by typing an example of it (thus Query by Example). You type the example on the **Criteria** line in the QBE grid in the column that would contain the matching values.

In this lesson, we will search for matching values in a single field. In the next lesson, we will use multiple criteria.

To select records with matching values through a query:

- Open the Query window and choose a table as discussed previously.

- Pick the desired fields.

- Enter the example of the value to be matched on the **Criteria** line in the column that would contain that value.

- Click the **Query View** button to see the resulting dynaset.

Activity 4.8: Using Numerical Criteria in a Query

We need a listing of the CDROMs that cost $179.

1. The **SALES** database should be open.

2. Click on the **Queries** tab.

3. Click the **New** button at the right edge of the Database window.

4. In the **New Query** dialog box, click on **Design View** and click the **OK** button.

5. Pick **CDROM** from the group of tables and click the **Add** button to place a list of its fields in the top half of the **Query1: Select Query** window.

6. Since **CDROM** is the only table in which we are interested, click the **Close** button to close the **Show Table** dialog box.

7. Double-click on **Title** in the list in the upper section of the window to place it in the first column of the QBE grid.

8. Double-click on **Cost** to put it in the second column of the QBE grid.

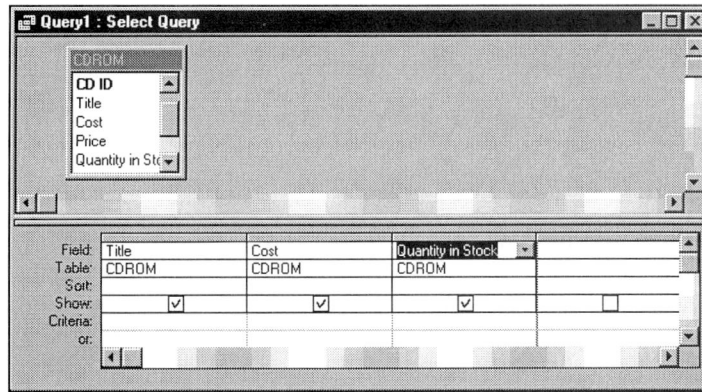

Figure 4 - 18

9. Scroll down to and double-click on **Quantity in Stock** to position it in the third column of the QBE grid (see Figure 4 - 18).

10. Click on the **Criteria** line in the **Cost** column of the QBE grid.

11. Type: **179** (see Figure 4 - 19).

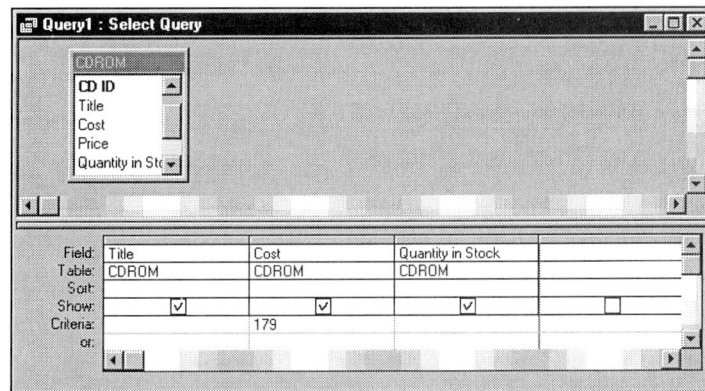

Figure 4 - 19

Do not type the dollar sign or any commas in numbers in a criterion. If you should get a "Type Mismatch" error, check your typing very carefully and correct the entry.

12. Click the **Query View** button on the toolbar to view the result (see Figure 4 - 20).

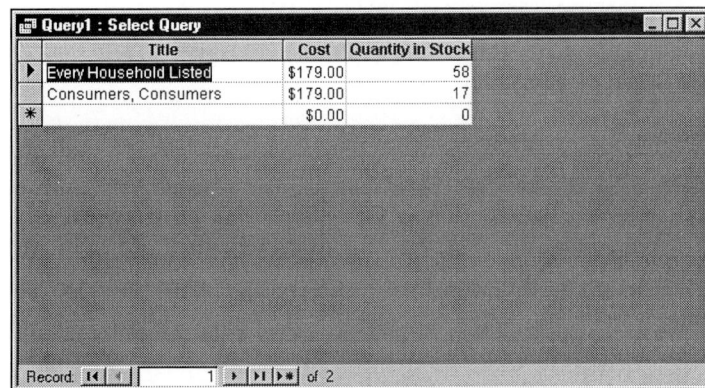

Figure 4 - 20

Examine the values for Cost. They should both be equal to $179.

13. Click the **Query View** button on the toolbar to return to the query design. Do not close the query.

THE INEQUALITY SYMBOLS IN QUERIES

Access interprets a single value on the **Criteria** line as requiring an exact match, that is the value in the table must *equal* the example. Though you could type the equal sign, it is always optional. Other *operators* are allowed besides an equal sign. These inequality symbols are listed in Table 4 - 1.

Symbol	Meaning with Numbers	Meaning with Dates	Meaning with Text
>	greater than	after	alphabetically after
<	less than	before	alphabetically before
>=	greater than or equal to	on or after	alphabetically after or equal to
<=	less than or equal to	on or before	alphabetically before or equal to
not	not equal to	not on	not equal to
or	or	or	or

Table 4 - 1

To search for a range of values:

• Set up the query as we have done previously.

• Enter the inequality symbol and value on the **Criteria** line in the column that would contain those values.

• Click the **Query View** button to see the resulting dynaset.

Activity 4.9: Using a Numerical Range in a Query

We need a listing of any CDROMs that have dropped below the reorder point of 20 pieces in stock.

1. The previous query should still be open.

   If the previous query is not still open, follow steps 1–9 from Activity 4–8 and proceed to step 3 in this activity.

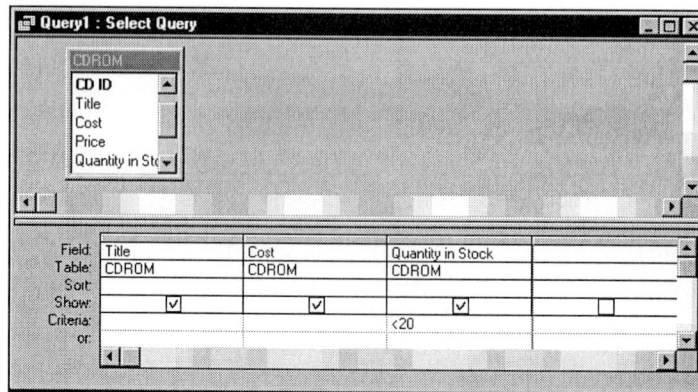

Figure 4 - 21

2. Erase the **179** on the **Criteria** line under **Cost**.

3. Click on the **Criteria** line in the **Quantity in Stock** column of the QBE grid.

4. Type: **<20** (see Figure 4 - 21).

5. Click the **Query View** button on the toolbar to view the result (see Figure 4 - 22).

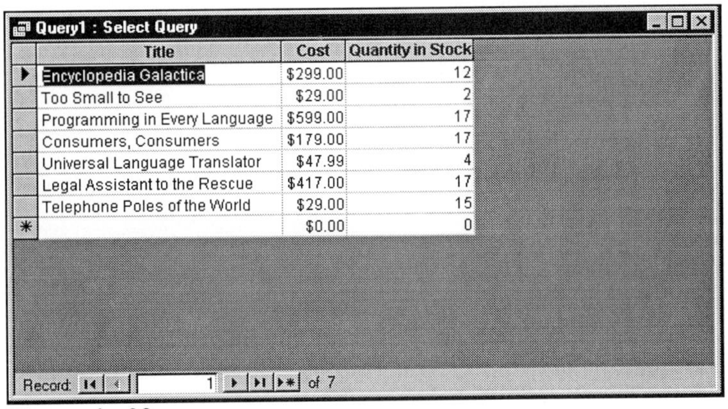

Title	Cost	Quantity in Stock
Encyclopedia Galactica	$299.00	12
Too Small to See	$29.00	2
Programming in Every Language	$599.00	17
Consumers, Consumers	$179.00	17
Universal Language Translator	$47.99	4
Legal Assistant to the Rescue	$417.00	17
Telephone Poles of the World	$29.00	15
*	$0.00	0

Record: 1 of 7

Figure 4 - 22

Examine the quantities. All seven should be less than 20.

PRINT PREVIEWING A QUERY RESULT

Since a reorder list could be extremely valuable, you would probably want to print the dynaset. Before you commit it to paper, however, you might want to see on the screen how a printout would look. The toolbar contains a **Print Preview** button (as well as a **Print** button).

To print preview a dynaset:

- Click the **Print Preview** button  on the toolbar while viewing a dynaset.

Activity 4.10: Printing a Dynaset

So we would not have to remember the reorder list, we could print that result. To view it first we will use **Print Preview**.

1. The dynaset from Activity 4.9 should still be on the screen. If not, click the **Query View** button.

2. Click the **Print Preview** button on the toolbar (see Figure 4 - 23).

   *Notice there is a **Print** button on this screen should you decide to print during **Print Preview**.*

3. The mouse cursor will become a magnifying glass shape with a plus sign inside it while on top of the preview page. Move that cursor on top of the text and click the mouse button to enlarge the preview to 100% size (see Figure 4 - 24).

   *You can move about the page with the **ARROW** keys or the Scroll Bars.*

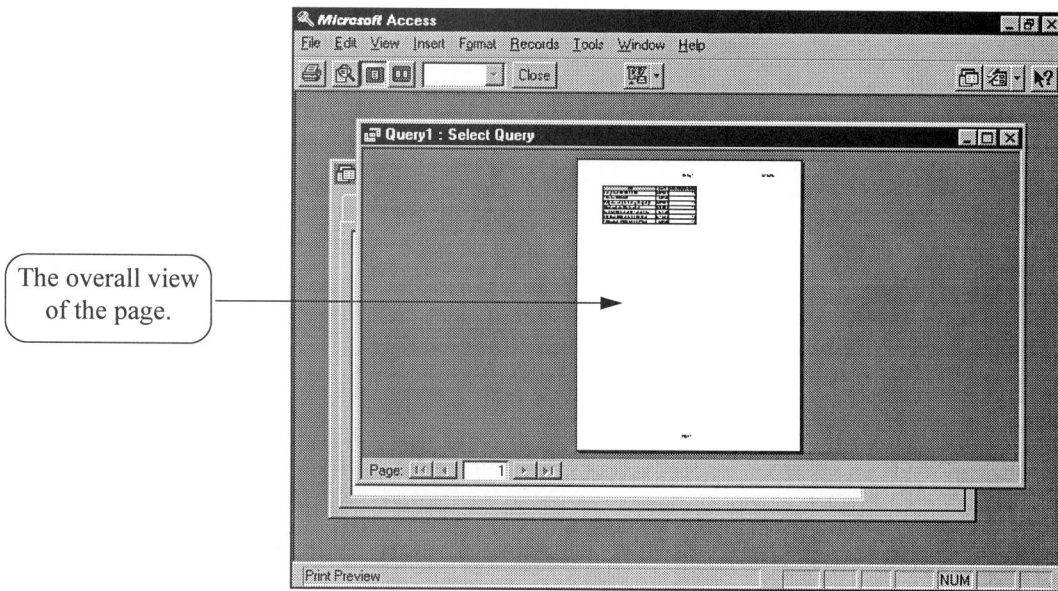

The overall view of the page.

Figure 4 - 23

4. To return to the full page, click the mouse on the white space of the page (the cursor will be a magnifying glass with a minus sign), or click the **Zoom** button on the toolbar.

5. After examining the preview, click the **Close** button on the toolbar to return to the dynaset.

6. Click the **Query View** button to return to the query design.

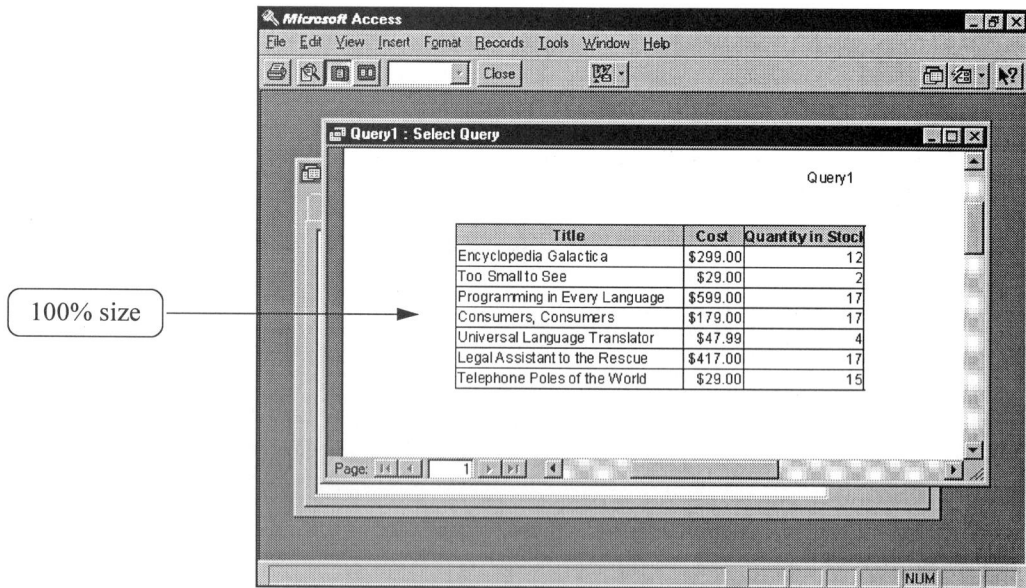

100% size

Title	Cost	Quantity in Stock
Encyclopedia Galactica	$299.00	12
Too Small to See	$29.00	2
Programming in Every Language	$599.00	17
Consumers, Consumers	$179.00	17
Universal Language Translator	$47.99	4
Legal Assistant to the Rescue	$417.00	17
Telephone Poles of the World	$29.00	15

Figure 4 - 24

TEXT CRITERIA IN A QUERY

The only difference between searching for matching text values and numeric values is that text criteria must be typed between quotation marks. For example, you would type

"NY" for the abbreviation for the state of New York. Often the quotes are optional as *Access* will fill them in for you. But *Access* does not always correctly guess where the quotes belong. For example, if the word **and** or the word **or** is within the text as with "Research and Development" or "Wet or Dry Vacuum," *Access* will not place the quotes correctly. Get into the habit of typing the quotes yourself and you will not fall into the misplaced quotes trap.

To search for matching text:

- Set up the query as we have done previously.

- Enter the example of the text value to be matched on the **Criteria** line in the column that would contain that value, being careful to type quotes at the beginning and end of the set of characters.

- Click the **Query View** button to see the resulting dynaset.

Activity 4.11: Searching for matching text

We need to look up the price of the "Too Small To See" CDROM. Since we will not need the **Cost** or **Quantity in Stock** fields, we could remove those two, or it might be easier to simply clear the entire QBE grid and start fresh.

1. Pick **EDIT/Clear Grid** in the menu.

2. Double-click the field named **CD ID** in the list of fields to place it in the first column.

3. Similarly, double-click **Title** and **Price**.

4. Click on the **Criteria** line in the **Title** column and enter: **"Too Small To See"** including the quotes (see Figure 4 - 25).

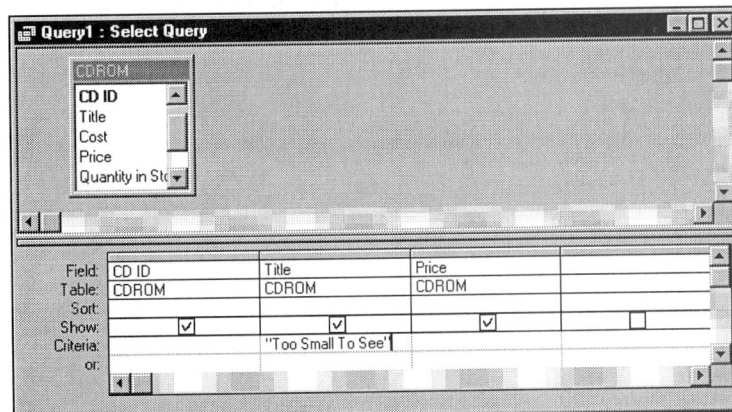

Figure 4 - 25

The text is not sensitive to the case that you type, thus; "too small to see" or "TOO SMALL TO SEE" or the mixed case example above will all succeed.

5. Click the **Query View** button on the toolbar to view the result.

We do not need to print the $49 price.

6. Click the **Query View** button on the toolbar to return to the query design.

DATE CRITERIA IN A QUERY

Enter dates in the QBE grid in slash format. *Access* will surround the date with pound signs. For example, July 4, 1996, would be represented as #7/4/96#. Since the inclusion of the pound signs is totally automatic, you do not need to be concerned about them, except to recognize that they will appear whenever you type a date criterion.

To search for a matching date:

- Set up the query as we have done previously.

- Enter the example of the date value to be matched on the **Criteria** line in the column that would contain that value as M/D/YY. For any date that is not in the 20th century, you should type all four digits for the year.

- Click the **Query View** button to see the resulting dynaset.

Activity 4.12: Searching for matching dates

We need to look up the titles of the CDROMs that were released before 5/2/95. Since we have not yet placed the **Release Date** field in the QBE grid, we must add it.

1. Erase the **"Too Small To See"** criterion from the **Title** column.

2. Double-click the field named **Release Date** in the list of fields to place it in the next available column.

   You may need to scroll downward in the field list to find Release Date.

3. On the **Criteria** line in the **Release Date** column, enter: **<5/2/95** (see Figure 4 - 26).

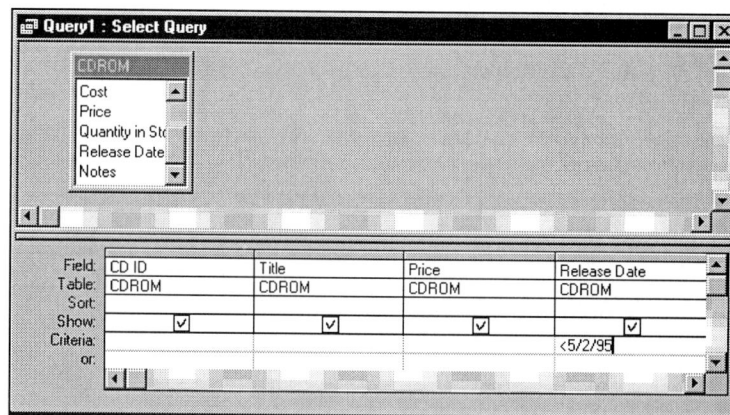

Figure 4 - 26

4. Click the **Query View** button on the toolbar to view the result (see Figure 4 - 27).

   Ten titles were released before 5/2/95.

5. Click the **Query View** button on the toolbar to return to the query design.

   Notice the pound signs that Access has added around the date.

6. Change the criterion to: **<=#5/2/95#**

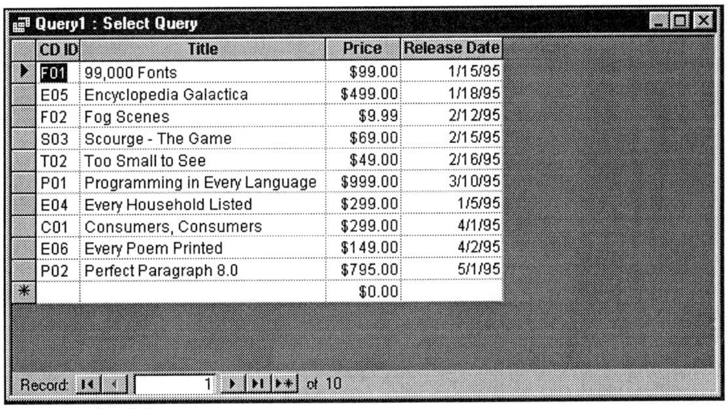

Query1 : Select Query

CD ID	Title	Price	Release Date
F01	99,000 Fonts	$99.00	1/15/95
E05	Encyclopedia Galactica	$499.00	1/18/95
F02	Fog Scenes	$9.99	2/12/95
S03	Scourge - The Game	$69.00	2/15/95
T02	Too Small to See	$49.00	2/16/95
P01	Programming in Every Language	$999.00	3/10/95
E04	Every Household Listed	$299.00	1/5/95
C01	Consumers, Consumers	$299.00	4/1/95
E06	Every Poem Printed	$149.00	4/2/95
P02	Perfect Paragraph 8.0	$795.00	5/1/95
*		$0.00	

Record: 1 of 10

Figure 4 - 27

7. Click the **Query View** button on the toolbar to view the result (see Figure 4 - 28).

   Twelve titles were released on or before 5/2/95.

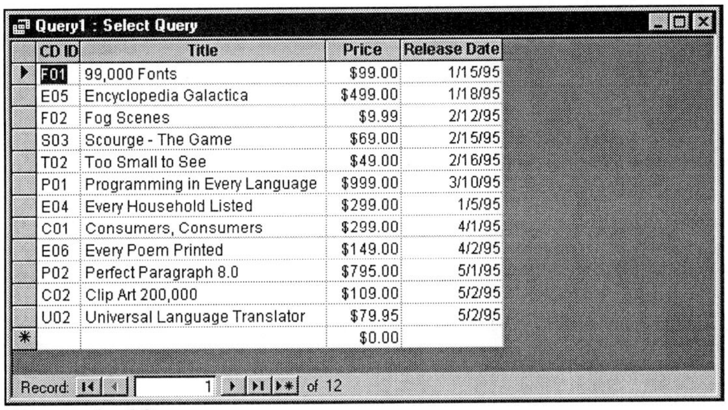

Query1 : Select Query

CD ID	Title	Price	Release Date
F01	99,000 Fonts	$99.00	1/15/95
E05	Encyclopedia Galactica	$499.00	1/18/95
F02	Fog Scenes	$9.99	2/12/95
S03	Scourge - The Game	$69.00	2/15/95
T02	Too Small to See	$49.00	2/16/95
P01	Programming in Every Language	$999.00	3/10/95
E04	Every Household Listed	$299.00	1/5/95
C01	Consumers, Consumers	$299.00	4/1/95
E06	Every Poem Printed	$149.00	4/2/95
P02	Perfect Paragraph 8.0	$795.00	5/1/95
C02	Clip Art 200,000	$109.00	5/2/95
U02	Universal Language Translator	$79.95	5/2/95
*		$0.00	

Record: 1 of 12

Figure 4 - 28

8. Print this result by clicking the **Print** button.
9. Click the **Query View** button on the toolbar to return to the query design.
10. Choose **FILE/Save.**
11. Type: **Before or on 5/2/95** and click the **OK** button (see Figure 4 - 29).

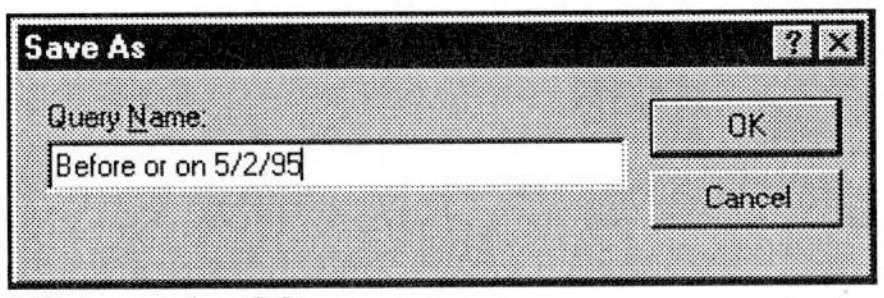

Figure 4 - 29

12. Choose **FILE/Close.**

SUMMARY

In this project we have explored single criterion queries. We practiced opening the Select Query window, selecting the desired fields, sorting by one or more fields, and matching a criterion. The criteria we used were of numerical, text, and date types. We used the inequality symbols for ranges of values. In the next lesson we will use multiple criteria and multiple tables in queries.

KEY TERMS

Criterion
Dynaset
Operator
Print Preview
QBE grid
Query by Example
Select Query

INDEPENDENT PROJECTS

Independent Project 4.1: The School Newspaper

This Independent Project continues the Newspaper Ad database from Independent Project 3.1. The newspaper's business manager has requested two lists.

The first is a listing of all the Full Page (FP) ads in order of the Date Paid. The **Issue Date** and the **Salesperson ID** fields are not important for this list, so those two will be left out of the result. The result of this query should look like Figure 4 - 30.

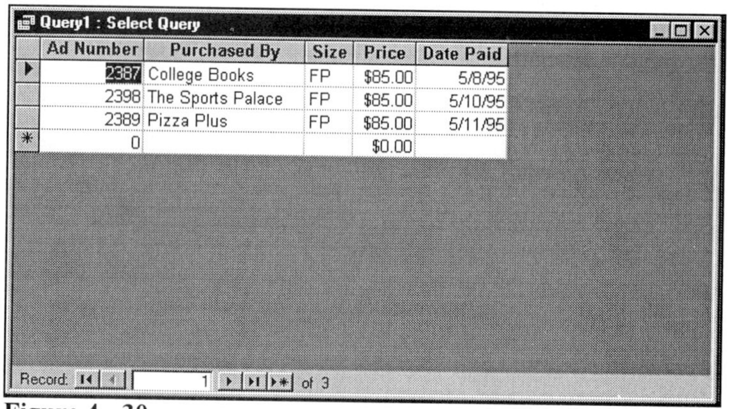

Ad Number	Purchased By	Size	Price	Date Paid
2387	College Books	FP	$85.00	5/8/95
2398	The Sports Palace	FP	$85.00	5/10/95
2389	Pizza Plus	FP	$85.00	5/11/95
0			$0.00	

Figure 4 - 30

The second is a list of all ads sold by Leslie Kaples sorted by Price, but it should only include the **Ad Number**, **Purchased By**, **Price**, and **Date Paid** fields. The result should resemble Figure 4 - 31.

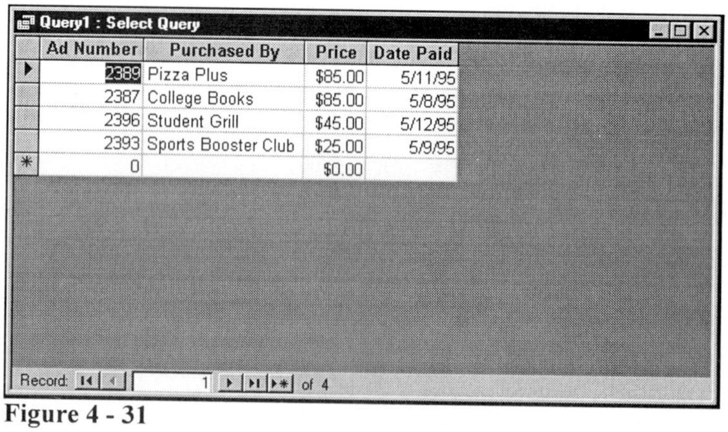

Ad Number	Purchased By	Price	Date Paid
2389	Pizza Plus	$85.00	5/11/95
2387	College Books	$85.00	5/8/95
2396	Student Grill	$45.00	5/12/95
2393	Sports Booster Club	$25.00	5/9/95
0		$0.00	

Figure 4 - 31

1. Run *Access.*

2. Open the **Exercise1** database in the Introductory dialog box. Alternatively, pick **FILE/Open Database** or click the **Open Database** tool on the toolbar, then click on the name **Exercise1** and click the **Open** button.

3. Click on the **Queries** tab at the top of the database window.

4. Click the **New** button to start a new query.

5. Pick **Design View** in the **New Query** dialog box and click **OK**.

6. Click on the name **Ads** in the list of tables in the **Show Table** dialog box and click the **Add** button.

7. Click **Close** to close the **Show Table** dialog box.

8. Double-click on the name **Ad Number** in the list of names to include that field in the QBE Grid.

9. Similarly, double-click on **Purchased By**, **Size**, **Price**, and **Date Paid** to include them in the QBE grid. You may need to scroll down to find **Date Paid**.

10. Click on the **Criteria** line in the **Size** column and enter: **"FP"** for Full Page.

11. Click the **Query View** button on the toolbar to see the three resulting listings. They still need to be sorted.

12. Click the **Query View** button to return to the query design.

13. Click on the **Sort** line in the **Date Paid** column. Click on the drop-down arrow and pick **Ascending**.

14. Click the **Query View** button on the toolbar to see the three resulting listings in sorted order.

15. Print the result by clicking the **Print** button.

16. Save the query as **Full Page Ads** by picking **FILE/Save**, entering the name, and clicking the **OK** button.

17. Close the query with **FILE/Close**.

18. To begin the second query, click on the **Queries** tab at the top of the database window if it is not already selected.

19. Click the **New** button to start a new query and pick **Design View** in the **New Query** dialog box. Click **OK**.

20. Click on the name **Ads** in the list of tables in the **Show Table** dialog box, click the **Add** button, and click **Close**.

21. Double-click on the **Ad Number** field to include it in the first column of the QBE grid.

22. Similarly, double-click on **Purchased By**, **Price**, **Date Paid**, and **Salesperson ID**.

23. Press the **END** key so you can see the **Salesperson ID** column.

24. Click on the **Criteria** line under **Salesperson ID** and enter: **"K17"**

25. Since the business manager did not want to see the Salesperson ID, click on the **Show** box to remove its check mark.

26. Click on the **Sort** line in the **Price** column, click on the drop-down arrow, and pick **Descending**.

27. Click the **Query View** button on the toolbar to see the result.

28. Print the result by clicking the **Print** button.

29. We do not need to save this query, so close it without saving with **FILE/Close**. When the alert box asks about saving, click the **No** button.

30. Close the database with **FILE/Close**.

31. If you need to exit from *Access*, do so properly.

Independent Project 4.2: The Bookstore

This Independent Project continues the Bookstore database from Independent Project 3.2. The owner has requested two lists.

    The first is a listing of the books that have fewer than 50 copies in stock. This listing should include the **Book Code**, **Title**, **Publisher Code**, and **Quantity in Stock**. Since this will be needed repeatedly as a check on books to be reordered, this query will be saved. The result of the first query should look like Figure 4 - 32.

    The second is a list of all books sold by Texts and Tomes (code TT12) sorted by Year of Publication and including the **Book Code**, **Title**, **Author**, **Year of Publication**, and **Publisher Code** fields. This is a temporary query and will be printed, but not saved. The result should resemble Figure 4 - 33.

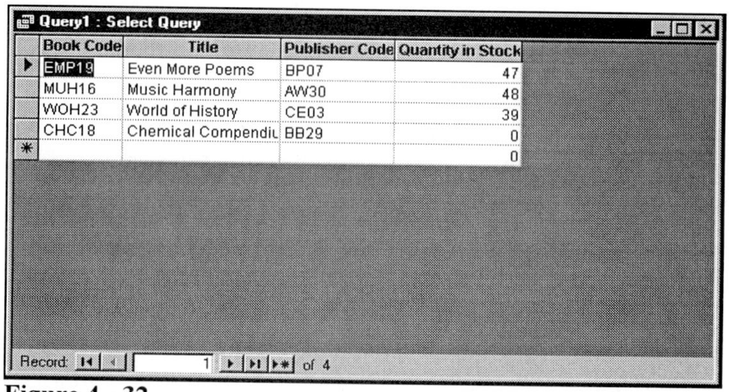

Book Code	Title	Publisher Code	Quantity in Stock
EMP19	Even More Poems	BP07	47
MUH16	Music Harmony	AW30	48
WOH23	World of History	CE03	39
CHC18	Chemical Compendiu	BB29	0
*			0

Record: 1 of 4

Figure 4 - 32

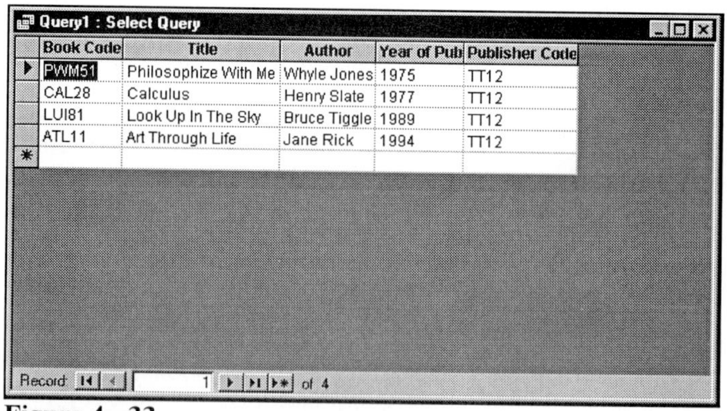

Book Code	Title	Author	Year of Pub	Publisher Code
PWM51	Philosophize With Me	Whyle Jones	1975	TT12
CAL28	Calculus	Henry Slate	1977	TT12
LUI81	Look Up In The Sky	Bruce Tiggle	1989	TT12
ATL11	Art Through Life	Jane Rick	1994	TT12
*				

Record: 1 of 4

Figure 4 - 33

1. Run *Access* and maximize its window.

2. Open the **Exercise2** database in the Introductory dialog box. Alternatively, pick **FILE/Open Database** or click the **Open Database** tool on the toolbar, then click on the name **Exercise2** and click the **Open** button.

3. Click on the **Queries** tab at the top of the Database window.

4. Click the **New** button to start a new query.

5. Pick **Design View** in the **New Query** dialog box and click **OK**.

6. Click on the name **Books** in the list of Tables in the **Show Table** dialog box and click the **Add** button.

7. Click **Close** to close the **Show Table** dialog box.

8. Double-click on the name **Book Code** in the list of names to include that field in the QBE grid.

9. Similarly, double-click on **Title**, **Publisher Code**, and **Quantity in Stock** to include them in the QBE grid.

10. Click on the **Criteria** line in the **Quantity in Stock** column and enter: **<50**

11. Click the **Query View** button on the toolbar to see the four resulting listings (see Figure 4 - 32).

12. Print the result by clicking the **Print** button.

13. Save the query as **Low Quantities** by picking **FILE/Save**, entering the name, and clicking the **OK** button.

14. Close the query with **FILE/Close**.

15. To begin the second query, click on the **Queries** tab at the top of the Database window if it is not already selected.

16. Click the **New** button to start a new query and pick **Design View** in the **New Query** dialog box. Click **OK**.

17. Click on the name **Books** in the list of tables in the **Show Table** dialog box, click the **Add** button, and click **Close**.

18. Double-click on the **Book Code** field to include it in the first column of the QBE Grid.

19. Similarly, double-click on **Title**, **Author**, **Year of Publication**, and **Publisher Code**.

20. Press the **END** key so you can see the **Publisher Code** column.

21. Click on the **Criteria** line under **Publisher Code** and enter: **"TT12"**

22. Click on the **Sort** line in the **Year of Publication** column, click on the drop-down arrow, and pick **Ascending**.

23. Click the **Query View** button on the toolbar to see the result (see Figure 4 - 33).

24. Print the result by clicking the **Print** button.

25. We do not need to save this query, so close it without saving with **FILE/Close**. When the alert box asks about saving, click the **No** button.

26. Close the database with **FILE/Close**.

27. If you need to exit from *Access* and/or Windows, do so properly.

Independent Project 4.3: The Real Estate Office

This Independent Project continues the Real Estate Office database from Independent Project 3.3. The office manager has requested three lists.

A client has asked about commercial properties that are on the first floor of a building. This first listing should include the **Code**, **Address**, **City**, **State**, **Zip**, **Size**, **Floor**, **Price**, and **Available** fields and be sorted by **Date Available**. This is a temporary query and will be printed, but not saved. The result of this first query should look like Figure 4 - 34.

Query1 : Select Query

Code	Address	City	State	Zip	Size	Floor	Price	Available
MC29	Maple Court	New Canaan	CT	06840	450	1	$125,000.00	5/15/95
RP13	3 Research Park	Stamford	CT	06902	18000	1	$3,400,000.00	6/1/95
RP12	2 Research Park	Stamford	CT	06902	18000	1	$3,400,000.00	6/1/95
ES52	5 Elm St.	Greenwich	CT	06830	4800	1	$72,000.00	6/1/95
RP15	5 Research Park	Stamford	CT	06902	21000	1	$4,100,000.00	8/1/95
RP16	6 Research Park	Stamford	CT	06902	19000	1	$3,900,000.00	10/1/95
*					0	0	$0.00	

Record: 1 of 6

Figure 4 - 34

The second is a list of all properties priced below $1,000,000. Include the **Code, Address, City, State, Zip, Size, Purchase or Rent, Price, Available**, and **Agency Code** fields. Since this query is a common requirement in the office, it will be saved as well as printed. This dynaset should match Figure 4 - 35.

Query1 : Select Query

Code	Address	City	State	Zip	Size	Purc	Price	Available	Agency
ES52	5 Elm St.	Greenwich	CT	06830	4800	R	$72,000.00	6/1/95	SC18
FA28	18 Frost Ave.	Greenwich	CT	06830	3700	R	$52,000.00	8/1/95	RR11
GP25	12 Gedney Place	Danbury	CT	06810	8900	R	$105,000.00	7/15/95	SC18
LW17	1 Lewis Way	Danbury	CT	06810	12000	R	$125,000.00	7/1/95	PP24
MC29	Maple Court	New Canaan	CT	06840	450	P	$125,000.00	5/15/95	PP15
RR19	952 River Rd.	Stamford	CT	06901	3750	R	$49,000.00	9/1/95	PP24
*					0		$0.00		

Record: 1 of 6

Figure 4 - 35

The third is a list of all properties that will be available on or before 8/1/95 sorted by date available. Include the **Code, Address, City, State, Zip, Size, Purchase or Rent, Price, Available**, and **Agency Code** fields. This one will be printed, but not saved. The result of this third query should resemble Figure 4 - 36.

Below $1,000,000 : Select Query

Code	Address	City	State	Zip	Size	Purc	Price	Available	Agency
MC29	Maple Court	New Canaan	CT	06840	450	P	$125,000.00	5/15/95	PP15
RP13	3 Research Park	Stamford	CT	06902	18000	P	$3,400,000.00	6/1/95	GW14
RP12	2 Research Park	Stamford	CT	06902	18000	P	$3,400,000.00	6/1/95	PP15
ES52	5 Elm St.	Greenwich	CT	06830	4800	R	$72,000.00	6/1/95	SC18
LW17	1 Lewis Way	Danbury	CT	06810	12000	R	$125,000.00	7/1/95	PP24
GP25	12 Gedney Place	Danbury	CT	06810	8900	R	$105,000.00	7/15/95	SC18
RP15	5 Research Park	Stamford	CT	06902	21000	P	$4,100,000.00	8/1/95	RP12
FA28	18 Frost Ave.	Greenwich	CT	06830	3700	R	$52,000.00	8/1/95	RR11
*					0		$0.00		

Record: 1 of 8

Figure 4 - 36

1. Run *Access* and **maximize** its window.

2. Open the **Exercise3** database.

3. Click on the **Queries** tab at the top of the **Database** window.

4. Begin a new query using **Design View**.

5. Add **Commercial Listings** to the query window and close the **Show Table** dialog box.

6. Include the **Code, Address, City, State, Zip, Size, Floor, Price**, and **Available** fields.

7. Enter the criteria to limit listings to the **first floor** of a building.

8. Include the operator to sort by date **Available** in **Ascending** order.

9. View the resulting listings (see Figure 4 - 34).

10. **Print** the result.

11. To begin the second query, either clear the grid or modify the existing fields in the QBE grid.

12. Include the **Code, Address, City, State, Zip, Size, Purchase or Rent, Price, Available**, and **Agency Code** fields. (*Access* will not scroll the QBE grid sideways; therefore, you will not see the first few fields as you select them, but they are there.)

13. Enter the criterion for **Price below $1,000,000**. Be careful to type the correct number of zeros and do **not** include the $ or commas.

14. View the result (see Figure 4 - 35).

15. Save the query as **Below $1,000,000**. In this name you may type the $ and commas.

16. **Print** the result.

17. Return to the design.

18. Begin setting up the third query by removing any criteria.

19. See the list of required fields in the paragraph above step 1 and make any adjustments that are necessary.

20. Enter the criterion for date available **on or before 8/1/95**.

21. Set the sort operator for ascending date **Available**.

22. View the result (see Figure 4 - 36).

23. Print the result.

24. We do not need to save this query, so close it without saving.

25. Close the database.

26. If you need to exit from *Access*, do so properly.

Independent Project 4.4: The Veterinarian

This Independent Project continues the veterinarian database from Independent Project 3.4. She has requested three lists. Include all fields in each query, print each dynaset, and save each query.

- All dogs.

- All animals weighing less than 20 pounds.

- Any animal born on or before 1/1/92.

Lesson 5

Multiple Criteria and Multi-Table Queries

Objectives

In this lesson you will learn how to:

- Specify multiple criteria for selecting records

- Use additional query operators

- Use wildcard characters in queries

- Join data from two or more tables with a multiple table query

PROJECT DESCRIPTION

In the previous lesson, the queries needed to match only a single value. It is more likely that the data you are seeking must match multiple criteria. For example, you may need all of the CDROMs released before a certain date that were published by a particular publisher. The date restriction must be matched as well as the restriction on publisher. Additionally, the data you need in the dynaset may reside in two or more tables. With multiple tables you use a query to join the data into a single dynaset.

In this lesson we will run several queries to obtain inventory information. The queries will be based on the **CDROM** table and use multiple criteria. Then we will query the CDROM table together with various other tables to gather additional information about the orders for CDROMs.

MULTIPLE CRITERIA

There are only two types of queries with multiple criteria: *And Queries* and *Or Queries*. An *And Query* contains two (or more) criteria, both of which must be matched simultaneously. An example would be all of the CDROMs that were released after 5/2/95 *and* are priced below $100. The resulting dynaset would contain only listings that satisfied both conditions.

An *Or Query* will have two or more conditions, any one of which may be matched. All of the CDROMs that were released after 5/2/95 *or* are priced below $100 would be an example. The dynaset for this last example would have some listings released after 5/2/95 no matter what their price, some priced below $100 no matter when they were released, and possibly some records that match both parts of the criteria.

A query with multiple criteria is set up the same way a single criterion query is. Then, in the **Query1: Select Query** window two or more examples to be matched are entered in the **Criteria** section of the QBE grid. The multiple criteria might be entered in different fields, or within one field. For example, all prices greater than $100 and less than $500 would place both conditions in the **Price** field, whereas all items priced greater than $100 and released after 5/2/95 would put criteria in two different fields.

Just as in English where we call a sentence compound when its two parts are connected by the word *and*, multiple criteria queries are also called *compound*.

To query with multiple criteria:

- Open the **Query** window in the normal way by clicking the **Queries** tab at the top of the **Database** window, clicking the **New** button at its right edge, choosing **Design View**, and clicking the **OK** button.

- Add the desired table or tables from the **Show Table** dialog box.

- Select the desired fields.

- Enter the first criterion.

- Enter a second criterion.

- Enter any additional criteria.

- View the resulting dynaset.

To enter criteria for an *and* query:

- Type more than one criterion in the same **Criteria** row of the QBE grid.

Activity 5.1: An And Query

We need a list of the expensive CDROMs on which we might be overstocked. Any CDROM that costs more than $100 **and** of which we have more than 50 in stock is possibly overstocked.

1. Open the **Sales** database if it is not already open on the workspace.

2. Click on the **Queries** tab at the top of the **Database** window.

3. Click the **New** button at the right edge of the **Database** window.

4. In the **New Query** dialog box, click on **Design View** and click the **OK** button.

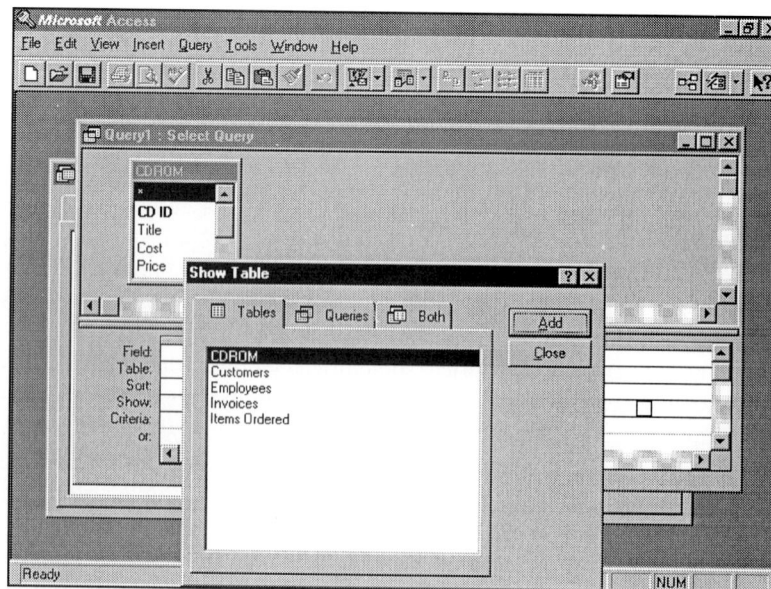

Figure 5 - 1

5. Pick the **CDROM** table and click the **Add** button to place a list of its fields in the top half of the **Query1: Select Query** window (see Figure 5 - 1).

6. Click the **Close** button to close the **Show Table** dialog box.

7. Double-click the **Title** field in the list of fields to include it in the first column in the QBE grid.

8. Also double-click the **Cost** and **Quantity In Stock** fields.

9. Click on the **Criteria** line in the **Cost** column of the QBE grid and enter: **>100**

10. Click on the **Criteria** line in the **Quantity in Stock** column and enter: **>50** (Figure 5 - 2).

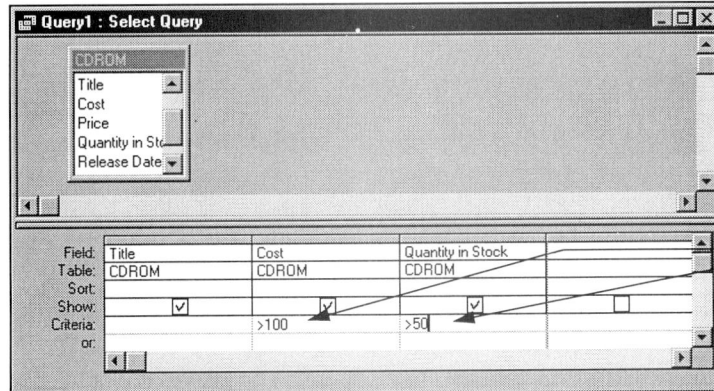

Figure 5 - 2

11. Click the **Query View** button on the toolbar to see the resulting dynaset.

   Each of the two listings has a Cost above $100 as well as a Quantity greater than 50 (see Figure 5 - 3).

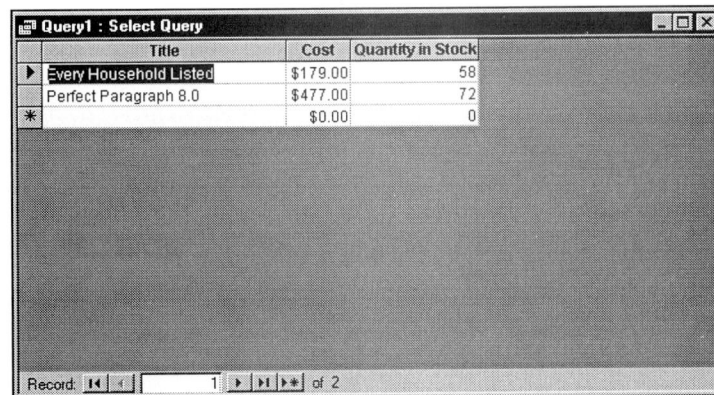

Figure 5 - 3

12. Click the **Query View** button to return to the query design.

To enter criteria for an *or* query:

- If the criteria are based on different fields, type the first criterion on the **Criteria** line and the second criterion on the **or** line of the QBE grid.

- If the criteria are all in the same field, type the first criterion and a space, type the word **or**, type a space and the second criterion.
- For more than two criteria, use additional lines in separate fields, or the word **or** additional times within a single field.

Activity 5.2: A Multiple Field Or Query

Our manager redefines "possibly overstocked" to mean any CDROM that costs more than $100 *or* of which we have more than 50 in stock. We need a new list of the CDROMs on which we may be overstocked. This will be an important query that we will need over and over; thus we will save this query.

1. Delete the **>50** on the **Criteria** line of the **Quantity in Stock** column.
2. Move down onto the **or** line of the **Quantity in Stock** column and enter: **>50** (Figure 5 - 4).

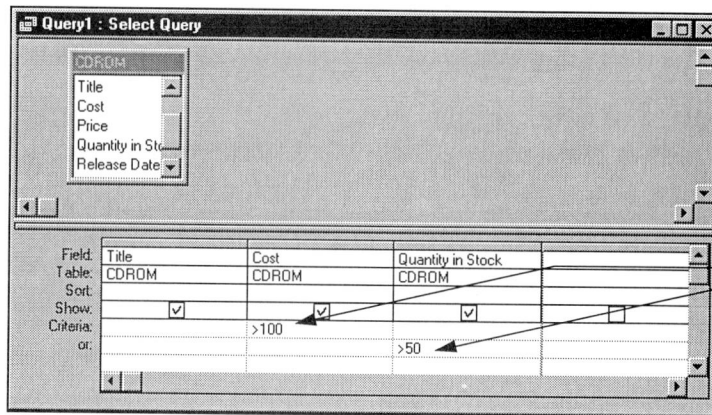

Figure 5 - 4

3. Click the **Query View** button to see the resulting dynaset.

   Of the 10 listings (see Figure 5 - 5), four have only a Cost above $100, four have only a Quantity greater than 50, and two have both.

Title	Cost	Quantity in Stock
Encyclopedia Galactica	$299.00	12
Fog Scenes	$5.99	130
Scourge - The Game	$41.00	89
Programming in Every Language	$599.00	17
Every Household Listed	$179.00	58
Consumers, Consumers	$179.00	17
Perfect Paragraph 8.0	$477.00	72
Clip Art 200,000	$65.00	290
Legal Assistant to the Rescue	$417.00	17
Everything There Is to Know	$77.00	60
	$0.00	0

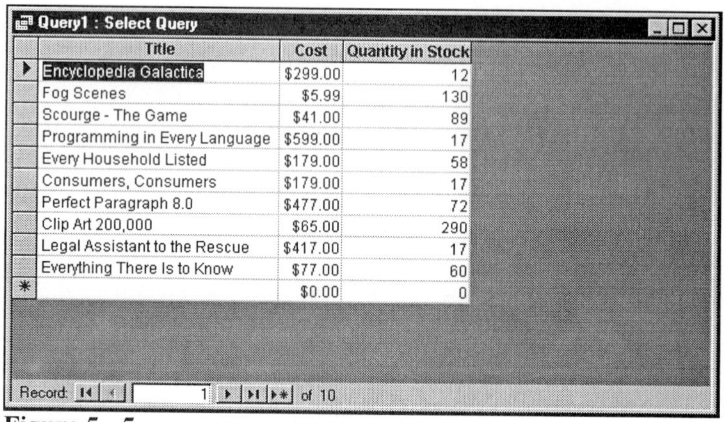

Figure 5 - 5

4. Choose **FILE/Save** to begin saving this query design.

   A query can be saved while either the design or the dynaset is showing in the window.

5. Enter the name: **Overstocked** and click **OK**.

6. Print the result by clicking the **Print** button.

7. Click the **Query View** button to return to the query design.

INCLUDING EVERY FIELD IN THE QBE GRID

Occasionally you need every field from a table included in the QBE grid. While you could double-click each field, there is a quicker method for selecting all fields.

To select every field into the QBE grid:

- Double-click the header that contains the table name at the top of the list of fields in the upper section of the Query window. All of the names will be highlighted.

- Move the mouse on top of any one of the names, hold down (do not click) the mouse button, and drag that name to the **Field** line of the QBE grid. When you release the mouse button, all fields will be installed.

- As *Access* usually does not scroll the QBE grid to show you the active field when you use this technique, press the **HOME** key to move to the first field.

Activity 5.3: Including All Fields

Our manager also asks for a listing of all of the data on CDROMs numbered C01, E04, or L01. Since this query is based on the same CDROM table, we do not need to begin all over, but the currently selected fields and criteria are not what we need. Therefore, we will again use Clear Grid to start a new design based on the same table. Since we need all data on the three CDROMs, we will include all fields in the QBE grid.

1. Choose **EDIT/Clear Grid**.

2. Double-click on the table name **CDROM** at the top of the list of fields in the upper section of the window to select all of the fields.

   All of the field names in the list will be highlighted (see Figure 5 - 6).

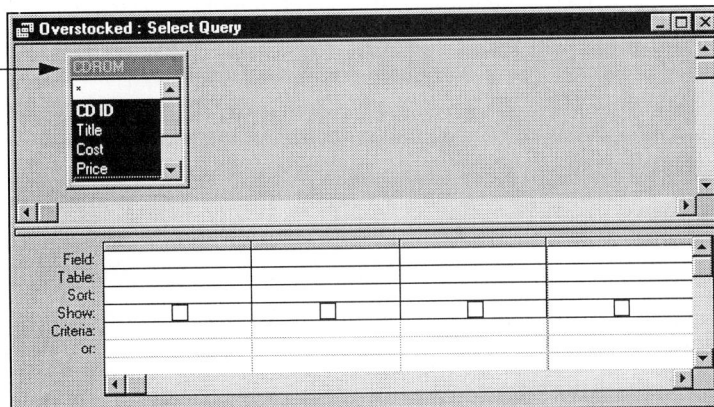

Double-click on the table name to select all fields.

Figure 5 - 6

3. Move the mouse on top of any one name in the highlighted list, hold down the mouse button, and drag that name down to the **Field** line of the first column in the QBE grid. Release the mouse button.

    *The highlighted field is **Notes**, but it is not currently showing in the window.*

4. Press the **HOME** key to move the highlight onto the first field, **CD ID** (see Figure 5 - 7).

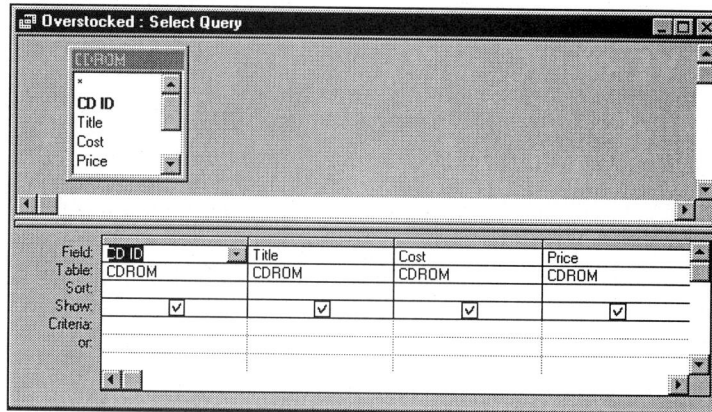

Figure 5 - 7

ADDITIONAL QUERY OPERATORS

An *operator* in a query is a symbol, word, or group of words that specify the range of values to be matched. We have already used the operators =, >, and <, as well as some combinations of those. Additional operators are listed in Table 5 - 1.

Operator	Example
between ___ and ___	between #4/1/95# and #4/30/95#
or	"C01" or "E04"
not	not "Windows"
null	null

Table 5 - 1

Activity 5.4: A Single Field Or Query

Our manager asked for all data on CDROMs numbered C01, E04, or L01. Since these ID numbers need to be specified in the same field, we can use the **or** operator rather than separate **or** lines.

1. Click on the **Criteria** line in the **CD ID** column.

    *If you were too close to the left edge of the QBE grid, the entire **Criteria** line may have been highlighted. If so, click again closer to the center of the column on the **Criteria** line so the cursor is a blinking vertical line.*

2. Type: **"C01" or "E04" or "L01"**

Be careful that you type zeros in the above criterion. Also, you can widen the column in the QBE grid by dragging the line at the right edge of the selector bar for the desired column, just like changing a column width in a table (Figure 5 - 8).

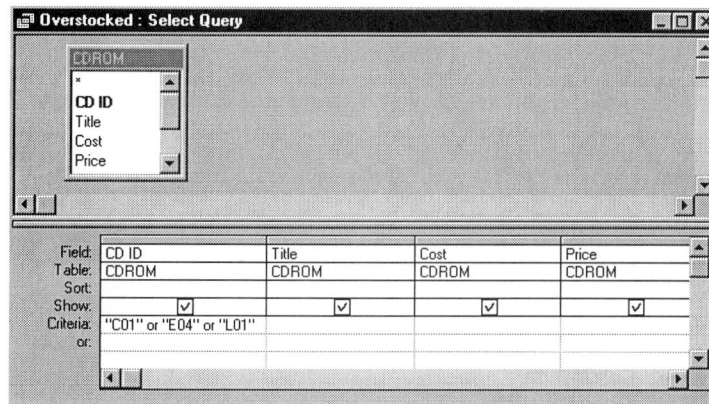

Figure 5 - 8

3. Click the **Query View** button to see the resulting dynaset.

    The three ID numbers should be listed in the dynaset (Figure 5 - 9).

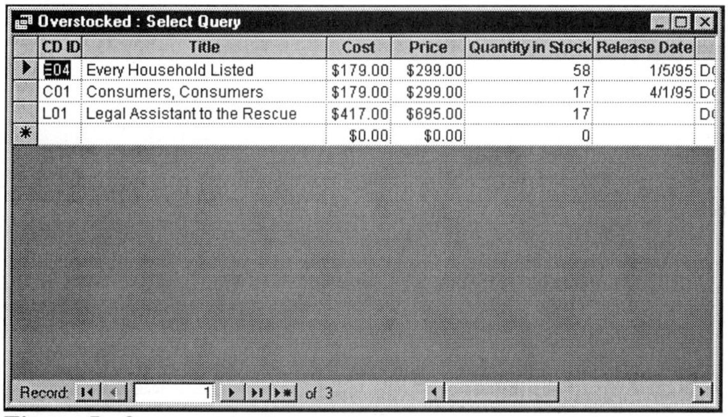

Figure 5 - 9

4. Print the result by clicking the **Print** button.
5. Click the **Query View** button to return to the query design.

THE *BETWEEN* OPERATOR

When you need the data entries that fall between a starting and an ending value, use the **between** operator. While in English *between* often means between but not equal to the given values, in *Access* the specified end points will be included as well.

To specify a criterion using *between*:

•   On the **Criteria** line in the QBE grid type the word **between** and a space, then the beginning value and a space, the word **and** and a space, and finally the ending value.

Activity 5.5: Using the Between Operator

We need a list of all of the CDROMs released between 2/15/95 and 4/30/95.

1. Erase the previous criterion in the **CD ID** column.

   *A quick way to erase a long criterion is to press the **F2** key to highlight the entire criterion, then the **DELETE** key to erase it.*

2. Move to the **Release Date** column.

3. On the **Criteria** line enter: **between 2/15/95 and 4/30/95** (Figure 5 - 10).

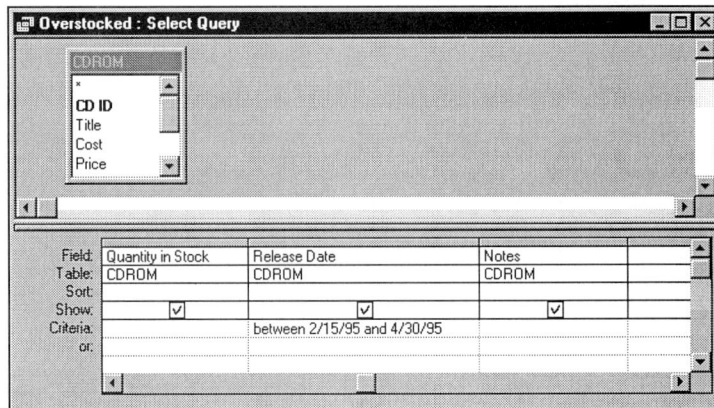

Figure 5 - 10

4. Click the **Query View** button to see the resulting dynaset.

   The five dates in the dynaset should be between or on the starting and ending dates (see Figure 5 - 11).

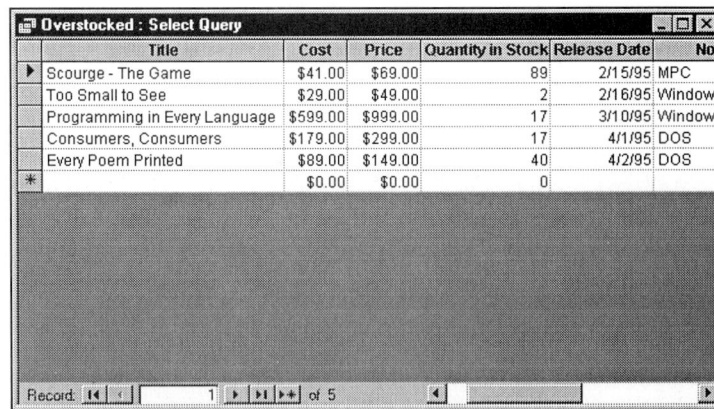

Figure 5 - 11

5. Print the result by clicking the **Print** button.

6. Click the **Query View** button to return to the query design.

THE *NOT* OPERATOR

Surprisingly often in queries, you know exactly what you do not want. To query for all entries that do not match a value, use the **not** operator.

To use the *not* operator:

● On the **Criteria** line in the QBE grid type the word **not** and a space, followed by the value to be excluded.

Activity 5.6: The Not Operator

1. Erase the previous criterion.

2. Move to the **Criteria** line in the **Notes** column.

3. Enter: **Not "Windows"** (see Figure 5 - 12).

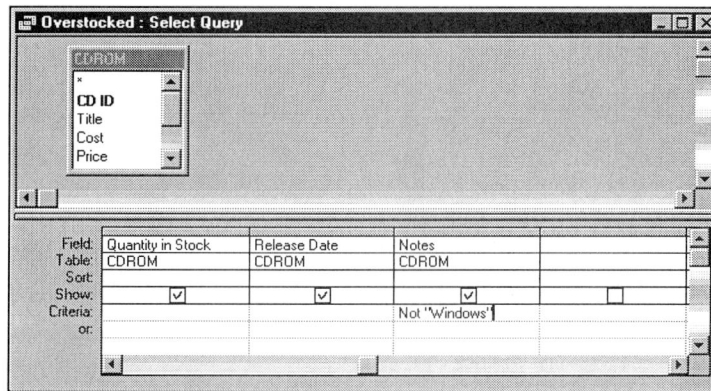

Figure 5 - 12

4. Click the **Query View** button to see the resulting dynaset.

   The eight listings in the dynaset (see Figure 5 - 13) will contain a variety of Notes that are not Windows, although one has "Windows - B&W." Since Windows - B&W is not exactly Windows, it matches our criterion, too. Shortly we will see how to eliminate this entry that includes the word Windows, even though it's not exactly the same.

CD ID	Title	Cost	Price	Quantity	Release Date	Notes
E05	Encyclopedia Galactica	$299.00	$499.00	12	1/18/95	MPC
F02	Fog Scenes	$5.99	$9.99	130	2/12/95	Windows - B&W
S03	Scourge - The Game	$41.00	$69.00	89	2/15/95	MPC
E04	Every Household Listed	$179.00	$299.00	58	1/5/95	DOS
C01	Consumers, Consumers	$179.00	$299.00	17	4/1/95	DOS
E06	Every Poem Printed	$89.00	$149.00	40	4/2/95	DOS
L01	Legal Assistant to the Rescue	$417.00	$695.00	17		DOS
T03	Telephone Poles of the World	$29.00	$49.00	15	5/14/95	MPC
*		$0.00	$0.00	0		

Record: 1 of 8

Figure 5 - 13

5. Print the result by clicking the **Print** button.

6. Click the **Query View** button to return to the query design.

THE *NULL* OPERATOR

Every time we need a set of records we type the value to be matched. In the columns where we do not type a value, there is no restriction on the data. What if we needed the records where there was no entry in that field, that is, where the field was empty?

We cannot leave the **Criteria** line empty since that means no restriction. The solution is the operator **null**. Null means empty.

To use the null operator:

- On the **Criteria** line in the QBE grid type the word **null** in the desired column. Actually the operator is **Is Null**, but *Access* will always fill in the **Is** for you.

Activity 5.7: The Null Operator

We need a list of those CDROMs that do not yet have a Release Date filled in.

1. Erase the previous criterion.

2. Move to the **Criteria** line of the **Release Date** column and enter: **null** (see Figure 5 - 14).

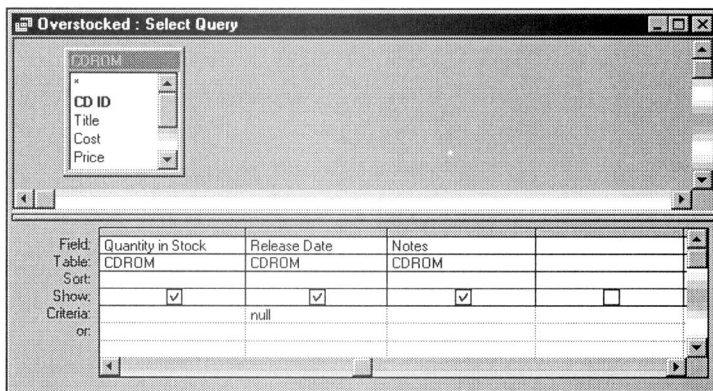

Figure 5 - 14

3. Click the **Query View** button to see the resulting dynaset.

   *The two listings in the dynaset will have empty **Release Date** fields (see Figure 5 - 15).*

Figure 5 - 15

4. Click the **Query View** button to return to the query design.

WILDCARDS

Earlier, we queried for the records that did not have "Windows" in the **Notes** field. While most listings in the dynaset contained completely different entries, one had the entry "Windows - B&W." A portion of the entry matched, but not the whole entry. How do we match portions of entries?

Wildcard characters allow you to match a portion of the entry in a field. The wildcard characters are * and **?**. The * represents any number of characters from no characters at all to the maximum. Thus, "**Windows***" would represent any entry that begins with the characters "Windows" including just Windows with no more characters and Windows followed by any other set of characters. "***Windows***" would stand for any entry that contains "Windows" anywhere within it, for the wild cards stand for possible characters in front of Windows and after Windows.

The **?** represents exactly one character, no more and no less. As an example, 5/?/95 would represent any single-digit day in May of 1995. 5/??/95 would represent the two-digit days. To represent any day in May of 1995, use the asterisk as in 5/*/95.

When you use a wildcard in a criterion, the word "like" must begin the entry. Thus, the two examples with Windows and May of 1995 would really be entered as **like "*Windows*"** and **like "5/*/95"**. As with the word Is when we used Null, *Access* will automatically fill in the word **like** for you. Also, when you use a wildcard with a date, that is the only time the date will not be surrounded by pound signs; quotation marks are used instead.

To use wildcards in a query:

*   Open the query in the normal way.

*   Select fields as usual.

*   Fill in criteria that include one or more wildcard characters.

Activity 5.8: Using Wildcards in the Notes Field

We need listings of every CDROM that has **Windows** anywhere within the **Notes** field.

1. Erase the previous criterion.

2. Move to the **Criteria** line of the **Notes** column, and enter: **like "*Windows*"** (see Figure 5 - 16).

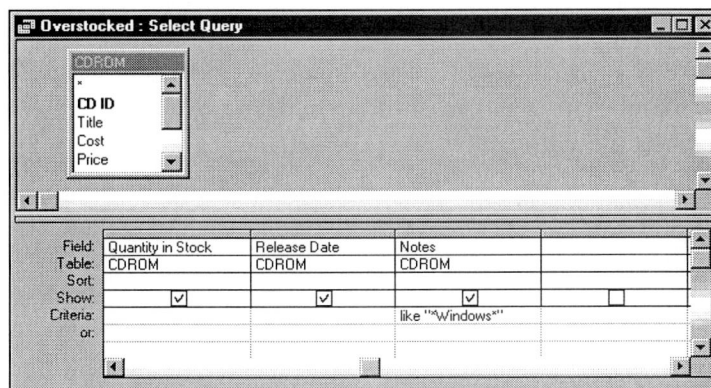

Figure 5 - 16

3. Click the **Query View** button to see the resulting dynaset.

   *The eight listings (see Figure 5 - 17) in the dynaset will have "Windows" somewhere within the **Notes** field.*

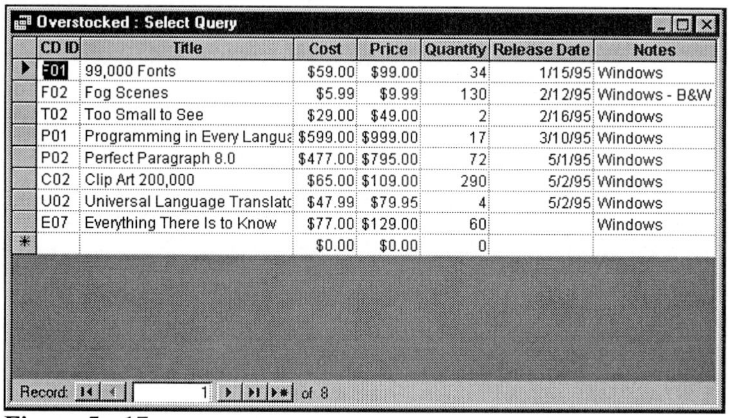

Overstocked : Select Query

CD ID	Title	Cost	Price	Quantity	Release Date	Notes
F01	99,000 Fonts	$59.00	$99.00	34	1/15/95	Windows
F02	Fog Scenes	$5.99	$9.99	130	2/12/95	Windows - B&W
T02	Too Small to See	$29.00	$49.00	2	2/16/95	Windows
P01	Programming in Every Langua	$599.00	$999.00	17	3/10/95	Windows
P02	Perfect Paragraph 8.0	$477.00	$795.00	72	5/1/95	Windows
C02	Clip Art 200,000	$65.00	$109.00	290	5/2/95	Windows
U02	Universal Language Translato	$47.99	$79.95	4	5/2/95	Windows
E07	Everything There Is to Know	$77.00	$129.00	60		Windows
*		$0.00	$0.00	0		

Record: 1 of 8

Figure 5 - 17

4. Print the result by clicking the **Print** button.

5. Click the **Query View** button to return to the query design.

Activity 5.9: Using Wildcards in the TITLE Field

We need to see the listings of each CDROM that has the word **every** anywhere within its title. Since we only need to see the data, we will not save this query when we are finished.

1. Erase the previous criterion.

2. Move to the **Criteria** line of the **Title** column, and enter: **like "*every*"** (see Figure 5 - 18).

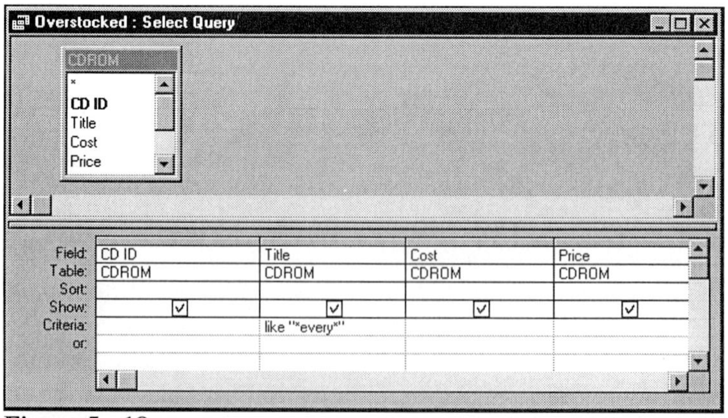

Overstocked : Select Query

CDROM
*
CD ID
Title
Cost
Price

Field:	CD ID	Title	Cost	Price
Table:	CDROM	CDROM	CDROM	CDROM
Sort:				
Show:	☑	☑	☑	☑
Criteria:		like '"*every*"'		
or:				

Figure 5 - 18

3. Click the **Query View** button to see the resulting dynaset.

   Each of the four listings in the dynaset will have "every" somewhere within its title Figure 5 - 19).

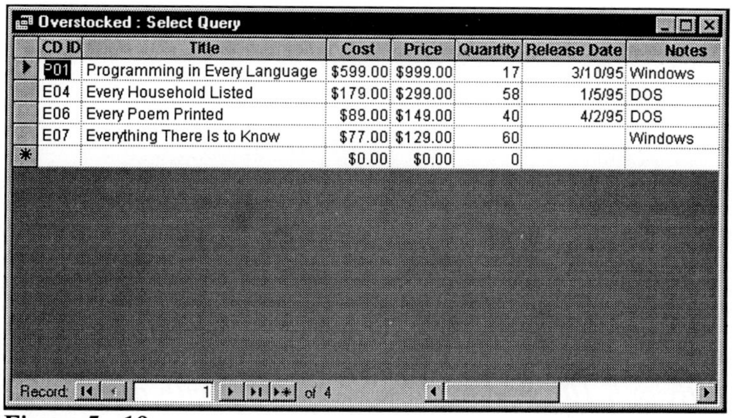

Figure 5 - 19

4. Print the result by clicking the **Print** button.

5. Click the **Query View** button to return to the query design.

6. Choose **FILE/Close**. When asked about saving, click the **No** button.

The Database window should be the active window again.

MULTIPLE TABLE QUERIES

The best design for the majority of databases is to have multiple tables holding the data. For the reasons given in Lesson 3, it is usually the only way to handle the data efficiently. Yet with a multi-table design, reports and calculations will often need to access data from more than one table at a time. To join the data from multiple tables you use a *join* query.

A join query is merely a select query with more than one table in the upper section of the query window. When you install more than one table in the query window, you must then *link* the tables by showing *Access* which field (or fields) in one table is the same as a field in another table. Every table included in the query must be linked to some other table. If you do not establish the link between two tables, each record in the first table will be joined with every record in the second table. Without a link, two tables with 1,000 records each would produce a dynaset with 1,000,000 listings!

Access 2.0 will often guess what the link is and automatically connect the two matching fields if they have the same name and one of them is a Primary Key. This is still another reason for a careful and consistent design and assigning of primary keys. Should *Access* guess correctly, you have no more to do. Should it guess incorrectly, however, you must click the mouse on the incorrect link line that *Access* drew, press the **DELETE** key to erase it, and properly link the tables yourself.

When you include more than one table in the upper section of the **Query** window and properly link the tables, you may place fields from each table in the QBE grid. Of course, you may sort, enter criteria, and do all the normal activities we have performed with single tables when you employ multiple table queries.

To join data from multiple tables through a query:

• Open a new **Query** window and choose the first table.

• Choose the second table.

• Choose any additional tables, and then close the **Show Table** dialog box.

- Establish the link between tables by clicking on the common field in the first table and dragging from that field onto the matching field in the second table.

- Link any additional tables.

- Pick the desired fields for the QBE grid.

- Enter any values to be matched on the **Criteria** line in the column that would contain those values.

- Include any sorting operators.

- Click the **Query View** button to see the resulting join as a dynaset.

Activity 5.10: Joining Multiple Tables with a Query

We need a dynaset with the names of the employees who sold each invoice. Since the invoice data is in the **Invoices** table with only the Employee ID to represent the salesperson, and the employees' names are in the **Employees** table, we must join the needed fields from the two tables. The common field in each of the two tables is **Employee ID**.

1. Open the **Sales** database if it is not already open on the workspace.

2. Click on the **Queries** tab at the top of the **Database** window.

3. Click the **New** button at the right side of the **Database** window.

4. In the **New Query** dialog box, click on **Design View** and click the **OK** button.

5. Pick the **Employees** table and click the **Add** button to place a list of its fields in the top half of the **Query1: Select Query** window.

6. Pick the **Invoices** table and click the **Add** button to place a list of its fields next to **Employees**.

   *Access will connect the common field in each table for you since Employee ID is the primary key in **Employees**, and a field with the same name exists in **Invoices**. This is the correct link (see Figure 5 - 20).*

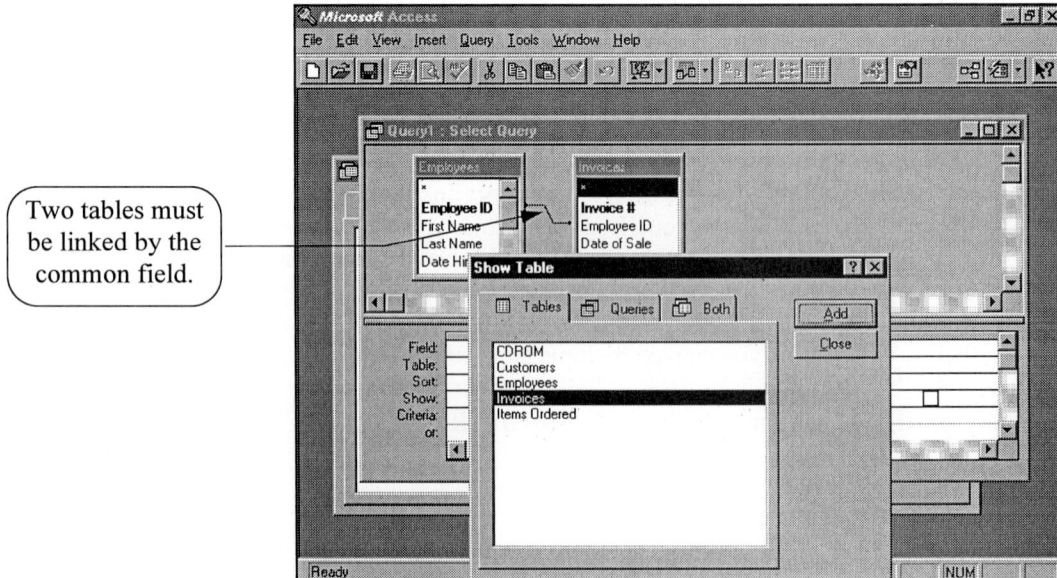

Figure 5 - 20

7. Click the **Close** button to close the **Show Table** dialog box.
8. Double-click **First Name** in the **Employees** table list to include it in the QBE grid.
9. Double-click **Last Name**.
10. Double-click the gray title bar of the **Invoices** table list to highlight all of its fields.
11. Move the mouse on top of any one of the highlighted field names and drag that name down to the third column of the QBE grid to install all four fields from **Invoices** (see Figure 5 - 21).

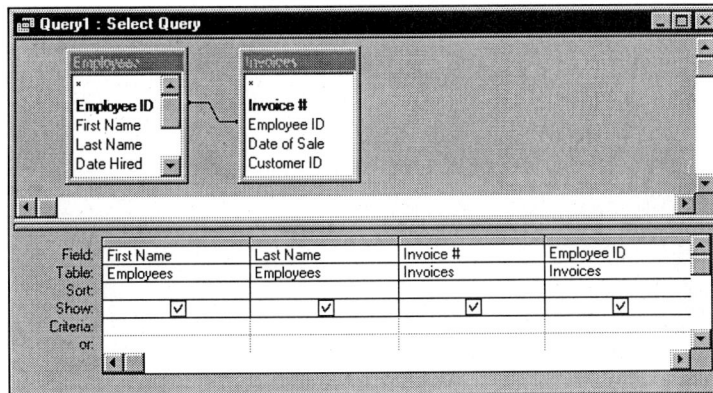

Figure 5 - 21

12. Click the **Query View** button to see the result.

    The two sales people Daphne Green and George Jeffers are matched to the invoices they sold. Notice that the Employee ID matches the name for each invoice (see Figure 5 - 22).

Query1 : Select Query

First Name	Last Name	Invoice #	Employee ID	Date of Sale	Customer ID
Daphne	Green	14902	10	6/2/95	AW31
Daphne	Green	14903	10	6/2/95	ED14
Daphne	Green	14908	10	5/19/95	AW31
Daphne	Green	14910	10	6/3/95	RF41
Daphne	Green	14911	10	6/4/95	BB12
Daphne	Green	14913	10	5/20/95	OR54
Daphne	Green	14915	10	6/2/95	AW31
Daphne	Green	14916	10	6/7/95	ED14
Daphne	Green	14919	10	6/8/95	FI85
Daphne	Green	14924	10	6/10/95	PA34
Daphne	Green	14927	10	6/12/95	AL05
Daphne	Green	14929	10	6/15/95	RA11
George	Jeffers	14904	11	6/2/95	AI29
George	Jeffers	14905	11	6/2/95	YT01
George	Jeffers	14906	11	6/2/95	TT10
George	Jeffers	14907	11	6/2/95	JE09
George	Jeffers	14909	11	6/3/95	YO19
George	Jeffers	14912	11	6/1/95	HA14

Record: 1 of 25

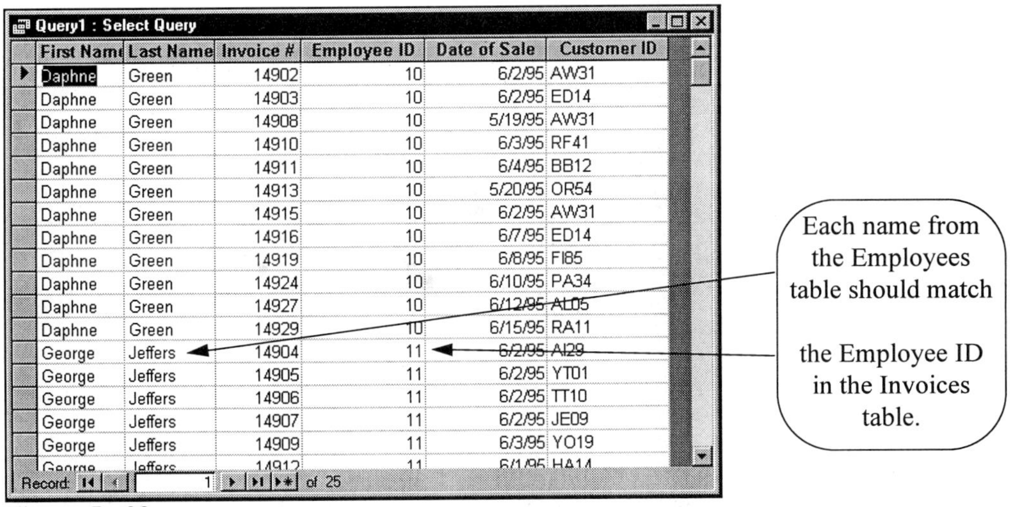

Figure 5 - 22

Also notice the Customer ID number for each invoice. Who is the customer? The next query will join the customer names to this listing by matching the Customer IDs to the ***Customers*** *table.*

13. Print the result by clicking the **Print** button.
14. Return to the design by clicking the **Query View** button.

Activity 5.11: Joining a Third Table into the Query

We would like the names of the customers who bought the items on each invoice. We still need all of the previous data from the **Employees** and **Invoices** tables, but want to add the customer names from the **Customers** table. So we need a third table, the **Customers** table. When finished, we will save this query with the name **Employees Sales to Customers** as we would probably need these results frequently.

1. Choose **QUERY/Show Table** in the menu or click the **Show Table** button on the toolbar.

2. Double-click on **Customers** in the **Show Table** dialog box, then close it.

   *Again Access figures out that the primary key **Customer ID** matches the field of the same name in **Invoices**, and draws the link line. This line is also correct (Figure 5 - 23).*

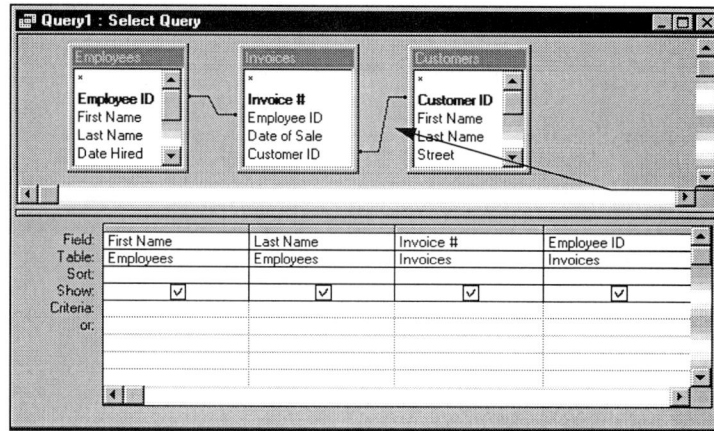

The **Invoices** and **Customers** tables are linked by the common field **Customer ID**.

Figure 5 - 23

3. Maximize the **Select Query** window.

4. Click anywhere in the **Employee ID** column in the QBE grid.

5. Pick **EDIT/Delete Column** to remove that column.

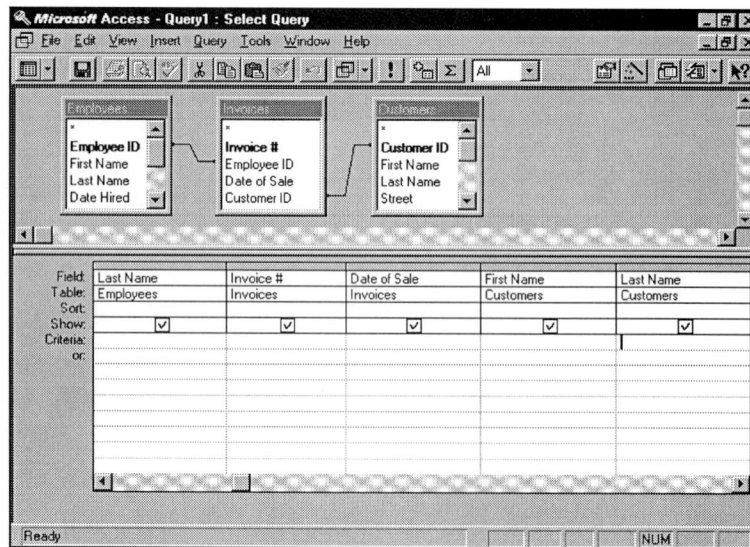

Figure 5 - 24

6. Similarly, click in the **Customer ID** column and pick **EDIT/Delete Column** to remove that column.

   *We do not need to see the **Customer ID** field now that we can see the customers' names.*

7. In the **Customers** field list, double-click the **First Name** and **Last Name** fields to include them in the QBE grid (Figure 5 - 24).

   You will probably need to scroll to the right to see the last field.

8. Click the **Query View** button to see the result.

   This dynaset joins data from three tables. Notice some of the customers' names occur multiple times (Figure 5 - 25). This is the very redundancy we eliminated with separate tables. We have instructed the computer to temporarily show the redundant names.

Employees.Fir	Employees.La	Invoice #	Date of Sale	Customers.First N	Customers.Last Nam
Daphne	Green	14902	6/2/95		Arrow Way Freight
Daphne	Green	14903	6/2/95		Edible Delights
George	Jeffers	14904	6/2/95		AreaWide Insurance
George	Jeffers	14905	6/2/95		Your Trip Travel
George	Jeffers	14906	6/2/95		Timed Travel, Inc
George	Jeffers	14907	6/2/95	Jennifer	Jerome
Daphne	Green	14908	5/19/95		Arrow Way Freight
George	Jeffers	14909	6/3/95	Larry	Yorko
Daphne	Green	14910	6/3/95		Regent Foods
Daphne	Green	14911	6/4/95		Balloon Bonanza
George	Jeffers	14912	6/1/95	Hazel	Harrington
Daphne	Green	14913	5/20/95	Donalio	Oradelio
Daphne	Green	14915	6/2/95		Arrow Way Freight
Daphne	Green	14916	6/7/95		Edible Delights
George	Jeffers	14917	6/7/95		AreaWide Insurance
Daphne	Green	14919	6/8/95	Terry	Fielder
George	Jeffers	14920	6/8/95	Caroline	Truefoe
George	Jeffers	14921	6/9/95	Laura	Ifalo
George	Jeffers	14922	6/10/95	Harry	Thompson

Figure 5 - 25

8. Choose **FILE/Save** to save this query.

9. Type the name **Employees Sales to Customers** in the **Save As** dialog box and click **OK**.

10. Print the result by clicking the **Print** button.

11. Close the query with **FILE/Close**.

Activity 5.12: A Second Multiple Table Query

We need a dynaset with the items sold on each invoice. The **Invoices** table does not contain that data since we could not predict how many items a customer would purchase. The items on each invoice are listed in the **Items Ordered** table. We will join **Invoices** and **Items Ordered**.

1. Open the **Sales** database if it is not already open on the workspace.

2. Click on the **Queries** tab at the top of the **Database** window.

3. Click the **New** button at the right edge of the **Database** window.

4. In the **New Query** dialog box, click on **Design View** and click the **OK** button.

5. Pick the **Invoices** table and click the **Add** button to place a list of its fields in the top half of the **Query1: Select Query** window.

6. Pick the **Items Ordered** table and click the **Add** button to place a list of its fields next to Invoices.

Access will connect the common field in each table for you since Invoice # is the primary key in Invoices and one of the primary keys in Items Ordered. The primary keys are displayed in bold letters in the field list (see Figure 5 - 26).

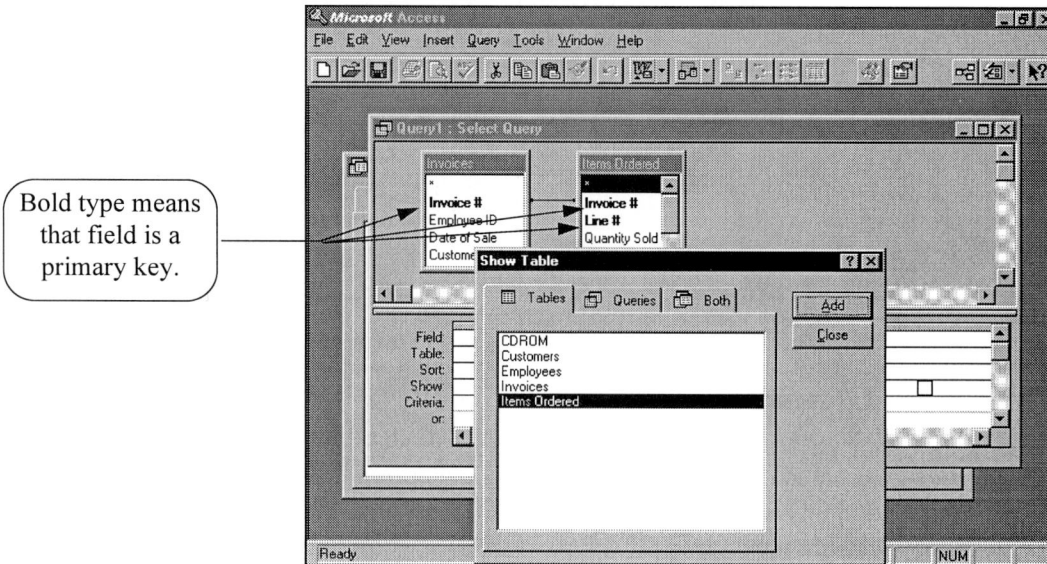

Bold type means that field is a primary key.

Figure 5 - 26

7. Click the **Close** button to close the **Show Table** dialog box.

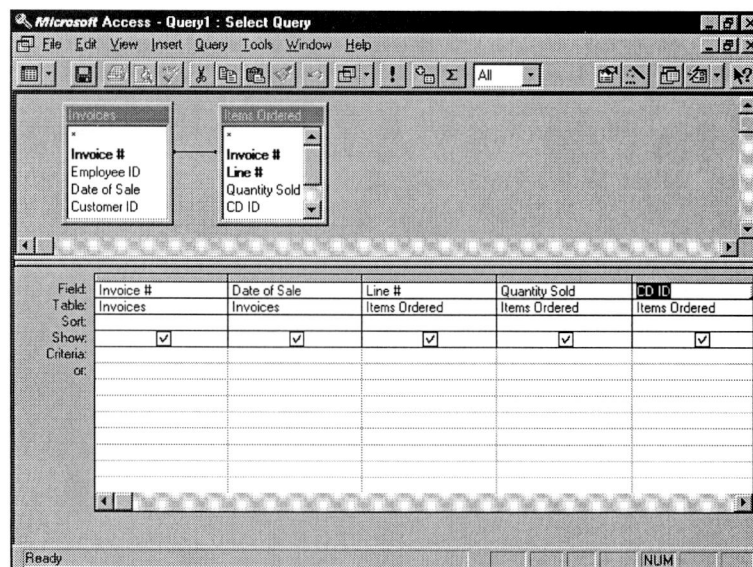

Figure 5 - 27

8. Double-click **Invoice #** in the **Invoices** table list to include it in the QBE grid.
9. Double-click **Date of Sale**.
10. From the **Items Ordered** field list, double-click the **Line #** field.
11. Also double-click the **Quantity Sold** and the **CD ID** fields (see Figure 5 - 27).
12. Click the **Query View** button to see the result.

    Notice that this dynaset shows the invoice numbers multiple times (see Figure 5 - 28), once for each item ordered on that invoice. This redundancy was avoided in the tables by designing separate tables.

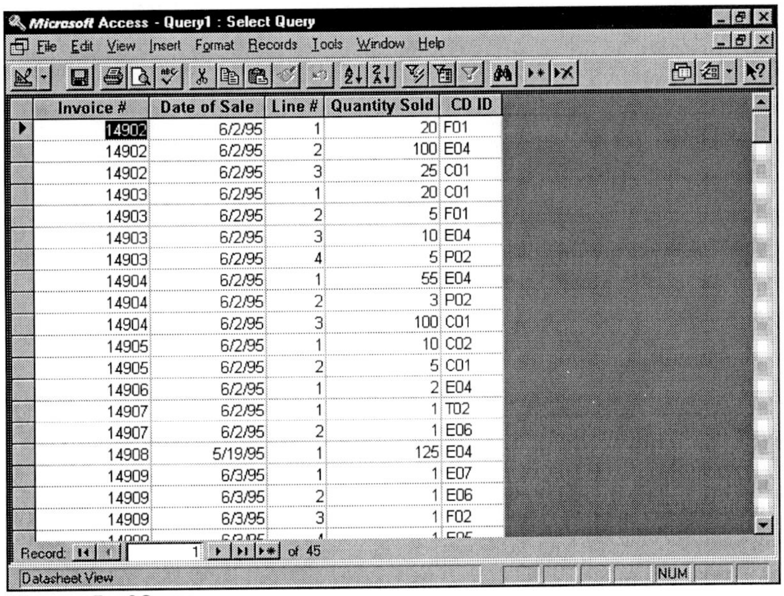

Invoice #	Date of Sale	Line #	Quantity Sold	CD ID
14902	6/2/95	1	20	F01
14902	6/2/95	2	100	E04
14902	6/2/95	3	25	C01
14903	6/2/95	1	20	C01
14903	6/2/95	2	5	F01
14903	6/2/95	3	10	E04
14903	6/2/95	4	5	P02
14904	6/2/95	1	55	E04
14904	6/2/95	2	3	P02
14904	6/2/95	3	100	C01
14905	6/2/95	1	10	C02
14905	6/2/95	2	5	C01
14906	6/2/95	1	2	E04
14907	6/2/95	1	1	T02
14907	6/2/95	2	1	E06
14908	5/19/95	1	125	E04
14909	6/3/95	1	1	E07
14909	6/3/95	2	1	E06
14909	6/3/95	3	1	F02

Figure 5 - 28

13. Choose **FILE/Save** to save this query.
14. Type the name **Invoice Items** in the **Save As** dialog box and click **OK**.
15. Print the result by clicking the **Print** button.
16. Close the query with **FILE/Close**.

ALTERING A QUERY

A saved query can be opened in design mode and altered to suit a new set of requirements.

Activity 5.13: Joining a Third Table into the Existing Invoice Items Query

We would like the names of the products ordered on each invoice. We still need all of the previous data from the **Invoices** and **Items Ordered** tables, but want to add the CDROM names from the **CDROM** table. So we need a third table, the **CDROM** table.

This amended query will be an improvement on the old design, so we will save it with the same name to replace that old design.

1. Click on the **Queries** tab at the top of the **Database** window.

2. Click on **Invoice Items** to highlight that name.

3. Click the **Design** button at the right side of the **Database** window.

4. Choose **QUERY/Show Table** in the menu or click the **Show Table** button on the toolbar.

5. Click on **CDROM** in the **Show Table** dialog box and click the **Add** button (see Figure 5 - 29), and then **close** the dialog box.

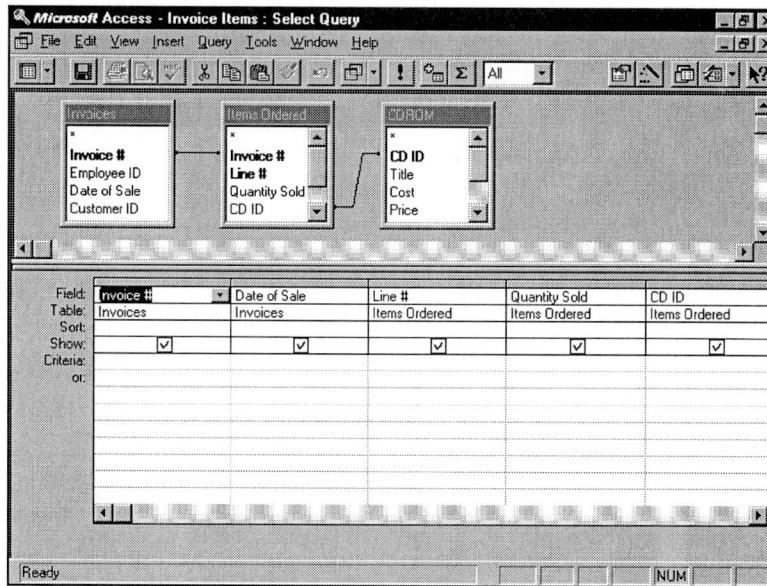

Figure 5 - 29

*Access figures out that the primary key **CD ID** in **CDROM** matches the field of the same name in **Items Ordered**, and draws the link line for you (see Figure 5 - 29).*

6. **Maximize** the **Select Query** window if it is not already maximized.

7. Click anywhere in the **CD ID** field in the QBE grid and pick **EDIT/Delete Column**.

8. In the **CDROM** field list, double-click the **Title** and **Price** fields to include them in the QBE grid.

   *You may not be able to see **Price** in the sixth column off the right edge of the screen, but it is there. You could scroll to the right with the scroll bar to see it.*

9. Click the **Query View** button to see the result (see Figure 5 - 30).

   This dynaset joins data from three tables. This time the redundancy occurs in the Titles and Prices of the CDROMs.

10. Choose **FILE/Save** to save this query with the same name and replace the old design.

11. Print the result by clicking the **Print** button.

12. Return to the design by clicking the **Query View** button.

    How could we add the Customers' names to this result? How about the Employees' names?

13. Close the query with **FILE/Close**.

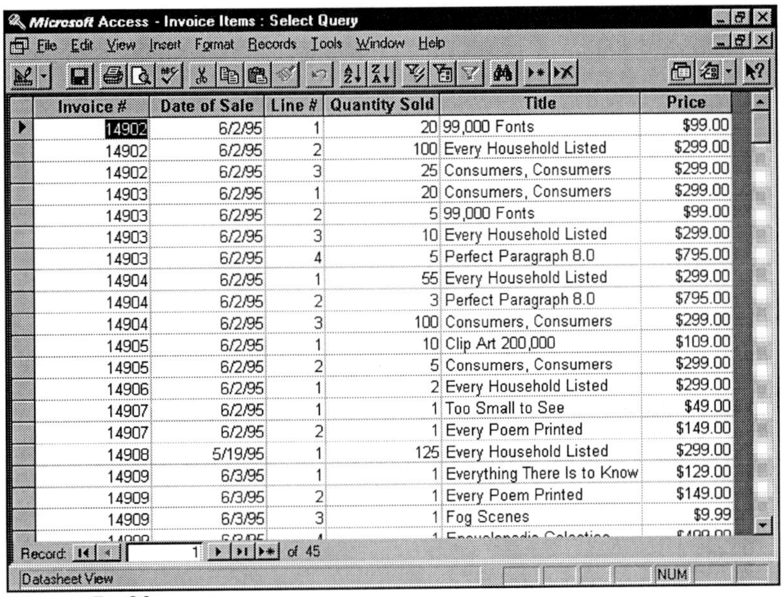

Invoice #	Date of Sale	Line #	Quantity Sold	Title	Price
14902	6/2/95	1	20	99,000 Fonts	$99.00
14902	6/2/95	2	100	Every Household Listed	$299.00
14902	6/2/95	3	25	Consumers, Consumers	$299.00
14903	6/2/95	1	20	Consumers, Consumers	$299.00
14903	6/2/95	2	5	99,000 Fonts	$99.00
14903	6/2/95	3	10	Every Household Listed	$299.00
14903	6/2/95	4	5	Perfect Paragraph 8.0	$795.00
14904	6/2/95	1	55	Every Household Listed	$299.00
14904	6/2/95	2	3	Perfect Paragraph 8.0	$795.00
14904	6/2/95	3	100	Consumers, Consumers	$299.00
14905	6/2/95	1	10	Clip Art 200,000	$109.00
14905	6/2/95	2	5	Consumers, Consumers	$299.00
14906	6/2/95	1	2	Every Household Listed	$299.00
14907	6/2/95	1	1	Too Small to See	$49.00
14907	6/2/95	2	1	Every Poem Printed	$149.00
14908	5/19/95	1	125	Every Household Listed	$299.00
14909	6/3/95	1	1	Everything There Is to Know	$129.00
14909	6/3/95	2	1	Every Poem Printed	$149.00
14909	6/3/95	3	1	Fog Scenes	$9.99

Figure 5 - 30

SUMMARY

In this project we have used multiple criteria and multiple table queries. We used multiple criteria for *And queries* and *Or queries*. We also used the *between*, *or*, *not*, and *null* operators, as well as wildcard characters in queries. The multiple table queries joined data from more than one table into a single dynaset. This was achieved by linking the common field in one table to the matching field in the second table.

In the next lesson we will design reports and labels for both tables and queries. The final lesson will explore calculating with queries, as well as Action Queries, which can alter the data throughout a table.

KEY TERMS

And Query
Compound
Join
Link
Operator
Or Query
Wildcard

INDEPENDENT PROJECTS

Independent Project 5.1: The School Newspaper

This Independent Project continues working with the Newspaper Ad database from Independent Project 4.1. The newspaper's editor needs a list of any companies with "sport" in their names to get ready for the Homecoming issue. The list should include all fields. Also, the business manager wants a listing of where the sales force lives, together with the businesses to whom they are selling ads. It should include the **Purchased By** field from the **Ads** table, as well as the **First Name**, **Last Name**, and **Room** fields from the **Sales Force** table. The two tables will need to be linked by their common field, **Salesperson ID**.

The first query result should look like Figure 5 - 31. The second will correspond to Figure 5 - 32.

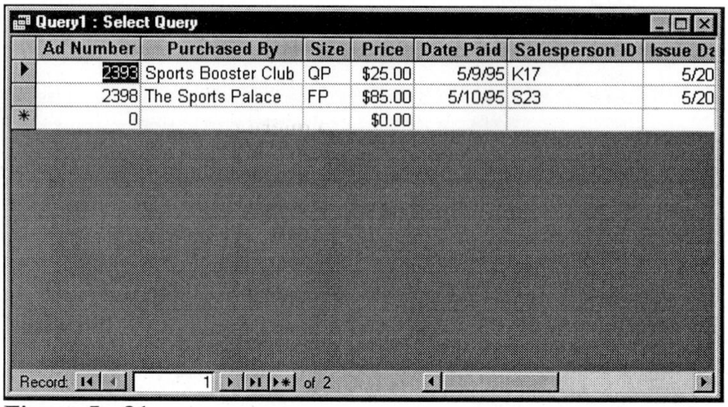

Query1 : Select Query

	Ad Number	Purchased By	Size	Price	Date Paid	Salesperson ID	Issue Da
▶	2393	Sports Booster Club	QP	$25.00	5/9/95	K17	5/20
	2398	The Sports Palace	FP	$85.00	5/10/95	S23	5/20
✱	0			$0.00			

Record: 1 of 2

Figure 5 - 31

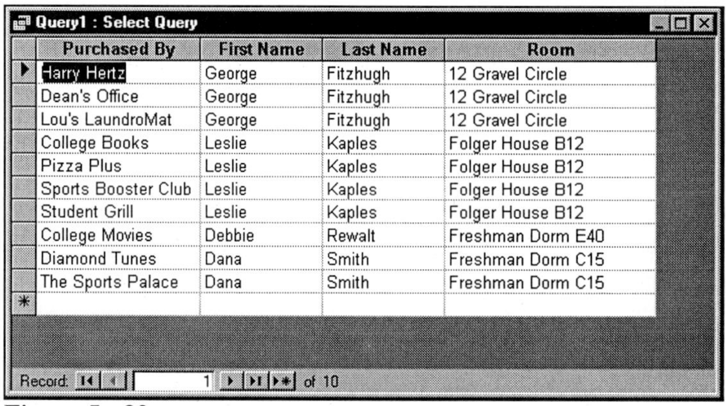

Query1 : Select Query

	Purchased By	First Name	Last Name	Room
▶	Harry Hertz	George	Fitzhugh	12 Gravel Circle
	Dean's Office	George	Fitzhugh	12 Gravel Circle
	Lou's LaundroMat	George	Fitzhugh	12 Gravel Circle
	College Books	Leslie	Kaples	Folger House B12
	Pizza Plus	Leslie	Kaples	Folger House B12
	Sports Booster Club	Leslie	Kaples	Folger House B12
	Student Grill	Leslie	Kaples	Folger House B12
	College Movies	Debbie	Rewalt	Freshman Dorm E40
	Diamond Tunes	Dana	Smith	Freshman Dorm C15
	The Sports Palace	Dana	Smith	Freshman Dorm C15
✱				

Record: 1 of 10

Figure 5 - 32

1. Run *Access* and maximize its window.

2. Open the **Exercise1** database in the Introductory dialog box. Alternatively, pick **FILE/Open Database** or click the **Open Database** tool on the toolbar, then click on the name **Exercise1** and click the **Open** button.

3. Click on the **Queries** tab at the top of the database window.

4. Click the **New** button to start a new query.

5. Pick **Design View** in the **New Query** dialog box and click **OK**.

6. Click on the name **Ads** in the list of tables in the **Show Table** dialog box and click the **Add** button.

7. Click **Close** to close the **Show Table** dialog box.

8. Double-click on the name **Ads** in the gray box at the top of the list of names to select all fields.

9. Move the mouse on top of any name in the highlighted list, hold down the mouse button, and drag that name down to the **Field** line of the first column in the QBE grid. When you release the mouse button, the entire set of field names will be installed.

10. Press the **HOME** key to jump to the first column.

11. Click on the **Criteria** line in the **Purchased By** column and enter: **like "*Sport*"**

12. Click the **Query View** button to see the resulting listings (see Figure 5 - 31).

13. Print the result by clicking the **Print** button.

14. Click the **Query View** button to return to the query design. You do not need to save this query, so we will build the second query from here.

15. Clear the current selection of fields from the QBE grid with **EDIT/Clear Grid**.

16. To add the **Sales Force** table, either click the **Show Table** button on the toolbar or pick **QUERY/Show Table**.

17. Click on the name **Sales Force** in the **Show Table** Tables list and click the **Add** button. *Access* should automatically link the two tables by the common field **Salesperson ID**.

18. Click **Close** to close the **Show Table** dialog box.

19. Double-click on the name **Purchased By** in the **Ads** table field list to include it in the QBE grid.

20. Double-click on **First Name**, then **Last Name**, and finally **Room** in the **Sales Force** field list.

21. Click the **Query View** button to see the resulting listings (see Figure 5 - 32).

22. Print the result by clicking the **Print** button.

23. Save the query as **Company vs Room** by picking **FILE/Save**, entering the name, and clicking the **OK** button. Do not type a period in the save name as periods are not legal.

24. Close the query with **FILE/Close**.

25. Close the database with **FILE/Close**.

26. If you need to exit from *Access*, do so properly.

Independent Project 5.2: The Bookstore

This Independent Project continues working with the Bookstore database from Independent Project 4.2. The owner needs a list of books that are priced below $30 and that have between 50 and 100 in stock. It should include all fields. Since this is a one-time request, you will print, but not save, this query. She also wants a complete listing of publisher's Name, Title, Author's name, and Year of Publication. It should be sorted by publisher's name. The two tables, **Publishers** and **Books**, will need to be linked by their common field, **Publisher Code**. As this listing may be required repeatedly, this one will be saved.

The first query result should look like Figure 5 - 33. The second will correspond to Figure 5 - 34.

Book Code	Title	Author	Year of Pub	Publisher Code	Cost	Price	Quantity in Stock
ATL11	Art Through Life	Jane Rick	1994	TT12	$13.50	$22.95	86
LUI81	Look Up In The Sky	Bruce Tiggle	1989	TT12	$17.00	$28.95	63
MOR47	Modern Russian	Igora Bylov	1990	CE03	$17.00	$28.50	59
POG17	The Physics of Glass	Kate Rice	1993	BP07	$4.75	$7.95	80
*					$0.00	$0.00	0

Figure 5 - 33

Name	Title	Author	Year of Pub
Atlantic Works	Music Harmony	Eliza Smith	1986
Atlantic Works	Music Composition	Eliza Smith	1985
Books Plus	The Physics of Glass	Kate Rice	1993
Books Plus	Even More Poems	Sina Grant	1976
Bulky Books	Chemical Compendium		1995
College Editions	World of History	James Dyce	1988
College Editions	Modern Russian	Igora Bylov	1990
College Editions	Economically Correct	Lester Dane	1974
Texts and Tomes	Philosophize With Me	Whyle Jones	1975
Texts and Tomes	Look Up In The Sky	Bruce Tiggle	1989
Texts and Tomes	Calculus	Henry Slate	1977
Texts and Tomes	Art Through Life	Jane Rick	1994

Figure 5 - 34

1. Run *Access* and maximize its window.

2. Open the **Exercise2** database in the introductory dialog box. Alternatively, pick **FILE/Open Database** or click the **Open Database** tool on the toolbar, then click on the name **Exercise2** and click the **Open** button.

3. Click on the **Queries** tab at the top of the Database window.

4. Click the **New** button to start a new query.

5. Pick **Design View** in the **New Query** dialog box and click **OK**.

6. Click on the name **Books** in the list of tables in the **Show Table** dialog box and click the **Add** button.

7. Click **Close** to close the **Show Table** dialog box.

8. Double-click on the name **Books** in the gray box at the top of the list of names to select all fields.

9. Move the mouse on top of any name in the highlighted list, hold down the mouse button, and drag that name down to the **Field** line of the first column in the QBE grid. When you release the mouse button, the entire set of field names will be installed.

10. Press the **END** key to jump to the last column.

11. Click on the **Criteria** line in the **Price** column and enter: **<30**

12. Click on the **Criteria** line in the **Quantity in Stock** column and enter: **between 50 and 100**

13. Click the **Query View** button on the toolbar.

14. **Maximize** the window so you can see the four resulting listings (see Figure 5 - 33).

15. Print the result by clicking the **Print** button.

16. Click the **Query View** button to return to the query design. You do not need to save this query, so we will build the second query from the current one.

17. Clear the current selection of fields from the QBE grid with **EDIT/Clear Grid**.

18. To add the Publishers table, either click the **Show Table** button on the toolbar or pick **QUERY/Show Table**.

19. Click on the name **Publishers** in the tables list and click the **Add** button. *Access* should automatically link the two tables by the common field **Publisher Code**.

20. Click **Close** to close the **Show Table** dialog box.

21. Double-click on the field **Name** in the **Publishers** table field list to include it in the QBE grid.

22. Press the **HOME** key so you can see the field.

23. Double-click on **Title**, then **Author**, and finally **Year of Publication** in the **Books** field list.

24. Click on the **Sort:** line in the **Name** column, click the **drop-down** arrow to open the list of sort operators, and click on **Ascending**.

25. Click the **Query View** button to see the resulting listings (see Figure 5 - 34).

26. Print the result by clicking the **Print** button.

27. Save the query as **Publishers' Books** by picking **FILE/Save**, entering the name, and clicking the **OK** button.

28. Close the query with **FILE/Close**.

29. Close the database with **FILE/Close**.

30. If you need to exit from *Access*, do so properly.

Independent Project 5.3: The Real Estate Office

This Independent Project continues working with the Real Estate Office database from the earlier lessons. The office manager needs a list of commercial properties that are larger than 4000 square feet in size and priced below $150,000. It should include all fields. Since this is a one-time request, you will print, but not save, this query. He also wants a complete listing of properties by agency name. The **Agency Name, Phone 1**, and **Fax** fields from the **Agencies** table should be included, as well as **Address, City, Size, Available**, and **Agent** fields from **Commercial Listings**. It should be sorted by Agency Name. The two tables, **Agencies** and **Commercial Listings**, will need to be linked by their common field, **Agency Code**. As this listing would be needed continually, this one will be saved and printed.

The first query result should look like Figure 5 - 35. The second will correspond to Figure 5 - 36.

Code	Address	City	State	Zip	Size	Floor	Purc	Price	Available	Agency	Agent
SS52	5 Elm St.	Greenwich	CT	06830	4800	1	R	$72,000.00	6/1/95	SC18	Brown
GP25	12 Gedney Place	Danbury	CT	06810	8900	3	R	$105,000.00	7/15/95	SC18	Equat
LW17	1 Lewis Way	Danbury	CT	06810	12000	2	R	$125,000.00	7/1/95	PP24	Smith
*					0	0		$0.00			

Figure 5 - 35

Agency Name	Phone 1	Fax	Address	City	Size	Available	Agent
George Winkle	972-9538	972-9625	3 Research Park	Stamford	18000	6/1/95	Purcell
Priceless Properties	359-1111	359-1212	2 Research Park	Stamford	18000	6/1/95	Ruth
Priceless Properties	359-1111	359-1212	Maple Court	New Canaan	450	5/15/95	Green
Profitable Properties	748-3471	748-0102	952 River Rd.	Stamford	3750	9/1/95	Smith
Profitable Properties	748-3471	748-0102	1 Lewis Way	Danbury	12000	7/1/95	Smith
Regal Real Estate	359-0050	359-0055	18 Frost Ave.	Greenwich	3700	8/1/95	Funchall
Right Properties	748-9410	748-9411	6 Research Park	Stamford	19000	10/1/95	Williams
Right Properties	748-9410	748-9411	5 Research Park	Stamford	21000	8/1/95	Williams
Smith and Cross	661-2831	661-2001	12 Gedney Place	Danbury	8900	7/15/95	Equat
Smith and Cross	661-2831	661-2001	5 Elm St.	Greenwich	4800	6/1/95	Brown
*					0		

Figure 5 - 36

1. Run *Access* and **maximize** its window.

2. Open the **Exercise3** database.

3. Click on the **Queries** tab.

4. Begin a new query using **Design View**.

5. Add **Commercial Listings** to the query window and close the **Show Table** dialog box.

6. Double-click on the name **Commercial Listings** to select all fields and drag any single name down to the **Field** line to install all fields into the QBE grid.

7. Move to the **Size** column.

8. Enter the criteria for **Size larger than 4000** square feet and **Price below $150,000** using the proper notation for examples in an *Access* query.

9. View the resulting listings (see Figure 5 - 35).

10. **Print** the result.

11. Return to the query design. You do not need to save this query.

12. Clear the QBE grid.

13. Add the **Agencies** table to the top section of the query window. *Access* should automatically link the two tables by the common field **Agency Code**.

    NOTE: *If Access does not link the two tables, you must have typed a different name for the **Agency Code** field in the **Commercial Listings** table. To establish the link between tables yourself, click on the field that represents **Agency Code** in **Commercial Listings** and drag from that name onto **Agency Code** in the **Agencies** table. The normal link line will be drawn and you will be ready to continue.*

14. Place the **Agency Name**, **Phone 1**, and **Fax** fields from the **Agencies** table into the QBE grid.

15. Include **Address**, **City**, **Size**, **Available**, and **Agent** from the **Commercial Listings** table.

16. Sort in ascending order by **Agency Name**.

17. View the resulting listings (see Figure 5 - 36).

18. **Save** the query as **Properties by Agency**.

19. **Print** the result.

20. **Close** the query.

21. **Close** the database.

22. If you need to exit from *Access*, do so properly.

Independent Project 5.4: The Veterinarian

This Independent Project continues working with the Veterinarian database from the earlier lessons. She needs the following two lists. Include all fields, print the resulting dynaset, and save each query.

- A list of dogs that weigh less than 50 pounds.

- A list of animals with "er" anywhere within their given name.

She also needs a listing of the owners with their pets. Include the fields named below, print the resulting dynaset, and save the query.

- A list that includes name, area code, and phone from the owners table and the name, type of animal, and date of last visit from the pets table.

  NOTE: *If Access does not automatically link the two tables, you must have typed a different name for the* **Owner Code** *field in the* **Pets** *table. To establish the link between tables yourself, click on the field that represents* **Owner Code** *in* **Pet Owners** *and drag from that name onto the owners code field in the* **Pets** *table. The normal link line will be drawn and you will be ready to continue.*

Lesson 6 Reports

Objectives

In this lesson you will learn how to:

- Design a report with the **Report Wizard**
- Preview a report design

- Modify a report design
- Print a report

PROJECT DESCRIPTION

Although working on the screen is ideal for editing and viewing a table's data, often a paper print-out is required to share the data with others. A typical business needs dozens of standard and special-purpose reports to review such activities as sales, inventory, accounts receivable, and customer distribution, to mention just a few topics. In this lesson we will see how to design and print two different types of reports, as well as mailing labels.

The first report will print a list of customers who have outstanding balances, as shown in Figure 6 - 1. This report is a *tabular* design. Tabular means it looks like a table of data.

Outstanding Balances Thursday, March 07, 1996

Cust ID	First Name	Last Name	Area Code	Phone	Credit Limit	Outstanding Balance
AW31		Arrow Way Freight	404	873-4909	$5,000.00	$562.00
JE09	Jennifer	Jerome	603	446-8021	$100.00	$59.10
PA34	Jerome	Packard	608	828-5512	$100.00	$49.00
RF41		Regent Foods	704	523-6106	$5,000.00	$1,982.00
TR30	Caroline	Truefoe	706	860-2971	$200.00	$129.00
YT01		Your Trip Travel	719	380-9210	$3,000.00	$593.40

Figure 6 - 1

The second report will include *grouping* and will print the customers in groups by state as illustrated in Figure 6 - 2.

165

Customers by State

State	Last Name	First Name	Customer ID	City	Zip	Credit Limit
CA						
	Area Wide Insurance		AI29	Nevada City	95959	$10,000.00
	Thompson	Harry	TH92	Irvine	92714	$500.00
	Udarell	Susan	UD20	San Jose	95112	$100.00
				Sum		**$10,600.00**
CO						
	Edible Delights		ED14	Loveland	80538	$5,000.00
	Your Trip Travel		YT01	Colorado Springs	80915	$3,000.00
				Sum		**$8,000.00**
FL						
	Oradelio	Donalio	OR54	Boca Raton	33433	$0.00

Figure 6 - 2

The third report will produce *mailing labels* for the complete customer list as illustrated in Figure 6 - 3.

Laura Ifalo
4529 Garrett Ave.
Peabody, MA 01960

Jennifer Jerome
82 Marlow Ln.
Marlow, NH 03456

Samantha Killian
89 Harvard Place
South Plainfield, NJ 07090

Timed Travel, Inc
1000 Flying Cloud Drive
New York, NY 10118

Dana Allington
89 Canter Rd.
Astoria, NY 11103

Regent Foods
6990 Industrial Blvd.
Charlotte, NC 28273

Arrow Way Freight
2395 E. Third Ave.
Atlanta, GA 30308

Caroline Truefoe
10204 Elm Rd.
Martinez, GA 30907

Donalio Oradelio
90 South Main
Boca Raton, FL 33433

Jerome Packard
Saleno Court
Middleton, WI 53562

Irving Razelroth
12 Skyway
Jefferson, SD 57038

Hazel Harrington
12093 Brighton Dr.
Morton Grove, IL 60053

Figure 6 - 3

DESIGNING A REPORT

The two steps in producing a designed report are to create the design, and then print the report. While this is somewhat more involved than just clicking the print button on the toolbar as we have done previously, a designed report offers far more flexibility. A report design can place fields anywhere on the page, not just in the row and column format of a table. You may select which fields you want included in the design and leave out unneeded fields. Computed results can be included, both as grand totals at the end of the report, and on each line to calculate results for each listing like a percentage of the total. Once a design is created, it can be saved and used over and over again.

A report may be designed for either a table or a query. A single table report would be limited to the fields within that one table along with any calculations that could be directly computed from its data. It would print all of the records in the table. A query can, of course, join data from two or more tables, so that a report could include a more comprehensive range of data. Since a query can restrict the included listings as well, a report designed around a query would print only the records that matched the query's criteria.

The report itself will usually have a *header* (see Figure 6 - 4) at the beginning (the head) of a report to introduce the overall report and a *footer* (see Figure 6 - 4) at the end (the foot) of the report to include any summary results. The report header normally contains the title of the report and may also have a date or other introductory information. The report footer often has final results like grand totals.

Each page can also have a header and footer (see Figure 6 - 4). The page header is usually where the column headings belong. The page footer typically contains the page number.

Each header or footer is placed in its own section in the design and is separated from the preceding section by a gray bar (see the right side of Figure 6 - 4). Since a typical report will have a Report Header, Page Header, Page Footer, and Report Footer, there will be several sections.

The section for the fields that will print each listing from the table or query is the *Detail* section, another section separated with a gray bar (see Figure 6 - 4 and Figure 6 - 16). Each section bar has its name on it with an arrow pointing downward toward the section contents.

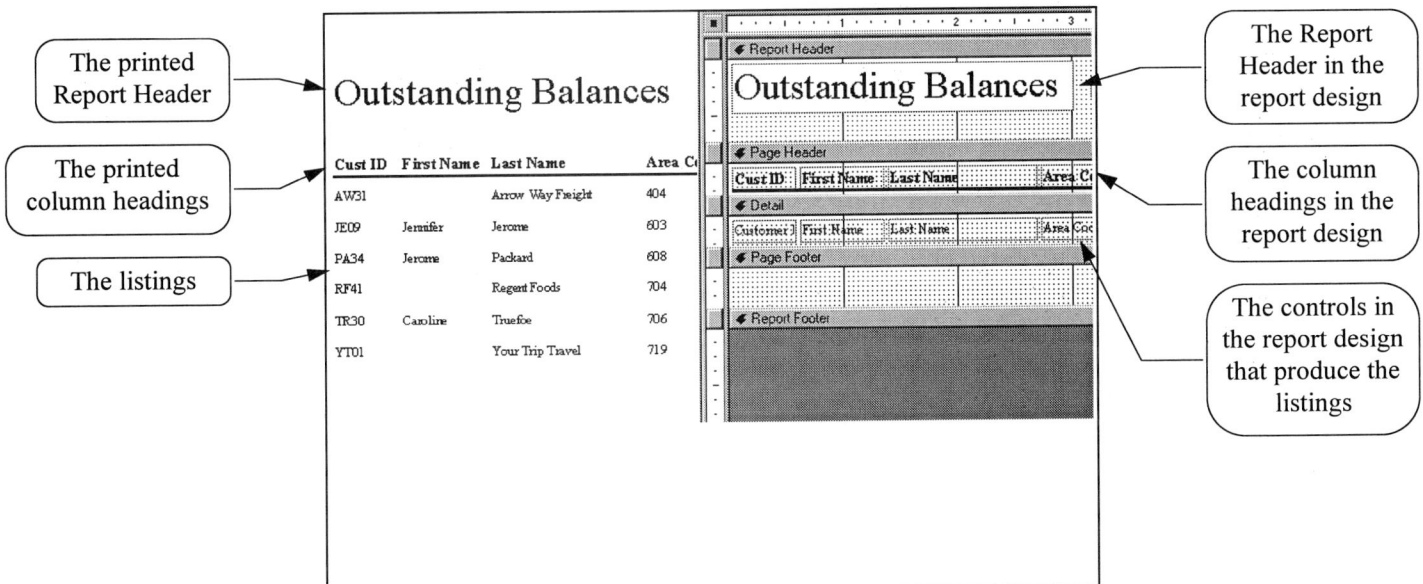

Figure 6 - 4

THE REPORT WIZARD

While it would be possible to design a report by selecting and placing each individual item onto the layout yourself, that would be very tedious. A typical report design will have 30 to 40 items that must be carefully placed and lined up with one another. A much easier solution is to employ the *Report Wizard*. The *Report Wizard* asks a sequence of questions as to how you want the design to look, and then produces the design for you. This eliminates the tedium, yet allows considerable flexibility. Once the *Report Wizard* is finished producing the report design, you may, of course, alter the design in any way desired in the **Report** window.

There are five different Report Wizards, each one of which can produce a different basic design. In the **New Report** dialog box (see Figure 6 - 7) you select which basic design you want to use. The choice Design View switches to a blank report design screen where you would need to place each desired item one by one, a process to be avoided, if possible. Report Wizard is the general-purpose choice. It allows you to choose the fields, any grouping or sorting, and summary calculations. The choice AutoReport: Columnar produces a single column design like a form. This style is not usually an efficient way to organize the data on paper and, thus, is not used as often as a tabular design. AutoReport: Tabular generates a general-purpose listing. It is often a good starting point for a regular list of a table's data. The Chart Wizard leads you through the creation of a graph. The Label Wizard produces designs for labels.

We will explore three common designs: tabular, tabular with grouping, and mailing labels.

To design a tabular report with the Report Wizard:

- If you will be producing the report from a query, prepare and save the query.

- Click the **Reports** tab at the top of the **Database** window.

- Click the **New** button at the right edge of the **Database** window.

- From the list at the top of the **New Report** dialog box, pick **Report Wizard**.

- From the drop-down list at the bottom of the **New Report** dialog box, pick the table or query that is the basis for the report and click **OK**.

- Select the fields you need on the report from the list the Wizard presents.

- Choose any grouping levels.

- Pick any fields by which to sort the report.

- Select **Tabular** for the layout and pick the page orientation.

- Choose the style for the report.

- Enter the title for the report and decide whether to preview the report or go directly to the design to make modifications.

Activity 6.1: The Query to Be Used in a Tabular Report

Management needs to review a list of those customers who have an outstanding balance. The required fields are **Customer ID**, **First Name**, **Last Name**, **Area Code**, **Phone number**, **Credit Limit**, and **Outstanding Balance**. The **Customers** table contains customers who both do and don't have an outstanding balance, so we first need to query to select only those customers who have a balance.

1. The **Sales** database should be opened.

2. Click the **Queries** tab at the top of the **Database** window.

3. Click the **New** button at the right edge of the **Database** window.

4. Click on **Design View** in the **New Query** dialog box and click **OK**.

5. Click on **Customers** in the list of tables and click the **Add** button. Then close the **Show Table** dialog box.

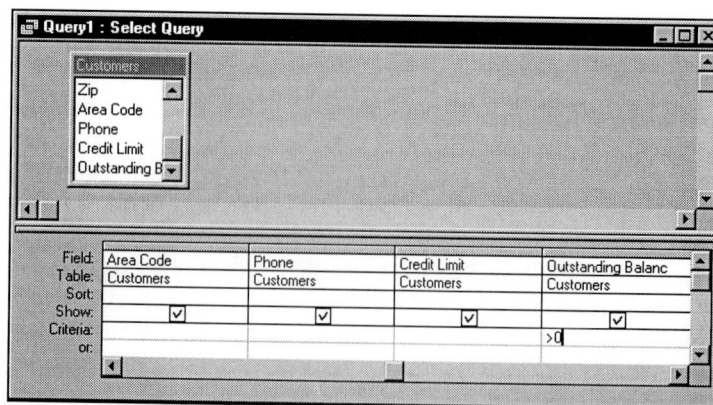

Figure 6 - 5

6. Double-click each of the required fields in the following order: **Customer ID, First Name, Last Name, Area Code, Phone, Credit Limit,** and **Outstanding Balance**.

7. Press the **LEFT ARROW** key so you can see the last two fields in the QBE grid.

8. Click on the **Criteria** line in the **Outstanding Balance** column and enter: **>0** (Figure 6 - 5).

9. Click the **Query View** button on the toolbar to visually check the result.

   There should be six records with outstanding balances (see Figure 6 - 6).

Customer ID	First Name	Last Name	Area Code	Phone	Credit Limit	Outstanding Balance
AW31		Arrow Way Freight	404	873-4909	$5,000.00	$562.00
JE09	Jennifer	Jerome	603	446-8021	$100.00	$59.10
PA34	Jerome	Packard	608	828-5512	$100.00	$49.00
RF41		Regent Foods	704	523-6106	$5,000.00	$1,982.00
TR30	Caroline	Truefoe	706	860-2971	$200.00	$129.00
YT01		Your Trip Travel	719	380-9210	$3,000.00	$593.40
*					$0.00	$0.00

Record: 1 of 6

Figure 6 - 6

10. Pick **FILE/Save**.

11. Enter the name **Outstanding Balances** and click the **OK** button.

12. Close the query with **FILE/Close**.

Activity 6.2: A Tabular Report

Now that we have the desired records with outstanding balances, we can create the report. The source of the data for the report will be the **Outstanding Balances** query, and we will use the *Report Wizard* to design a tabular report.

1. Click the **Reports** tab at the top of the **Database** window.

2. Click the **New** button at the right edge of the **Database** window.

3. Click the drop-down arrow to open the list to **Choose the table or query where the object's data comes from:** in the **New Report** dialog box and click on **Outstanding Balances**.

   You may need to scroll down the list.

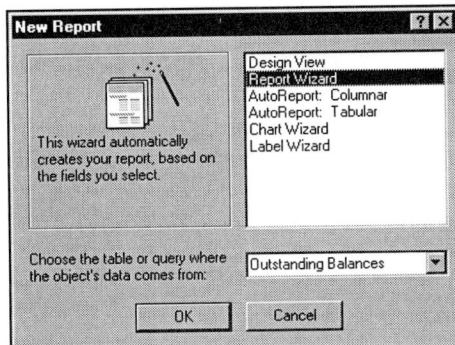

New Report

This wizard automatically creates your report, based on the fields you select.

Design View
Report Wizard
AutoReport: Columnar
AutoReport: Tabular
Chart Wizard
Label Wizard

Choose the table or query where the object's data comes from: Outstanding Balances

OK   Cancel

Figure 6 - 7

4. Click on **Report Wizard** in the list at the top of the **New Report** dialog box (see Figure 6 - 7).

5. Click the **OK** button.

6. In the first **Report Wizard** dialog box, click the >> button to send the complete list of fields from the **Available Fields** list to the **Selected Fields** list (see Figure 6 - 8).

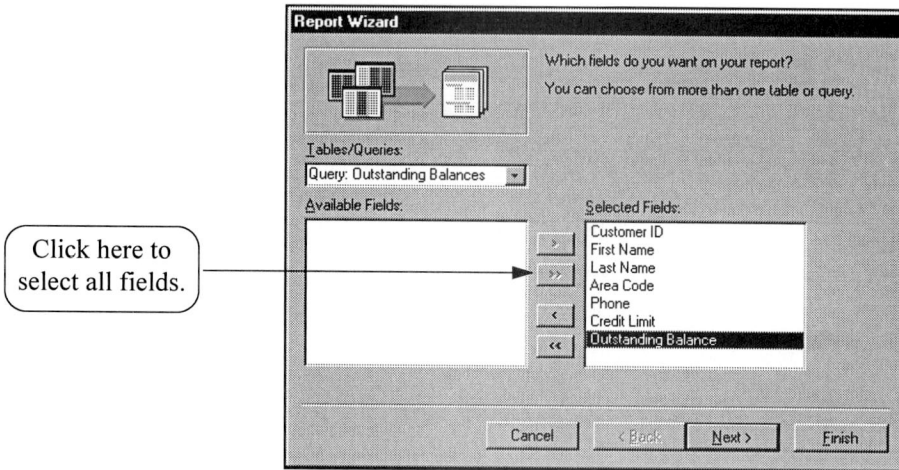

Figure 6 - 8

The ***Tables/Queries*** *list already has the correct selection since we picked Outstanding Balances in the previous dialog box. To pick individual fields in any order, click on the name of the field in the* **Available Fields** *list and click the* ***single arrowhead*** *button that points to the right. The arrowheads pointing to the left will bring one or all of the fields back so you can reselect.*

7. Click the **Next>** button.

8. We do not need grouping until the next report, so make no changes in the **Do you want to add any grouping levels?** and click the **Next>** button (see Figure 6 - 9).

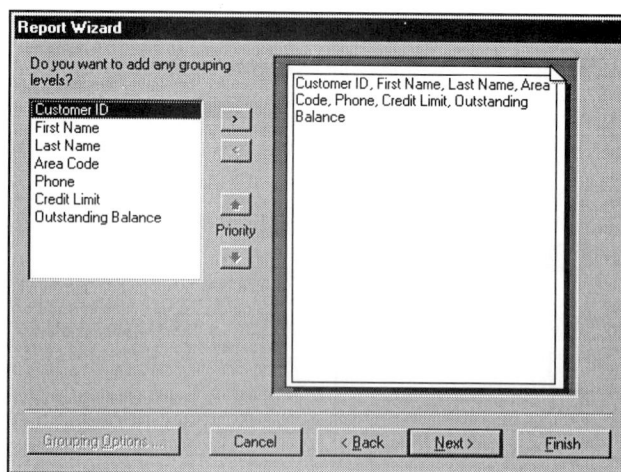

Figure 6 - 9

The next question is by which fields, if any, do you wish to sort the listings (see Figure 6 - 10). Click the drop-down arrow to open the first list and pick the most important field by which to sort. Continue with the second most important, etc. You may select up to four fields by which to sort.

9. As we do not want to sort this report, click the **Next>** button without selecting any fields (see Figure 6 - 10).

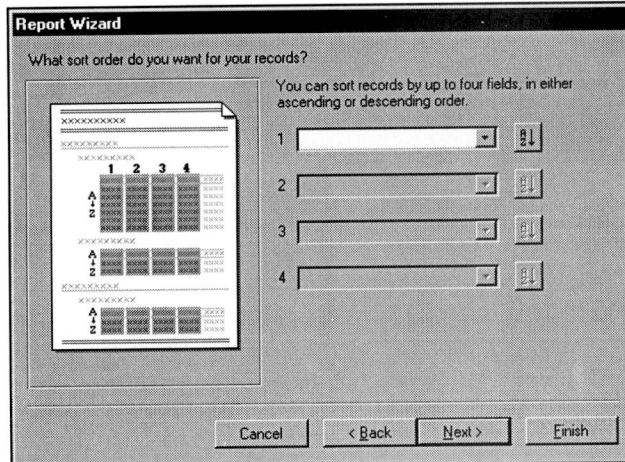

Figure 6 - 10

10. Make certain **Tabular** is the selection for **Layout**, click on **Landscape** for **Orientation**, and check **Adjust the field width so all fields fit on a page** if it is not already checked (see Figure 6 - 11).

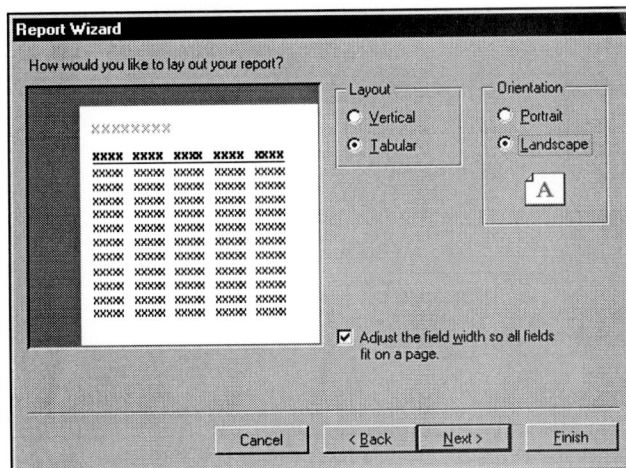

Figure 6 - 11

11. Click the **Next >** button.

    *What style is the next question. We will use **Formal**, but click on each of the other choices to explore the variety of styles.*

12. Click on **Formal** and click **Next>** (Figure 6 - 12).

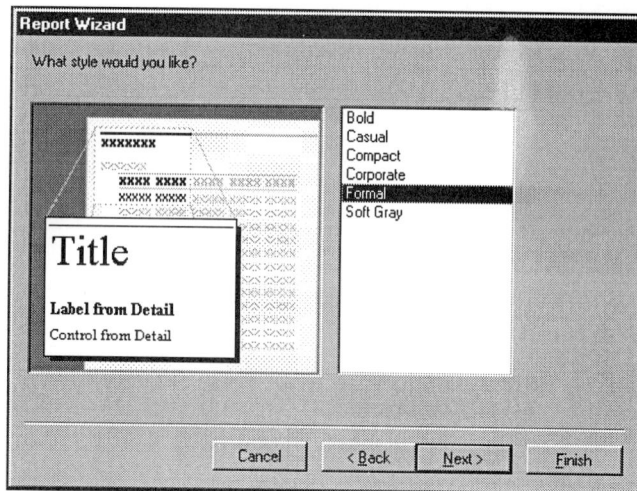

Figure 6 - 12

The final set of questions (notice the finish flag in Figure 6 - 13) asks for a title for the report, whether to go to preview mode or design mode, and whether you want Help displayed simultaneously. The title is both the name by which the report will be saved within the database (and must not duplicate an existing report name) and the main title that will go at the top of the first page of the report.

13. The query name **Outstanding Balances** is perfect as a title (and name) for this report and we want none of the other options, so click **Preview the report** and then the **Finish** button (see Figure 6 - 13).

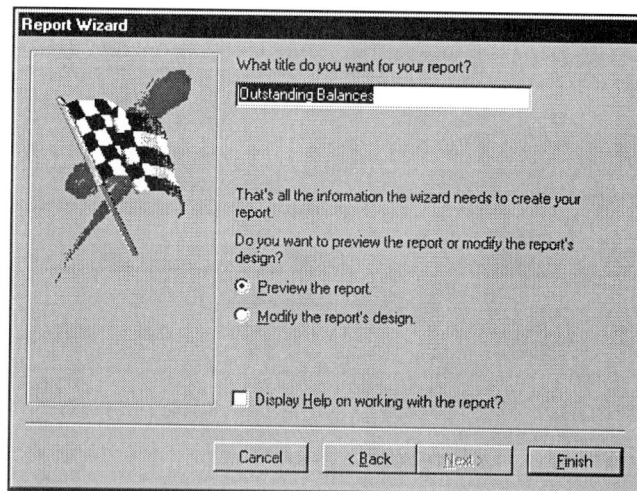

Figure 6 - 13

The Wizard completes the design and moves to the Print Preview screen so you can see the result (see Figure 6 - 14).

14. **Maximize** the preview window.

15. So you can see the overall page (see Figure 6 - 15) click the **Zoom** button on the toolbar or click anywhere on the white page.

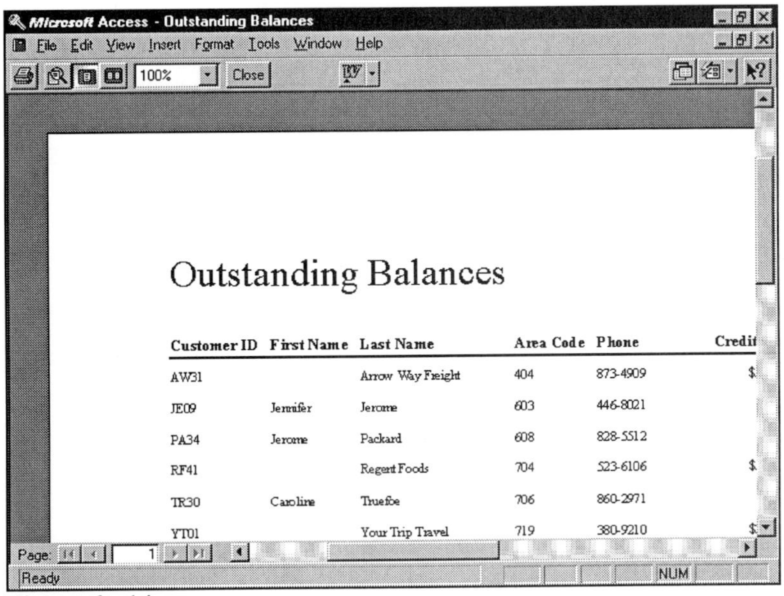

Figure 6 - 14

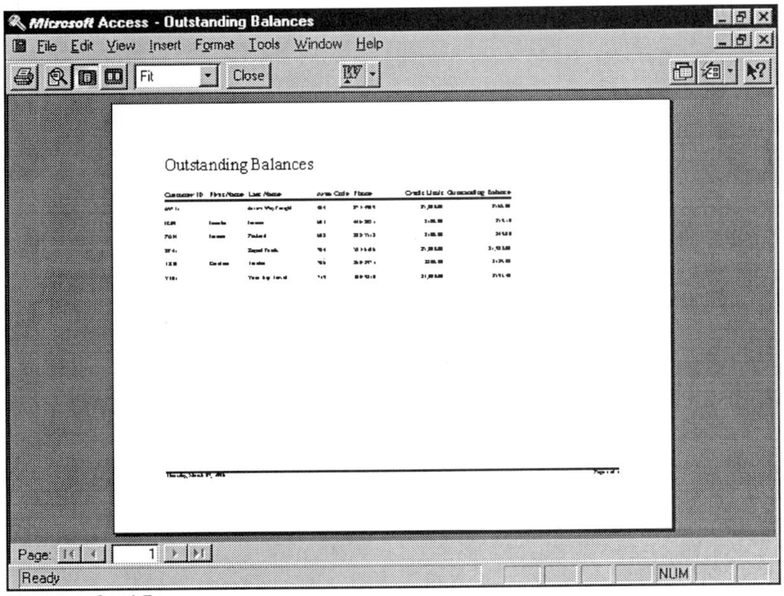

Figure 6 - 15

16. Click the **Close** button on the toolbar.

    The Report Design screen appears (see Figure 6 - 16). This is the design the Wizard worked out for you. An additional toolbar named the Toolbox may have appeared on the desktop. The Toolbox is used to place additional items onto the report design.

17. To hide the Toolbox until we need it, open the **VIEW** menu. If **Toolbox** has a checkmark in front of it, click on **Toolbox** to remove the checkmark. If there is no checkmark in front of **Toolbox**, close the menu by clicking on **VIEW** again.

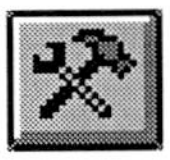

    *You could also click the **Toolbox** button on the toolbar to show or hide it.*

    If you will be continuing on to the next section, leave the design on the screen.

CHANGING A REPORT DESIGN

Any changes to a report design are performed in the **Report** window (Figure 6 - 16). The existing design is divided into the sections that were discussed earlier, namely the Report Header, Page Header, Detail section, Page Footer, and Report Footer. Each section begins with the gray bar and extends downward to the next section bar.

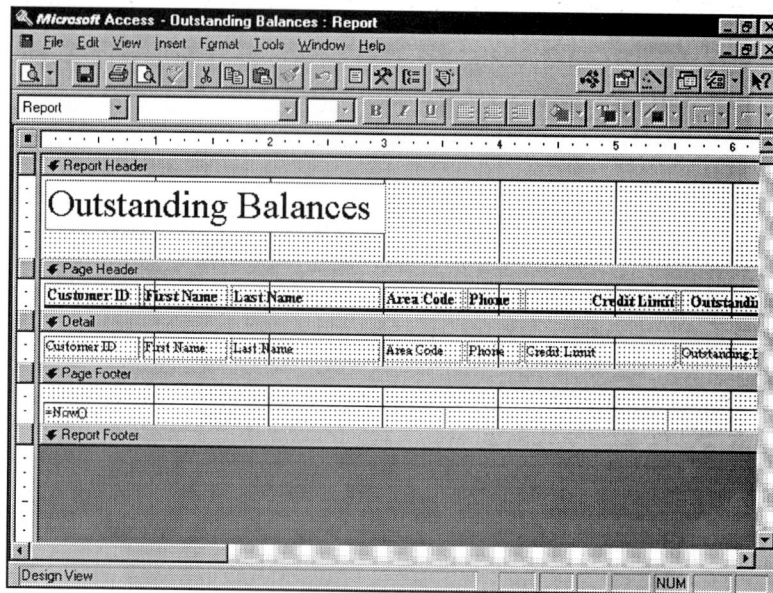

Figure 6 - 16

A new toolbar appears automatically when you switch to the report design screen. The Formatting toolbar contains tools for selecting and altering the appearance of the items on the design.

Each item included in the design is a *control*. The field controls and label controls are shown as boxes. The controls that represent the ruling lines are the lines drawn on the design screen.

The design can be changed by altering the controls and sections. Clicking on a control or selecting its name in the Select Object list on the Formatting toolbar will produce *handles* at each corner and the middle of each side. The top left handle is the *move handle*. The others are *sizing* handles (see Figure 6 - 17).

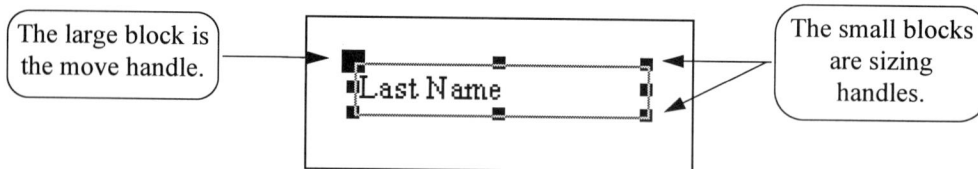

The large block is the move handle.

Last Name

The small blocks are sizing handles.

Figure 6 - 17

To change the existing controls on a report design:

- Select the control by clicking on it or by picking its name in the **Select Object** drop-down list on the Formatting toolbar.

- Move it by dragging its *move handle* to a new position on the design or with the **Cut** and **Paste** buttons on the toolbar.

- Delete it by pressing the **DELETE** key.

- Resize it by dragging a *sizing handle* until the control is the appropriate size.

Activity 6.3: Changing the Tabular Report Design

We need to move the date from the bottom left corner of the report to a more prominent position next to the title at the top. Then we will delete the ruling line at the bottom of the design.

1. If the report design is not already on the screen, click on the **Reports** tab, click on the name **Outstanding Balance** in the list of reports, and click the **Design** button at the right side of the database window.

2. Locate the **=Now()** control at the bottom left corner of the report design and click on it once to select it (see Figure 6 - 18).

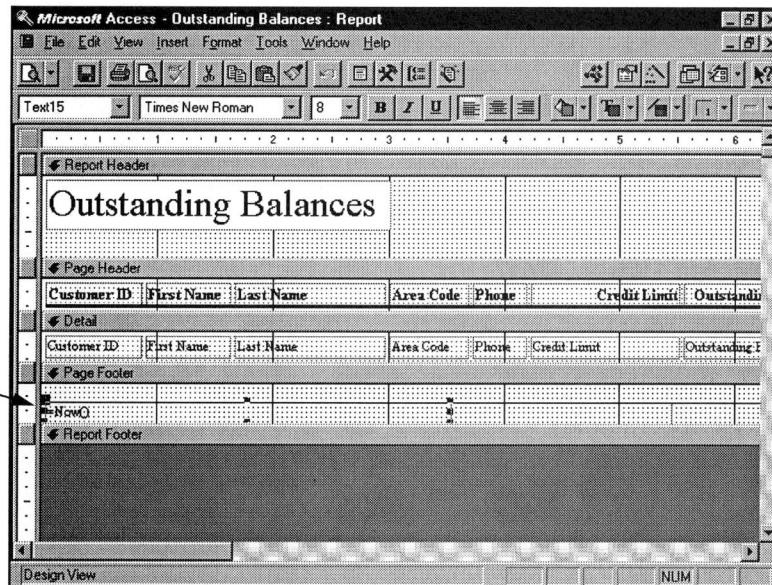

Select the **=Now()** control by clicking on it. Then click the **Cut** button on the toolbar.

Figure 6 - 18

Handles will appear on the control.

3. Click the **Cut** button on the toolbar to snip it from the design.

   *The control will disappear from the design. The control has gone to the Windows Clipboard, from which it can be retrieved with the **Paste** button.*

4. Click on the gray bar that says **Report Header** to select that section.

5. Click the **Paste** button.

The control returns, but is currently on top of the report title (see Figure 6 - 19).

> Click on the Report Header bar and click the **Paste** button to move the =Now() control to that section.

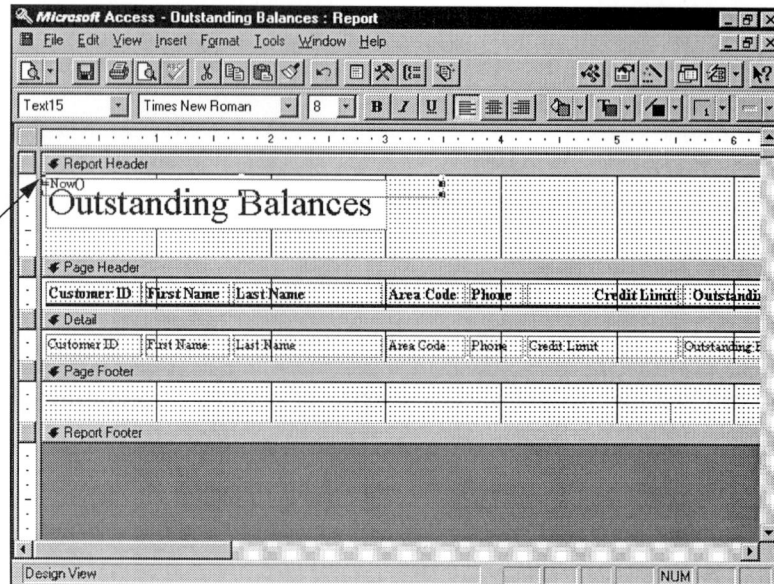

Figure 6 - 19

6. Position the mouse on top of the *move handle* for the =**Now()** control. The mouse pointer will become a pointing index finger. (You may need to try several times before you arrive on top of the *move* handle at the top left corner of the control.) Hold down the mouse button and drag the control to the right of the main title (see Figure 6 - 20).

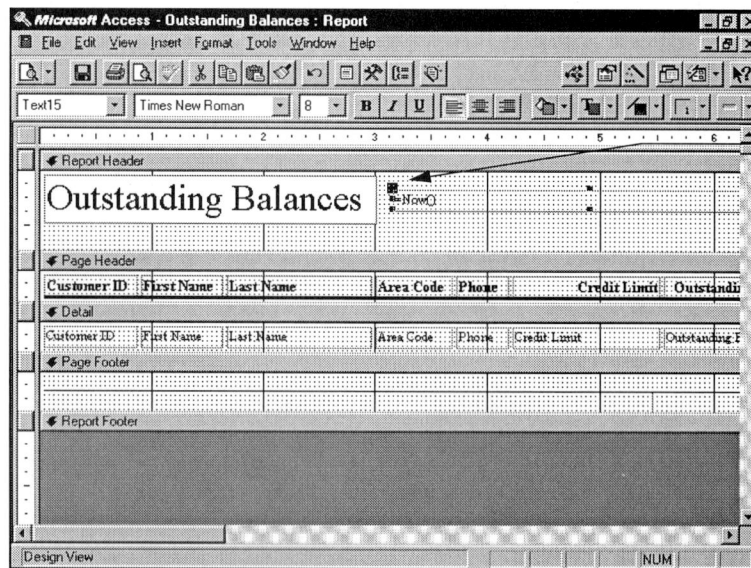

> Use the *move* handle to drag the control into position.

Figure 6 - 20

7. Click on the ruling line that remains where the date used to be at the bottom left corner of the design.

    Handles will appear on the line (see Figure 6 - 21).

8. Press the **Delete** key to remove the line.

9. Save the modified design with **FILE/Save**.

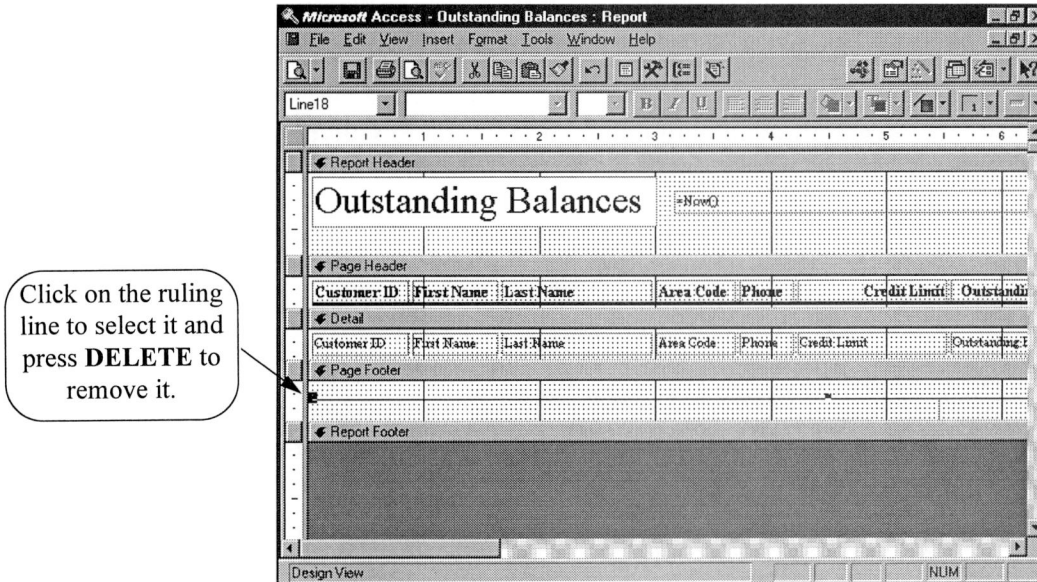

> Click on the ruling line to select it and press **DELETE** to remove it.

Figure 6 - 21

10. Click the **Report View** button or the **Print Preview** button (they look the same) to preview the report (see Figure 6 - 22).

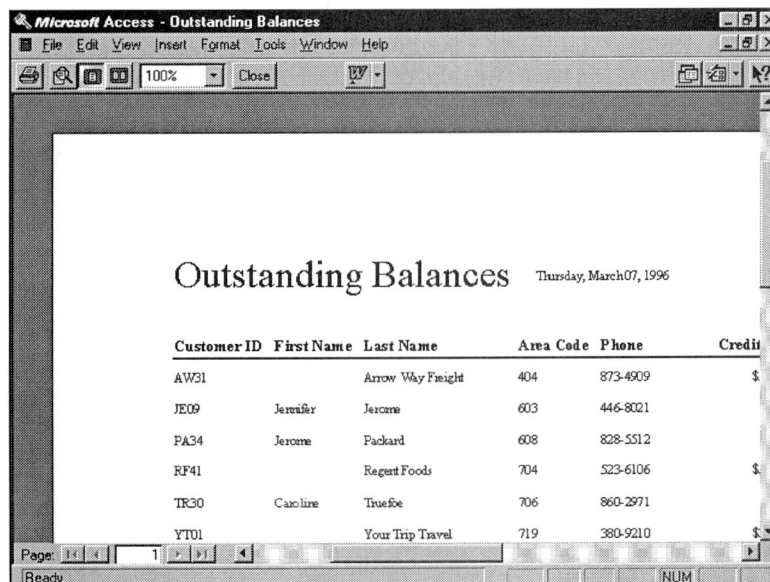

Figure 6 - 22

11. Print the report by clicking the **Print** button on the toolbar.

12. Close the report design with **FILE/Close**.

DESIGNING A TABULAR REPORT WITH GROUPING

Often a report will need to be *grouped* on the entries in one or more fields. *Grouped* means that all the records with one particular value in a field are assembled into a cluster, and each additional value in that field is placed in a separate gathering. Each group is then separated from the next and given a header section to introduce the group and a footer section to conclude the group. The header would typically contain the name of the group and the footer often holds subtotals for the group.

To design a report with grouping using the Report Wizard:

- Begin a new report using the choice **Report Wizard** in the **New Report** dialog box.

- Select the fields you need on the report from the list the Wizard presents.

- Choose any fields by which to group the report.

- Pick the fields by which to sort within each grouping and add any summary options.

- Choose the layout and page orientation for the report.

- Choose the style.

- Enter the title for the report and decide whether to preview the report or go directly to the design to make modifications.

Activity 6.4: A Report with Grouping

Management would like a report that shows which states the various customers come from. The report should list their Customer ID, First Name, Last Name, City, State, Zip Code, and Credit Limit. The report should be grouped by state and sorted alphabetically by customer name within each state. Since the report will include every listing, we will base the report on the data table itself rather than a query.

1. Click the **Reports** tab at the top of the **Database** window.

2. Click the **New** button at the right edge of the **Database** window.

3. Click the drop-down arrow to open the list of tables and queries at the bottom of the **New Report** dialog box and pick **Customers**.

4. Click on **Report Wizard** at the top of the **New Report** dialog box and click the **OK** button.

5. In the list of **Available Fields**, click on **Customer ID** and click the single arrowhead button that points to the right to transfer it to the **Selected Fields** list (see Figure 6 - 23).

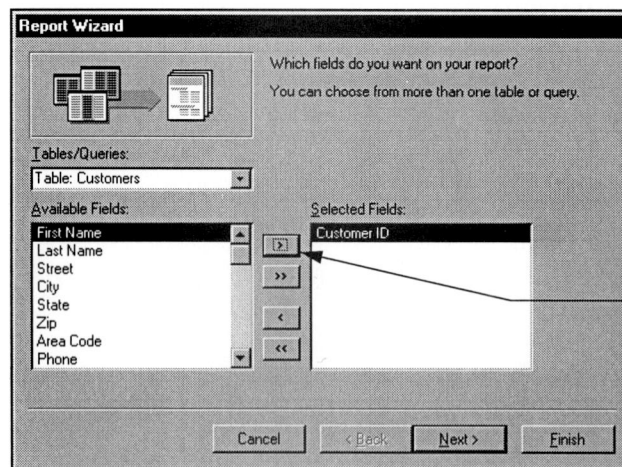

Figure 6 - 23

6. Click on **First Name** in the **Available Fields** list and click the single arrowhead button to transfer it to the **Selected Fields** list.

7. Click on **Last Name** and click the single arrowhead button.

8. Similarly, click on **City**, then **State**, then **Zip**, then **Credit Limit**, clicking the single arrowhead button each time (see Figure 6 - 24).

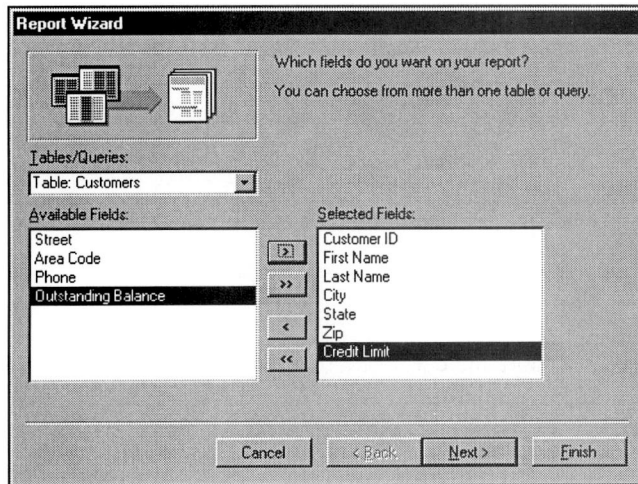

Figure 6 - 24

9. Click the **Next** > button.

   The next question is by which fields, if any, do you wish to group the listings. Select a field and use the arrowhead button. Grouping may be up to four levels deep.

10. Click on **State** to highlight it and click the single arrowhead button to transfer it to a separate box at the top of the illustrated report (see Figure 6 - 25).

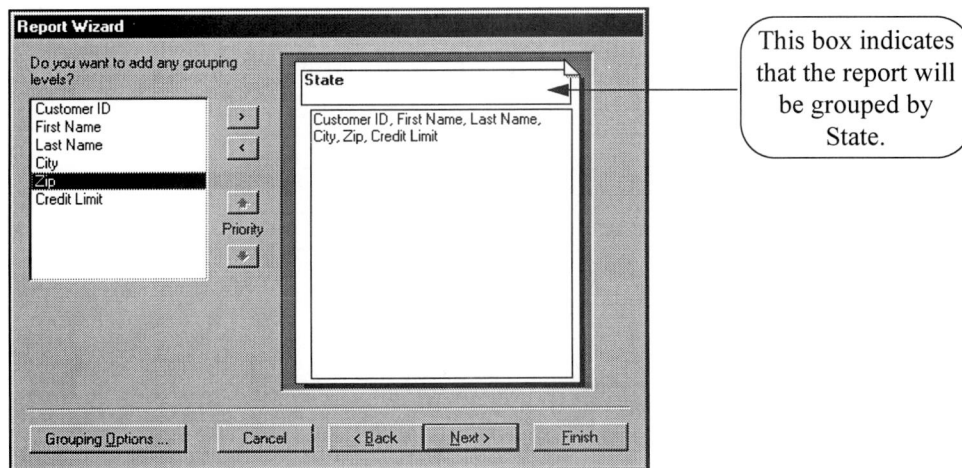

This box indicates that the report will be grouped by State.

Figure 6 - 25

11. Click the **Next** > button.

    The report needs to be sorted in name order. We will sort by Last Name. Then, should any two or more customers have the same last name, we will sort secondarily by their First Name.

12. Click on the drop-down list arrow and pick **Last Name** in the list. Ascending (A-Z) order is correct, so do not click the **AZ** sort order button (see Figure 6 - 26).

13. Similarly, click the drop-down arrow for the second list and pick **First Name**. Leave A-Z as the desired sort order by *not* clicking the **AZ** sort order button (see Figure 6 - 26).

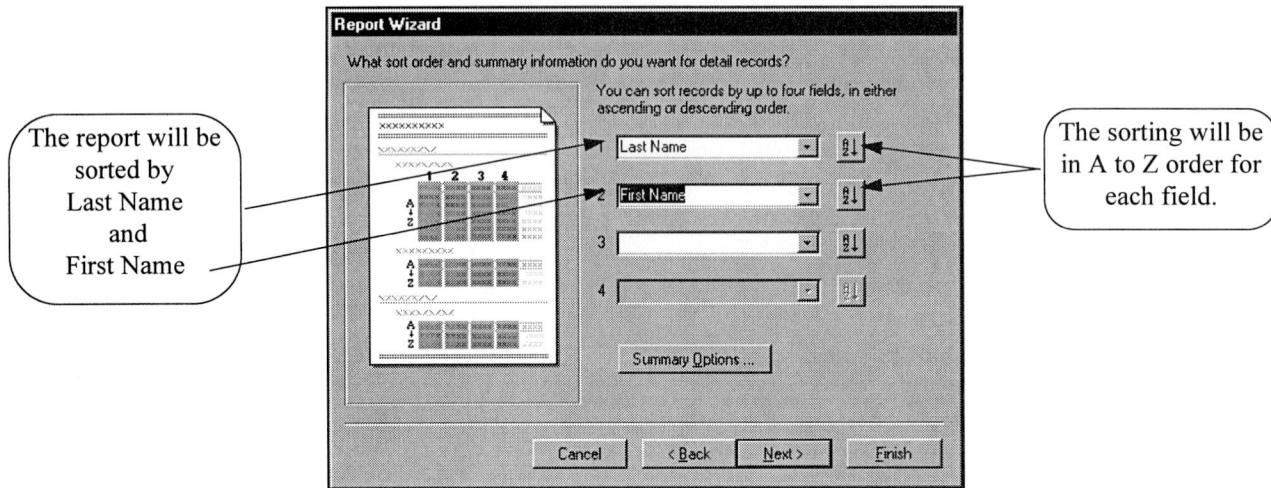

Figure 6 - 26

14. We would like sums for the Credit Limits, so click the **Summary Options** button.

15. Click the **Sum** check box on the **Credit Limit** line (see Figure 6 - 27). Make certain **Detail and Summary** is selected in the **Show** box, and do not check **Calculate percent....** Click the **OK** button.

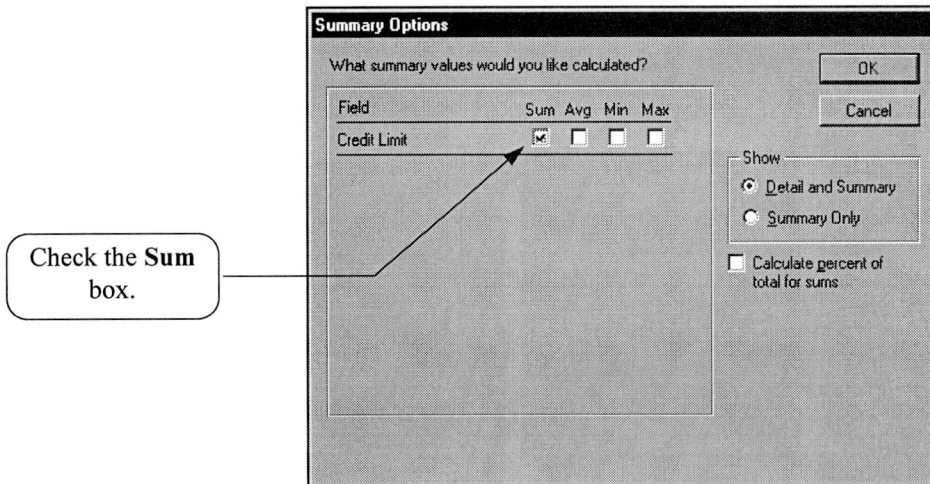

Figure 6 - 27

*The Detail will be the listings of customer records that we want on the report. The option for **Summary Only** would show the sums, but no individual customer listings.*

16. Click the **Next >** button.

17. Pick **Stepped** for the Layout and **Landscape** for the Orientation. Since you almost always want all fields on a single page, not two or more side by side pages, leave the check on **Adjust the field width so all fields fit on a page** (see Figure 6 - 28). Click **Next>**.

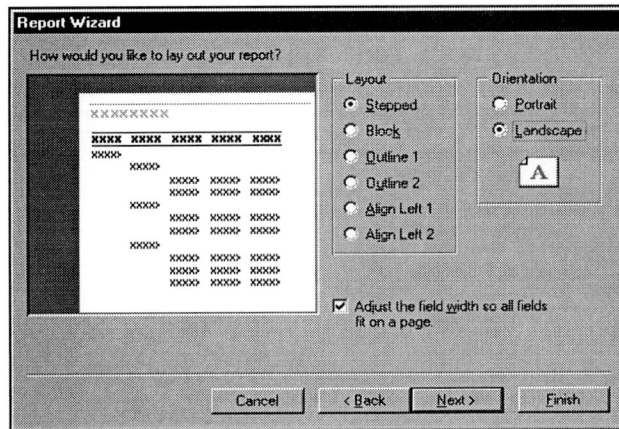

Figure 6 - 28

18. For style we will use **Formal**. Click on **Formal** and click the **Next>** button (see Figure 6 - 29).

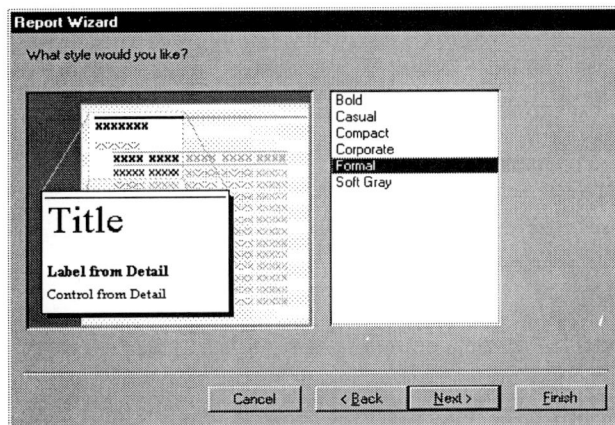

Figure 6 - 29

19. For the title enter: **Customers by State**

20. We want to **Preview the report** and do not want the Display Help option (see Figure 6 - 30). Click the **Finish** button.

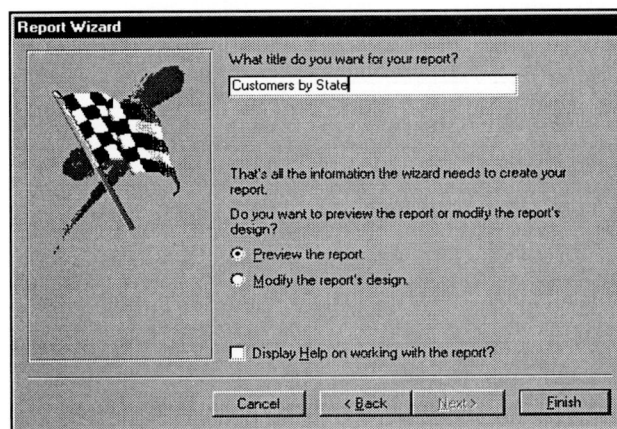

Figure 6 - 30

When complete, the Wizard displays the Print Preview screen so you can see the result (see Figure 6 - 31).

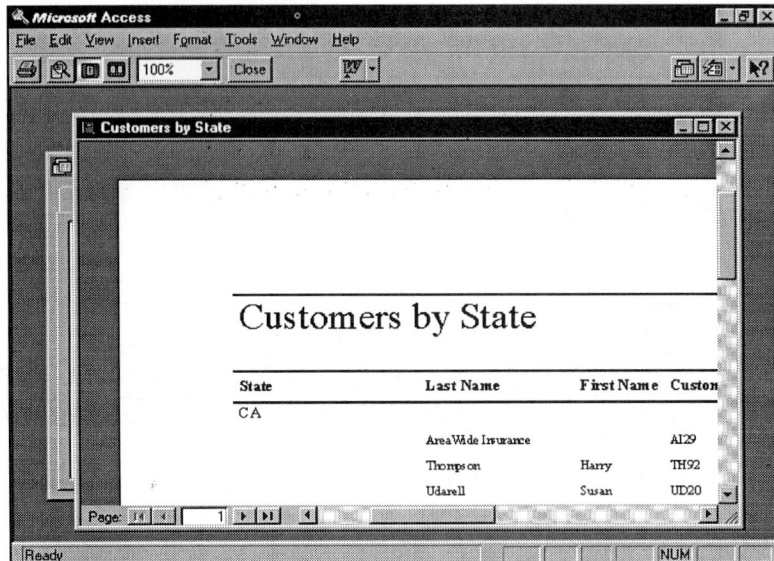

Figure 6 - 31

21. **Maximize** the **Preview** window.

    Notice the groups for each state with the customer names in alphabetical order within each group (see Figure 6 - 31). CA, the first state in the report, is one line above the actual listings. CA is the group header.

22. If the overall page is not showing, click the **Zoom** button on the toolbar or click anywhere on the white page.

23. Click the magnifying glass mouse pointer on the top right corner of the report page to zoom into the right side of the report.

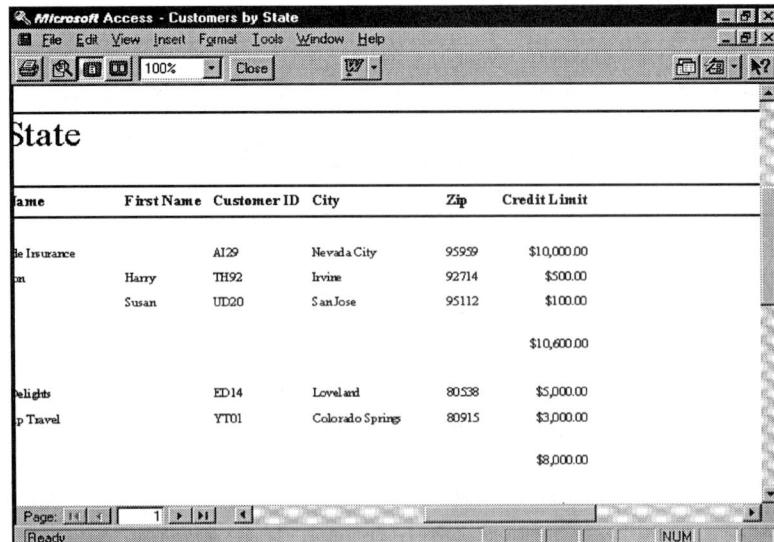

Figure 6 - 32

Notice the subtotals for Credit Limit (see Figure 6 - 32). The sub-totals are the footers for the groups.

24. Click the **Close** button on the toolbar.

*The report design screen appears (see Figure 6 - 33). Notice the **State Header** and **State Footer,** which are the group header and group footer sections.*

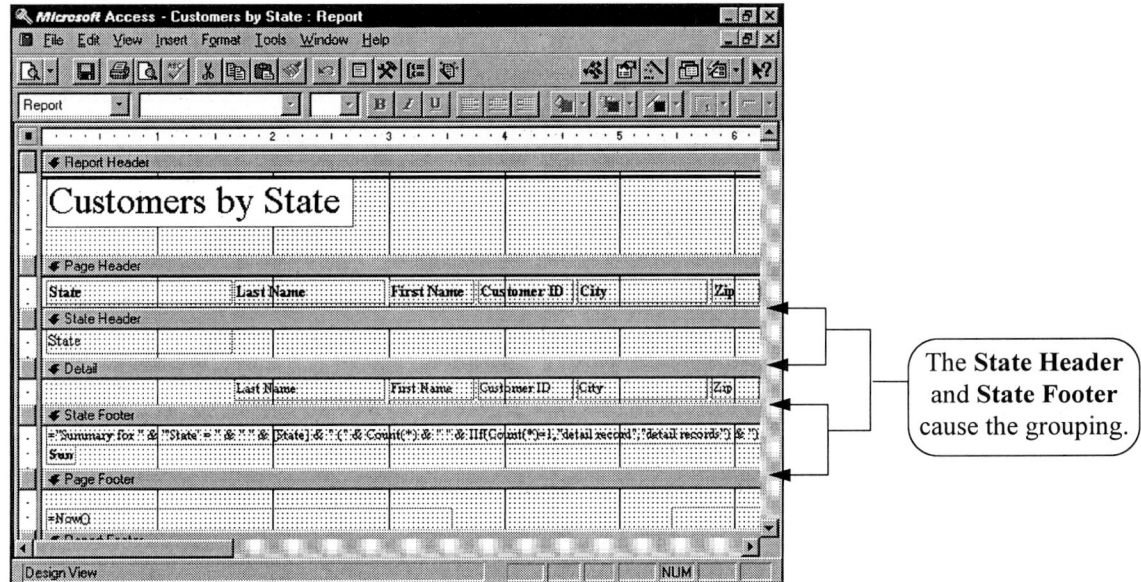

Figure 6 - 33

CHANGING THE FORMATTING OF CONTROLS

Any changes to the appearance of an item on the report is called *formatting*. The formatting of several items on our report that is grouped by state should be changed to improve its appearance and make it more readable.

While alterations to the font, size, bold, italics, underline, alignment, color, or border style can be made with the toolbar buttons, additional changes must be made in the *Properties List*. The Properties List is the complete collection of settings for a control.

To change the formatting of controls on a report design:

- Select the desired control by clicking on it.

- Click the toolbar buttons for font, size, bold, italics, underline, alignment, color, or border style.

- For additional formatting, open the Properties List by clicking the **Properties** button ![icon] on the toolbar or with **VIEW/Properties** and change its settings.

Activity 6.5: Formatting the Report Design

We will increase the size of the state names and make them bold so they stand out better. Also, the title might look better centered on the page. The line that says "Summary for 'State' = CA (3 detail records)" could be eliminated to simplify the design. Finally, the label "Sum" should be at the right side of the report near the subtotals, not at the left, so we will move it.

1. Click on the **State** control in the **State Header** (see Figure 6 - 34). This is not the State control in the Page Header; that control represents the label at the top of the column.

   Handles will appear on each corner and side.

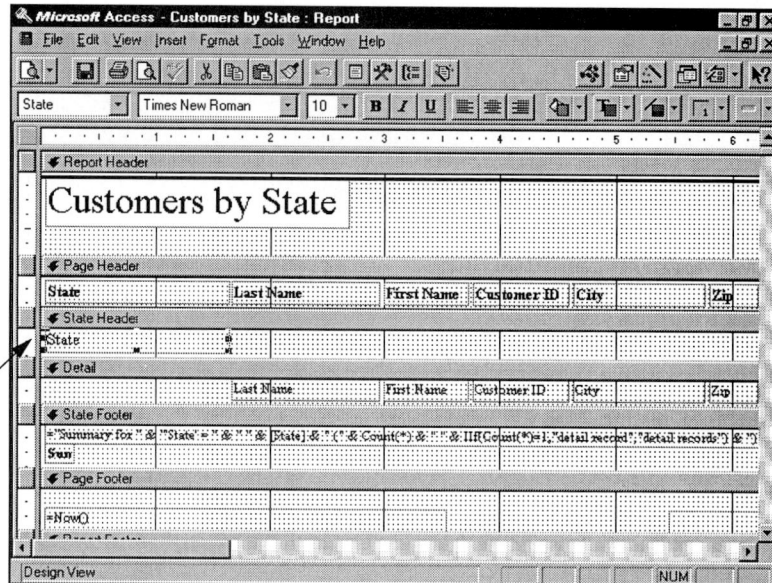

Click on the **State** control to select it so you can change its formatting.

Figure 6 - 34

2. Open the list of font sizes and click on **14**.

3. Click on the **Bold** button on the toolbar.

4. Scroll over to the right edge of the report design and notice that it reaches 9 inches on the ruler at the top of the design.

   In landscape orientation the paper is 11 inches wide. The Report Wizard allows 1 inch for each of the left and right page margins. 11 minus the 2 inches for the margins leaves 9 inches of design width.

5. Scroll back to the left edge of the design.

6. Click on the main title **Customers by State** to select that control.

7. Click the **Properties** button on the toolbar to open the Properties List for the title. Alternatively, pick **VIEW/Properties**.

8. Click on the **Width** line on the **Format** page and replace the old value with **8.5** (Figure 6 - 35).

   You do not need to type the inch mark. 8.5 inches was chosen because the title starts a little to the right of the left edge of the design (as do all of the other controls at the left side of the design). Making it the full 9 inches wide would have pushed it over the right margin, causing a second side-by-side page.

9. Close the Properties List with **VIEW/Properties** or the toolbar button.

10. Click the **Center** button on the toolbar to center the title on the page.

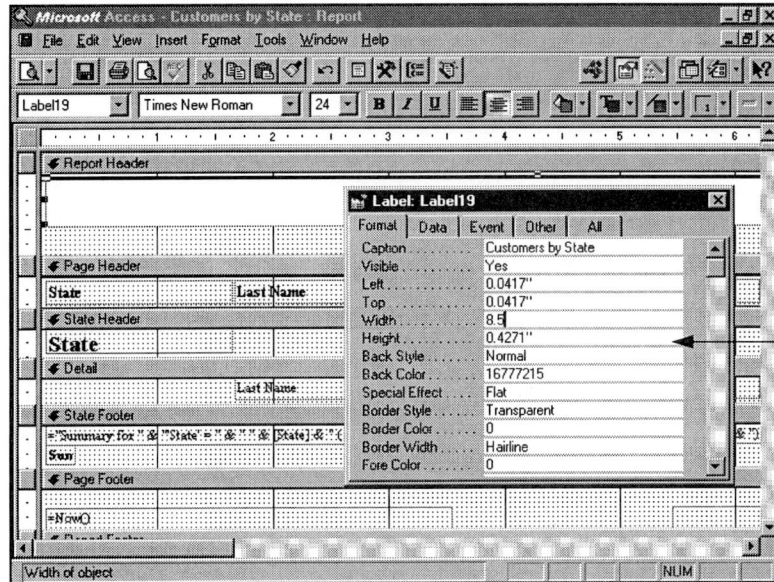

Figure 6 - 35

The title will be repositioned in the center of the page (see Figure 6 - 36).

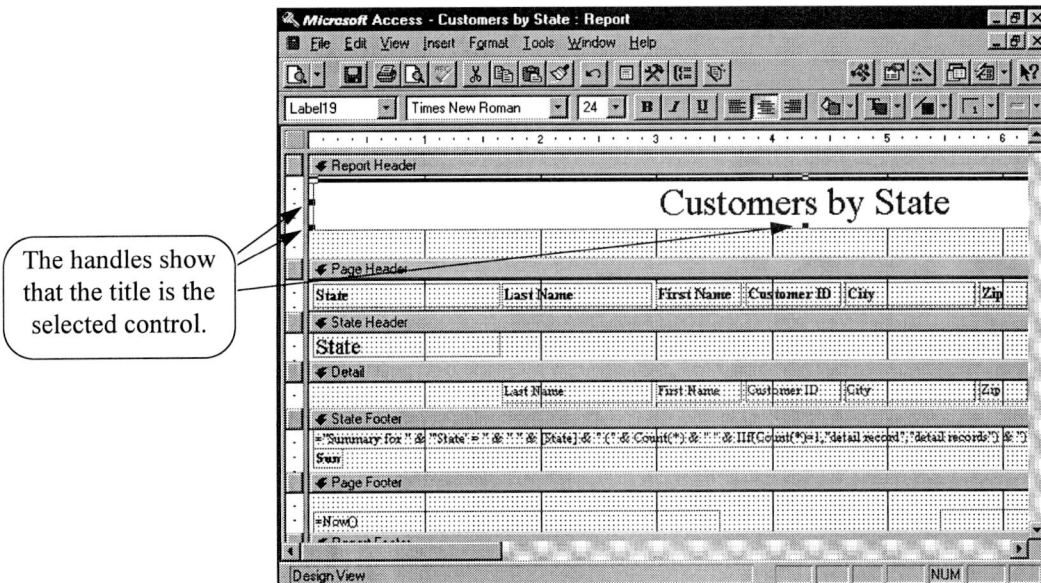

Figure 6 - 36

11. In the **State Footer**, click on the control that begins =**"Summary for "** & **"'State' = " & " "** & **[State]** to select it (Figure 6 - 37). Press the **DELETE** key to remove it from the design.

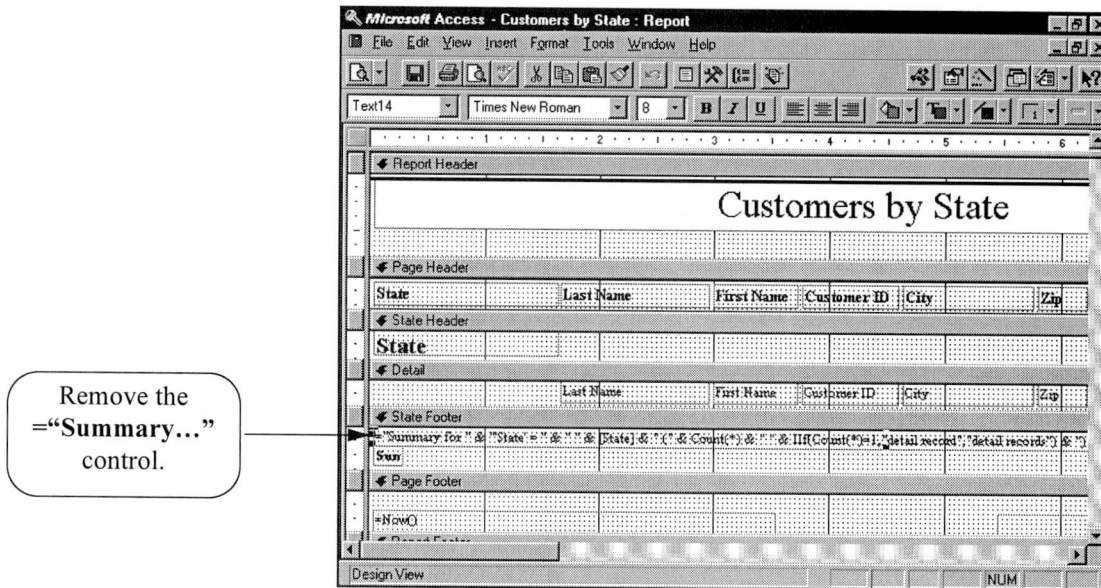

Remove the
="**Summary...**"
control.

Figure 6 - 37

12. Scroll so you can see the right edge of the design and notice that the control for **=Sum([Credit Limit])** begins at about 6 inches on the top ruler. Scroll back to the left edge of the design.

13. Click on the label **Sum** in the **State Footer** to select that control.

14. Open the Properties List with **VIEW/Properties** or the toolbar button.

15. Move to the line for **Left** on the **Format** tab and replace the old value with **5** to reposition the label at 5 inches across (see Figure 6 - 38).

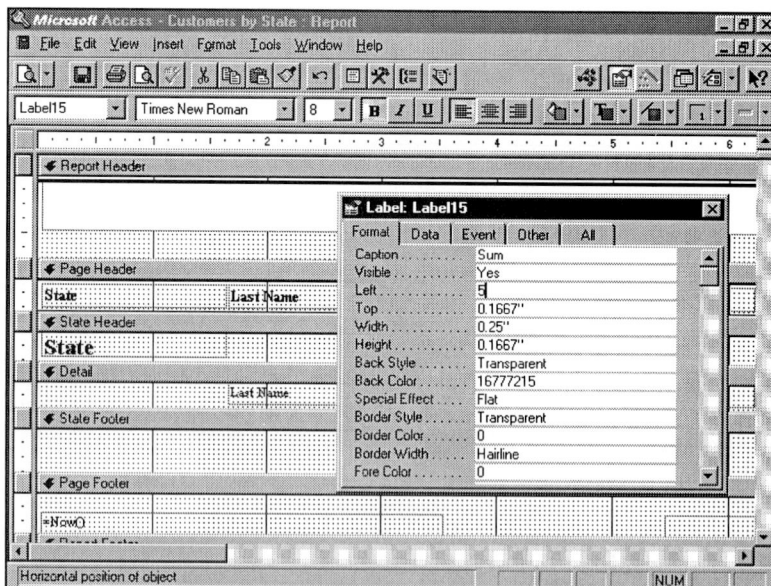

Figure 6 - 38

You could also drag the label to the same location with the mouse. The advantage of using the Properties List is that the vertical position will not change. With dragging, the mouse usually moves up or down the design while you are trying to move only to the right.

16. Click the **Properties** button on the toolbar to close the Properties List.

17. Scroll over to the right side of the design and click on the **=Sum([Credit Limit])** to select it.

18. Click the **Bold** button on the toolbar so the value matches the label, which is already bold.

19. Click the **Report View** button on the toolbar to view the changes.

The title should be centered, the state name should be larger and bold, the very long label is gone, and the Sum label should be at the right side next to the calculated sum, which is now bold (see Figure 3 - 39). You may need to scroll around to see each change.

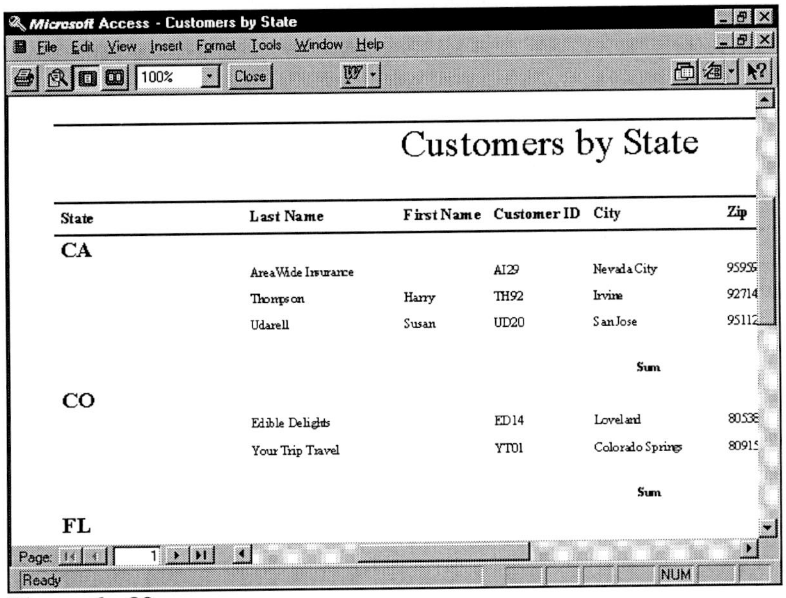

Figure 6 - 39

20. Save the changed design with **FILE/Save**.

21. Print the report by clicking the **Print** button.

22. Close the design with **FILE/Close**.

DESIGNING MAILING LABELS

A mailing label design is another common type of report. The *Label Wizard* can design labels for you.

To design a mailing label report with the Label Wizard:

- Click the **Reports** tab at the top of the **Database** window.

- Click the **New** button at the right edge of the **Database** window.

- From the drop-down list in the **New Report** dialog box, pick the desired table or query on which to report.

- Pick **Label Wizard** in the list in the **New Report** dialog box and click the **OK** button.

- Choose sheet or continuous labels, then the Avery label dimensions and number of labels across.

- Set the font, size, weight, and color.

- Choose the contents for each line of the label design by clicking the field name and sending it to the **Prototype label** box and typing any desired punctuation.

- Pick any fields by which to sort the labels.

- Type the name by which the design will be saved and choose to either see the labels as they will print, or to move directly to the design window.

Activity 6.6: Mailing Labels

A mailing will be sent to all customers, so we need a set of mailing labels. These will be regular mailing labels with First and Last Name on the top line, Street on the second line, and City-State - Zip on the third line. They should be sorted into zip code order, then by name within each zip code.

1. Click the **Reports** tab at the top of the **Database** window.

2. Click the **New** button at the right edge of the **Database** window.

3. Click on **Customers** in the drop-down list of tables and queries in the **New Report** dialog box, then click on **Label Wizard** in the open list. Click the **OK** button.

    *There are several different varieties of labels listed in the **What label size do you want?** dialog box (Figure 6 - 40). If you will be printing to a laser printer or on plain paper rather than gummed labels, click on **Sheet feed** in the **Label Type** box and pick **Avery number 5160**. If you will be printing to strips of labels in a dot matrix printer, click on **Continuous** for **Label Type** and pick **4145** as the Avery number. If you are not sure, ask your instructor which to select.*

4. Click on **Sheet feed** in the **Label Type** box and pick **Avery number 5160**. Unit of Measure should remain **English** (see Figure 6 - 40). Click the **Next>** button.

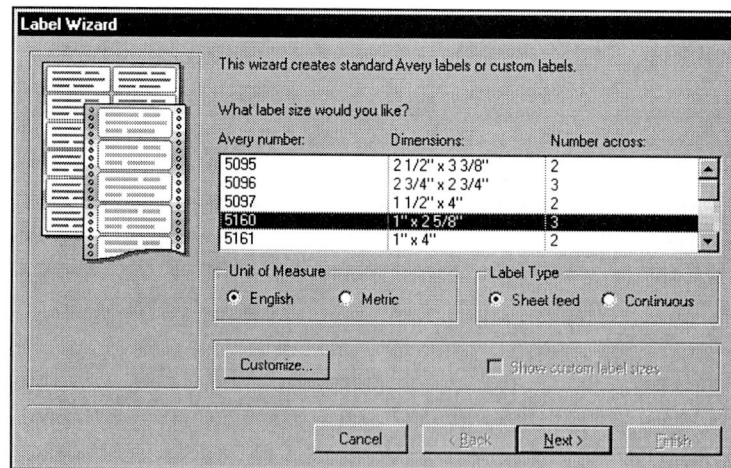

Figure 6 - 40

Avery 5160 is the standard size for three across and ten down labels on sheets that go in a laser printer.

5. Set the Font name: to **Arial**, the Font size: to **9**, the Font weight: to **Medium**, and the Text color: to **Black**. Do not check **Italic** or **Underline** (see Figure 6 - 41).

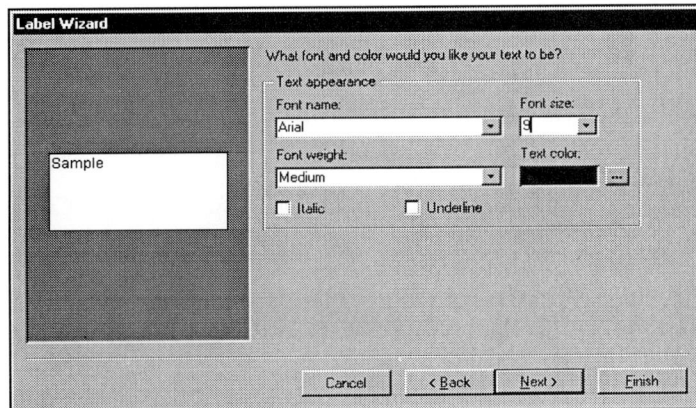

Figure 6 - 41

6. Click the **Next >** button.

7. To begin the first line of the label design, click on **First Name** in the **Available fields** list and click the arrowhead button to transfer it to the **Prototype label** box (see Figure 6 - 42).

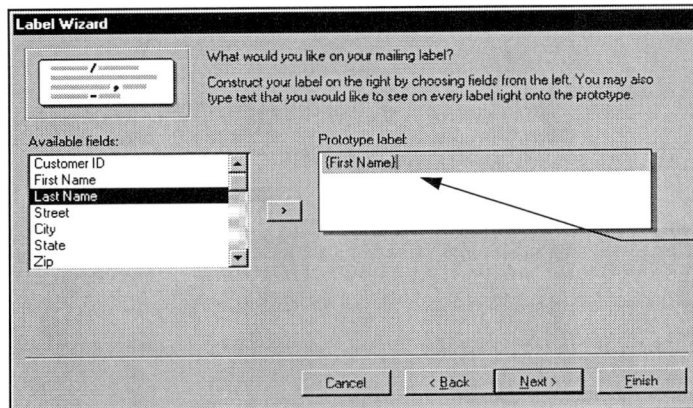

Begin the label design with the **First Name** field.

Figure 6 - 42

8. Press the **SPACEBAR** to place a space between the first and last names.

9. Click on **Last Name** and click the **arrowhead** button to transfer it to the Prototype label box (see Figure 6 - 43).

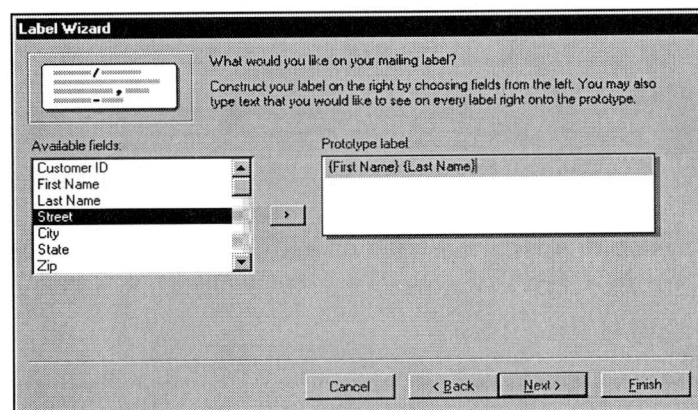

Figure 6 - 43

That completes the top line of the mailing label, so we're ready to begin the second line.

10. Press the **ENTER** key to begin the second line.

11. Click on **Street** and click the **arrowhead** button to transfer it to the Prototype label box.

    ***Street** is the only field on the second line.*

    *If you mistakenly include the wrong field, just press the **BACKSPACE** key. If you have a mistake on an earlier line in the label design, click the mouse at the right end of the mistaken component and press the **BACKSPACE** key. Then click on the correct item in the **Available fields** list and click the arrowhead button to include it at the position of the cursor. Click the mouse or press arrow keys to return to your working position in the **Prototype label**.*

12. Press the **ENTER** key to begin the third line.

13. Click on **City** and click the **arrowhead** button.

14. Type a **comma** for the comma to separate city from state.

15. Press the **SPACEBAR**.

16. Click on **State** and click the **arrowhead** button.

17. Press the **SPACEBAR** twice to separate State from Zip with two spaces.

18. Click on **Zip** and click the **arrowhead** button (see Figure 6 - 44).

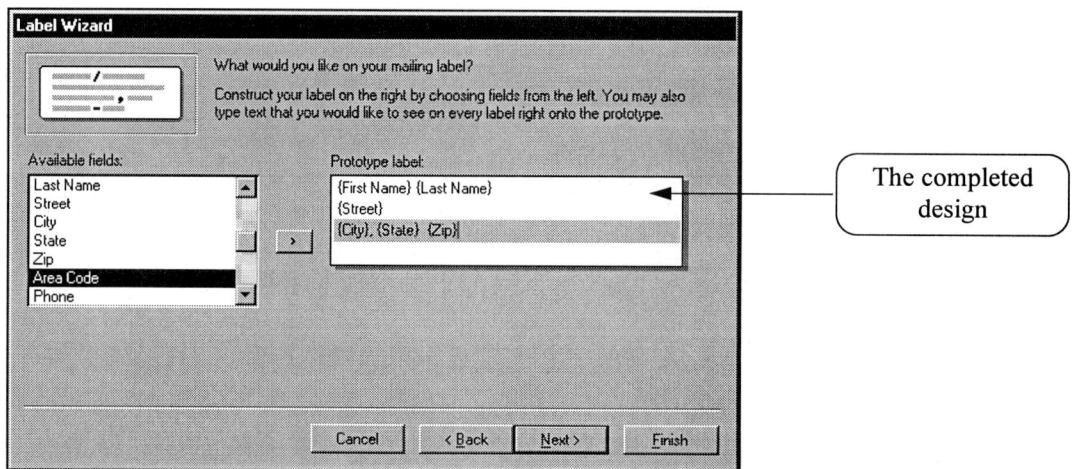

Figure 6 - 44

19. Click the **Next >** button.

    *The Wizard asks for the fields by which to sort (see Figure 6 - 45). The Post Office prefers zip code order so we will sort by **Zip**. For people in the same zip code, we will select **Last Name** as the second most important field for sorting.*

20. Click on **Zip** in the Available fields list to highlight it and click the single arrowhead button that points to the right to transfer **Zip** to the **Sort by** column (see Figure 6 - 45).

21. Similarly, click on **Last Name** to highlight it and click the **single arrowhead** button to transfer it to the **Sort by** column (see Figure 6 - 45).

22. Click the **Next >** button.

23. Type the name **Customer Mailing Labels** in the **What name would you like for your report?** box (see Figure 6 - 46).

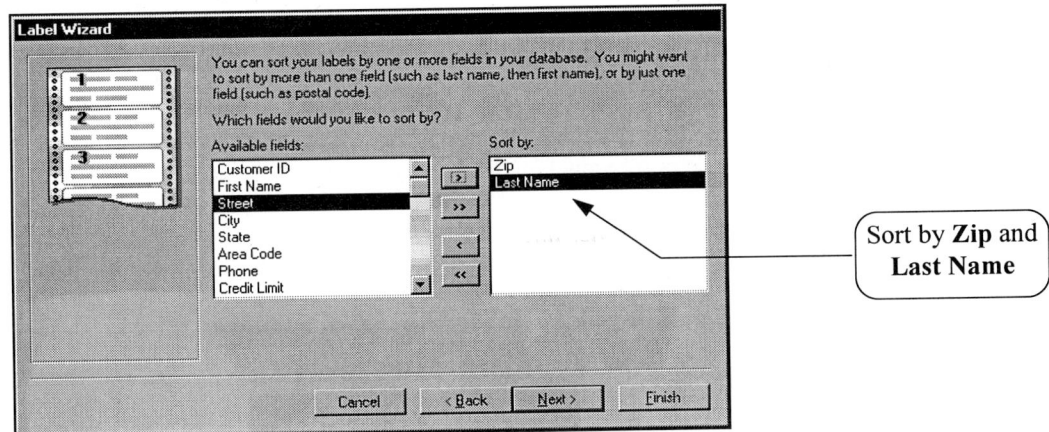

Figure 6 - 45

24. We want to **See the mailing labels as they will look printed**, so click that option and click the **Finish** button. Do not check the Display Help... check box (see Figure 6 - 46).

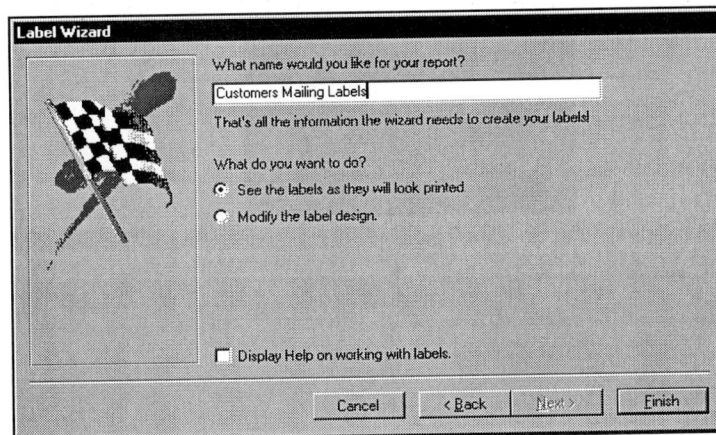

Figure 6 - 46

*The Wizard puts the design together and displays the **Print Preview** screen (see Figure 6 - 47).*

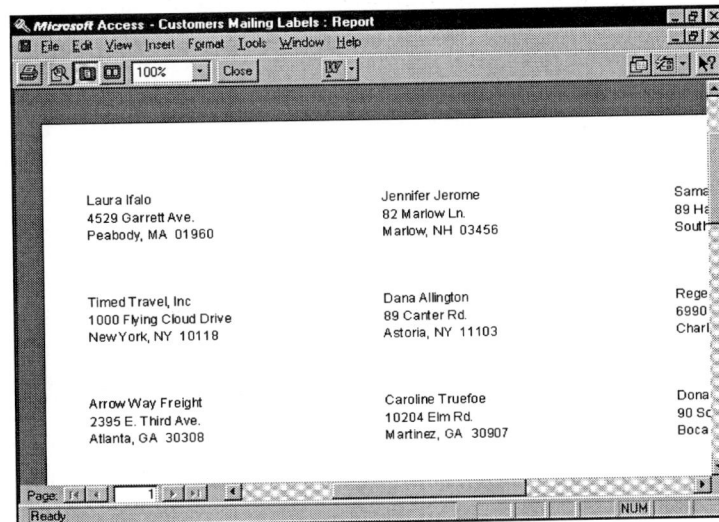

Figure 6 - 47

25. **Maximize** the **Preview** window.

   Notice that the labels are three across and in zip code order (see Figure 6 - 47).

26. Click anywhere on the white page to see the overall page (see Figure 6 - 48).

27. Print the report by clicking the **Print** button.

28. Close the design with **FILE/Close**.

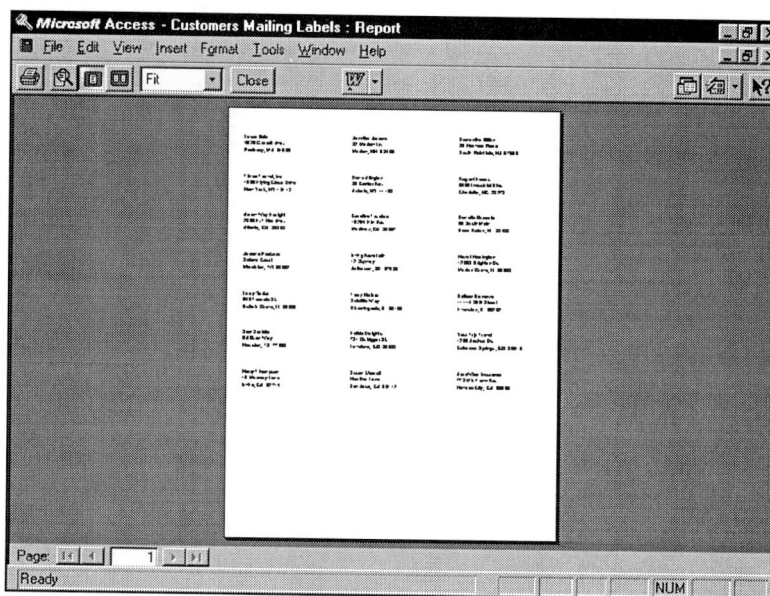

Figure 6 - 48

SUMMARY

In this Project, we have produced three different types of reports based on the data in the **Customers** table. The tabular report contained listings from a query that selected only customers with an outstanding balance. We customized the design by moving the date and deleting one of the ruling lines. The second design included grouping the customers by state. We changed the formatting on some of its controls. The third design was for mailing labels, which were sorted by zip code and last name.

In the final lesson we will see how to calculate with queries and how to alter the data in a table with the Action Queries.

KEY TERMS

Control	Grouped	Label Wizard
Detail Section	Report	Properties List
Footer	Handle	Report Wizard
Formatting	Header	Tabular Report

INDEPENDENT PROJECTS

Independent Project 6.1: The School Newspaper

This Independent Project continues working with the Newspaper Ad database from Independent Project 5.1. The newspaper's business manager requires a report of the sales of ads grouped by the salespersons. The name of the salesperson, **Ad Number**, **Price**, and **Purchased By** fields are needed. Since the data reside in two separate tables, you will need to prepare a query to join the data from Sales Force and Ads first.

The top portion of the finished report should resemble Figure 6 - 49.

Advertisement Sales

Last Name	Ad Number	Price	Purchased By	Issue Date
Fitzhugh				
	2391	$15.00	Harry Hertz	5/20/95
	2394	$15.00	Dean's Office	5/20/95
	2395	$25.00	Lou's LaundroMat	5/20/95
	Sum	$55.00		
	Percent	12.22%		
Kaples				
	2387	$85.00	College Books	5/20/95
	2389	$85.00	Pizza Plus	5/20/95
	2393	$25.00	Sports Booster Club	5/20/95
	2396	$45.00	Student Grill	5/20/95

Figure 6 - 49

1. Run *Access*.

2. Open the **Exercise1** database in the Introductory dialog box, with **FILE/Open Database**, or by clicking the **Open Database** tool on the toolbar.

3. Click on the **Queries** tab at the top of the database window.

4. Click the **New** button to start a new query.

5. Pick **Design View** in the **New Query** dialog box and click **OK**.

6. Click on **Ads** in the list of tables and click the **Add** button.

7. Click on **Sales Force** in the list of tables and click the **Add** button. *Access* should link the two tables by the **Salesperson ID** field automatically.

8. Close the **Show Table** dialog box.

9. Double-click the **Last Name** field in the **Sales Force** table to add it to the QBE grid.

10. From **Ads**, double-click on **Ad Number**, **Price**, **Purchased By**, and **Issue Date**.

11. **Maximize** the Query window.

12. View the results by clicking the **Query View** button to verify the query design.

13. Save the query by choosing **FILE/Save**, entering the name **Sales**, and clicking the **OK** button.

14. Close the query with **FILE/Close**.

15. Begin creating the report by clicking on the **Reports** tab at the top of the database window.

16. Click the **New** button.

17. Open the list of tables and queries by clicking the drop-down arrow and choose **Sales**.

18. Click on **Report Wizard** and click the **OK** button.

19. In the first **Report Wizard** dialog box, click on the button with the double arrow head pointing to the right to include all fields from the query and click the **Next>** button.

20. In the **Do you want to add any grouping levels?** dialog box, click on the button with the single arrow head pointing to the right to group only by **Last Name**. Click **Next>**.

21. For **What sort order...?** pick **Ad Number** in the first drop-down list. A-Z is correct.

22. Click the **Summary Options** button.

23. Check the **Sum** box in the **Price** row. Also, check the **Calculate percent of total for sums** check box. Click the **OK** button.

24. Click **Next>**.

25. Choose **Stepped** for Layout and **Portrait** for Orientation and click the **Next>** button.

26. For **What style...** pick **Formal**. Click **Next>**.

27. Type the title **Advertisement Sales**.

28. You want to **Preview the report**, so click on that option and click the **Finish** button.

29. **Maximize** the preview window.

30. The label that says "**Summary for 'Last Name'= Fitzhugh (3 detail records)**" just clutters the report, so you should remove it. To begin, click the **Close** button to switch to the report design.

31. In the **Last Name Footer** section, click on the control that begins =**"Summary for " & "'Last Name'= "**.

32. Press the **DELETE** key to remove that control.

33. Click on the label **Percent** in the **Last Name Footer** to select it. Notice that the calculation for the percentage, =**Sum([Price])/([Price Grand Total Sum])**, starts at about 2.5 inches on the top ruler.

34. Open the Properties List with **VIEW/Properties** or the toolbar button.

35. Move to the **Left** line on the **Format** tab and change the value to **2** inches.

36. Close the Properties List with **VIEW/Properties** or the toolbar button.

37. Click on the label **Sum** in the **Last Name Footer** to select it.

38. Open the Properties List with **VIEW/Properties** or the toolbar button.

39. Move to the **Left** line on the **Format** tab and change the value to **2** inches.

40. Close the Properties List with **VIEW/Properties** or the toolbar button.

41. Click the **Report View** button to examine the new results (see Figure 6 - 49).

42. Save the design changes to the report by picking **FILE/Save**.

43. Print the report by clicking the **Print** button on the toolbar.

44. Close the report with **FILE/Close**.

45. Close the database with **FILE/Close**.

45. Close the database with **FILE/Close**.

46. If you need to exit from *Access*, do so properly.

Independent Project 6.2: The Bookstore

This Independent Project continues working with the Bookstore database from the earlier lessons. The owner has requested a report that lists the publisher, fax number, book titles, and cost for every book. Since the data reside in two separate tables, you will need to prepare a query to join the data from **Publishers** and **Books** first.

The top portion of the finished report should resemble Figure 6 - 50.

1. Run *Access*.

2. Open the **Exercise2** database in the Introductory dialog box or with **FILE/Open Database** or by clicking the **Open Database** tool on the toolbar.

3. Click on the **Queries** tab at the top of the Database window.

4. Click the **New** button to start a new query.

5. Pick **Design View** in the **New Query** dialog box.

Books by Publisher

Name	Title	Area Code	Fax	Cost
Atlantic Works				
	Music Composition	403	436-7440	$19.50
	Music Harmony	403	436-7440	$19.50
Books Plus				
	Even More Poems	205	430-7190	$12.60
	The Physics of Glass	205	430-7190	$4.75
Bulky Books				
	Chemical Compendium	408	559-0018	$34.50
College Editions				
	Economically Correct	719	260-4546	$19.95
	Modern Russian	719	260-4546	$17.00

Figure 6 - 50

6. Click on **Publishers** in the list of tables and click the **Add** button.

7. Click on **Books** in the list of tables and click the **Add** button. *Access* should link the two tables by the **Publisher Code** field automatically.

8. Close the **Show Table** dialog box.

9. Double-click the **Name** field in the **Publishers** table to add it to the QBE grid.

10. Similarly, double-click on **Area Code, Fax, Title,** and **Cost**.

11. **Maximize** the Query window.

12. View the results by clicking the **Query View** button to verify the query design.

13. Save the query by choosing **FILE/Save**, entering the name **Publishers and Books**, and clicking the **OK** button.

14. Close the query with **FILE/Close**.

15. Begin creating the report by clicking on the **Reports** tab at the top of the **Database** window.

16. Click the **New** button.

17. Open the list of tables and queries by clicking the drop-down arrow and choose **Publishers and Books**.

18. Click on **Report Wizard** and click the **OK** button.

19. In the first **Report Wizard** dialog box, click on the button with the double arrow head pointing to the right to include all fields from the query and click the **Next>** button.

20. In the **Do you want to add any grouping levels?** dialog box, click on the button with the single arrow head pointing to the right to group only by **Name**. Click **Next>**.

21. For **What sort order...?**, pick **Title** in the drop-down list. A-Z is correct. Click **Next>**.

22. Choose **Stepped** for Layout and **Portrait** for Orientation and click the **Next>** button.

23. For **What style...**, pick **Formal** and click **Next>**.

24. Type the title **Books by Publisher**.

25. You want to **Preview the report**, so click on that option and click the **Finish** button.

26. **Maximize** the Report window.

27. Click the **Close** button to switch to the Design screen.

28. Click on the **Name** control in the **Name Header** to select it.

29. Click the **Bold** button on the toolbar to make the name bold.

30. Click the **Report View** button to examine the new results (see Figure 6 - 50).

31. Save the report by picking **FILE/Save**.

32. Print the report by clicking the **Print** button.

33. Close the report with **FILE/Close**.

34. Close the database with **FILE/Close**.

35. If you need to exit from *Access*, do so properly.

Independent Project 6.3: The Real Estate Office

This Independent Project continues working with the Real Estate Office database from the earlier lessons. The owner has requested a report that lists the commercial properties grouped by agency. From the **Agencies** table you should include the Agency Name and Phone 1. From the **Commercial Listings** table include the **Agent**, **Address**, **City**, and **Price**. Since the data reside in two separate tables, you will need to prepare a query to join the data first.

The top portion of the finished report should resemble Figure 6 - 51.

1. Run *Access*.

2. Open the **Exercise3** database.

3. Begin a new query using Design View.

4. Add **Agencies** and then **Commercial Listings** to the top section of the query window.

5. Close the **Show Table** dialog box.

> **[!]** **NOTE**: *Access should have linked the two tables by **Agency Code** but, if not, click on the **Agency Code** field in **Agencies** and drag across to the matching field in **Commercial Listings** to link the two tables by hand.*

Agency Listings

Agency Name	Agent	Phone 1	Address	City	Price
George Winkle					
	Purcell	972-9538	3 Research Park	Stamford	$3,400,000.00
Priceless Properties					
	Green	359-1111	Maple Court	New Canaan	$125,000.00
	Ruth	359-1111	2 Research Park	Stamford	$3,400,000.00
Profitable Properties					
	Smith	748-3471	952 River Rd.	Stamford	$49,000.00
	Smith	748-3471	1 Lewis Way	Danbury	$125,000.00
Regal Real Estate					
	Funchall	359-0050	18 Frost Ave.	Greenwich	$52,000.00

Figure 6 - 51

6. Add **Agency Name** and **Phone 1** from **Agencies** to the QBE grid.

7. Similarly, add **Agent**, **Address**, **City**, and **Price** from **Commercial Listings** to the QBE grid.

8. **Maximize** the Query window.

9. View the results to verify the query design.

10. **Save** the query as **Agency Listings**.

11. **Close** the query.

12. Begin creating the report by clicking on the **Reports** tab and the **New** button.

13. Use the **Agency Listings** query as the basis of the report and use the **Report Wizard**.

14. Include all fields from the query without changing the order.

15. Group by **Agency Name**.

16. Sort by **Agent**. No Summary Options are needed.

17. Use a **Stepped** Layout and **Landscape** Orientation.

18. Pick **Formal** style.

19. Accept the default title **Agency Listings**. You want to **Preview the report**.

20. **Maximize** the Report window so you can examine the report better.

21. **Close** the Preview window to switch to the report design.

22. Make the **Agency Name** bold.

23. In the **Report Header** select the title, **Agency Listings**. Open the Properties List and change its width to **6** inches. Close the Properties List.

24. **Center** the title.

25. Examine the new results on the print preview screen (see Figure 6 - 51).

26. **Save** the report changes.

27. **Print** the report.

28. **Close** the report.

29. **Close** the database.

30. If you need to exit from *Access*, do so properly.

Independent Project 6.4: The Veterinarian

This Independent Project continues working with the Veterinarian database from the earlier lessons. She has requested a report that lists the pets grouped by owner. She hands you a sample of what the report should look like (see Figure 6 - 52). Since the data reside in two separate tables, you will need to prepare a query to join the data first. Create the query and save it, then create the report, save the report design, and print the report.

Owners and Pets

Pet Owners.Name	Area Code	Phone	Pets.Name	Type	Date of Last Visit
Albert Smith					
	203	359-4181	Runner	horse	4/1/96
	203	359-4181	Wild Thing	dog	2/21/96
	203	359-4181	Fifi	cat	3/1/96
	203	359-4181	Homer	dog	3/9/96
Dan Wilson					
	203	972-3571	Wilhelm	horse	3/2/96
	203	972-3571	Spot	dog	3/22/96
Mureen Utley					
	203	359-8152	Kuddles	cat	3/31/96
	203	359-8152	George	dog	4/11/96

Figure 6 - 52

7 Calculations and Action Queries

Objectives

In this lesson you will learn how to:

- Perform calculations in queries
- Calculate summary results with queries
- Query a query

- Group a summary result
- Perform an update query
- Carry out a delete query

PROJECT DESCRIPTION

Besides the capability of selecting matching records and sorting those results, queries can also perform calculations on the data in one or more tables. The calculated results can be anything from a simple arithmetic operation like **Sale Amount + Tax** or **Commission Rate * Total Sale** to more complicated calculations. Summary calculations are also possible like **Average Price** or **Sum of the Salaries**.

Yet another type of query, the *Action Query*, can alter the data in a table. One type of Action Query is the *Delete Query*. It can delete groups of records from a table. Another type is the *Update Query,* which can replace or update the entries in many or all records.

In the first part of this lesson we will calculate several sets of results from the CDROM table. The simple calculations will first produce a list of inventory values (see Figure 7 - 3), and then a price list for a 25% off sale (see Figure 7 - 7). In the second part we will calculate summary results, including the average price of a CDROM and the total inventory value. The third part of this lesson will use grouping within a summary calculation, where we will calculate the minimum and maximum price for each type of CDROM (see Figure 7 - 15). In the last part we will use action queries to change the data in the **CDROM** table. We will lower all prices by 7%, and then delete the out-of-date CDROMs.

CALCULATIONS IN QUERIES

To perform calculations with queries, set up the query with the required table in the top of the **Query** window and the desired fields in the QBE grid. Then, create a new field in the QBE grid by typing on the **Field** line the name you want it to have in the resulting dynaset followed by a colon and the desired calculation. The value in a field can be included in a calculation by enclosing the field name between square brackets. For example, the values in the **Price** field would be included in a calculation as **[Price]**.

Suppose you needed to calculate a 10% commission based on the amount in a field named **Sale Amount**, and wanted to name the result **Commission**. You would enter on the **Field** line in a new column of the QBE grid: **Commission:[Sale Amount]*0.10**. To create a calculation for Total Cost where the field containing the amount of the sale is named **Sale Amount** and the field holding the shipping expense is named Shipping, type on the **Field** line of the QBE grid: **Total Cost:[Sale Amount]+[Shipping]**.

To set up a Calculation Query:

- Click the **Queries** tab at the top of the **Database** window.

- Click the **New** button at the right edge of the **Database** window.

- Choose **Design View** in the list of the **New Query** dialog box and click **OK**.

- Add the desired table (or tables) from the **Show Table** dialog box.

- Select any fields you will need to see in addition to the calculated result.

- Create the calculation in a new column in the QBE grid.

- View the resulting dynaset.

Activity 7.1: A Calculation Query for Inventory Value

Your manager asks you to calculate the inventory value of the CDROMs currently in stock. Since inventory value is calculated as **Cost*Quantity in Stock**, we need to create a calculated field with that formula in a query. After we have the calculated values, we will sort the list from largest inventory value to smallest.

1. The **Sales** database should be opened.

2. Click on the **Queries** tab.

3. Click the **New** button at the right edge of the **Database** window.

4. In the **New Query** dialog box, click on **Design View** and the **OK** button.

5. Since we are interested in the **CDROM** table, pick **CDROM** in the list of tables and click the **Add** button.

6. **CDROM** is the only table we need to calculate Inventory Value, so click the **Close** button to close the **Show Table** dialog box.

7. Double-click on the **Title** field in the list of fields to include it as the first field in the QBE grid.

8. Press **TAB** to jump to the second column.

9. Type: **Inventory Value:[Cost]*[Quantity in Stock]** to create the calculation (Figure 7 - 1).

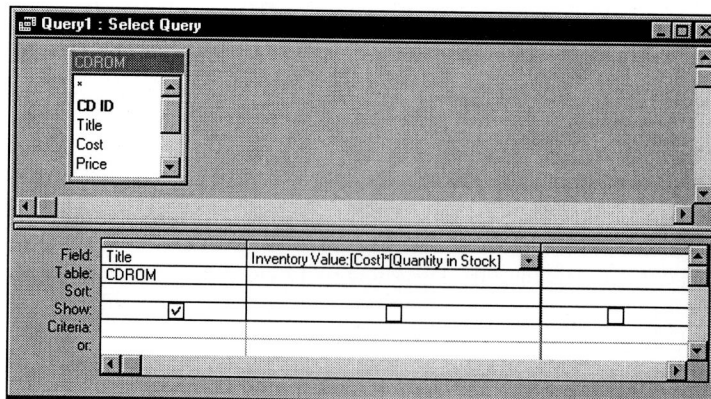

Figure 7 - 1

*Although the **Show** box is not currently checked, Access will check it for you automatically.*

10. So you can see the entire entry, move the mouse pointer on top of the right edge of the selector bar and drag it further to the right to widen the calculated column in the QBE grid.

11. Click the **Query View** button on the toolbar to see the resulting dynaset (Figure 7 - 2).

Title	Inventory Value
Consumers, Consumers	$3,043.00
Clip Art 200,000	$18,850.00
Every Household Listed	$10,382.00
Encyclopedia Galactica	$3,588.00
Every Poem Printed	$3,560.00
Everything There Is to Know	$4,620.00
99,000 Fonts	$2,006.00
Fog Scenes	$779.22
Legal Assistant to the Rescue	$7,089.00
Programming in Every Language	$10,183.00
Perfect Paragraph 8.0	$34,344.00
Scourge - The Game	$3,649.00
Too Small to See	$58.00
Telephone Poles of the World	$435.00

Figure 7 - 2

Each product should be listed together with its calculated inventory value, but they are not in order of inventory value.

12. Return to the query design by clicking the **Query View** button on the toolbar.

13. Click the mouse on the **Sort** line of the **Inventory Value** column.

14. Click the drop-down arrow to open the list of sort operators and pick **Descending**.

15. Click the **Query View** button on the toolbar to see the resulting dynaset (see Figure 7 - 3).

Title	Inventory Value
Perfect Paragraph 8.0	$34,344.00
Clip Art 200,000	$18,850.00
Every Household Listed	$10,382.00
Programming in Every Language	$10,183.00
Legal Assistant to the Rescue	$7,089.00
Everything There Is to Know	$4,620.00
Scourge - The Game	$3,649.00
Encyclopedia Galactica	$3,588.00
Every Poem Printed	$3,560.00
Consumers, Consumers	$3,043.00
99,000 Fonts	$2,006.00
Fog Scenes	$779.22
Telephone Poles of the World	$435.00
Universal Language Translator	$191.96

Figure 7 - 3

The product with the largest inventory value should be on top.

16. Pick **FILE/Save**, enter the name: **Inventory Value**, and click **OK** to save this query.

17. Click the **Print** button on the toolbar to print the dynaset.

18. Click the **Query View** button to return to the query design.

Activity 7.2: Calculating Discounted Prices

The company decides to run a holiday 25% off sale. You need to calculate the new, reduced prices. If you take 25% off, that leaves 75% of the regular price. Thus, the calculation is **Price*0.75**.

Since CDROM is already in the **Query** window, we will merely modify the current query. This is a one-time sale, and so it does not need to be saved.

1. If the query design is not already open, click on **Inventory Value** in the **Queries** panel of the Database window and click the **Design** button.

2. Click anywhere within the **Inventory Value** column.

3. Pick **EDIT/Delete Column** to remove that column.

4. Double-click on **Price** in the list of fields to include it in the second column of the QBE grid.

5. On the **Field** line of the empty third column type: **Discounted Price:[Price]*0.75** to create the calculation.

6. Widen the field so you can see the entire entry as in Figure 7 - 4.

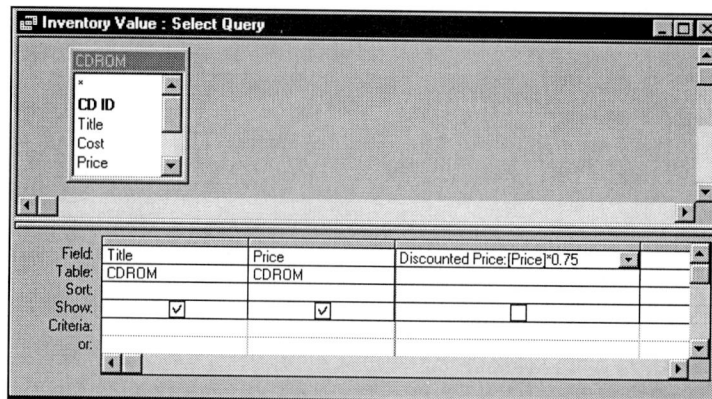

Figure 7 - 4

7. Click the **Query View** button on the toolbar to see the resulting dynaset (see Figure 7 - 5).

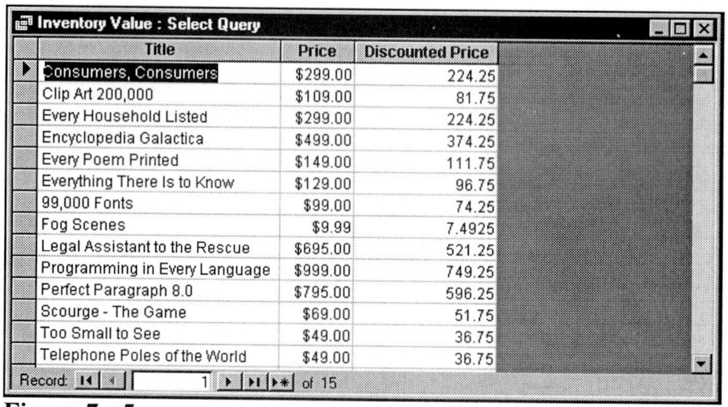

Figure 7 - 5

Each product will be listed together with its regular price and the discounted price, but the calculated results are not formatted to look like prices.

8. Return to the query design by clicking the **Query View** button on the toolbar.

9. With the cursor anywhere in the **Discounted Price** column, click the **Properties** button on the toolbar or pick **VIEW/Properties** (see Figure 7 - 6).

The Properties List for this field in the query opens. Although our previous exposure to Properties was on a report or form design, almost everything in Access has a Properties List that controls its details and options.

10. On the **General** tab, click on the **Format** line, click the drop-down arrow to open the list of formats, and pick **Currency**.

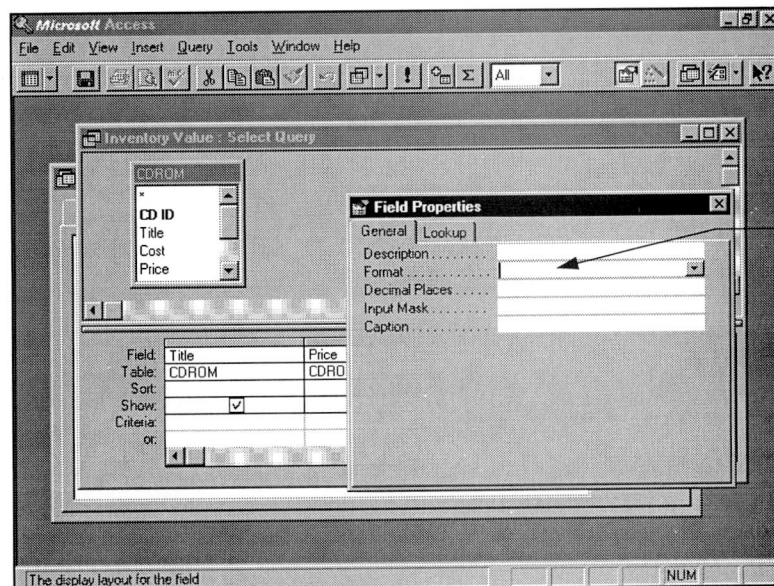

Click on the **Format** line and the drop-down arrow to choose a format.

Figure 7 - 6

11. Close the Properties List by clicking the **Properties** button again or with **VIEW/Properties**.

12. Click the **Query View** button on the toolbar to see the result (see Figure 7 - 7).

Figure 7 - 7

13. Click the **Print** button on the toolbar to print the dynaset.

14. Choose **FILE/Close** to close the query.

    As this is a one-time sale, we do not need to save this query.

15. Click the **No** button in answer to **Do you want to save changes...**.

SUMMARY CALCULATIONS IN QUERIES

Rather than producing a calculated result for each listing as in the previous section, a *summary calculation* produces an overall result. Examples would include the count of how many products are in the **CDROM** table, the average price of all products, or the total inventory value of the entire **CDROM** table.

To perform a Summary Calculation Query:

- Click the **Queries** tab at the top of the **Database** window.

- Click the **New** button at the right edge of the **Database** window.

- Choose **Design View** in the **New Query** dialog box and click the **OK** button.

- Add the desired table (or tables) from the **Show Table** dialog box.

- Select the field(s) you want summarized.

- Switch the query into a summary query by clicking the **Totals** button Σ on the toolbar or choosing **VIEW/Totals** in the menu. This will add a **Total** line to the QBE grid (see Figure 7 - 8), where you select the desired summary calculation.

- Open the drop-down list on the new **Total** line, and pick the summary operation.

- View the resulting dynaset.

Activity 7.3: A Summary Calculation Query for Average Price

We want to know the average price of a CDROM. We will not save this query.

1. The **Sales** database should be open.

2. Click on the **Queries** tab.

3. Click the **New** button at the right edge of the **Database** window.

4. In the **New Query** dialog box, click on **Design View** and click the **OK** button.

5. Since we are interested in the CDROM table, pick **CDROM** and click the **Add** button.

6. CDROM is the only table we need to calculate Average Price, so click the **Close** button to close the **Show Table** dialog box.

7. Double-click on the **Price** field in the list of fields to include it in the QBE grid.

8. Click the **Totals** button on the toolbar to include the **Total** line in the QBE grid (see Figure 7 - 8).

    *The **Group By** operator will appear on the **Totals** line. We will discuss its meaning in the section on Grouping two sections ahead.*

9. Click on the **Total** line in the **Price** column and click the drop-down arrow that appears in order to open the list of operations.

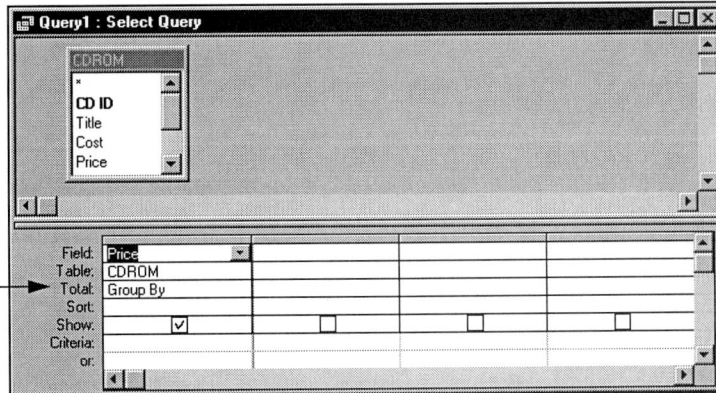

The **Total** line

Figure 7 - 8

10. Choose **Avg** by clicking on it (see Figure 7 - 9).

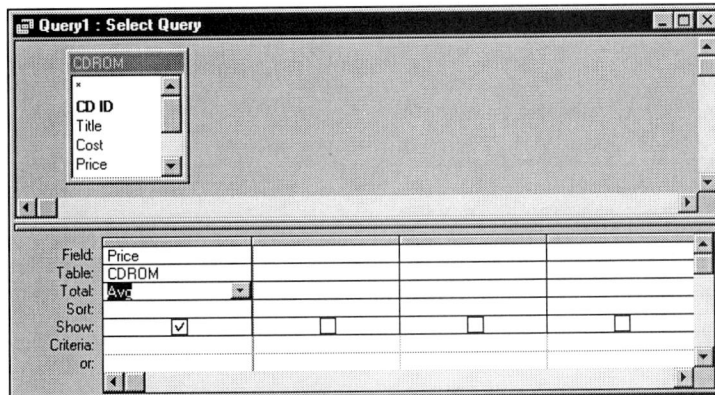

Figure 7 - 9

11. Click the **Query View** button on the toolbar to see the result.

    The answer for the average price should be $288.60.

12. Choose **FILE/Close** to close the query.

13. Click the **No** button in answer to **Do you want to save changes...**.

QUERYING A QUERY

Just as a table can be the basis for a query, so can another query. Instead of selecting a table name from the list in the **Show Table** dialog box, click on the **Queries** tab and select from the queries that are listed. In all other ways the operation is identical to a query based on a table.

To perform a Query based on a Query:

- Begin a new query.

- Click on the **Queries** tab (see Figure 7 - 10) at the top of the **Show Table** dialog box.

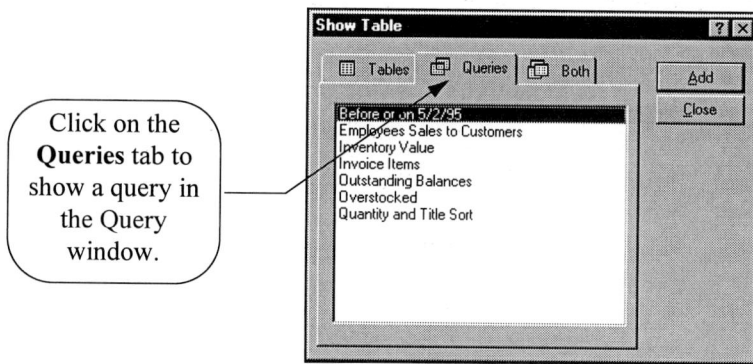

Click on the **Queries** tab to show a query in the Query window.

Figure 7 - 10

- Add the desired query and close the **Show Table** dialog box.
- Add any desired field(s) and set up any calculations.
- View the resulting dynaset.

Activity 7.4: A Summary Calculation for Total Inventory Value

From the Inventory Value query we did earlier, we want to know the total inventory value of all the products combined. We will save this query.

1. The **Sales** database should be open.
2. Click on the **Queries** tab.
3. Click the **New** button at the right edge of the **Database** window.
4. In the **New Query** dialog box, click on **Design View** and click the **OK** button.
5. Since we are interested in the results from the Inventory Value query we performed earlier, click the **Queries** tab at the top of the **Show Table** dialog box (see Figure 7 - 10).
6. Pick **Inventory Value** and click the **Add** button.
7. Close the **Show Table** dialog box.
8. Double-click on the **Inventory Value** field in the list of fields to include it in the QBE grid.
9. Click the **Totals** button on the toolbar to include the **Total** line in the QBE grid.

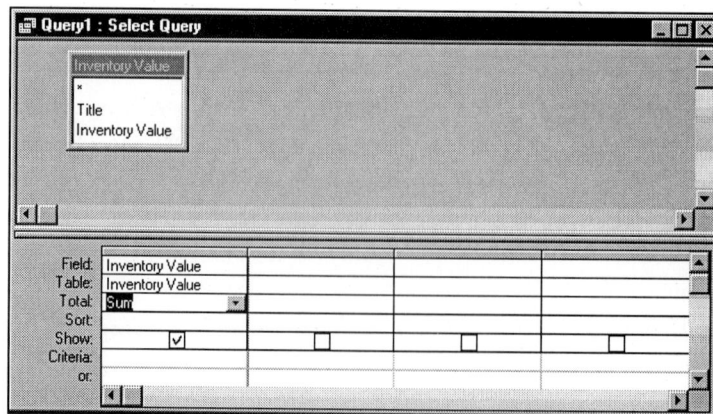

Figure 7 - 11

10. Click on the **Total** line in the **Inventory Value** column and click the drop-down arrow that appears in the column to open the list of operations.

11. Choose **Sum** (see Figure 7 - 11).

12. Click the **Query View** button on the toolbar to see the result.

    The total inventory value should be $102,778.18.

13. Save the query by picking **FILE/Save As/Export**, entering the name: **Total Inventory Value** in the **New Name** text box, and clicking the **OK** button.

14. Choose **FILE/Close** to close the query.

GROUPING IN CALCULATIONS

The **CDROM** table has classifications for the types of CDROMs in the **Notes** field. We need to know the maximum and minimum price for each category.

This last phrase, for each category, means we do not want the one maximum and minimum for all the items in the table; we want the CDROMs grouped by type and then the maximum and minimum within each grouping. The *Group By* operator that appears automatically when you switch a query to a Totals query does exactly that. It makes groups based on the values in each field that contains the Group By operator and summarizes the groups. Our grouping field will be **Notes**.

Since the **Group By** operator appears automatically on the **Totals** line, you must be careful not to include in the QBE grid any fields that contain different values within a single group. If you do, *Access* will group more finely than you intended. For example, if we included the titles for the CDROMs in the QBE grid, the maximum and minimum would be grouped by each different title instead of by the type. There is no way to remove the **Group By** operator; thus you may not include the title field if you want to group by the type.

To use the Group By operator in summary queries:

- Set up the query.

- Switch the query into a summary Query by clicking the **Totals** button on the toolbar or choose **VIEW/Totals** in the menu.

- In the field that is to be summarized, open the drop-down list on the **Total** line, and pick the summary operation.

- In all other fields leave the **Group By** operator.

- View the resulting dynaset.

Activity 7.5: Grouping in Summary Calculations

We need the maximum and minimum price for each type of CDROM. To calculate those results, we need to perform a summary calculation using the **Notes** and **Price** fields from the **CDROM** table. We will save this query.

1. The **Sales** database should be open.

2. Click on the **Queries** tab.

3. Click the **New** button at the right edge of the **Database** window.

4. In the **New Query** dialog box, click on **Design View** and click the **OK** button.

5. Pick **CDROM** and click the **Add** button.

6. Close the **Show Table** dialog box.

7. Scroll down to and double-click on the **Notes** field in the list of fields.

8. Double-click on the **Price** field.

9. Click the **Totals** button on the toolbar to include the **Total** line in the QBE grid.

10. Click on the **Total** line in the **Price** column and click the drop-down arrow that appears in order to open the list of operations.

11. Choose **Min** (see Figure 7 - 12).

12. Leave **Group By** in the **Notes** column (see Figure 7 - 12).

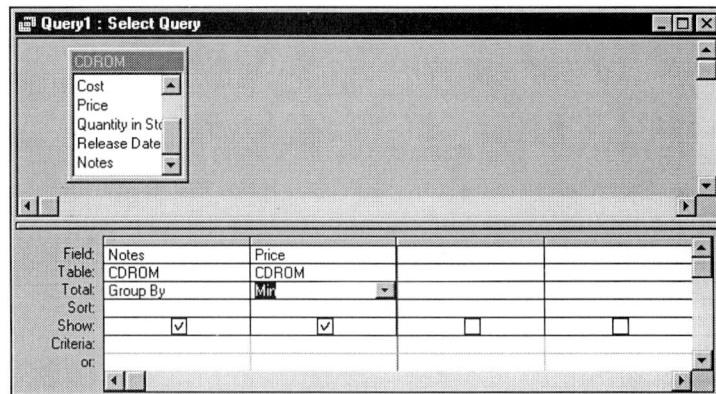

Figure 7 - 12

13. Click the **Query View** button on the toolbar to see the result (see Figure 7 - 13).

Notes	MinOfPrice
DOS	$149.00
MPC	$49.00
Windows	$49.00
Windows - B&W	$9.99

Record: 1 of 4

Figure 7 - 13

*Each type from the **Notes** field should have one line with a minimum price. But we also need the maximum price.*

14. Click the **Query View** button to return to the design.

15. Double-click on the **Price** field again to include a second copy of that field in the QBE grid (see Figure 7 - 14).

16. Click on the **Totals** line in this second **Price** column and click the drop-down arrow that appears in order to open the list of operations.

17. Choose **Max** (see Figure 7 - 14).

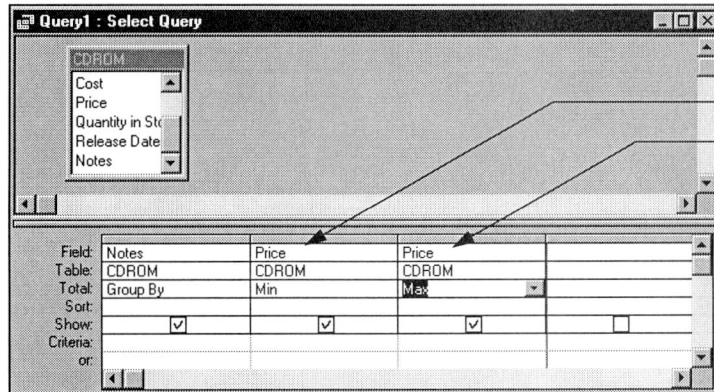

Include two copies of the **Price** field to perform two summary operations.

Figure 7 - 14

18. Click the **Query View** button on the toolbar to see the result (see Figure 7 - 15).

Figure 7 - 15

For each type of CDROM, both the minimum and the maximum price should be listed.

19. Save the query by picking **FILE/Save**, entering the name: **Min & Max Price by CDROM Type** in the **New Name** text box, and clicking the **OK** button.

20. Click the **Print** button on the toolbar.

21. Choose **FILE/Close** to close the query.

THE UPDATE QUERY

Just as we often need to edit the data in various records to keep it up to date, there are occasions when many or all of the records need the same change to one or more fields. For example, when an area code changes, dozens of customers may need their records updated. Perhaps the manager decides to lower all prices of CDROMs by 7%. Such mass changes would be tedious and prone to error if edited one record at a time. The solution is the Update Query.

An Update Query will alter the values in one or more fields in selected records or every record throughout an entire table in one operation. You set up a regular query, then convert it to an Update Query with the menu choice **QUERY/Update**. This adds a new line to the QBE grid named **Update To** and removes the **Sort** and **Show** lines (Figure 7 - 16). The **Update To** line is where you specify the new value or calculated value for the field.

To perform an Update Query:

- Open the **Select Query** window.

- Pick **QUERY/Update** in the menu.

- Add the field(s) that will be updated.

- Add the fields and enter any criteria to restrict which records will be updated.

- To perform the update, click the **Run** button ![Run button] on the toolbar or choose **QUERY/Run** in the menu.

Activity 7.6: An Update Query

Because of increased competition, we need to lower our prices. The decision is made to lower them 7%. Lowering prices by 7% leaves 93% of the original price. Thus, we will update the prices to 93% times the original price. We will save this query.

1. The **Sales** database should be open.

2. Click on the **Queries** tab.

3. Click the **New** button at the right edge of the **Database** window.

4. In the **New Query** dialog box, click on **Design View** and click the **OK** button.

5. Since we need to change prices in the **CDROM** table, pick **CDROM** and click the **Add** button.

6. Close the **Show Table** dialog box.

7. Double-click on the **Price** field in the list of fields to include it as the first field in the QBE grid.

8. Pick **QUERY/Update** to switch the query type (Figure 7 - 16).

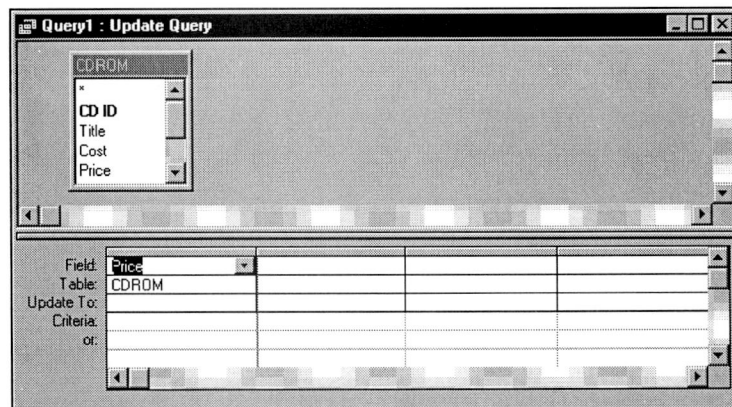

Figure 7 - 16

9. Click on the **Update To** line in the **Price** column and enter **[Price]*0.93** (see Figure 7 - 17).

   Since the original price was 100%, reducing the prices by 7% would leave 93%.

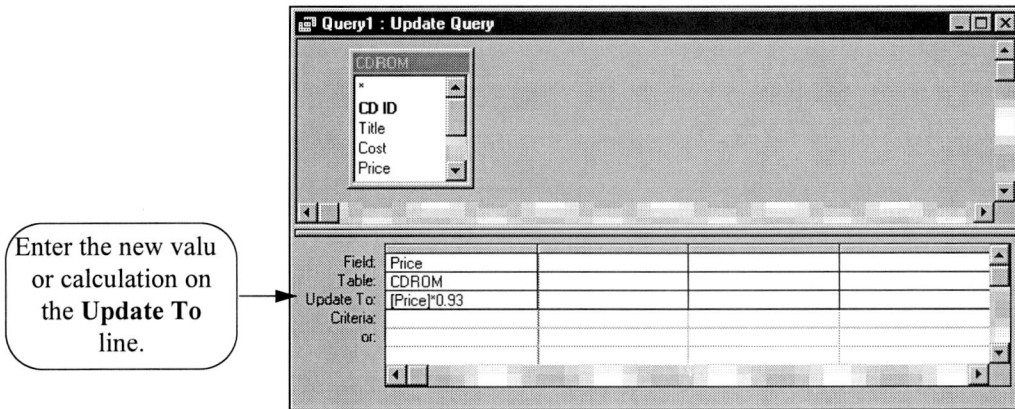

Enter the new value or calculation on the **Update To** line.

Figure 7 - 17

10. Before we make the changes, click the **Query View** button on the toolbar to see the original prices as shown in Figure 7 - 18.

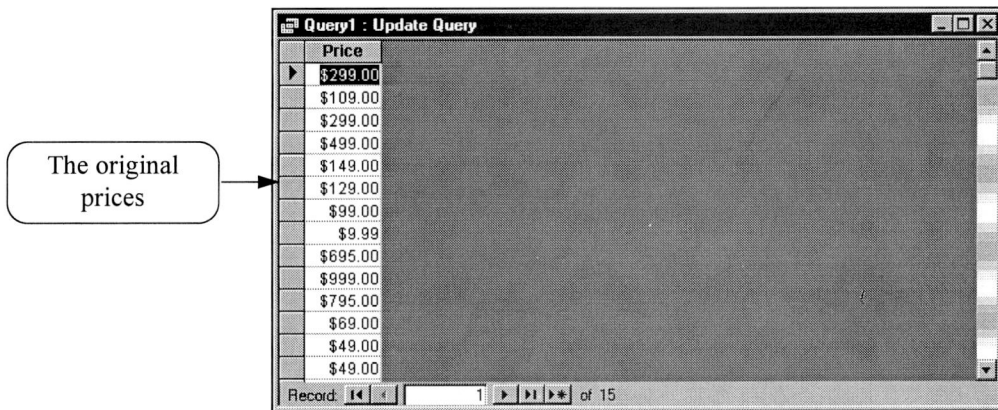

The original prices

Figure 7 - 18

11. Write down the first price.

12. Return to the design by clicking the **Query View** button on the toolbar.

13. Click the **Run** button on the toolbar to initiate the changes.

14. Click the **Yes** button in the **You are about to update 15 row(s).** alert box (Figure 7 - 19).

When you click the OK button, Access changes the data in the original table. Thus, you must be sure you mean to update the records.

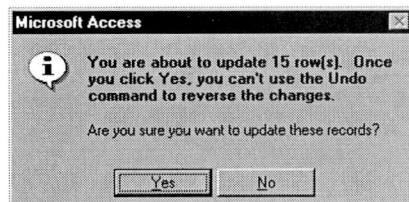

Figure 7 - 19

15. Click the **Query View** button on the toolbar to see the altered prices (Figure 7 - 20).

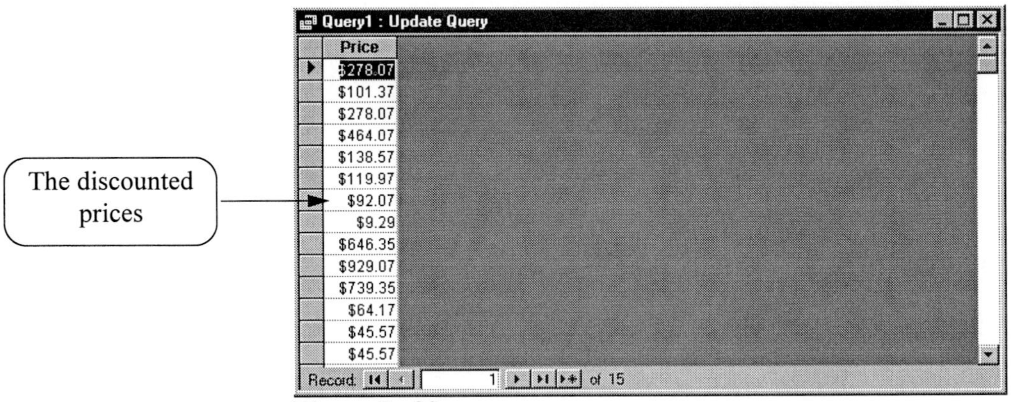

The discounted prices →

Figure 7 - 20

The new prices should be a bit lower than they were a minute ago. Compare the new first price with the original price you wrote down in Step 11.

16. Save the query by picking **FILE/Save As/Export**, entering the name: **Reduce Prices 7%** in the **New Name** text box, and clicking the **OK** button.

17. Choose **FILE/Close** to close the query.

Notice the different icon in front of the name of an action query (see Figure 7 - 21). That is to warn you that this query alters the data in the table if you run it.

An **Update Query** icon →

Figure 7 - 21

THE DELETE QUERY

Eventually a table contains outdated records and the owner may decide to delete those listings. In a previous lesson we deleted a single record by selecting it and pressing the **DELETE** key. While that method is fine for a few records, it would get tedious if there were dozens or hundreds of records to delete. For such an operation one would use a Delete Query.

When a Delete Query is run, the deletion of records is permanent. Therefore, it is common practice (and wise) to set up the same criteria in a Select Query first, and view the resulting listings to confirm that the desired records will be deleted. Once the criteria have been verified, convert the query to a Delete Query and run it.

The * (asterisk) symbol at the top of the field listings in the top section of the **Query** window (see Figure 7 - 22) is required for a Delete Query. The * represents all of the fields as a single block. It can be used in Select Queries too, but does not allow access to individual fields, so is rarely used that way. For Delete Queries, however, it is always placed in the first column of the QBE grid. The * will be preceded by the table name and a period. For our query using the **CDROM** table we will place **CDROM.*** on the **Field** line of the first column (see Figure 7 - 23). The fields for the criteria are then placed in the following columns and the criteria entered.

When the query is converted to a Delete Query, a **Delete** line will be added as the third line of the QBE grid (see Figure 7 - 26). The **Sort** and **Show:** lines disappear. The **CDROM.*** column will show the word **From**, and all other columns will display the word **Where**. The word **From** marks the table from which the records will be deleted. The word **Where** designates the criteria.

To perform a Delete Query:

- Open the **Query1: Select Query** window with the table that contains the records to be deleted.

- Add the * (asterisk) from the list of fields in the table in the upper panel of the window (see Figure 7 - 22).

Add the asterisk to the QBE grid to represent all fields for a Delete Query.

Figure 7 - 22

- Add the single field or combination of fields that hold the criteria as to which records should be deleted.

- Enter the criteria.

- View the resulting dynaset to confirm that the correct records have been selected.

- Switch the query into a Delete Query by choosing **QUERY/Delete** in the menu.

- Run the query.

Activity 7.7: A Delete Query

Since orders for DOS CDROMs have fallen substantially in the last sales period, the company has decided CDROMs for DOS are outdated and should be dropped from the inventory. Your job is to remove the DOS CDROM listings from the **CDROM** table. Since the **Notes** field contains the type DOS, that is the field where we will test for the criterion.

1. The **Sales** database should be open.

2. Click on the **Queries** tab.

3. Click the **New** button at the right edge of the **Database** window.

4. In the **New Query** dialog box, click on **Design View** and click the **OK** button.

5. Since we will delete the outdated DOS CDROMs, click on **CDROM**, click **Add**, and then close the **Show Table** dialog box.

6. Double-click the * at the top of the list of fields to install it in the first column of the QBE grid (see Figure 7 - 23).

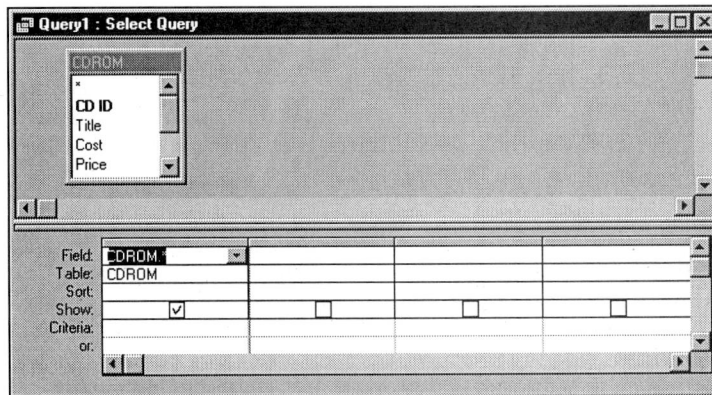

Figure 7 - 23

*The **Field** line will show **CDROM.*** in the first column.*

7. Double-click the **Notes** field to place it in the second column of the QBE grid.

8. On the **Criteria** line in the **Notes** column of the QBE grid, enter: **like "*DOS*"** (see Figure 7 - 24).

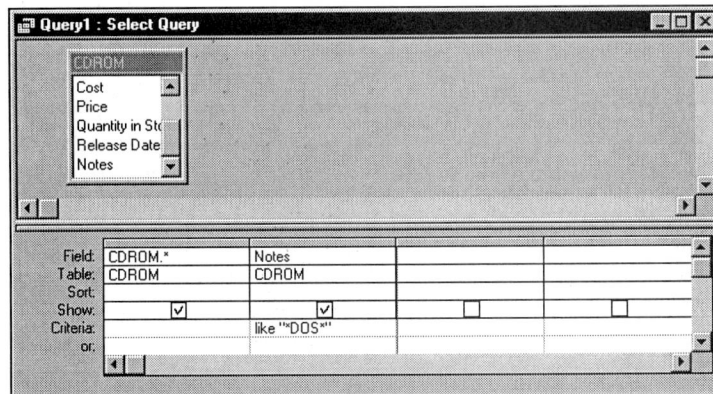

Figure 7 - 24

*The wildcards at the beginning and end of DOS will guarantee we find all records that contain DOS anywhere within the **Notes** field.*

9. Click the **Query View** button on the toolbar to examine the results (Figure 7 - 25).

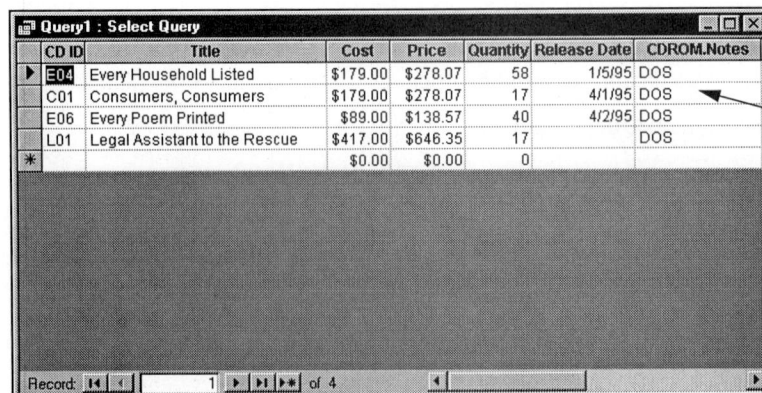

Figure 7 - 25

*The four records should all have DOS as their entry in the **Notes** field. These are the records we want to delete.*

10. Return to the design by clicking the **Query View** button on the toolbar.

11. Pick **QUERY/Delete** in the menus to switch the query to a Delete Query (Figure 7 - 26).

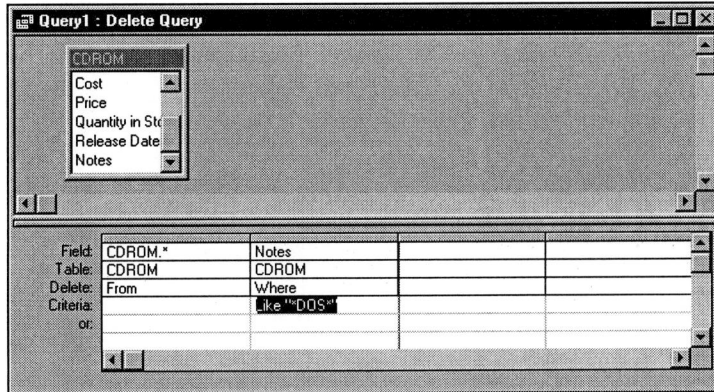

Figure 7 - 26

*The **Delete** line appears in the QBE grid. **From** is entered in the first column and **Where** in all other columns. Read this setup as **Delete From CDROM.* Where Notes is Like "*DOS*"**.*

12. Click the **Run** button on the toolbar.

*The message **You are about to delete 4 row(s)...** appears in an alert box (see Figure 7 - 27). You must be certain the correct records are about to be deleted, for, once you click the **Yes** button, there is no way to get the deleted records back. If you are not sure, click the **No** button and check the criteria again.*

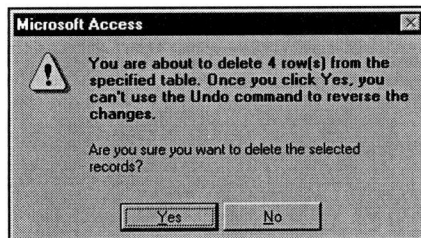

Figure 7 - 27

13. Click **Yes.** The records are deleted.

14. Pick **QUERY/Select** in the menus to switch back so we can check the results.

15. Click the **Query View** button on the toolbar to examine the results.

There should be no records listed, as the DOS CDROMs have been deleted.

16. Choose **FILE/Close** to close the query. Click the **No** button when *Access* asks about saving, as the query is no longer of any use and we do not need to save it.

SUMMARY

In this final project you have calculated several results from the CDROM table and updated its data. You calculated the individual inventory values, and later summed those results to calculate the total inventory value for the entire table. You calculated temporarily discounted holiday prices, then permanently discounted the prices 7% by updating the prices in the CDROM table. You calculated average, maximum, and minimum prices, including grouping the CDROMs by type. Finally, you deleted the outdated listings from the CDROM table.

KEY TERMS

Action Query	Delete Query	Grouping
Update Query	Summary Calculation	

INDEPENDENT PROJECTS

Independent Project 7.1: The School Newspaper

This Independent Project continues working with the Newspaper Ad database from Independent Project 6.1. The newspaper's business manager needs the following calculated results:

- The sum of all ads (see Figure 7 - 28). Only the sum of the Prices from the **Ads** table is needed.

- The sum of the ads grouped by size (see Figure 7 - 29). This needs the **Price** field and the **Size** field from the **Ads** table.

- The average price of an ad sold by each salesperson identified by name rather than ID number (see Figure 7 - 30). This will require the names from the **Sales Force** table in addition to the Price from the **Ads** table.

Additionally, the issue date has been moved up one day to beat the start of exams. Therefore, every entry in the **Issue Date** field needs to be changed from 5/20/95 to 5/19/95.

1. Run *Access*.

2. Open the **Exercise1** database in the Introductory dialog box or with **FILE/Open Database** or by clicking the **Open Database** tool on the toolbar, and then clicking on the name **Exercise1** and clicking the **OK** button.

3. Click on the **Queries** tab at the top of the database window.

4. Click the **New** button to start a new query.

5. In the **New Query** dialog box, click on **Design View** and click the **OK** button.

6. Click on the name **Ads** in the list of tables in the **Show Table** dialog box and click the **Add** button.

7. Click **Close** to close the **Show Table** dialog box.

8. Double-click on the name **Price** to place it in the first column of the QBE grid.

9. Click the **Totals** button on the toolbar to install the **Total** line.

10. Click on the **Total** line in the **Price** column to move to that line.

11. Click the drop-down arrow to open the list of summary calculations.

12. Click on **Sum**.

13. Click the **Query View** button on the toolbar to see the resulting sum (see Figure 7 - 28).

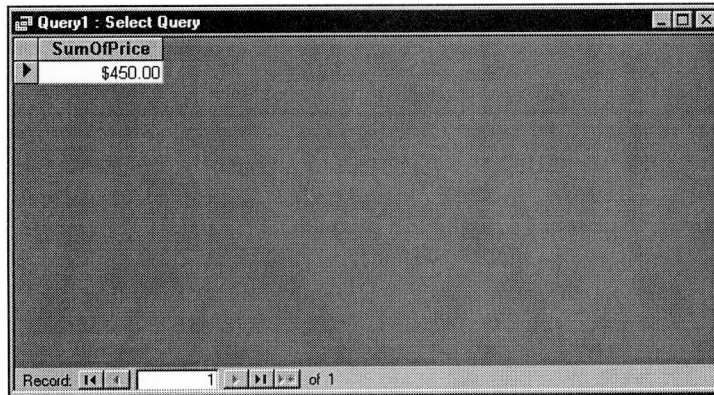

Figure 7 - 28

14. Print the result by clicking the **Print** button.

15. Click the **Query View** button to return to the query design.

16. For the second calculation you need only include the **Size** as a grouping field. Therefore, double-click on **Size** in the list of fields to place it in the second column of the QBE grid. Leave the **Group By** operator alone.

17. Click the **Query View** button on the toolbar to see the resulting sums (see Figure 7 - 29).

Figure 7 - 29

18. Print the result by clicking the **Print** button.

19. Click the **Query View** button to return to the query design.

20. The query for the average price of an ad sold by each salesperson needs the **Sales Force** table for the names in addition to the **Ads** table. Click the **Show Table** button on the toolbar or pick **QUERY/Show Table**.

21. Click on **Sales Force** and click the **Add** button to include its field list in the upper section of the Query window. *Access* will link the two tables on **Salesperson ID** automatically.

22. Click the **Close** button in the **Show Table** dialog box.

23. Pick **EDIT/Clear Grid** to clear the QBE grid.

24. Double-click on **First Name** in the **Sales Force** table to install it in the first column of the QBE grid. Leave **Group By** on the **Total** line.

25. Double-click on **Last Name** in the **Sales Force** table to install it in the second column of the QBE grid. Leave **Group By** on the **Total**: line.

26. Double-click on **Price** in the **Ads** table to install it in the third column.

27. Click on the **Total** line in the **Price** column, click the drop-down arrow to open the list of summary operators, and pick **Avg**.

28. Click the **Query View** button on the toolbar to see the resulting averages (Figure 7 - 30).

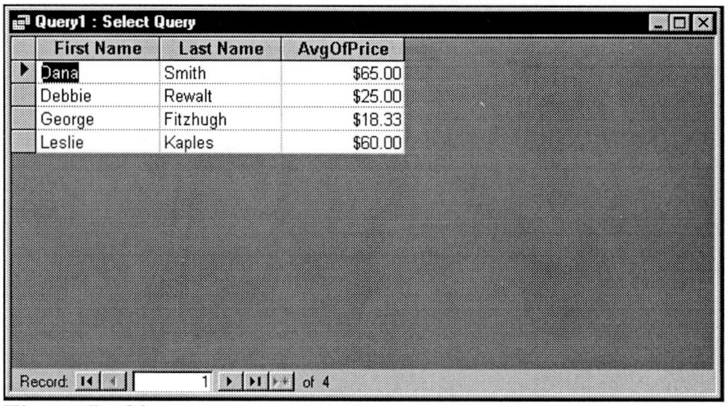

First Name	Last Name	AvgOfPrice
Dana	Smith	$65.00
Debbie	Rewalt	$25.00
George	Fitzhugh	$18.33
Leslie	Kaples	$60.00

Record: 1 of 4

Figure 7 - 30

29. Print the result by clicking the **Print** button.

30. Click the **Query View** button to return to the query design.

31. To prepare for updating the Issue Date, pick **EDIT/Clear Grid** to clear the QBE grid.

32. Double-click on **Issue Date** in the **Ads** table to install it in the first column of the QBE grid.

33. Click the **Totals** button on the toolbar to remove the **Total** line from the QBE grid.

34. Pick **QUERY/Update** in the menus to switch the query design to an update query.

35. On the **Update To** line in the Issue Date column of the QBE grid type: **5/19/95**

36. Click the **Run** button on the toolbar or pick **QUERY/Run**.

37. In the **You are about to update 10 row(s).** alert box, click **Yes**.

38. Close the query with **FILE/Close**. Click **No** in the **Do you want to save changes...** alert box.

39. In the Database window, click on the **Tables** tab, click on **Ads**, and click the **Open** button to open the table.

40. Examine the **Issue Date** field. It should contain **5/19/95** in every record.

41. Close the table with **FILE/Close**.

42. Close the database with **FILE/Close**.

43. If you need to exit from *Access*, do so properly.

Independent Project 7.2: The Bookstore

This Independent Project continues working with the Books database from the earlier lessons. The owner needs the following calculated results:

- The profit margin of each book. The Profit Margin is calculated as **(Price - Cost)/Cost**. The **Title**, **Cost**, and **Price** fields should be included as well (see Figure 7 - 31).

- The total inventory value (the **Sum of Cost * Quantity in Stock**) of all of the books (see Figure 7 - 32).

- The average price of the books from each publisher (see Figure 7 - 33). This needs the **Name** field from the **Publishers** table and the **Price** field from the **Books** table.

Additionally, the owner has decided not to deal with Atlantic Works (AW30) any further, so any of their books should be deleted from the **Books** table.

Query1 : Select Query

Title	Cost	Price	Profit Margin
Art Through Life	$13.50	$22.95	70.00%
Calculus	$25.40	$42.95	69.09%
Chemical Compendiu	$34.50	$49.95	44.78%
Economically Correct	$19.95	$32.95	65.16%
Even More Poems	$12.60	$21.00	66.67%
Look Up In The Sky	$17.00	$28.95	70.29%
Modern Russian	$17.00	$28.50	67.65%
Music Composition	$19.50	$32.95	68.97%
Music Harmony	$19.50	$32.95	68.97%
The Physics of Glass	$4.75	$7.95	67.37%
Philosophize With Me	$18.50	$30.95	67.30%
World of History	$20.95	$34.95	66.83%
*	$0.00	$0.00	

Record: 1 of 12

Figure 7 - 31

Inventory Value
$15,222.00

Figure 7 - 32

Name	AvgOfPrice
Atlantic Works	$32.95
Books Plus	$14.48
Bulky Books	$49.95
College Editions	$32.13
Texts and Tomes	$31.45

Figure 7 - 33

1. Run *Access*.

2. Open the **Exercise2** database by selecting it in the Introductory dialog box or with **FILE/Open Database** or by clicking the **Open Database** tool on the toolbar, then clicking on the name **Exercise2** and clicking the **OK** button.

3. Click on the **Queries** tab at the top of the database window.

4. Click the **New** button to start a new query.

5. In the **New Query** dialog box, click on **Design View** and click the **OK** button.

6. Click on the name **Books** in the list of tables in the **Show Table** dialog box and click the **Add** button.

7. Click **Close** to close the **Show Table** dialog box.

8. Double-click on the name **Title** to place it in the first column of the QBE grid.

9. Similarly, double-click on **Cost** and **Price**.

10. Click on the **Field** line in the fourth column and type: **Profit Margin:([Price]-[Cost])/[Cost]**

11. Press the down arrow, then double-click on the right edge of the **selector** to get a Best Fit for the column so you can see the entire calculation. You may need to scroll to the right first.

12. Click the **Query View** button on the toolbar to see the results.

13. While the calculations were successful, the resulting values are a jumble of decimal places. To begin formatting the results, click the **Query View** button to return to the query design.

14. Click anywhere within the calculation on the **Field** line in the fourth column.

15. Click the **Properties** button on the toolbar.

16. Click on the **Format** line in the properties list and click the drop-down arrow that appears.

17. Click on **Percent**, then close the **Field Properties** list by clicking the **Properties** button on the toolbar again.

18. Click the **Query View** button on the toolbar to see the results (see Figure 7 - 31).

19. Print the result by clicking the **Print** button.

20. Click the **Query View** button to return to the query design.

21. Save this query by picking **FILE/Save** and typing the name **Profit Margin**. Click the **OK** button.

22. Clear the QBE grid with **EDIT/Clear Grid**.

23. For the inventory value calculation you need only to enter the calculation and switch to a Totals query. To begin, press **HOME**.

24. Enter: **Inventory Value:[Cost] * [Quantity in Stock]**

25. Press the down arrow, then double-click on the right edge of the **selector** to get a Best Fit for the column so you can see the entire calculation.

26. Click the **Totals** button on the toolbar.

27. Click on the **Total** line in the column with the calculation, click on the drop-down arrow to open the list of operators, and choose **Sum**.

28. Click the **Query View** button on the toolbar to see the resulting sum (see Figure 7 - 32).

29. Print the result by clicking the **Print** button.

30. Click the **Query View** button to return to the query design.

31. Save this query by picking **FILE/Save As/Export** and typing the new name **Inventory Value**. Click the **OK** button.

32. Clear the QBE grid with **EDIT/Clear Grid**.

33. To begin the third query for the average price of a book for each publisher, click the **Add Table** button on the toolbar or pick **QUERY/Add Table**.

34. Click on **Publishers** and click the **Add** button to include its field list in the upper section of the Query window. *Access* will link the two tables on **Publisher Code** automatically.

35. Click the **Close** button in the **Show Table** dialog box.

36. Double-click on **Name** in the **Publishers** table to install it in the first column of the QBE grid. Leave **Group By** on the **Total** line.

37. Double-click on **Price** in the **Books** table to install it in the second column of the QBE grid.

38. Click on the **Total** line in the **Price** column, click the drop-down arrow to open the list of summary operators, and pick **Avg**.

39. Click the **Query View** button on the toolbar to see the resulting averages (see Figure 7 - 33).

40. Print the result by clicking the **Print** button.

41. Click the **Query View** button to return to the query design. You do not need to save this query.

42. To prepare for deleting the books from Atlantic Works, pick **EDIT/Clear Grid** to clear the QBE grid.

43. Click on the **Totals** button on the toolbar to remove the **Total** line.

44. Press **HOME** to jump to the first column.

45. Scroll to the top of the list of fields in the **Books** list and double-click on the * to install it into the QBE grid. The first column will contain the entry **Books.*** which is required for a delete query.

46. Double-click on **Publisher Code** and **Name** in the **Publishers** table to include those fields in the QBE grid.

47. Click the **Query View** button on the toolbar, and then press the **END** key to see the names of the publishers and their code numbers. Notice that Atlantic Works is code AW30.

48. Click the **Query View** button to return to the query design.

49. Click on the **Criteria** line in the **Publisher Code** column of the QBE grid.

50. Type **"AW30"** making sure the final character is a zero.

51. Click the **Query View** button on the toolbar to check that only Atlantic Works is being selected. Two books, Music Composition and Music Harmony, should be listed.

52. Click the **Query View** button to return to the query design.

53. Pick **QUERY/Delete** in the menus to convert the query to a delete query. The **Books.*** column should say **From** on the **Delete** line, and **Publisher Code** and **Name** should have **Where** on the **Delete** line.

54. Click the **Run** button on the toolbar or pick **QUERY/Run**.

55. In the **You are about to delete 2 row(s)...** alert box, click **Yes**.

56. Pick **QUERY/Select** from the menu to switch the query back to a select query.

57. Delete the **"AW30"** from the **Criteria** line in the **Publisher Code** column.

58. Click the **Query View** button on the toolbar to review the remaining books. Press the **END** key and Atlantic Works should not be listed.

59. Close the query with **FILE/Close**. Click **No** in the **Do you want to save changes...** alert box.

60. Close the database with **FILE/Close**.

61. If you need to exit from *Access*, do so properly.

Independent Project 7.3: The Real Estate Office

This Independent Project continues working with the Real Estate Office database from the earlier lessons. The manager needs the following calculated results:

- The price per square foot of each commercial listing that is for Rent. The Price per square foot is calculated as Price/Size. Code, Address, City, Size, Floor, and Purchase or Rent should be included as well (see Figure 7 - 34).

- The average price per square foot of the commercial listings grouped by whether they are for Purchase or Rent (see Figure 7 - 35).

- The earliest and latest dates available for the properties in Commercial Listings (Figure 7 - 36) grouped by agency name and whether they are for purchase or rent. This should include the Agency Name from the **Agency** table and the **Purchase or Rent** and **Date Available** fields from the **Commercial Listings** table.

Additionally, all of the listings for Research Park, Stamford, have been given to the Right Properties agency (RP12). The listings in Commercial Properties need to be updated.

Code	Address	City	Size	Floor	Purc	Price per Sq Ft
ES52	5 Elm St.	Greenwich	4800	1	R	$15.00
FA28	18 Frost Ave.	Greenwich	3700	2	R	$14.05
GP25	12 Gedney Place	Danbury	8900	3	R	$11.80
LW17	1 Lewis Way	Danbury	12000	2	R	$10.42
RR19	952 River Rd.	Stamford	3750	6	R	$13.07
*			0	0		

Figure 7 - 34

Purc	Price per Sq Ft
P	$211.21
R	$12.87

Figure 7 - 35

Agency Name	Purc	MinOfAvailable	MaxOfAvailable
George Winkle	P	6/1/95	6/1/95
Priceless Properties	P	5/15/95	6/1/95
Profitable Properties	R	7/1/95	9/1/95
Regal Real Estate	R	8/1/95	8/1/95
Right Properties	P	8/1/95	10/1/95
Smith and Cross	R	6/1/95	7/15/95

Figure 7 - 36

1. Run *Access*.
2. Open the **Exercise3** database.
3. Start a new query. Use **Design View**.
4. Add **Commercial Listings** and close the **Show Table** dialog box.
5. Install the **Code, Address, City, Size, Floor,** and **Purchase or Rent** fields into the QBE grid.
6. On the **Field** line in the seventh column type: **Price per Sq Ft:[Price]/[Size]**
7. Format this calculation for **Currency** in the Properties List.
8. Enter the criterion for Rent (**"R"**) in the **Purchase or Rent** column.
9. Click the **Query View** button on the toolbar to see the results (see Figure 7 - 34).
10. **Print** the result.
11. Return to the query design.
12. Save this query as **Price per Sq Ft**.
13. To begin the grouping by **Purchase or Rent**, move to the first column of the QBE grid.
14. Remove the **Code, Address, City, Size,** and **Floor** fields.
15. Remove the criterion in the **Purchase or Rent** column.
16. Switch the query to a **Totals** query.
17. Make the **Price per Sq Ft** field an Average.
18. View the resulting averages (see Figure 7 - 35).
19. **Print** the result.

20. Return to the query design.

21. Use **FILE/Save As/Export** to save this query as **P or R Price per Sq Ft**.

22. Clear the QBE grid to get ready for the third query.

23. Add the **Agencies** table to the top of the Query window. *Access* should create the link on **Agency Code** automatically.

24. Add the **Agency Name**, **Purchase or Rent**, and **Available** fields to the QBE grid.

25. On the **Total** line open the drop-down list of operators and switch **Available** to **Min**. Leave **Group By** for the other two columns.

26. Double-click on **Available** again to install a second copy of that field in the next column of the QBE grid, and from the list of operators on the **Total** line pick **Max**.

27. View the result (see Figure 7 - 36).

28. **Print** the result.

29. Return to the query design.

30. Use **FILE/Save As/Export** to save this query as **Agency First and Last Dates**.

31. To prepare for updating the agency for the Research Park properties, clear the QBE grid.

32. Remove the **Agencies** table by clicking on the gray selector that names the table at the top of the list of fields in the top section of the query window and pressing the **DELETE** key. (This is not required but keeps the workspace tidier.)

33. Remove the **Total** line by clicking the **Totals** button on the toolbar.

34. Add **Address** to the QBE grid.

35. Enter: **like "*Research Park*"** on the **Criteria** line.

36. Add **Agency Code** to the QBE grid.

37. View the result to check it for accuracy. There should be four listings.

38. Return to the query design.

39. Switch the query to an **Update Query**.

40. On the **Update To** line in the **Agency Code** column type: **RP12**

41. Run the query with the **Run** button.

42. In the **You are about to update 4 row(s)...** alert box, click **Yes**.

43. Switch the query back to a Select Query.

44. View the result. All four listings should now have RP12 for the Agency Code.

45. **Close** the query without saving.

46. **Close** the database.

47. If you need to exit from *Access*, do so properly.

Independent Project 7.4: The Veterinarian

This Independent Project continues working with the Veterinarian database from the earlier lessons. She needs the following calculated results. Create and save each query (except do not save the Delete Query), then print each dynaset.

- The average weight of each type of animal.

- The age of the cats. Age is calculated as **(#today's date#-date of birth)/365**. Substitute the current date for the words "**today's date**". Note that you must type the pound signs around the current date. Also, the parentheses are mandatory. Include the pet name, type of animal, date of birth, and age, remembering to enclose the date of birth field in square brackets.

- The count of how many of each type of pet belongs to each owner. This will need both tables.

Additionally, Paula Smith has moved to another region of the country. Her pets' listings should be deleted from the table with a delete query.

Appendix:
Features Reference

The following table contains a summary of the main features presented in the lessons. As you know, most features in *Access* can be performed in a variety of ways. Many of the menu bar commands can also be selected from the Quick Menus. Listed mouse shortcuts involve the use of the buttons on the toolbars and other mouse techniques. Shortcut keys are keystrokes of function keys or keyboard keys with or without **CTRL**, **SHIFT**, or **ALT** being held down. A few features require that the text or column be selected prior to executing the command. If you need more detail on using these features, the table contains a reference to the lesson describing its use.

Features	Mouse Shortcut	Menu Bar Commands	Shortcut Keys	Lessons
Add a table to query	Click Show Table button on toolbar	QUERY/Show Table		5
Best Fit a field	Double-click right edge of Field Selector box	FORMAT/Column Width/Best Fit		2
Change a query to a Delete query	Click the drop-down arrow next to the Query Type button on toolbar and pick Delete	QUERY/Delete		7
Change a query to an Update query	Click the drop-down arrow next to the Query Type button on toolbar and pick Update	QUERY/Update		7
Clear all fields from QBE Grid		EDIT/Clear Grid		4
Close a database	Click the Close button	FILE/Close	CTRL+F4	I
Close a design window	Click the Close button	FILE/Close	CTRL+F4	1
Close a table	Click the Close button	FILE/Close	CTRL+F4	I
Create a form	Click New button in database window when Forms tab is selected	INSERT/Form	ALT-N when Forms tab is selected	3
Create a new database	Click New Database toolbar button	FILE/New Database	CTRL-N	1
Create a new table	Click New button in database window while Tables tab is active	INSERT/Table	ALT-N in database window while Table tab is active	1
Create a query	Click New button in database window when Queries tab is selected	INSERT/Query	ALT-N when Queries tab is selected	4
Create a report	Click New button in database window when Reports tab is selected	INSERT/Report	ALT-N when Reports tab is selected	6

Features	Mouse Shortcut	Menu Bar Commands	Shortcut Keys	Lessons
Delete a field from QBE Grid		EDIT/Delete Column	DELETE when field is selected	5
Delete a record	Click Cut button on toolbar when record is selected	EDIT/Delete Record when anywhere within the record or EDIT/Delete when entire record is selected	DELETE when record is selected	2
Edit Mode	Click mouse in field		F2	2
Exit Access	Click the Close button	FILE/Exit	ALT+F4	I
Help	Click Help button on toolbar, then click on object	HELP/Microsoft Access Help Topics	F1	I
Import a table		FILE/Get External Data/Import		3
Include a field in QBE grid	Double-click field name or click and drag name to QBE grid		type name on Field: line	4
Include all fields in QBE Grid	Double-click table name, then drag any single field to QBE Grid			4
Include Totals in a query	Click the Totals button on toolbar	VIEW/Totals		7
Join multiple tables in query	Click common field in one table and drag to common field in second table			5
Link to a table		FILE/Get External Data/Link Tables		3
Modify a table's structure	Click Table View button on toolbar when table is open	VIEW/Table Design when table is open		
Move a field	Click on Field Selector, then drag to new position			2
Move to first field	Use scroll bar, then click in field		HOME	2
Move to first record	Click First Record Navigation Button	EDIT/Go To/ First	CTRL+UP ARROW	2
Move to last field	Use scroll bar, then click in field		END	2
Move to last record	Click First Record Navigation Button	EDIT/Go To/ Last	CTRL+DOWN ARROW	2
Move to next field	Click in next field		TAB	1
Move to next record	Click Next Record Navigation Button	EDIT/Go To/ Next	DOWN ARROW	2
Move to previous field	Click in previous field		SHIFT+TAB	2
Move to previous record	Click Previous Record Navigation Button	EDIT/Go To/ Previous	UP ARROW	2
Navigation (or Replace) Mode	Double-click mouse in field		F2	2
Open a database	Click Open Database toolbar button	FILE/Open Database	CTRL+O	I and 2

Features	Mouse Shortcut	Menu Bar Commands	Shortcut Keys	Lessons
Open a table	Double-click table name or click Open button in database window when name is highlighted		ENTER when name is highlighted	1
Open Print Preview window	Click the Print Preview button on the toolbar	FILE/Print Preview		4
Open the Properties List	Click the Properties button on the toolbar or double-click the control	VIEW/Properties		3
Open the Toolbox	Click the Toolbox button on the toolbar	VIEW/Toolbox		3
Primary Key	Click Primary Key button on toolbar	EDIT/Primary Key		1
Print	Click Print button on toolbar	FILE/Print	CTRL+P	1
Print Preview	Click Print Preview button on toolbar	FILE/Print Preview		4
Rename a table	Click on the name when it is highlighted	EDIT/Rename when highlight is on table name		3
Run Access	Double-click Access icon		ENTER when name is highlighted	1
Run an action query	Click Run button on toolbar	QUERY/Run		7
Save a design	Click Save button on toolbar	FILE/Save	CTRL-S	1
Search	Click Find button on toolbar	EDIT/Find	CTRL-F	2
Select a control on a form	Click on the control		TAB repeatedly until control is selected	3
Select a control on a report	Click on the control		TAB repeatedly until control is selected	6
Select a record	Click on Record Selector box	EDIT/Select Record	SHIFT+SPACEBAR	2
Size a field	Drag right edge of Field Selector box	FORMAT/Column Width		2
Sort a dynaset	Click on Sort: line in desired field in QBE grid and choose Ascending or Descending in drop-down list		type Ascending or Descending on Sort: line	4
Switch panes	Click in the other pane		F6	1
View a dynaset	Click the Query View button on toolbar	VIEW/Datasheet		4
View query design window	Click the Query View button on toolbar	VIEW/Query Design		4

Index

NOTES

NOTES

NOTES

NOTES

NOTES

NOTES

NOTES

NOTES

NOTES

NOTES

NOTES

NOTES

NOTES